THE SAVOY OPERAS

MACMILLAN AND CO., Limited

MACMILLAN AND CO., Limited
LONDON · BOMBAY · CALCUTTA · MADRAS
MELBOURNE

THE MACMILLAN COMPANY
NEW YORK · BOSTON · CHICAGO
DALLAS · SAN FRANCISCO

THE MACMILLAN CO. OF CANADA, Ltd.
TORONTO

THE
SAVOY OPERAS

BEING THE COMPLETE TEXT OF THE
GILBERT AND SULLIVAN OPERAS AS
ORIGINALLY PRODUCED IN THE YEARS
1875–1896

BY

Sir W. S. GILBERT

MACMILLAN AND CO., LIMITED
ST. MARTIN'S STREET, LONDON
1926

PRINTED IN GREAT BRITAIN

CONTENTS

TRIAL BY JURY

DRAMATIS PERSONÆ.

THE LEARNED JUDGE.
THE PLAINTIFF.
THE DEFENDANT.
COUNSEL FOR THE PLAINTIFF.
USHER.
FOREMAN OF THE JURY.
ASSOCIATE.
FIRST BRIDESMAID.

First produced at the Royalty Theatre, March 25, 1875.

TRIAL BY JURY

SCENE.—*A Court of Justice.*

Barristers, Attorneys, and Jurymen discovered.

CHORUS.

Hark, the hour of ten is sounding :
Hearts with anxious fears are bounding,
Hall of Justice crowds surrounding,
    Breathing hope and fear—
For to-day in this arena,
Summoned by a stern subpœna,
Edwin, sued by Angelina,
    Shortly will appear.

Enter USHER.

SOLO—USHER.

Now, Jurymen, hear my advice—
All kinds of vulgar prejudice
    I pray you set aside :
With stern judicial frame of mind
From bias free of every kind,
    This trial must be tried.

CHORUS.

From bias free of every kind,
This trial must be tried.

(*During Chorus*, USHER *sings fortissimo,* " *Silence in
        Court !* ")

3

USHER.

Oh, listen to the plaintiff's case :
Observe the features of her face—
　　The broken-hearted bride.
Condole with her distress of mind :
From bias free of every kind,
　　This trial must be tried !

CHORUS.

From bias free, etc.

USHER.

And when amid the plaintiff's shrieks,
The ruffianly defendant speaks—
　　Upon the other side ;
What *he* may say you needn't mind—
From bias free of every kind,
　　This trial must be tried !

CHORUS.

From bias free, etc.

Enter DEFENDANT.

RECIT.—DEFENDANT.

Is this the Court of the Exchequer ?

ALL.
It is !

DEFENDANT (*aside*).
Be firm, be firm, my pecker,
Your evil star's in the ascendant !

ALL.
Who are you ?

DEFENDANT
I'm the Defendant !

Chorus of Jurymen (*shaking their fists*).

> Monster, dread our damages.
>> We're the jury,
>> Dread our fury!

Defendant.

> Hear me, hear me, if you please,
>> These are very strange proceedings—
> For permit me to remark
>> On the merits of my pleadings,
> You're at present in the dark.

(Defendant *beckons to* Jurymen—*they leave the box and gather round him as they sing the following*):

> That's a very true remark—
>> On the merits of his pleadings
> We're at present in the dark!
> Ha! ha!—ha! ha!

SONG—Defendant.

> When first my old, old love I knew,
>> My bosom welled with joy;
> My riches at her feet I threw—
>> I was a love-sick boy!
> No terms seemed too extravagant
>> Upon her to employ—
> I used to mope, and sigh, and pant,
>> Just like a love-sick boy!
>>> Tink-a-Tank—Tink-a-Tank.

> But joy incessant palls the sense;
>> And love, unchanged, will cloy,
> And she became a bore intense
>> Unto her love-sick boy!
> With fitful glimmer burnt my flame,
>> And I grew cold and coy,
> At last, one morning, I became
>> Another's love-sick boy.
>>> Tink-a-Tank—Tink-a-Tank.

CHORUS OF JURYMEN (*advancing stealthily*).

Oh, I was like that when a lad !
    A shocking young scamp of a rover,
I behaved like a regular cad ;
    But that sort of thing is all over.
I'm now a respectable chap
    And shine with a virtue resplendent,
And, therefore, I haven't a scrap
    Of sympathy with the defendant !
        He shall treat us with awe,
        If there isn't a flaw,
Singing so merrily—Trial-la-law !
Trial-la-law—Trial-la-law !
Singing so merrily—Trial-la-law !

> (*They enter the Jury-box.*)

RECIT.—USHER (*on Bench*).

Silence in Court, and all attention lend.
Behold your Judge !   In due submission bend !

Enter JUDGE *on Bench.*

CHORUS.

All hail great Judge !
    To your bright rays
We never grudge
    Ecstatic praise.
            All hail !
May each decree
    As statute rank
And never be
    Reversed in banc.
            All hail !

RECIT.—JUDGE.

For these kind words accept my thanks, I pray.
A Breach of Promise we've to try to-day.
But firstly, if the time you'll not begrudge,
I'll tell you how I came to be a Judge.

ALL.

He'll tell us how he came to be a Judge!

SONG—JUDGE.

When I, good friends, was called to the bar,
   I'd an appetite fresh and hearty,
But I was, as many young barristers are,
   An impecunious party.
I'd a swallow-tail coat of a beautiful blue—
   A brief which I bought of a booby—
A couple of shirts and a collar or two,
   And a ring that looked like a ruby!

CHORUS.

   A couple of shirts, etc.

JUDGE.

In Westminster Hall I danced a dance,
   Like a semi-despondent fury;
For I thought I should never hit on a chance
   Of addressing a British Jury—
But I soon got tired of third-class journeys,
   And dinners of bread and water;
So I fell in love with a rich attorney's
   Elderly, ugly daughter.

CHORUS.

   So he fell in love, etc.

JUDGE.

The rich attorney, he jumped with joy,
   And replied to my fond professions:
" You shall reap the reward of your pluck, my boy,
   At the Bailey and Middlesex Sessions.
You'll soon get used to her looks," said he,
   " And a very nice girl you'll find her!
She may very well pass for forty-three
   In the dusk, with a light behind her! "

CHORUS.

She may very well, etc.

JUDGE.

The rich attorney was good as his word ;
  The briefs came trooping gaily,
And every day my voice was heard
  At the Sessions or Ancient Bailey.
All thieves who could my fees afford
  Relied on my orations,
And many a burglar I've restored
  To his friends and his relations.

CHORUS.

And many a burglar, etc.

JUDGE.

At length I became as rich as the Gurneys—
  An incubus then I thought her,
So I threw over that rich attorney's
  Elderly, ugly daughter.
The rich attorney my character high
  Tried vainly to disparage—
And now, if you please, I'm ready to try
  This Breach of Promise of Marriage !

CHORUS.

And now if you please, etc.

JUDGE.

For now I am a Judge !

ALL.

And a good Judge too.

JUDGE.

Yes, now I am a Judge !

ALL.

And a good Judge too !

JUDGE.

Though all my law is fudge,
Yet I'll never, never budge,
But I'll live and die a Judge !

ALL.

And a good Judge too !

JUDGE (*pianissimo*).

It was managed by a job—

ALL.

And a good job too !

JUDGE.

It was managed by a job !

ALL.

And a good job too !

JUDGE.

It is patent to the mob,
That my being made a nob
Was effected by a job.

ALL.

And a good job too !

Enter COUNSEL *for* PLAINTIFF. *He takes his place
in front row of Counsels' seats.*

RECIT.—COUNSEL.

Swear thou the Jury !

USHER.

Kneel, Jurymen, oh, kneel !

(*All the* JURY *kneel in the Jury-box, and so are hidden
from audience.*)

USHER.

Oh, will you swear by yonder skies,
Whatever question may arise,
'Twixt rich and poor, 'twixt low and high,
That you will well and truly try ?

JURY (*raising their hands, which alone are visible*).
To all of this we make reply,
By the dull slate of yonder sky :
That we will well and truly try.

(*All rise with the last note.*)

RECIT.—COUNSEL.

Where is the Plaintiff ?
Let her now be brought.

RECIT.—USHER.

Oh, Angelina !   Come thou into Court !
Angelina ! Angelina ! !

Enter the BRIDESMAIDS.

CHORUS OF BRIDESMAIDS.

Comes the broken flower—
  Comes the cheated maid—
Though the tempest lower,
  Rain and cloud will fade !
Take, oh take these posies :
  Though thy beauty rare
Shame the blushing roses,
  They are passing fair !
    Wear the flowers till they fade ;
    Happy be thy life, oh maid !

(*The* JUDGE, *having taken a great fancy to* FIRST BRIDES-
MAID, *sends her a note by* USHER, *which she reads,
kisses rapturously, and places in her bosom.*)

Enter PLAINTIFF.

SOLO—Plaintiff.

O'er the season vernal,
 Time may cast a shade ;
Sunshine, if eternal,
 Makes the roses fade !
Time may do his duty ;
 Let the thief alone—
Winter hath a beauty,
 That is all his own.
   Fairest days are sun and shade :
   I am no unhappy maid !

(*The* Judge *having by this time transferred his admiration
to* Plaintiff, *directs the Usher to take the note from*
First Bridesmaid *and hand it to* Plaintiff, *who
reads it, kisses it rapturously, and places it in her
bosom.*)

Chorus of Bridesmaids.
Comes the broken flower, etc.

Judge.

Oh, never, never, never, since I joined the human race,
Saw I so exquisitely fair a face.

The Jury (*shaking their forefingers at him*).
 Ah, sly dog !   Ah, sly dog !

Judge (*to* Jury).

How say you ?   Is she not designed for capture ?

Foreman (*after consulting with the* Jury).

We've but one word, my lord, and that is—Rapture.

Plaintiff (*curtseying*).

Your kindness, gentlemen, quite overpowers !

Jury.

We love you fondly and would make you ours !

THE BRIDESMAIDS (*shaking their forefingers at* JURY).
Ah, sly dogs !   Ah, sly dogs !

RECIT.—COUNSEL *for* PLAINTIFF.
May it please you, my lud !
Gentlemen of the jury !

ARIA.

With a sense of deep emotion,
    I approach this painful case ;
For I never had a notion
    That a man could be so base,
Or deceive a girl confiding,
Vows, *etcetera*, deriding.

ALL.

He deceived a girl confiding,
Vows, *etcetera*, deriding.

(PLAINTIFF *falls sobbing on* COUNSEL'S *breast and
remains there.*)

COUNSEL.

See my interesting client,
    Victim of a heartless wile !
See the traitor all defiant
    Wear a supercilious smile !
Sweetly smiled my client on him,
Coyly woo'd and gently won him.

ALL.

Sweetly smiled, etc.

COUNSEL.

Swiftly fled each honeyed hour
    Spent with this unmanly male !
Camberwell became a bower,
    Peckham an Arcadian Vale,
Breathing concentrated otto !—
An existence *à la* Watteau.

ALL.

Bless us, concentrated otto ! etc.

COUNSEL.

Picture, then, my client naming,
   And insisting on the day :
Picture him excuses framing—
   Going from her far away ;
Doubly criminal to do so,
For the maid had bought her *trousseau* !

ALL.

Doubly criminal, etc.

COUNSEL (*to* PLAINTIFF, *who weeps*).

Cheer up, my pretty—oh, cheer up !

JURY.

Cheer up, cheer up, we love you !

(COUNSEL *leads* PLAINTIFF *fondly into Witness-box ; he takes a tender leave of her, and resumes his place in Court.*)

(PLAINTIFF *reels as if about to faint.*)

JUDGE.

That she is reeling
   Is plain to see !

FOREMAN.

If faint you're feeling
   Recline on me !

(*She falls sobbing on to the* FOREMAN'S *breast.*)

PLAINTIFF (*feebly*).

I shall recover
   If left alone.

ALL (*shaking their fists at* DEFENDANT).
Oh, perjured lover,
Atone ! atone !

FOREMAN.
Just like a father
I wish to be. (*Kissing her.*)

JUDGE (*approaching her*).
Or, if you'd rather,
Recline on me !

(*She jumps on to Bench, sits down by the* JUDGE,
and falls sobbing on his breast.)

COUNSEL.
Oh ! fetch some water
From far Cologne !

ALL.
For this sad slaughter
Atone ! atone !

JURY (*shaking fists at* DEFENDANT).
Monster, monster, dread our fury—
There's the Judge, and we're the Jury !
Come !   Substantial damages,
Dam—

USHER.
Silence in Court !

SONG—DEFENDANT.
Oh, gentlemen, listen, I pray,
    Though I own that my heart has been ranging,
Of nature the laws I obey,
    For nature is constantly changing.
The moon in her phases is found,
    The time and the wind and the weather,
The months in succession come round,
    And you don't find two Mondays together.
        Consider the moral, I pray,
            Nor bring a young fellow to sorrow,
        Who loves this young lady to-day,
            And loves that young lady to-morrow.

BRIDESMAIDS (*rushing forward, and kneeling to* JURY)
    Consider the moral, etc.

You cannot eat breakfast all day,
   Nor is it the act of a sinner,
When breakfast is taken away,
   To turn your attention to dinner ;
And it's not in the range of belief,
   That you could hold him as a glutton,
Who, when he is tired of beef,
   Determines to tackle the mutton.
     But this I am willing to say,
       If it will appease her sorrow,
     I'll marry this lady to-day,
       And I'll marry the other to-morrow !

BRIDESMAIDS (*rushing forward as before*).
    But this he is willing to say, etc.

RECIT.—JUDGE.

That seems a reasonable proposition,
To which, I think, your client may agree.

COUNSEL.

But, I submit, my lord, with all submission,
To marry two at once is Burglaree !

    (*Referring to law book*.)
In the reign of James the Second,
It was generally reckoned
As a very serious crime
To marry two wives at one time.

(*Hands book up to* JUDGE, *who reads it*.)

ALL.

Oh, man of learning !

QUARTETTE.

JUDGE.

A nice dilemma we have here,
   That calls for all our wit :

COUNSEL.

And at this stage, it don't appear
    That we can settle it.

DEFENDANT (*in Witness-box*).

If I to wed the girl am loth
    A breach 'twill surely be—

PLAINTIFF.

And if he goes and marries both,
    It counts as Burglaree !

ALL.

A nice dilemma, etc.

DUET—PLAINTIFF *and* DEFENDANT.

PLAINTIFF (*embracing him rapturously*).

I love him—I love him—with fervour unceasing
    I worship and madly adore ;
My blind adoration is always increasing,
    My loss I shall ever deplore.
Oh, see what a blessing, what love and caressing
    I've lost, and remember it, pray,
When you I'm addressing, are busy assessing
    The damages Edwin must pay !

DEFENDANT (*repelling her furiously*).

I smoke like a furnace—I'm always in liquor,
    A ruffian—a bully—a sot ;
I'm sure I should thrash her, perhaps I should kick her,
    I am such a very bad lot !
I'm not prepossessing, as you may be guessing,
    She couldn't endure me a day ;
Recall my professing, when you are assessing
    The damages Edwin must pay !

(*She clings to him passionately ; after a struggle, he
    throws her off into arms of* COUNSEL.)

JURY.

We would be fairly acting,
But this is most distracting !

RECIT.—JUDGE.

The question, gentlemen—is one of liquor ;
    You ask for guidance—this is my reply :
He says, when tipsy, he would thrash and kick her,
    Let's make him tipsy, gentlemen, and try !

COUNSEL.

With all respect
I do object !

PLAINTIFF.

I do object !

DEFENDANT.

I don't object !

ALL.

With all respect
We do object !

JUDGE (*tossing his books and papers about*).

All the legal furies seize you !
No proposal seems to please you,
I can't stop up here all day,
I must shortly go away.
Barristers, and you, attorneys,
Set out on your homeward journeys ;
Gentle, simple-minded Usher,
Get you, if you like, to Russ*her* ;
Put your briefs upon the shelf,
I will marry her myself !

(*He comes down from Bench to floor of Court.*
He embraces ANGELINA.)

FINALE.

PLAINTIFF.

Oh, joy unbounded,
With wealth surrounded,
The knell is sounded
    Of grief and woe.

COUNSEL.

With love devoted
On you he's doated.
To castle moated
    Away they go.

DEFENDANT.

I wonder whether
They'll live together
In marriage tether
    In manner true ?

USHER.

It seems to me, sir,
Of such as she, sir,
A judge is he, sir,
    And a good judge too.

JUDGE.

Yes, I am a Judge.

ALL.

And a good Judge too !

JUDGE.

Yes, I am a Judge.

ALL.

And a good Judge too !

JUDGE.

Though homeward as you trudge,
You declare my law is fudge,
Yet of beauty I'm a judge.

ALL.

And a good Judge too !

CURTAIN.

THE SORCERER

DRAMATIS PERSONÆ.

SIR MARMADUKE POINTDEXTRE (*an Elderly Baronet*).

ALEXIS (*of the Grenadier Guards—his Son*).

DR. DALY (*Vicar of Ploverleigh*).

NOTARY.

JOHN WELLINGTON WELLS (*of J. W. Wells & Co., Family Sorcerers*).

LADY SANGAZURE (*a Lady of Ancient Lineage*).

ALINE (*her Daughter—betrothed to Alexis*).

MRS. PARTLET (*a Pew-opener*).

CONSTANCE (*her Daughter*).

Chorus of Villagers.

ACT I.—Exterior of Sir Marmaduke's Mansion.   Mid-day.

(*Twelve hours are supposed to elapse between Acts I. and II.*)

ACT II.—Exterior of Sir Marmaduke's Mansion.   Midnight.

First produced at the Opéra Comique on November 17, 1877.

22

THE SORCERER

ACT I.

SCENE.—*Exterior of Sir Marmaduke's Elizabethan Mansion.*

CHORUS OF VILLAGERS.

Ring forth, ye bells,
  With clarion sound—
Forget your knells,
  For joys abound.
Forget your notes
  Of mournful lay,
And from your throats
  Pour joy to-day.

For to-day young Alexis—young Alexis Pointdextre
Is betrothed to Aline—to Aline Sangazure,
And that pride of his sex is—of his sex is to be next her,
  At the feast on the green—on the green, oh, be sure !

Ring forth, ye bells, etc.

[*Exeunt the men into house.*

Enter MRS. PARTLET *with* CONSTANCE, *her daughter.*

RECITATIVE.

MRS. P.   Constance, my daughter, why this strange
                depression ?
              The village rings with seasonable joy,
              Because the young and amiable Alexis,

23

Heir to the great Sir Marmaduke Pointdextre,
Is plighted to Aline, the only daughter
Of Annabella, Lady Sangazure.
You, you alone are sad and out of spirits ;
What is the reason ? Speak, my daughter,
    speak !

CON.   Oh, mother, do not ask !   If my complexion
From red to white should change in quick suc-
    cession,
And then from white to red, oh, take no notice !
If my poor limbs should tremble with emotion,
Pay no attention, mother—it is nothing !
If long and deep-drawn sighs I chance to utter,
Oh, heed them not, their cause must ne'er be
    known !

[MRS. PARTLET *motions to* CHORUS *to leave her with*
CONSTANCE. *Exeunt Ladies of* CHORUS.

ARIA.—CONSTANCE.

When he is here,
  I sigh with pleasure—
When he is gone,
  I sigh with grief.
My hopeless fear
  No soul can measure—
His love alone
  Can give my aching heart relief !

When he is cold,
  I weep for sorrow—
When he is kind,
  I weep for joy.
My grief untold
  Knows no to-morrow—
My woe can find
  No hope, no solace, no alloy !

Mrs. P. Come, tell me all about it ! Do not fear—
I, too, have loved ; but that was long ago !
Who is the object of your young affections ?

Con. Hush, mother ! He is here !

Enter Dr. Daly. *He is pensive and does not see them.*

Mrs. P. (*amazed*). Our reverend vicar !

Con. Oh, pity me, my heart is almost broken !

Mrs. P. My child, be comforted. To such an union
I shall not offer any opposition.
Take him—he's yours ! May you and he be
happy !

Con. But, mother dear, he is not yours to give !

Mrs. P. That's true, indeed !

Con. He might object !

Mrs. P. He might.
But come—take heart—I'll probe him on the
subject.
Be comforted—leave this affair to me.

RECITATIVE—Dr. Daly.

The air is charged with amatory numbers—
Soft madrigals, and dreamy lovers' lays.
Peace, peace, old heart ! Why waken from its slumbers
The aching memory of the old, old days ?

BALLAD.

Time was when Love and I were well acquainted.
Time was when we walked ever hand in hand.
A saintly youth, with worldly thought untainted,
None better-loved than I in all the land !
Time was, when maidens of the noblest station,
Forsaking even military men,
Would gaze upon me, rapt in adoration—
Ah me, I was a fair young curate then !

Had I a headache ? sighed the maids assembled ;
Had I a cold ? welled forth the silent tear ;

Did I look pale ? then half a parish trembled ;
    And when I coughed all thought the end was near !
I had no care—no jealous doubts hung o'er me—
    For I was loved beyond all other men.
Fled gilded dukes and belted earls before me—
    Ah me, I was a pale young curate then !

(*At the conclusion of the ballad*, MRS. PARTLET *comes
        forward with* CONSTANCE.)

MRS. P.   Good day, reverend sir.

DR. D.   Ah, good Mrs. Partlet, I am glad to see you.
And your little daughter, Constance ! Why, she is quite
a little woman, I declare !

CON. (*aside*).   Oh, mother, I cannot speak to him !

MRS. P.   Yes, reverend sir, she is nearly eighteen, and
as good a girl as ever stepped.   (*Aside to* DR. D.).   Ah,
sir, I'm afraid I shall soon lose her !

DR. D. (*aside to* MRS. P.).   Dear me, you pain me very
much.   Is she delicate ?

MRS. P.   Oh no, sir—I don't mean that—but young
girls look to get married.

DR. D.   Oh, I take you.   To be sure.   But there's
plenty of time for that.   Four or five years hence, Mrs.
Partlet, four or five years hence.   But when the time *does*
come, I shall have much pleasure in marrying her myself—

CON. (*aside*).   Oh, mother !

DR. D.   To some strapping young fellow in her own
rank of life.

CON. (*in tears*).   He does *not* love me !

MRS. P.   I have often wondered, reverend sir (if you'll
excuse the liberty), that *you* have never married.

DR. D. (*aside*).   Be still, my fluttering heart !

MRS. P.   A clergyman's wife does so much good in a
village.   Besides that, you are not as young as you were,
and before very long you will want somebody to nurse
you, and look after your little comforts.

DR. D.   Mrs. Partlet, there is much truth in what you
say.   I am indeed getting on in years, and a helpmate

would cheer my declining days. Time was when it might have been ; but I have left it too long—I am an old fogy, now, am I not, my dear ? (*to* CONSTANCE)—a very old fogy, indeed. Ha ! ha ! No, Mrs. Partlet, my mind is quite made up. I shall live and die a solitary old bachelor.

CON. Oh, mother, mother ! (*Sobs on* MRS. PARTLET'S *bosom.*)

MRS. P. Come, come, dear one, don't fret. At a more fitting time we will try again—we will try again.

[*Exeunt* MRS. PARTLET *and* CONSTANCE.

DR. D. (*looking after them*). Poor little girl ! I'm afraid she has something on her mind. She is rather comely. Time was when this old heart would have throbbed in double-time at the sight of such a fairy form ! But tush ! I am puling ! Here comes the young Alexis with his proud and happy father. Let me dry this tell-tale tear !

Enter SIR MARMADUKE *and* ALEXIS.

RECITATIVE.

DR. D. Sir Marmaduke—my dear young friend, Alexis—
On this most happy, most auspicious plighting—
Permit me, as a true old friend, to tender
My best, my very best congratulations !

SIR M. Sir, you are most obleeging !

ALEXIS. Dr. Daly,
My dear old tutor, and my valued pastor,
I thank you from the bottom of my heart !

(*Spoken through music.*)

DR. D. May fortune bless you ! may the middle distance
Of your young life be pleasant as the foreground—
The joyous foreground ! and, when you have reached it,

May that which now is the far-off horizon
(But which will then become the middle dis-
tance),
In fruitful promise be exceeded only
By that which will have opened, in the meantime,
Into a new and glorious horizon !

SIR M.   Dear Sir, that is an excellent example
Of an old school of stately compliment
To which I have, through life, been much
addicted.
Will you obleege me with a copy of it,
In clerkly manuscript, that I myself
May use it on appropriate occasions ?

DR. D.   Sir, you shall have a fairly-written copy
Ere Sol has sunk into his western slumbers !

                                        [*Exit* DR. DALY.

SIR M. (*to* ALEXIS, *who is in a reverie*).   Come, come,
my son—your *fiancée* will be here in five minutes.   Rouse
yourself to receive her.

ALEXIS.   Oh rapture !

SIR M.   Yes, you are a fortunate young fellow, and I
will not disguise from you that this union with the House
of Sangazure realizes my fondest wishes.   Aline is rich,
and she comes of a sufficiently old family, for she is
the seven thousand and thirty-seventh in direct descent
from Helen of Troy.   True, there was a blot on the
escutcheon of that lady—that affair with Paris—but
where is the family, other than my own, in which there
is no flaw ?   You are a lucky fellow, sir—a very lucky
fellow !

ALEXIS.   Father, I am welling over with limpid joy !
No sicklying taint of sorrow overlies the lucid lake of liquid
love, upon which, hand in hand, Aline and I are to float
into eternity !

SIR M.   Alexis, I desire that of your love for this young
lady you do not speak so openly.   You are always singing
ballads in praise of her beauty, and you expect the very

menials who wait behind your chair, to chorus your
ecstasies.   It is not delicate.

    ALEXIS.   Father, a man who loves as I love—

    SIR M.   Pooh pooh, sir ! fifty years ago I madly loved
your future mother-in-law, the Lady Sangazure, and I have
reason to believe that she returned my love.   But were we
guilty of the indelicacy of publicly rushing into each other's
arms, exclaiming—

       " Oh, my adored one ! "   " Beloved boy ! "
       " Ecstatic rapture ! "   " Unmingled joy ! "

which seems to be the modern fashion of love-making ?
No ! it was " Madam, I trust you are in the enjoyment
of good health "—" Sir, you are vastly polite, I protest I
am mighty well "—and so forth.   Much more delicate—
much more respectful.   But see—Aline approaches—let us
retire, that she may compose herself for the interesting
ceremony in which she is to play so important a part.

             [*Exeunt* SIR MARMADUKE *and* ALEXIS.

Enter ALINE, *on terrace, preceded by Chorus of Girls.*

CHORUS OF GIRLS.

With heart and with voice
    Let us welcome this mating :
To the youth of her choice,
    With a heart palpitating,
       Comes the lovely Aline !

May their love never cloy !
    May their bliss be unbounded !
With a halo of joy
    May their lives be surrounded !
       Heaven bless our Aline !

RECITATIVE—ALINE.

My kindly friends, I thank you for this greeting,
And as you wish me every earthly joy,
I trust your wishes may have quick fulfilment !

ARIA—ALINE.

Oh, happy young heart !
    Comes thy young lord a-wooing
With joy in his eyes,
    And pride in his breast—
Make much of thy prize,
    For he is the best
That ever came a-suing.
    Yet—yet we must part,
                    Young heart !
    Yet—yet we must part !

Oh, merry young heart,
    Bright are the days of thy wooing !
But happier far
    The days untried—
No sorrow can mar,
    When Love has tied
The knot there's no undoing.
    Then, never to part,
                    Young heart !
    Then, never to part !

Enter LADY SANGAZURE.

RECITATIVE—LADY S.

My child, I join in these congratulations :
Heed not the tear that dims this aged eye !
Old memories crowd upon me.   Though I sorrow,
'Tis for myself, Aline, and not for thee !

Enter ALEXIS, *preceded by Chorus of Men.*

CHORUS OF MEN AND WOMEN.

With heart and with voice
    Let us welcome this mating ;
To the maid of his choice,
    With a heart palpitating,
        Comes Alexis the brave !

Sir Marmaduke *enters.* Lady Sangazure *and he exhibit signs of strong emotion at the sight of each other, which they endeavour to repress.* Alexis *and* Aline *rush into each other's arms.*

RECITATIVE.

Alexis.   Oh, my adored one !
Aline.   Beloved boy !
Alexis.   Ecstatic rapture !
Aline.   Unmingled joy !

[*They retire up.*

DUET—Sir Marmaduke *and* Lady Sangazure.

Sir M. (*with stately courtesy*).
          Welcome joy, adieu to sadness !
             As Aurora gilds the day,
          So those eyes, twin orbs of gladness,
             Chase the clouds of care away.
          Irresistible incentive
             Bids me humbly kiss your hand ;
          I'm your servant most attentive—
             Most attentive to command !

(*Aside with frantic vehemence.*)
          Wild with adoration !
          Mad with fascination !
          To indulge my lamentation
             No occasion do I miss !
          Goaded to distraction
          By maddening inaction,
          I find some satisfaction
             In apostrophe like this :
          " Sangazure immortal,
             " Sangazure divine,
          " Welcome to my portal,
             " Angel, oh be mine ! "

(*Aloud with much ceremony.*)
          Irresistible incentive
             Bids me humbly kiss your hand ;

I'm your servant most attentive—
    Most attentive to command !

LADY S. Sir, I thank you most politely
    For your graceful courtesee ;
    Compliment more true and knightly
      Never yet was paid to me !
    Chivalry is an ingredient
      Sadly lacking in our land—
    Sir, I am your most obedient,
      Most obedient to command !

(Aside with great vehemence.)

Wild with adoration !
Mad with fascination !
To indulge my lamentation
    No occasion do I miss !
Goaded to distraction
By maddening inaction,
I find some satisfaction
    In apostrophe like this :
    " Marmaduke immortal,
      " Marmaduke divine,
    " Take me to thy portal,
      " Loved one, oh be mine ! "

(Aloud with much ceremony.)

Chivalry is an ingredient
    Sadly lacking in our land ;
Sir, I am your most obedient,
    Most obedient to command !

(During this the NOTARY *has entered, with marriage
contract.)*

RECIT.—NOTARY.

All is prepared for sealing and for signing,
    The contract has been drafted as agreed ;
Approach the table, oh, ye lovers pining,
    With hand and seal come execute the deed !

(ALEXIS *and* ALINE *advance and sign,* ALEXIS *supported by* SIR MARMADUKE, ALINE *by her Mother.*)

CHORUS.

See they sign, without a quiver, it—
Then to seal proceed.
They deliver it—they deliver it
As their Act and Deed !

ALEXIS.   I deliver it—I deliver it
As my Act and Deed !

ALINE.   I deliver it—I deliver it
As my Act and Deed !

CHORUS.

With heart and with voice
Let us welcome this mating ;
Leave them here to rejoice,
With true love palpitating,
Alexis the brave,
And the lovely Aline !

[*Exeunt all but* ALEXIS *and* ALINE.

ALEXIS. At last we are alone ! My darling, you are now irrevocably betrothed to me. Are you not very, very happy ?

ALINE. Oh, Alexis, can you doubt it ? Do I not love you beyond all on earth, and am I not beloved in return ? Is not true love, faithfully given and faithfully returned, the source of every earthly joy ?

ALEXIS. Of that there can be no doubt. Oh, that the world could be persuaded of the truth of that maxim ! Oh, that the world would break down the artificial barriers of rank, wealth, education, age, beauty, habits, taste, and temper, and recognise the glorious principle, that in marriage alone is to be found the panacea for every ill !

ALINE. Continue to preach that sweet doctrine, and you will succeed, oh, evangel of true happiness !

c

ALEXIS.   I hope so, but as yet the cause progresses but slowly.   Still I have made some converts to the principle, that men and women should be coupled in matrimony without distinction of rank.   I have lectured on the subject at Mechanics' Institutes, and the mechanics were unanimous in favour of my views.   I have preached in workhouses, beershops, and Lunatic Asylums, and I have been received with enthusiasm.   I have addressed navvies on the advantages that would accrue to them if they married wealthy ladies of rank, and not a navvy dissented !

ALINE.   Noble fellows !   And yet there are those who hold that the uneducated classes are not open to argument ! And what do the countesses say ?

ALEXIS.   Why, at present, it can't be denied, the aristocracy hold aloof.

ALINE.   Ah, the working man is the true Intelligence after all !

ALEXIS.   He is a noble creature when he is quite sober. Yes, Aline, true happiness comes of true love, and true love should be independent of external influences.   It should live upon itself and by itself—in itself love should live for love alone !

BALLAD—ALEXIS.

Love feeds on many kinds of food, I know,
    Some love for rank, and some for duty :
Some give their hearts away for empty show,
    And others love for youth and beauty.
To love for money all the world is prone :
    Some love themselves, and live all lonely :
Give me the love that loves for love alone—
    I love that love—I love it only !

What man for any other joy can thirst,
    Whose loving wife adores him duly ?
Want, misery, and care may do their worst,
    If loving woman loves you truly.

A lover's thoughts are ever with his own—
None truly loved is ever lonely :
Give me the love that loves for love alone—
I love that love—I love it only !

ALINE.   Oh, Alexis, those are noble principles !

ALEXIS.   Yes, Aline, and I am going to take a desperate step in support of them.   Have you ever heard of the firm of J. W. Wells & Co., the old-established Family Sorcerers in St. Mary Axe ?

ALINE.   I have seen their advertisement.

ALEXIS.   They have invented a philtre, which, if report may be believed, is simply infallible.   I intend to distribute it through the village, and within half an hour of my doing so there will not be an adult in the place who will not have learnt the secret of pure and lasting happiness. What do you say to that ?

ALINE.   Well, dear, of course a filter is a very useful thing in a house ; but still I don't quite see that it is the sort of thing that places its possessor on the very pinnacle of earthly joy.

ALEXIS.   Aline, you misunderstand me.   I didn't say a filter—I said a philtre.

ALINE (*alarmed*).   You don't mean a love-potion ?

ALEXIS.   On the contrary—I *do* mean a love-potion.

ALINE.   Oh, Alexis !   I don't think it would be right. I don't indeed.   And then—a real magician !   Oh, it would be downright wicked.

ALEXIS.   Aline, is it, or is it not, a laudable object to steep the whole village up to its lips in love, and to couple them in matrimony without distinction of age, rank, or fortune ?

ALINE.   Unquestionably, but—

ALEXIS.   Then unpleasant as it must be to have recourse to supernatural aid, I must nevertheless pocket my aversion, in deference to the great and good end I have in view.   (*Calling*) Hercules.

Enter a Page from tent.

PAGE.   Yes, sir.

ALEXIS. Is Mr. Wells there?

PAGE. He's in the tent, sir—refreshing.

ALEXIS. Ask him to be so good as to step this way.

PAGE. Yes, sir. [*Exit Page.*

ALINE. Oh, but, Alexis! A real Sorcerer! Oh, I shall be frightened to death!

ALEXIS. I trust my Aline will not yield to fear while the strong right arm of her Alexis is here to protect her.

ALINE. It's nonsense, dear, to talk of your protecting me with your strong right arm, in face of the fact that this Family Sorcerer could change me into a guinea-pig before you could turn round.

ALEXIS. He *could* change you into a guinea-pig, no doubt, but it is most unlikely that he would take such a liberty. It's a most respectable firm, and I am sure he would never be guilty of so untradesmanlike an act.

Enter MR. WELLS *from tent.*

MR. W. Good day, sir. (ALINE *much terrified.*)

ALEXIS. Good day—I believe you are a Sorcerer.

MR. W. Yes, sir, we practise Necromancy in all its branches. We've a choice assortment of wishing-caps, divining-rods, amulets, charms, and counter-charms. We can cast you a nativity at a low figure, and we have a horoscope at three-and-six that we can guarantee. Our Abudah chests, each containing a patent Hag who comes out and prophesies disasters, with spring complete, are strongly recommended. Our Aladdin lamps are very chaste, and our Prophetic Tablets, foretelling everything —from a change of Ministry down to a rise in Unified— are much enquired for. Our penny Curse—one of the cheapest things in the trade—is considered infallible. We have some very superior Blessings, too, but they're very little asked for. We've only sold one since Christmas— to a gentleman who bought it to send to his mother-in-law —but it turned out that he was afflicted in the head, and it's been returned on our hands. But our sale of penny Curses, especially on Saturday nights, is tremendous. We can't turn 'em out fast enough.

SONG—Mr. WELLS.

Oh ! my name is John Wellington Wells,
I'm a dealer in magic and spells,
    In blessings and curses
    And ever-filled purses,
In prophecies, witches, and knells.

If you want a proud foe to " make tracks "—
If you'd melt a rich uncle in wax—
    You've but to look in
    On our resident Djinn,
Number seventy, Simmery Axe !

We've a first-class assortment of magic ;
  And for raising a posthumous shade
With effects that are comic or tragic,
  There's no cheaper house in the trade.
Love-philtre—we've quantities of it ;
  And for knowledge if any one burns,
We keep an extremely small prophet, a prophet
  Who brings us unbounded returns :

      For he can prophesy
      With a wink *of* his eye,
      Peep with security
      Into futurity,
      Sum up your history,
      Clear up a mystery,
      Humour proclivity
      For a nativity—for a nativity ;
      With mirrors so magical,
      Tetrapods tragical,
      Bogies spectacular,
      Answers oracular,
      Facts astronomical,
      Solemn or comical,
      And, if you want it, he
      Makes a reduction on taking a quantity !

Oh !
If any one anything lacks,
He'll find it all ready in stacks,
    If he'll only look in
    On the resident Djinn,
Number seventy, Simmery Axe !

    He can raise you hosts
                Of ghosts,
And that without reflectors ;
    And creepy things
                With wings,
And gaunt and grisly spectres.
    He can fill you crowds
                Of shrouds,
And horrify you vastly ;
    He can rack your brains
                With chains,
And gibberings grim and ghastly !

    Then, if you plan it, he
    Changes organity,
    With an urbanity,
    Full of Satanity,
    Vexes humanity
    With an inanity
    Fatal to vanity—
Driving your foes to the verge of insanity !

    Barring tautology,
    In demonology,
    'Lectro-biology,
    Mystic nosology,
    Spirit philology,
    High-class astrology,
    Such is his knowledge, he
Isn't the man to require an apology !

                Oh !
My name is John Wellington Wells,
I'm a dealer in magic and spells,

In blessings and curses
And ever-filled purses,
In prophecies, witches, and knells.

If any one anything lacks,
He'll find it all ready in stacks,
If he'll only look in
On the resident Djinn,
Number seventy, Simmery Axe !

ALEXIS. I have sent for you to consult you on a very
important matter. I believe you advertise a Patent Oxy-
Hydrogen Love-at-first-sight Philtre ?

MR. W. Sir, it is our leading article. (*Producing a
phial.*)

ALEXIS. Now I want to know if you can confidently
guarantee it as possessing all the qualities you claim for it
in your advertisement ?

MR. W. Sir, we are not in the habit of puffing our
goods. Ours is an old-established house with a large
family connection, and every assurance held out in the
advertisement is fully realised. (*Hurt.*)

ALINE (*aside*). Oh, Alexis, don't offend him ! He'll
change us into something dreadful—I know he will !

ALEXIS. I am anxious from purely philanthropical
motives to distribute this philtre, secretly, among the
inhabitants of this village. I shall of course require a
quantity. How do you sell it ?

MR. W. In buying a quantity, sir, we should strongly
advise your taking it in the wood, and drawing it off as
you happen to want it. We have it in four-and-a-half and
nine gallon casks—also in pipes and hogsheads for laying
down, and we deduct 10 per cent for prompt cash.

ALEXIS. I should mention that I am a Member of the
Army and Navy Stores.

MR. W. In that case we deduct 25 per cent.

ALEXIS. Aline, the villagers will assemble to carouse
in a few minutes. Go and fetch the tea-pot.

ALINE.   But, Alexis—

ALEXIS.   My dear, you must obey me, if you please.
Go and fetch the tea-pot.

ALINE (*going*).   I'm sure Dr. Daly would disapprove
of it !

[*Exit* ALINE.

ALEXIS.   And how soon does it take effect ?

MR. W.   In twelve hours.   Whoever drinks of it loses
consciousness for that period, and on waking falls in love,
as a matter of course, with the first lady he meets who
has also tasted it, and his affection is at once returned.
One trial will prove the fact.

Enter ALINE *with large tea-pot.*

ALEXIS.   Good : then, Mr. Wells, I shall feel obliged
if you will at once pour as much philtre into this tea-pot
as will suffice to affect the whole village.

ALINE.   But bless me, Alexis, many of the villagers are
married people !

MR. W.   Madam, this philtre is compounded on the
strictest principles.   On married people it has no effect
whatever.   But are you quite sure that you have nerve
enough to carry you through the fearful ordeal ?

ALEXIS.   In the good cause I fear nothing.

MR. W.   Very good, then, we will proceed at once to
the Incantation.

(*The stage grows dark.*)

INCANTATION.

MR. W.   Sprites of earth and air—
                 Fiends of flame and fire—
                      Demon souls,
                      Come here in shoals,
                 This dreadful deed inspire !
                      Appear, appear, appear.

MALE VOICES.   Good master, we are here !

Mr. W.   Noisome hags of night—
                Imps of deadly shade—
                Pallid ghosts,
                Arise in hosts,
                And lend me all your aid.
                Appear, appear, appear!
Female Voices.   Good master, we are here!
Alexis (*aside*).   Hark, they assemble,
                These fiends of the night!
Aline (*aside*).   Oh, Alexis, I tremble,
                Seek safety in flight!

ARIA—Aline.

Let us fly to a far-off land,
    Where peace and plenty dwell—
Where the sigh of the silver strand
    Is echoed in every shell.
To the joy that land will give,
    On the wings of Love we'll fly;
In innocence there to live—
    In innocence there to die!

Chorus of Spirits.

Too late—too late
    It may not be!
That happy fate
    Is not for thee!

Alexis, Aline, *and* Mr. Wells.

Too late—too late,
    That may not be!
That happy fate
    Is not for $\begin{cases} \text{me!} \\ \text{thee!} \end{cases}$

Mr. Wells.

Now shrivelled hags, with poison bags,
    Discharge your loathsome loads!

C 2

Spit flame and fire, unholy choir !
Belch forth your venom, toads !
Ye demons fell, with yelp and yell,
Shed curses far afield—
Ye fiends of night, your filthy blight
In noisome plenty yield !

MR. WELLS (*pouring phial into tea-pot—flash*).
                                    Number One !
CHORUS.   It is done !
MR. W. (*same business*). Number Two ! (*flash*).
CHORUS.   One too few !
MR. W. (*same business*). Number Three ! (*flash*).
CHORUS.   Set us free !
                Set us free—our work is done.
                          Ha ! ha ! ha !
                Set us free—our course is run !
                          Ha ! ha ! ha !

ALINE and ALEXIS (*aside*).

Let us fly to a far-off land,
    Where peace and plenty dwell—
Where the sigh of the silver strand
    Is echoed in every shell.

CHORUS OF FIENDS.

Ha ! ha ! ha ! ha ! ha ! ha ! ha ! ha ! ha ! ha !

Stage grows light. MR. WELLS *beckons villagers. Enter
    villagers and all the dramatis personæ, dancing
    joyously.* MRS. PARTLET *and* MR. WELLS *then
    distribute tea-cups.*

CHORUS.

Now to the banquet we press ;
    Now for the eggs, the ham ;
Now for the mustard and cress,
    Now for the strawberry jam !

Now for the tea of our host,
  Now for the rollicking bun,
Now for the muffin and toast,
  Now for the gay Sally Lunn !

WOMEN.   The eggs and the ham, and the strawberry
    jam !

MEN.   The rollicking bun, and the gay Sally Lunn !
    The rollicking, rollicking bun !

RECIT.—SIR MARMADUKE.

Be happy all—the feast is spread before ye ;
  Fear nothing, but enjoy yourselves, I pray !
Eat, aye, and drink—be merry, I implore ye,
  For once let thoughtless Folly rule the day.

TEA-CUP BRINDISI.

Eat, drink, and be gay,
  Banish all worry and sorrow,
Laugh gaily to-day,
  Weep, if you're sorry, to-morrow !
Come, pass the cup round—
  I will go bail for the liquor ;
It's strong, I'll be bound,
  For it was brewed by the vicar !

CHORUS.

None so knowing as he
At brewing a jorum of tea,
    Ha ! ha !
A pretty stiff jorum of tea.

TRIO—MR. WELLS, ALINE, and ALEXIS (aside).

See—see—they drink—
  All thought unheeding,
The tea-cups clink,
  They are exceeding !

> Their hearts will melt
>   In half-an-hour—
> Then will be felt
>   The potion's power!

(*During this verse* CONSTANCE *has brought a small tea-pot,
    kettle, caddy, and cosy to* DR. DALY. *He makes tea
    scientifically.*)

BRINDISI, 2nd Verse—DR. DALY (*with the tea-pot*).

> Pain, trouble, and care,
>   Misery, heart-ache, and worry,
> Quick, out of your lair!
>   Get you all gone in a hurry!
> Toil, sorrow, and plot,
>   Fly away quicker and quicker—
> Three spoons to the pot—
>   That is the brew of your vicar!

CHORUS.

> None so cunning as he
> At brewing a jorum of tea,
>   Ha! ha!
> A pretty stiff jorum of tea!

ENSEMBLE—ALEXIS *and* ALINE (*aside*).

> Oh love, true love—unworldly, abiding!
>   Source of all pleasure—true fountain of joy,—
> Oh love, true love—divinely confiding,
>   Exquisite treasure that knows no alloy,—
> Oh love, true love, rich harvest of gladness,
>   Peace-bearing tillage—great garner of bliss,—
> Oh love, true love, look down on our sadness—
>   Dwell in this village—oh, hear us in this!

*It becomes evident by the strange conduct of the characters
    that the charm is working. All rub their eyes, and
    stagger about the stage as if under the influence of a
    narcotic.*

TUTTI (*aside*).   ALEXIS, MR. WELLS, *and* ALINE (*aside*).

Oh, marvellous illusion !	A marvellous illusion !
Oh, terrible surprise !	A terrible surprise
What is this strange confusion	Excites a strange confusion
That veils my aching eyes ?	Within their aching eyes—
I must regain my senses,	They must regain their senses,
Restoring Reason's law,	Restoring Reason's law,
Or fearful inferences	Or fearful inferences
Society will draw !	Society will draw !

Those who have partaken of the philtre struggle in vain against its effects, and, at the end of the chorus, fall insensible on the stage.

END OF ACT I.

ACT II.

SCENE.—*Exterior of* SIR MARMADUKE'S *mansion by moonlight. All the peasantry are discovered asleep on the ground, as at the end of Act I.*

Enter MR. WELLS, *on tiptoe, followed by* ALEXIS *and* ALINE. MR. WELLS *carries a dark lantern.*

TRIO—ALEXIS, ALINE, *and* MR. WELLS.

'Tis twelve, I think,
   And at this mystic hour
The magic drink
   Should manifest its power.
Oh, slumbering forms,
   How little have ye guessed
The fire that warms
   Each apathetic breast !

ALEXIS. But stay, my father is not here !
ALINE. And pray where is my mother dear ?
MR. WELLS.   I did not think it meet to see
    A dame of lengthy pedigree,
    A Baronet and K.C.B.,
    A Doctor of Divinity,
    And that respectable Q.C.,
    All fast asleep, al-fresco-ly;
    And so I had them taken home
    And put to bed respectably !
    I trust my conduct meets your approba-
        tion.

ALEXIS.   Sir, you have acted with discrimination,
               And shown more delicate appreciation
               Than we expect in persons of your
                   station.
MR. WELLS.   But stay—they waken, one by one—
               The spell has worked·—the deed is done !
               I would suggest that we retire
               While Love, the Housemaid, lights her
                   kitchen fire !

          [*Exeunt* MR. WELLS, ALEXIS, *and* ALINE, *on
               tiptoe, as the villagers stretch their arms,
               yawn, rub their eyes, and sit up.*

MEN.   Why, where be oi, and what be oi a doin',
              A sleepin' out, just when the dews du rise ?
GIRLS.   Why, that's the very way your health to ruin,
              And don't seem quite respectable likewise !
MEN (*staring at girls*). Eh, that's you !
                              Only think o' that now !
GIRLS (*coyly*).   What may you be at, now ?
                              Tell me, du !
MEN (*admiringly*).   Eh, what a nose,
                              And eh, what eyes, miss !
                          Lips like a rose,
                              And cheeks likewise, miss !
GIRLS (*coyly*).   Oi tell you true,
                              Which I've never done, sir,
                          Oi loike you
                              As I never loiked none, sir !
ALL.   Eh, but oi du loike you !
MEN.   If you'll marry me, I'll dig for
                              you and rake for you !
GIRLS.   If you'll marry me, I'll scrub
                              for you and bake for you !
MEN.   If you'll marry me, all others
                              I'll forsake for you !
ALL.   All this will I du, if you'll
                              marry me !

GIRLS.	If you'll marry me, I'll cook for you and brew for you !
MEN.	If you'll marry me, I've guineas not a few for you !
GIRLS.	If you'll marry me, I'll take you in and du for you !
ALL.	All this will I du, if you'll marry me !
	Eh, but oi du loike you !

COUNTRY DANCE.

At end of dance, enter CONSTANCE *in tears, leading* NOTARY, *who carries an ear-trumpet.*

ARIA—CONSTANCE.

Dear friends, take pity on my lot,
　　My cup is not of nectar !
I long have loved—as who would not ?—
　　Our kind and reverend rector.
Long years ago my love began
　　So sweetly—yet so sadly—
But when I saw this plain old man,
Away my old affection ran—
　　I found I loved him madly.
　　　　Oh !

(*To* NOTARY.)	You very, very plain old man, I love, I love you madly !
CHORUS.	You very, very plain old man, She loves, she loves you madly !
NOTARY.	I am a very deaf old man, And hear you very badly !
CONSTANCE.	I know not why I love him so ; It is enchantment, surely ! He's dry and snuffy, deaf and slow Ill-tempered, weak, and poorly ! He's ugly, and absurdly dressed, And sixty-seven nearly,

He's everything that I detest,
But if the truth must be confessed,
    I love him very dearly !
        Oh !

(*To* NOTARY.) You're everything that I detest,
    But still I love you dearly !

CHORUS.   You're everything that girls detest,
    But still she loves you dearly !

NOTARY.   I caught that line, but for the rest,
    I did not hear it clearly !

(*During this verse* ALINE *and* ALEXIS *have entered
at back unobserved.*)

ALINE *and* ALEXIS.

ALEXIS.   Oh joy ! oh joy !
     The charm works well,
       And all are now united.

ALINE.   The blind young boy
     Obeys the spell,
       Their troth they all have plighted !

ENSEMBLE.

ALINE *and* ALEXIS.	CONSTANCE.	NOTARY.
Oh joy ! oh joy !	Oh, bitter joy !	Oh joy ! oh joy !
The charm works well,	No words can tell	No words can tell
And all are now united !	How my poor heart is	My state of mind de-
The blind young boy	blighted !	lighted.
Obeys the spell,	They'll soon employ	They'll soon employ
Their troth they all have	A marriage bell,	A marriage bell,
plighted.	To say that we're united.	To say that we're united.
True happiness	I do confess	True happiness
Reigns everywhere,	A sorrow rare	Reigns everywhere,
And dwells with both	My humbled spirit	And dwells with both
the sexes,	vexes,	the sexes,
And all will bless	And none will bless	And all will bless
The thoughtful care	Example rare	Example rare
Of their beloved Alexis !	Of their beloved Alexis !	Of their beloved Alexis !

[*All, except* ALEXIS *and* ALINE, *exeunt lovingly.*

ALINE. How joyful they all seem in their new-found
happiness ! The whole village has paired off in the
happiest manner. And yet not a match has been made
that the hollow world would not consider ill-advised !

ALEXIS. But we are wiser—far wiser—than the world. Observe the good that will become of these ill-assorted unions. The miserly wife will check the reckless expenditure of her too frivolous consort, the wealthy husband will shower innumerable bonnets on his penniless bride, and the young and lively spouse will cheer the declining days of her aged partner with comic songs unceasing !

ALINE. What a delightful prospect for him !

ALEXIS. But one thing remains to be done, that my happiness may be complete. We must drink the philtre ourselves, that I may be assured of your love for ever and ever.

ALINE. Oh, Alexis, do you doubt me ? Is it necessary that such love as ours should be secured by artificial means ? Oh, no, no, no !

ALEXIS. My dear Aline, time works terrible changes, and I want to place our love beyond the chance of change.

ALINE. Alexis, it is already far beyond that chance. Have faith in me, for my love can never, never change !

ALEXIS. Then you absolutely refuse ?

ALINE. I do. If you cannot trust me, you have no right to love me—no right to be loved *by* me.

ALEXIS. Enough, Aline, I shall know how to interpret this refusal.

BALLAD—ALEXIS.

Thou hast the power thy vaunted love
To sanctify, all doubt above,
    Despite the gathering shade :
To make that love of thine so sure
That, come what may, it must endure
    Till time itself shall fade.
        Thy love is but a flower
        That fades within the hour !
    If such thy love, oh, shame !
    Call it by other name—
        It is not love !

Thine is the power and thine alone,
To place me on so proud a throne
That kings might envy me !
A priceless throne of love untold,
More rare than orient pearl and gold.
But no !   Thou wouldst be free !
Such love is like the ray
That dies within the day :
If such thy love, oh, shame !
Call it by other name—
It is not love !

Enter DR. DALY.

DR. D. (*musing*).   It is singular—it is very singular. It has overthrown all my calculations. It is distinctly opposed to the doctrine of averages. I cannot understand it.

ALINE.   Dear Dr. Daly, what has puzzled you ?

DR. D.   My dear, this village has not hitherto been addicted to marrying and giving in marriage. Hitherto the youths of this village have not been enterprising, and the maidens have been distinctly coy. Judge then of my surprise when I tell you that the whole village came to me in a body just now, and implored me to join them in matrimony with as little delay as possible. Even your excellent father has hinted to me that before very long it is not unlikely that he also may change his condition.

ALINE.   Oh, Alexis—do you hear that ?   Are you not delighted ?

ALEXIS.   Yes.   I confess that a union between your mother and my father would be a happy circumstance indeed. (*Crossing to* DR. DALY.)   My dear sir—the news that you bring us is very gratifying.

DR. D.   Yes—still, in my eyes, it has its melancholy side. This universal marrying recalls the happy days— now, alas, gone for ever—when I myself might have— but tush ! I am puling. I am too old to marry—and yet, within the last half-hour, I have greatly yearned for companionship. I never remarked it before, but the young maidens of this village are very comely. So likewise are the middle-aged. Also the elderly. All are comely—and (*with a deep sigh*) all are engaged !

ALINE. Here comes your father.

Enter SIR MARMADUKE *with* MRS. PARTLET, *arm-in-arm*.

ALINE *and* ALEXIS (*aside*). Mrs. Partlet !

SIR M. Dr. Daly, give me joy. Alexis, my dear boy, you will, I am sure, be pleased to hear that my declining days are not unlikely to be solaced by the companionship of this good, virtuous, and amiable woman.

ALEXIS (*rather taken aback*). My dear father, this is not altogether what I expected. I am certainly taken somewhat by surprise. Still it can hardly be necessary to assure you that any wife of yours is a mother of mine. (*Aside to* ALINE.) It is not quite what I could have wished.

MRS. P. (*crossing to* ALEXIS). Oh, sir, I entreat your forgiveness. I am aware that socially I am not heverythink that could be desired, nor am I blessed with an abundance of worldly goods, but I can at least confer on your estimable father the great and priceless dowry of a true, tender, and lovin' 'art !

ALEXIS (*coldly*). I do not question it. After all, a faithful love is the true source of every earthly joy.

SIR M. I knew that my boy would not blame his poor father for acting on the impulse of a heart that has never yet misled him. Zorah is not perhaps what the world calls beautiful—

DR. D. Still she is comely—distinctly comely. (*Sighs*.)

ALINE. Zorah is very good, and very clean, and honest, and quite, quite sober in her habits : and that is worth far more than beauty, dear Sir Marmaduke.

DR. D. Yes ; beauty will fade and perish, but personal cleanliness is practically undying, for it can be renewed whenever it discovers symptoms of decay. My dear Sir Marmaduke, I heartily congratulate you. (*Sighs*.)

QUINTETTE.

ALEXIS, ALINE, SIR MARMADUKE, ZORAH, *and* DR. DALY.

ALEXIS.

I rejoice that it's decided,
    Happy now will be his life,
For my father is provided
    With a true and tender wife.

ENSEMBLE.

She will tend him, nurse him, mend him,
    Air his linen, dry his tears ;
Bless the thoughtful fates that send him
    Such a wife to soothe his years !

ALINE.

No young giddy thoughtless maiden,
    Full of graces, airs, and jeers—
But a sober widow, laden
    With the weight of fifty years !

SIR M.

No high-born exacting beauty,
    Blazing like a jewelled sun—
But a wife who'll do her duty,
    As that duty should be done !

MRS. P.

I'm no saucy minx and giddy—
    Hussies such as them abound—
But a clean and tidy widdy
    Well be-known for miles around !

DR. D.

All the village now have mated,
    All are happy as can be—
I to live alone am fated :
    No one's left to marry me !

ENSEMBLE.   She will tend him, etc.

> [*Exeunt* SIR MARMADUKE, MRS. PARTLET,
> *and* ALINE, *with* ALEXIS. DR. DALY
> *looks after them sentimentally, then exit
> with a sigh.*
>
> *Enter* MR. WELLS.

RECITATIVE—MR. WELLS.

Oh, I have wrought much evil with my spells !
    And ill I can't undo !
This is too bad of you, J. W. Wells—
    What wrong have they done you ?
And see—another love-lorn lady comes—
    Alas, poor stricken dame !
A gentle pensiveness her life benumbs—
    And mine, alone, the blame !

LADY SANGAZURE *enters.   She is very melancholy.*

LADY S.   Alas ! ah me ! and well-a-day !
              I sigh for love, and well I may,
              For I am very old and grey.
                    But stay !

(*Sees* MR. WELLS, *and becomes fascinated by him.*)

RECITATIVE.

LADY S.   What is this fairy form I see before me ?
MR. W.   Oh, horrible !—she's going to adore me !
          This last catastrophe is overpowering !
LADY S.   Why do you glare at one with visage lowering ?
          For pity's sake recoil not thus from me !
MR. W.   My lady, leave me—this may never be !

DUET—LADY SANGAZURE *and* MR. WELLS.

MR. W.   Hate me ! I drop my H's—have through life !
LADY S.   Love me ! I'll drop them too !
MR. W.   Hate me ! I always eat peas with a knife !
LADY S.   Love me ! I'll eat like you !

Mr. W.	Hate me! I spend the day at Rosherville!
Lady S.	Love me! that joy I'll share!
Mr. W.	Hate me! I often roll down One Tree Hill!
Lady S.	Love me! I'll join you there!

Lady S.	Love me! my prejudices I will drop!
Mr. W.	Hate me! that's not enough!
Lady S.	Love me! I'll come and help you in the shop!
Mr. W.	Hate me! the life is rough!
Lady S.	Love me! my grammar I will all forswear!
Mr. W.	Hate me! abjure my lot!
Lady S.	Love me! I'll stick sunflowers in my hair!
Mr. W.	Hate me! they'll suit you not!

RECITATIVE—Mr. WELLS.

At what I am going to say be not enraged—
I may not love you—for I am engaged!

Lady S. (*horrified*).　　Engaged!

Mr. W.　　　　　　　　　　　Engaged!

To a maiden fair,
With bright brown hair,
　And a sweet and simple smile,
Who waits for me
By the sounding sea,
　On a South Pacific isle.

Mr. W. (*aside*).	A lie!	No maiden waits me there!
Lady S. (*mournfully*).		She has bright brown hair;
Mr. W. (*aside*).	A lie!	No maiden smiles on me!
Lady S. (*mournfully*).		By the sounding sea!

ENSEMBLE.

Lady Sangazure.	Mr. Wells.
Oh, agony, rage, despair!	Oh, agony, rage, despair!
The maiden has bright brown hair,	Oh, where will this end—oh, where?
And mine is as white as snow!	I should like very much to know!
False man, it will be your fault,	It will certainly be my fault,
If I go to my family vault,	If she goes to her family vault,
And bury my life-long woe!	To bury her life-long woe!

BOTH.   The family vault—the family vault.

It will certainly be $\begin{Bmatrix} your \\ my \end{Bmatrix}$ fault,

If $\begin{Bmatrix} I\ go \\ she\ goes \end{Bmatrix}$ to $\begin{Bmatrix} my \\ her \end{Bmatrix}$ family vault,

To bury $\begin{Bmatrix} my \\ her \end{Bmatrix}$ life-long woe !

[*Exit* LADY SANGAZURE, *in great anguish,
accompanied by* MR. WELLS.

Enter ALINE.

RECITATIVE.

Alexis !   Doubt me not, my loved one !   See,
Thine uttered will is sovereign law to me !
All fear—all thought of ill I cast away !
It is my darling's will, and I obey !

(*She drinks the philtre.*)

The fearful deed is done,
　　My love is near !
I go to meet my own
　　In trembling fear !
If o'er us aught of ill
　　Should cast a shade,
It was my darling's will,
　　And I obeyed !

(*As* ALINE *is going off, she meets* DR. DALY, *entering
pensively.   He is playing on a flageolet.   Under the
influence of the spell she at once becomes strangely
fascinated by him, and exhibits every symptom of
being hopelessly in love with him.*)

SONG—DR. DALY.

Oh, my voice is sad and low
And with timid step I go—
For with load of love o'erladen
I enquire of every maiden,
　"Will you wed me, little lady ?
　Will you share my cottage shady ? "

Little lady answers " No !
Thank you for your kindly proffer—
Good your heart, and full your coffer ;
Yet I must decline your offer—
    I'm engaged to So-and-so ! "
        So-and-so !
        So-and-so ! (*flageolet solo*)
She's engaged to So-and-so !
What a rogue young hearts to pillage ;
What a worker on Love's tillage !
Every maiden in the village
    Is engaged to So-and-so !
        So-and-so !
        So-and-so ! (*flageolet solo*)
    All engaged to So-and-so !

(*At the end of the song* DR. DALY *sees* ALINE, *and, under
the influence of the potion, falls in love with her.*)

ENSEMBLE—ALINE *and* DR. DALY.

Oh, joyous boon ! oh, mad delight ;
Oh, sun and moon ! oh, day and night !
    Rejoice, rejoice with me !
Proclaim our joy, ye birds above—
Ye brooklets, murmur forth our love,
    In choral ecstasy :

ALINE.	Oh, joyous boon !
DR. D.	Oh, mad delight !
ALINE.	Oh, sun and moon !
DR. D.	Oh, day and night !
BOTH.	Ye birds, and brooks, and fruitful trees,

With choral joy delight the breeze—
    Rejoice, rejoice with me !

Enter ALEXIS.

ALEXIS (*with rapture*). Aline, my only love, my happiness !

The philtre—you have tasted it ?

ALINE (*with confusion*). Yes ! Yes !

ALEXIS. Oh, joy, mine, mine for ever, and for aye !
(*Embraces her.*)

ALINE. Alexis, don't do that—you must not !

(DR. DALY *interposes between them.*)

ALEXIS (*amazed*). Why ?

DUET—ALINE *and* DR. DALY.

ALINE.   Alas ! that lovers thus should meet :
        Oh, pity, pity me !
    Oh, charge me not with cold deceit ;
        Oh, pity, pity me !
    You bade me drink—with trembling awe
    I drank, and, by the potion's law,
    I loved the very first I saw !
        Oh, pity, pity me !

DR. D.   My dear young friend, consolèd be—
        We pity, pity you.
    In this I'm not an agent free—
        We pity, pity you.
    Some most extraordinary spell
    O'er us has cast its magic fell—
    The consequence I need not tell.
        We pity, pity you.

ENSEMBLE.

Some most extraordinary spell

O'er $\begin{Bmatrix} \text{us} \\ \text{them} \end{Bmatrix}$ has cast its magic fell—

The consequence $\begin{Bmatrix} \text{we} \\ \text{they} \end{Bmatrix}$ need not tell.

$\begin{Bmatrix} \text{We} \\ \text{They} \end{Bmatrix}$ pity, pity $\begin{Bmatrix} \text{thee !} \\ \text{me.} \end{Bmatrix}$

ALEXIS (*furiously*). False one, begone—I spurn thee,
        To thy new lover turn thee !
        Thy perfidy all men shall know.

ALINE (*wildly*).   I could not help it!
ALEXIS (*calling off*).   Come one, come all!
DR. D.   We could not help it!
ALEXIS (*calling off*).   Obey my call!
ALINE (*wildly*).   I could not help it!
ALEXIS (*calling off*).   Come hither, run!
DR. D.   We could not help it!
ALEXIS (*calling off*).   Come, every one!

Enter all the characters except LADY SANGAZURE *and*
MR. WELLS.

CHORUS.

Oh, what is the matter, and what is the clatter?
  He's glowering at her, and threatens a blow!
Oh, why does he batter the girl he did flatter?
  And why does the latter recoil from him so?

RECITATIVE—ALEXIS.

Prepare for sad surprises—
My love Aline despises!
No thought of sorrow shames her—
Another lover claims her!
Be his, false girl, for better or for worse—
But, ere you leave me, may a lover's curse——

DR. D. (*coming forward*). Hold! Be just. This poor child drank the philtre at your instance. She hurried off to meet you—but, most unhappily, she met me instead. As you had administered the potion to both of us, the result was inevitable. But fear nothing from me—I will be no man's rival. I shall quit the country at once—and bury my sorrow in the congenial gloom of a Colonial Bishopric.

ALEXIS. My excellent old friend! (*Taking his hand —then turning to* MR. WELLS, *who has entered with* LADY SANGAZURE.) Oh, Mr. Wells, what, what is to be done?

MR. W. I do not know—and yet—there is one means by which this spell may be removed.

ALEXIS.   Name it—oh, name it !

MR. W.   Or you or I must yield up his life to Ahrimanes.   I would rather it were you.   I should have no hesitation in sacrificing my own life to spare yours, but we take stock next week, and it would not be fair on the Co.

ALEXIS.   True.   Well, I am ready !

ALINE.   No, no—Alexis—it must not be !   Mr. Wells, if he must die that all may be restored to their old loves, what is to become of me ?   I should be left out in the cold, with no love to be restored to !

MR. W.   True—I did not think of that.   (*To the others.*)   My friends, I appeal to you, and I will leave the decision in your hands.

FINALE.

MR. W.	Or I or he
	Must die !
	Which shall it be ?
	Reply !
SIR M.	Die thou !
	Thou art the cause of all offending !
DR. D.	Die thou !
	Yield thou to this decree unbending !
ALL.	Die thou !
MR. W.	So be it ! I submit ! My fate is sealed.
	To public execration thus I yield !

(*Falls on trap.*)

Be happy all—leave me to my despair—
I go—it matters not with whom—or where !

(*Gong.*)

All quit their present partners, and rejoin their old lovers.
SIR MARMADUKE *leaves* MRS. PARTLET, *and goes to* LADY SANGAZURE.   ALINE *leaves* DR. DALY, *and goes to* ALEXIS.   DR. DALY *leaves* ALINE, *and goes to* CONSTANCE.   NOTARY *leaves* CONSTANCE, *and goes to* MRS. PARTLET.   *All the* CHORUS *make a corresponding change.*

ALL.

GENTLEMEN.	Oh, my adored one !
LADIES.	Unmingled joy !
GENTLEMEN.	Ecstatic rapture !
LADIES.	Beloved boy !

(*They embrace.*)

SIR. M.   Come to my mansion, all of you !   At least
We'll crown our rapture with another feast !

ENSEMBLE.

SIR MARMADUKE, LADY SANGAZURE, ALEXIS,
and ALINE.

Now to the banquet we press—
Now for the eggs and the ham—
Now for the mustard and cress—
Now for the strawberry jam !

CHORUS.   Now to the banquet, etc.

DR. DALY, CONSTANCE, NOTARY, *and* MRS. PARTLET.

Now for the tea of our host—
Now for the rollicking bun—
Now for the muffin and toast—
Now for the gay Sally Lunn !

CHORUS.   Now for the tea, etc.

(*General Dance.*)

During the symphony MR. WELLS *sinks through trap,
amid red fire.*

CURTAIN.

H.M.S. PINAFORE

OR

THE LASS THAT LOVED A SAILOR

DRAMATIS PERSONÆ.

THE RT. HON. SIR JOSEPH PORTER, K.C.B. (*First Lord of the Admiralty*).

CAPTAIN CORCORAN (*Commanding H.M.S. Pinafore*).

TOM TUCKER (*Midshipmite*).

RALPH RACKSTRAW (*Able Seaman*).

DICK DEADEYE (*Able Seaman*).

BILL BOBSTAY (*Boatswain's Mate*).

BOB BECKET (*Carpenter's Mate*).

JOSEPHINE (*the Captain's Daughter*).

HEBE (*Sir Joseph's First Cousin*).

MRS. CRIPPS (LITTLE BUTTERCUP) (*a Portsmouth Bumboat Woman*).

First Lord's Sisters, his Cousins, his Aunts, Sailors, Marines, etc.

SCENE.—Quarter-deck of H.M.S. *Pinafore*, off Portsmouth.

ACT I.—Noon.   ACT II.—Night.

First produced at the Opéra Comique on May 25, 1878.

H.M.S. PINAFORE

OR

THE LASS THAT LOVED A SAILOR

ACT I.

SCENE.—*Quarter-deck of H.M.S. Pinafore.   Sailors, led by* BOATSWAIN, *discovered cleaning brasswork, splicing rope, etc.*

CHORUS.

We sail the ocean blue,
And our saucy ship's a beauty;
We're sober men and true,
And attentive to our duty.
When the balls whistle free
O'er the bright blue sea,
We stand to our guns all day;
When at anchor we ride
On the Portsmouth tide,
We have plenty of time to play.

Enter LITTLE BUTTERCUP, *with large basket on her arm*

RECIT.

Hail, men-o'-war's men—safeguards of your nation,
Here is an end, at last, of all privation;
You've got your pay—spare all you can afford
To welcome Little Buttercup on board.

ARIA.

For I'm called Little Buttercup—dear Little Buttercup,
   Though I could never tell why,
But still I'm called Buttercup—poor Little Buttercup,
   Sweet Little Buttercup I !

I've snuff and tobaccy, and excellent jacky,
   I've scissors, and watches, and knives ;
I've ribbons and laces to set off the faces
   Of pretty young sweethearts and wives.

I've treacle and toffee, I've tea and I've coffee,
   Soft tommy and succulent chops ;
I've chickens and conies, and pretty polonies,
   And excellent peppermint drops.

Then buy of your Buttercup—dear Little Buttercup ;
   Sailors should never be shy ;
So, buy of your Buttercup—poor Little Buttercup ;
   Come, of your Buttercup buy !

BOAT.   Aye, Little Buttercup—and well called—for
you're the rosiest, the roundest, and the reddest beauty in
all Spithead.

BUT.   Red, am I ? and round—and rosy ! May be,
for I have dissembled well ! But hark ye, my merry
friend—hast ever thought that beneath a gay and frivolous
exterior there may lurk a canker-worm which is slowly
but surely eating its way into one's very heart ?

BOAT.   No, my lass, I can't say I've ever thought that.

Enter DICK DEADEYE. *He pushes through sailors,*
        and comes down.

DICK.   *I* have thought it often. (*All recoil from him.*)

BUT.   Yes, you look like it ! What's the matter with
the man ? Isn't he well ?

BOAT.   Don't take no heed of *him* ; that's only poor
Dick Deadeye.

DICK.   I say—it's a beast of a name, ain't it—Dick
Deadeye ?

BUT. It's not a nice name.

DICK. I'm ugly too, ain't I?

BUT. You are certainly plain.

DICK. And I'm three-cornered too, ain't I?

BUT. You are rather triangular.

DICK. Ha! ha! That's it. I'm ugly, and they hate me for it; for you all hate me, don't you?

ALL. We do!

DICK. There!

BOAT. Well, Dick, we wouldn't go for to hurt any fellow-creature's feelings, but you can't expect a chap with such a name as Dick Deadeye to be a popular character—now can you?

DICK. No.

BOAT. It's asking too much, ain't it?

DICK. It is. From such a face and form as mine the noblest sentiments sound like the black utterances of a depraved imagination. It is human nature—I am resigned.

RECIT.

BUT. (*looking down hatchway*).

But, tell me—who's the youth whose faltering feet
    With difficulty bear him on his course?

BOAT. That is the smartest lad in all the fleet—
    Ralph Rackstraw!

BUT. Ha! That name! Remorse! remorse!

Enter RALPH *from hatchway.*

MADRIGAL—RALPH.

    The Nightingale
Sighed for the moon's bright ray,
    And told his tale
In his own melodious way!
He sang " Ah, well-a-day! "

ALL.   He sang " Ah, well-a-day! "

The lowly vale
For the mountain vainly sighed,
To his humble wail
The echoing hills replied.
They sang " Ah, well-a-day ! "

ALL. They sang " Ah, well-a-day ! "

RECIT.

I know the value of a kindly chorus,
But choruses yield little consolation
When we have pain and sorrow too before us !
I love—and love, alas, above my station !

BUT. (*aside*). He loves—and loves a lass above his station!
ALL (*aside*). Yes, yes, the lass is much above his station!

[*Exit* LITTLE BUTTERCUP.

BALLAD—RALPH.

A maiden fair to see,
The pearl of minstrelsy,
A bud of blushing beauty ;
For whom proud nobles sigh,
And with each other vie
To do her menial's duty.

ALL. To do her menial's duty.

A suitor, lowly born,
With hopeless passion torn,
And poor beyond denying,
Has dared for her to pine
At whose exalted shrine
A world of wealth is sighing.

ALL. A world of wealth is sighing !

Unlearned he in aught
Save that which love has taught
(For love had been his tutor) ;
Oh, pity, pity me—
Our captain's daughter she,
And I that lowly suitor !

ALL. And he that lowly suitor !

BOAT. Ah, my poor lad, you've climbed too high : our worthy captain's child won't have nothin' to say to a poor chap like you. Will she, lads ?

ALL. No, no !

DICK. No, no, captains' daughters don't marry fore-mast hands.

ALL (*recoiling from him*). Shame ! shame !

BOAT. Dick Deadeye, them sentiments o' yourn are a disgrace to our common natur'.

RALPH. But it's a strange anomaly, that the daughter of a man who hails from the quarter-deck may not love another who lays out on the fore-yard arm. For a man is but a man, whether he hoists his flag at the main-truck or his slacks on the main-deck.

DICK. Ah, it's a queer world !

RALPH. Dick Deadeye, I have no desire to press hardly on you, but such a revolutionary sentiment is enough to make an honest sailor shudder.

BOAT. My lads, our gallant captain has come on deck ; let us greet him as so brave an officer and so gallant a seaman deserves.

Enter CAPTAIN CORCORAN.

RECIT.

CAPT. My gallant crew, good morning.

ALL (*saluting*). Sir, good morning !

CAPT. I hope you're all quite well.

ALL (*as before*). Quite well ; and you, sir ?

CAPT. I am in reasonable health, and happy
　　　　To meet you all once more.

ALL (*as before*). You do us proud, sir !

SONG—CAPT.

CAPT. I am the Captain of the *Pinafore* ;

ALL. And a right good captain, too !

CAPT. 　　You're very, very good,
　　　　　And be it understood,
　　　　I command a right good crew,

ALL.   We're very, very good,
            And be it understood,
            He commands a right good crew.
CAPT.   Though related to a peer,
            I can hand, reef, and steer,
            And ship a selvagee ;
            I am never known to quail
            At the fury of a gale,
            And I'm never, never sick at sea !
ALL.   What, never ?
CAPT.   No, never !
ALL.   What, *never* ?
CAPT.   Hardly ever !
ALL.   He's hardly ever sick at sea !
        Then give three cheers, and one cheer more,
        For the hardy Captain of the *Pinafore* !

CAPT.   I do my best to satisfy you all—
ALL.   And with you we're quite content.
CAPT.   You're exceedingly polite,
            And I think it only right
            To return the compliment.
ALL.   We're exceedingly polite,
            And he thinks it's only right
            To return the compliment.
CAPT.   Bad language or abuse,
            I never, never use,
            Whatever the emergency ;
            Though " Bother it " I may
            Occasionally say,
            I never use a big, big D—
ALL.   What, never ?
CAPT.   No, never !
ALL.   What, *never* ?
CAPT.   Hardly ever !
ALL.   Hardly ever swears a big, big D—
        Then give three cheers, and one cheer more,
        For the well-bred Captain of the *Pinafore* !
                        [*After song exeunt all but* CAPTAIN

Enter LITTLE BUTTERCUP.

RECITATIVE.

BUT.   Sir, you are sad!   The silent eloquence
       Of yonder tear that trembles on your eyelash
       Proclaims a sorrow far more deep than common;
       Confide in me—fear not—I am a mother!
CAPT.   Yes, Little Buttercup, I'm sad and sorry—
       My daughter, Josephine, the fairest flower
       That ever blossomed on ancestral timber,
       Is sought in marriage by Sir Joseph Porter,
       Our Admiralty's First Lord, but for some reason
       She does not seem to tackle kindly to it.

BUT. (*with emotion*).   Ah, poor Sir Joseph! Ah, I
       know too well
       The anguish of a heart that loves but vainly!
       But see, here comes your most attractive daughter.
       I go—Farewell!   [*Exit.*
CAPT. (*looking after her*).   A plump and pleasing
       person!   [*Exit.*

Enter JOSEPHINE, *twining some flowers which she
carries in a small basket.*

BALLAD—JOSEPHINE.

Sorry her lot who loves too well,
   Heavy the heart that hopes but vainly,
Sad are the sighs that own the spell,
   Uttered by eyes that speak too plainly;
      Heavy the sorrow that bows the head
      When love is alive and hope is dead!

Sad is the hour when sets the sun—
   Dark is the night to earth's poor daughters,
When to the ark the wearied one
   Flies from the empty waste of waters!
      Heavy the sorrow that bows the head
      When love is alive and hope is dead!

Enter CAPTAIN.

CAPT. My child, I grieve to see that you are a prey to melancholy. You should look your best to-day, for Sir Joseph Porter, K.C.B., will be here this afternoon to claim your promised hand.

JOS. Ah, father, your words cut me to the quick. I can esteem—reverence—venerate Sir Joseph, for he is a great and good man; but oh, I cannot love him! My heart is already given.

CAPT. (*aside*). It is then as I feared. (*Aloud.*) Given? And to whom? Not to some gilded lordling?

JOS. No, father—the object of my love is no lordling. Oh, pity me, for he is but a humble sailor on board your own ship!

CAPT. Impossible!

JOS. Yes, it is true—too true.

CAPT. A common sailor? Oh fie!

JOS. I blush for the weakness that allows me to cherish such a passion. I hate myself when I think of the depth to which I have stooped in permitting myself to think tenderly of one so ignobly born, but I love him! I love him! I love him! (*Weeps.*)

CAPT. Come, my child, let us talk this over. In a matter of the heart I would not coerce my daughter—I attach but little value to rank or wealth, but the line must be drawn somewhere. A man in that station may be brave and worthy, but at every step he would commit solecisms that society would never pardon.

JOS. Oh, I have thought of this night and day. But fear not, father, I have a heart, and therefore I love; but I am your daughter, and therefore I am proud. Though I carry my love with me to the tomb, he shall never, never know it.

CAPT. You *are* my daughter after all. But see, Sir Joseph's barge approaches, manned by twelve trusty oarsmen and accompanied by the admiring crowd of sisters, cousins, and aunts that attend him wherever he goes. Retire, my daughter, to your cabin—take this, his photograph, with you—it may help to bring you to a more reasonable frame of mind.

Jos.   My own thoughtful father !

      [*Exit* JOSEPHINE.   CAPTAIN *remains and
            ascends the poop-deck.*

BARCAROLLE (*invisible*).

Over the bright blue sea
Comes Sir Joseph Porter, K.C.B.,
    Wherever he may go
Bang-bang the loud nine-pounders go !
    Shout o'er the bright blue sea
For Sir Joseph Porter, K.C.B.

(*During this the Crew have entered on tiptoe,
    listening attentively to the song.*)

CHORUS OF SAILORS.

Sir Joseph's barge is seen,
    And its crowd of blushing beauties,
We hope he'll find us clean,
    And attentive to our duties.
We sail, we sail the ocean blue,
    And our saucy ship's a beauty.
We're sober, sober men and true
    And attentive to our duty.
We're smart and sober men,
    And quite devoid of fe-ar,
In all the Royal N.
    None are so smart as we are.

Enter Sir JOSEPH'S FEMALE RELATIVES.

They dance round stage.

REL.   Gaily tripping,
                Lightly skipping,
            Flock the maidens to the shipping.
SAILORS.   Flags and guns and pennants dipping !
            All the ladies love the shipping.
REL.   Sailors sprightly
                Always rightly
            Welcome ladies so politely.
SAILORS.   Ladies who can smile so brightly,
            Sailors welcome most politely.

CAPT. (*from poop*).   Now give three cheers, I'll lead the way
ALL.   Hurrah ! hurrah ! hurrah ! hurray !

Enter SIR JOSEPH *with* COUSIN HEBE.

SONG—SIR JOSEPH.

> I am the monarch of the sea,
> The ruler of the Queen's Navee,
> Whose praise Great Britain loudly chants.

COUSIN HEBE.   And we are his sisters, and his cousins,
and his aunts !

REL.   And we are his sisters, and his cousins, and
his aunts !

SIR JOSEPH.   When at anchor here I ride,
My bosom swells with pride,
And I snap my fingers at a foeman's taunts ;

COUSIN HEBE.   And so do his sisters, and his cousins, and
his aunts !

ALL.   And so do his sisters, and his cousins, and
his aunts !

SIR JOSEPH.   But when the breezes blow,
I generally go below,
And seek the seclusion that a cabin grants !

COUSIN HEBE.   And so do his sisters, and his cousins,
and his aunts !

ALL.   And so do his sisters, and his cousins, and
his aunts !
His sisters and his cousins,
Whom he reckons up by dozens,
And his aunts !

SONG—SIR JOSEPH.

When I was a lad I served a term
As office boy to an Attorney's firm.
I cleaned the windows and I swept the floor,
And I polished up the handle of the big front door.
I polished up that handle so carefullee
That now I am the Ruler of the Queen's Navee !

CHORUS.—He polished, etc.

As office boy I made such a mark
That they gave me the post of a junior clerk.
I served the writs with a smile so bland,
And I copied all the letters in a big round hand—
   I copied all the letters in a hand so free,
     That now I am the Ruler of the Queen's Navee !
       CHORUS.—He copied, etc.

In serving writs I made such a name
That an articled clerk I soon became ;
I wore clean collars and a brand-new suit
For the pass examination at the Institute.
   And that pass examination did so well for me,
     That now I am the Ruler of the Queen's Navee !
       CHORUS.—And that pass examination, etc.

Of legal knowledge I acquired such a grip
That they took me into the partnership.
And that junior partnership, I ween,
Was the only ship that I ever had seen.
   But that kind of ship so suited me,
     That now I am the Ruler of the Queen's Navee !
       CHORUS.—But that kind, etc.

I grew so rich that I was sent
By a pocket borough into Parliament.
I always voted at my party's call,
And I never thought of thinking for myself at all.
   I thought so little, they rewarded me
     By making me the Ruler of the Queen's Navee !
       CHORUS.—He thought so little, etc.

Now landsmen all, whoever you may be,
If you want to rise to the top of the tree,
If your soul isn't fettered to an office stool,
Be careful to be guided by this golden rule—
   Stick close to your desks and never go to sea,
     And you all may be Rulers of the Queen's Navee !
       CHORUS.—Stick close, etc.

SIR JOSEPH. You've a remarkably fine crew, Captain Corcoran.

CAPT. It *is* a fine crew, Sir Joseph.

SIR JOSEPH (*examining a very small midshipman*). A British sailor is a splendid fellow, Captain Corcoran.

CAPT. A splendid fellow indeed, Sir Joseph.

SIR JOSEPH. I hope you treat your crew kindly, Captain Corcoran.

CAPT. Indeed I hope so, Sir Joseph.

SIR JOSEPH. Never forget that they are the bulwarks of England's greatness, Captain Corcoran.

CAPT. So I have always considered them, Sir Joseph.

SIR JOSEPH. No bullying, I trust—no strong language of any kind, eh ?

CAPT. Oh, never, Sir Joseph.

SIR JOSEPH. What, *never* ?

CAPT. Hardly ever, Sir Joseph. They are an excellent crew, and do their work thoroughly without it.

SIR JOSEPH. Don't patronise them, sir—pray, don't patronise them.

CAPT. Certainly not, Sir Joseph.

SIR JOSEPH. That you are their captain is an accident of birth. I cannot permit these noble fellows to be patronised because an accident of birth has placed you above them and them below you.

CAPT. I am the last person to insult a British sailor, Sir Joseph.

SIR JOSEPH. You are the last person who did, Captain Corcoran. Desire that splendid seaman to step forward.

(DICK *comes forward.*)

SIR JOSEPH. No, no, the other splendid seaman.

CAPT. Ralph Rackstraw, three paces to the front— march !

SIR JOSEPH (*sternly*). If what ?

CAPT. I beg your pardon—I don't think I understand you.

SIR JOSEPH. If you *please*.

CAPT. Oh, yes, of course. If you please. (RALPH *steps forward*.)

SIR JOSEPH. You're a remarkably fine fellow.

RALPH. Yes, your honour.

SIR JOSEPH. And a first-rate seaman, I'll be bound.

RALPH. There's not a smarter topman in the Navy, your honour, though I say it who shouldn't.

SIR JOSEPH. Not at all. Proper self-respect, nothing more. Can you dance a hornpipe?

RALPH. No, your honour.

SIR JOSEPH. That's a pity: all sailors should dance hornpipes. I will teach you one this evening, after dinner. Now tell me—don't be afraid—how does your captain treat you, eh?

RALPH. A better captain don't walk the deck, your honour.

ALL. Aye! Aye!

SIR JOSEPH. Good. I like to hear you speak well of your commanding officer; I daresay he don't deserve it, but still it does you credit. Can you sing?

RALPH. I can hum a little, your honour.

SIR JOSEPH. Then hum this at your leisure. (*Giving him MS. music.*) It is a song that I have composed for the use of the Royal Navy. It is designed to encourage independence of thought and action in the lower branches of the service, and to teach the principle that a British sailor is any man's equal, excepting mine. Now, Captain Corcoran, a word with you in your cabin, on a tender and sentimental subject.

CAPT. Aye, aye, Sir Joseph. (*Crossing.*) Boatswain, in commemoration of this joyous occasion, see that extra grog is served out to the ship's company at seven bells.

BOAT. Beg pardon. If what, your honour?

CAPT. If what? I don't think I understand you.

BOAT. If you *please*, your honour.

CAPT. What!

SIR JOSEPH. The gentleman is quite right. If you *please*.

CAPT. (*stamping his foot impatiently*).   If you *please*!
                                                      [*Exit.*

SIR JOSEPH.   For I hold that on the seas
                   The expression, " if you please ",
                        A particularly gentlemanly tone im-
                        plants.
COUSIN HEBE. And so do his sisters, and his cousins, and
                        his aunts !
ALL.   And so do his sisters, and his cousins, and
                        his aunts !

              [*Exeunt* SIR JOSEPH *and* RELATIVES.

BOAT.   Ah ! Sir Joseph's a true gentleman ; courteous
and considerate to the very humblest.

RALPH.   True, Boatswain, but we are not the very
humblest.   Sir Joseph has explained our true position to
us.   As he says, a British seaman is any man's equal
excepting his, and if Sir Joseph says that, is it not our
duty to believe him ?

ALL.   Well spoke ! well spoke !

DICK.   You're on a wrong tack, and so is he.   He
means well, but he don't know.   When people have to
obey other people's orders, equality's out of the question.

ALL (*recoiling*).   Horrible ! horrible !

BOAT.   Dick Deadeye, if you go for to infuriate this
here ship's company too far, I won't answer for being able
to hold 'em in.   I'm shocked ! that's what I am—shocked !

RALPH.   Messmates, my mind's made up.   I'll speak
to the captain's daughter, and tell her, like an honest man,
of the honest love I have for her.

ALL.   Aye, aye !

RALPH.   Is not my love as good as another's ?   Is not
my heart as true as another's ?   Have I not hands and
eyes and ears and limbs like another ?

ALL.   Aye, aye !

RALPH.   True, I lack birth——

BOAT.   You've a berth on board this very ship.

RALPH.   Well said—I had forgotten that.   Messmates
—what do you say ?   Do you approve my determination ?

ALL.   We do.
DICK.   *I* don't.
BOAT.   What is to be done with this here hopeless chap?
Let us sing him the song that Sir Joseph has kindly com-
posed for us.   Perhaps it will bring this here miserable
creetur to a proper state of mind.

GLEE—RALPH, BOATSWAIN, BOATSWAIN'S MATE,
and CHORUS.

A British tar is a soaring soul,
    As free as a mountain bird,
His energetic fist should be ready to resist
    A dictatorial word.
His nose should pant and his lip should curl,
His cheeks should flame and his brow should furl,
His bosom should heave and his heart should glow,
And his fist be ever ready for a knock-down blow.

    CHORUS.—His nose should pant, etc.

His eyes should flash with an inborn fire,
    His brow with scorn be wrung ;
He never should bow down to a domineering frown,
    Or the tang of a tyrant tongue.
His foot should stamp and his throat should growl,
His hair should twirl and his face should scowl ;
His eyes should flash and his breast protrude,
And this should be his customary attitude—(*pose*).

    CHORUS.—His foot should stamp, etc.

(*All dance off excepting* RALPH, *who remains,
    leaning pensively against bulwark.*)

Enter JOSEPHINE *from cabin.*

JOS.   It is useless—Sir Joseph's attentions nauseate me.
I know that he is a truly great and good man, for he told
me so himself, but to me he seems tedious, fretful, and
dictatorial.   Yet his must be a mind of no common order,
or he would not dare to teach my dear father to dance

a hornpipe on the cabin table. (*Sees* RALPH.) Ralph Rackstraw ! (*Overcome by emotion.*)

RALPH. Aye, lady—no other than poor Ralph Rackstraw !

JOS. (*aside*). How my heart beats ! (*Aloud.*) And why poor, Ralph ?

RALPH. I am poor in the essence of happiness, lady—rich only in never-ending unrest. In me there meet a combination of antithetical elements which are at eternal war with one another. Driven hither by objective influences—thither by subjective emotions—wafted one moment into blazing day, by mocking hope—plunged the next into the Cimmerian darkness of tangible despair, I am but a living ganglion of irreconcilable antagonisms. I hope I make myself clear, lady ?

JOS. Perfectly. (*Aside.*) His simple eloquence goes to my heart. Oh, if I dared—but no, the thought is madness ! (*Aloud.*) Dismiss these foolish fancies, they torture you but needlessly. Come, make one effort.

RALPH (*aside*). I will—one. (*Aloud.*) Josephine !

JOS. (*indignantly*). Sir !

RALPH. Aye, even though Jove's armoury were launched at the head of the audacious mortal whose lips, unhallowed by relationship, dared to breathe that precious word, yet would I breathe it once, and then perchance be silent evermore. Josephine, in one brief breath I will concentrate the hopes, the doubts, the anxious fears of six weary months. Josephine, I am a British sailor, and I love you !

JOS. Sir, this audacity ! (*Aside.*) Oh, my heart, my beating heart ! (*Aloud.*) This unwarrantable presumption on the part of a common sailor ! (*Aside.*) Common ! oh, the irony of the word ! (*Crossing, aloud.*) Oh, sir, you forget the disparity in our ranks.

RALPH. I forget nothing, haughty lady. I love you desperately, my life is in your hand—I lay it at your feet ! Give me hope, and what I lack in education and polite accomplishments, that I will endeavour to acquire.

Drive me to despair, and in death alone I shall look for consolation.   I am proud and cannot stoop to implore. I have spoken and I wait your word.

Jos.   You shall not wait long.   Your proffered love I haughtily reject.   Go, sir, and learn to cast your eyes on some village maiden in your own poor rank—they should be lowered before your captain's daughter !

DUET—JOSEPHINE *and* RALPH.

Jos.
 Refrain, audacious tar,
  Your suit from pressing,
 Remember what you are,
  And whom addressing !

(*Aside.*)
 I'd laugh my rank to scorn
  In union holy,
 Were he more highly born
  Or I more lowly !

RALPH.
 Proud lady, have your way,
  Unfeeling beauty !
 You speak and I obey,
  It is my duty !
 I am the lowliest tar
  That sails the water,
 And you, proud maiden, are
  My captain's daughter !

(*Aside.*)
 My heart with anguish torn
  Bows down before her,
 She laughs my love to scorn,
  Yet I adore her !

[*Repeat refrain, ensemble, then exit* JOSEPHINE *into cabin.*

RALPH (*Recit.*)   Can I survive this overbearing
  Or live a life of mad despairing,
  My proffered love despised, rejected ?
  No, no, it's not to be expected !
   (*Calling off.*)
 Messmates, ahoy !
  Come here !   Come here !

Enter Sailors, Hebe, *and* Relatives.

ALL.   Aye, aye, my boy,
                     What cheer, what cheer ?
                     Now tell us, pray,
                     Without delay,
                     What does she say—
                     What cheer, what cheer ?

RALPH (*to* COUSIN HEBE).
                 The maiden treats my suit with scorn,
                     Rejects my humble gift, my lady ;
                 She says I am ignobly born,
                     And cuts my hopes adrift, my lady.

ALL.   Oh, cruel one.

DICK.   She spurns your suit ?   Oho !   Oho !
             I told you so, I told you so.

SAILORS *and* RELATIVES.

             Shall $\begin{Bmatrix} \text{we} \\ \text{they} \end{Bmatrix}$ submit ?   Are $\begin{Bmatrix} \text{we} \\ \text{they} \end{Bmatrix}$ but slaves ?
             Love comes alike to high and low—
             Britannia's sailors rule the waves,
                 And shall they stoop to insult ?   No !

DICK.   You must submit, you are but slaves ;
                 A lady she !   Oho !   Oho !
             You lowly toilers of the waves,
                 She spurns you all—I told you so !

RALPH.   My friends, my leave of life I'm taking,
             For oh, my heart, my heart is breaking.
             When I am gone, oh, prithee tell
             The maid that, as I died, I loved her well !

ALL (*turning away, weeping*).
                 Of life, alas ! his leave he's taking,
                 For ah ! his faithful heart is breaking ;
                 When he is gone we'll surely tell
                 The maid that, as he died, he loved her well.

(*During Chorus* BOATSWAIN *has loaded pistol,
                 which he hands to* RALPH.)

RALPH. Be warned, my messmates all
        Who love in rank above you—
      For Josephine I fall !
(*Puts pistol to his head. All the sailors stop their ears.*)
        Enter JOSEPHINE *on deck.*

JOS.   Ah ! stay your hand ! I love you !
ALL.   Ah ! stay your hand—she loves you !
RALPH (*incredulously*). Loves me ?
JOS.   Loves you !
ALL.   Yes, yes—ah, yes,—she loves you !

ENSEMBLE.

SAILORS *and* RELATIVES *and* JOSEPHINE.

    Oh joy, oh rapture unforeseen,
    For now the sky is all serene ;
    The god of day—the orb of love—
    Has hung his ensign high above,
        The sky is all ablaze.

    With wooing words and loving song,
    We'll chase the lagging hours along,
    And if { I find / we find } the maiden coy,

    I'll / We'll } murmur forth decorous joy
        In dreamy roundelays !

DICK DEADEYE.

    He thinks he's won his Josephine,
    But though the sky is now serene,
    A frowning thunderbolt above
    May end their ill-assorted love
        Which now is all ablaze.
    Our captain, ere the day is gone,
    Will be extremely down upon
    The wicked men who art employ
    To make his Josephine less coy
        In many various ways.   [*Exit* DICK.

Jos.	This very night,
Hebe.	With bated breath
Ralph.	And muffled oar—
Jos.	Without a light,
Hebe.	As still as death,
Ralph.	We'll steal ashore.
Jos.	A clergyman
Ralph.	Shall make us one
Boat.	At half-past ten,
Jos.	And then we can
Ralph.	Return, for none
Boat.	Can part them then !
All.	This very night, etc.

(Dick *appears at hatchway*.)

Dick.   Forbear, nor carry out the scheme you've planned ;
　　　　She is a lady—you a foremast hand !
　　　　Remember, she's your gallant captain's daughter,
　　　　And you the meanest slave that crawls the water !

All.　　　　Back, vermin, back,
　　　　　　Nor mock us !
　　　　　Back, vermin, back,
　　　　　　You shock us !

[*Exit* Dick.

Let's give three cheers for the sailor's bride
Who casts all thought of rank aside—
Who gives up home and fortune too
For the honest love of a sailor true !
　　For a British tar is a soaring soul
　　　As free as a mountain bird !
　　His energetic fist should be ready to resist
　　　A dictatorial word !
His foot should stamp and his throat should growl,
His hair should twirl and his face should scowl,
His eyes should flash and his breast protrude,
And this should be his customary attitude—(*pose*).

General Dance.

End of Act I.

ACT II.

Same Scene.   Night.   Awning removed.   Moonlight.

CAPTAIN *discovered singing on poop-deck, and accompanying himself on a mandolin.*   LITTLE BUTTERCUP *seated on quarter-deck, gazing sentimentally at him.*

SONG—CAPTAIN.

Fair moon, to thee I sing,
 Bright regent of the heavens,
Say, why is everything
 Either at sixes or at sevens ?
I have lived hitherto
 Free from breath of slander,
Beloved by all my crew—
 A really popular commander.
But now my kindly crew rebel,
 My daughter to a tar is partial,
Sir Joseph storms, and, sad to tell,
 He threatens a court martial !
 Fair moon, to thee I sing,
  Bright regent of the heavens,
  Say, why is everything
   Either at sixes or at sevens ?

BUT.   How sweetly he carols forth his melody to the unconscious moon !   Of whom is he thinking ?   Of some high-born beauty ?   It may be !   Who is poor Little Buttercup that she should expect his glance to fall on one so lowly !   And yet if he knew—if he only knew !

CAPT. (*coming down*). Ah! Little Buttercup, still on board? That is not quite right, little one. It would have been more respectable to have gone on shore at dusk.

BUT. True, dear Captain—but the recollection of your sad pale face seemed to chain me to the ship. I would fain see you smile before I go.

CAPT. Ah! Little Buttercup, I fear it will be long before I recover my accustomed cheerfulness, for misfortunes crowd upon me, and all my old friends seem to have turned against me!

BUT. Oh no—do not say " all ", dear Captain. That were unjust to one, at least.

CAPT. True, for you are staunch to me. (*Aside.*) If ever I gave my heart again, methinks it would be to such a one as this! (*Aloud.*) I am touched to the heart by your innocent regard for me, and were we differently situated, I think I could have returned it. But as it is, I fear I can never be more to you than a friend.

BUT. I understand! You hold aloof from me because you are rich and lofty—and I poor and lowly. But take care! The poor bumboat woman has gipsy blood in her veins, and she can read destinies.

CAPT. Destinies?

BUT. There is a change in store for you!

CAPT. A change?

BUT. Aye—be prepared!

DUET—LITTLE BUTTERCUP *and* CAPTAIN.

BUT.　　Things are seldom what they seem,
　　　　　Skim milk masquerades as cream;
　　　　　Highlows pass as patent leathers;
　　　　　Jackdaws strut in peacock's feathers.

CAPT. (*puzzled*).　Very true,
　　　　　　　　　So they do.

BUT.　　Black sheep dwell in every fold;
　　　　　All that glitters is not gold;
　　　　　Storks turn out to be but logs;
　　　　　Bulls are but inflated frogs.

CAPT. (*puzzled*).   So they be,
            Frequentlee.

BUT.   Drops the wind and stops the mill ;
          Turbot is ambitious brill ;
          Gild the farthing if you will,
          Yet it is a farthing still.

CAPT. (*puzzled*).   Yes, I know,
            That is so.
       Though to catch your drift I'm striving,
         It is shady—it is shady ;
       I don't see at what you're driving,
         Mystic lady—mystic lady,

(*Aside.*) Stern conviction's o'er me stealing,
       That the mystic lady's dealing
       In oracular revealing.

BUT. (*aside*).   Stern conviction's o'er him stealing,
       That the mystic lady's dealing
       In oracular revealing.

BOTH.   Yes, I know—
         That is so !

CAPT.   Though I'm anything but clever,
      I could talk like that for ever :
      Once a cat was killed by care ;
      Only brave deserve the fair.

BUT.   Very true,
         So they do.

CAPT.   Wink is often good as nod ;
      Spoils the child who spares the rod ;
      Thirsty lambs run foxy dangers ;
      Dogs are found in many mangers.

BUT.   Frequentlee,
        I agree.

CAPT.   Paw of cat the chestnut snatches ;
      Worn-out garments show new patches ;
      Only count the chick that hatches ;
      Men are grown-up catchy-catchies.

BUT.   Yes, I know,
         That is so.

(*Aside.*) Though to catch my drift he's striving,
    I'll dissemble—I'll dissemble ;
When he sees at what I'm driving,
    Let him tremble—let him tremble !

ENSEMBLE.

Though a mystic tone $\begin{Bmatrix} I \\ you \end{Bmatrix}$ borrow,

$\left. \begin{matrix} \text{You will} \\ \text{I shall} \end{matrix} \right\}$ learn the truth with sorrow,

Here to-day and gone to-morrow ;
    Yes, I know—
    That is so !

[*At the end exit* LITTLE BUTTERCUP *melodramatically.*

CAPT. Incomprehensible as her utterances are, I nevertheless feel that they are dictated by a sincere regard for
me. But to what new misery is she referring ? Time
alone can tell !

Enter SIR JOSEPH.

SIR JOSEPH. Captain Corcoran, I am much disappointed with your daughter. In fact, I don't think she
will do.

CAPT. She won't do, Sir Joseph !

SIR JOSEPH. I'm afraid not. The fact is, that although
I have urged my suit with as much eloquence as is consistent with an official utterance, I have done so hitherto
without success. How do you account for this ?

CAPT. Really, Sir Joseph, I hardly know. Josephine
is of course sensible of your condescension.

SIR JOSEPH. She naturally would be.

CAPT. But perhaps your exalted rank dazzles her.

SIR JOSEPH. You think it does ?

CAPT. I can hardly say ; but she is a modest girl,
and her social position is far below your own. It may be
that she feels she is not worthy of you.

SIR JOSEPH. That is really a very sensible suggestion, and displays more knowledge of human nature than I had given you credit for.

CAPT. See, she comes. If your lordship would kindly reason with her and assure her officially that it is a standing rule at the Admiralty that love levels all ranks, her respect for an official utterance might induce her to look upon your offer in its proper light.

SIR JOSEPH. It is not unlikely. I will adopt your suggestion. But soft, she is here. Let us withdraw, and watch our opportunity.

Enter JOSEPHINE *from cabin.* FIRST LORD
and CAPTAIN *retire.*

SCENA—JOSEPHINE.
The hours creep on apace,
  My guilty heart is quaking !
Oh, that I might retrace
  The step that I am taking !
Its folly it were easy to be showing,
What I am giving up and whither going.
On the one hand, papa's luxurious home,
  Hung with ancestral armour and old brasses,
Carved oak and tapestry from distant Rome,
  Rare " blue and white " Venetian finger-glasses,
Rich oriental rugs, luxurious sofa pillows,
And everything that isn't old, from Gillow's.
And on the other, a dark and dingy room,
  In some back street with stuffy children crying,
Where organs yell, and clacking housewives fume,
  And clothes are hanging out all day a-drying.
With one cracked looking-glass to see your face in,
And dinner served up in a pudding basin !

A simple sailor, lowly born,
  Unlettered and unknown,
Who toils for bread from early morn
  Till half the night has flown !

No golden rank can he impart—
No wealth of house or land—
No fortune save his trusty heart
And honest brown right hand !
And yet he is so wondrous fair
That love for one so passing rare,
So peerless in his manly beauty,
Were little else than solemn duty !
Oh, god of love, and god of reason, say,
Which of you twain shall my poor heart obey !

SIR JOSEPH *and* CAPTAIN *enter.*

SIR JOSEPH. Madam, it has been represented to me that you are appalled by my exalted rank. I desire to convey to you officially my assurance, that if your hesitation is attributable to that circumstance, it is uncalled for.

JOS. Oh ! then your lordship is of opinion that married happiness is *not* inconsistent with discrepancy in rank ?

SIR JOSEPH. I am officially of that opinion.

JOS. That the high and the lowly may be truly happy together, provided that they truly love one another ?

SIR JOSEPH. Madam, I desire to convey to you officially my opinion that love is a platform upon which all ranks meet.

JOS. I thank you, Sir Joseph. I *did* hesitate, but I will hesitate no longer. (*Aside.*) He little thinks how eloquently he has pleaded his rival's cause !

TRIO.

FIRST LORD, CAPTAIN, *and* JOSEPHINE.

CAPT.   Never mind the why and wherefore,
Love can level ranks, and therefore,
Though his lordship's station's mighty,
Though stupendous be his brain,
Though your tastes are mean and flighty
And your fortune poor and plain,

CAPT. *and* Ring the merry bells on board-ship,
SIR JOSEPH. Rend the air with warbling wild,

　　　　For the union of $\begin{Bmatrix} his \\ my \end{Bmatrix}$ lordship

　　　　　　With a humble captain's child !
CAPT.　　　　For a humble captain's daughter—
JOS.　　　　For a gallant captain's daughter—
SIR JOSEPH. And a lord who rules the water—
JOS. (*aside*). And a *tar* who ploughs the water !
ALL.　　　　Let the air with joy be laden,
　　　　　　Rend with songs the air above,
　　　　For the union of a maiden
　　　　　　With the man who owns her love !

SIR JOSEPH. Never mind the why and wherefore,
　　　　　　Love can level ranks, and therefore,
　　　　Though your nautical relation (*alluding to* CAPT.)
　　　　　　In my set could scarcely pass—
　　　　Though you occupy a station
　　　　　　In the lower middle class—
CAPT. *and* Ring the merry bells on board-ship,
SIR JOSEPH. Rend the air with warbling wild,

　　　　For the union of $\begin{Bmatrix} my \\ his \end{Bmatrix}$ lordship

　　　　　　With a humble captain's child !
CAPT.　　　　For a humble captain's daughter—
JOS.　　　　For a gallant captain's daughter—
SIR JOSEPH. And a lord who rules the water—
JOS. (*aside*). And a *tar* who ploughs the water !
ALL.　　　　Let the air with joy be laden,
　　　　　　Rend with songs the air above,
　　　　For the union of a maiden
　　　　　　With the man who owns her love !

JOS.　　　　Never mind the why and wherefore,
　　　　　　Love can level ranks, and therefore
　　　　I admit the jurisdiction ;
　　　　　　Ably have you played your part ;
　　　　You have carried firm conviction
　　　　　　To my hesitating heart.

CAPT. *and*   Ring the merry bells on board-ship,
SIR JOSEPH.   Rend the air with warbling wild,

For the union of $\begin{Bmatrix} \text{my} \\ \text{his} \end{Bmatrix}$ lordship

     With a humble captain's child !
CAPT.   For a humble captain's daughter—
JOS.   For a gallant captain's daughter—
SIR JOSEPH.   And a lord who rules the water—
JOS. (*aside*).   And a *tar* who ploughs the water !
(*Aloud.*)   Let the air with joy be laden.
CAPT. *and* SIR JOSEPH.   Ring the merry bells on board-
        ship—
JOS.   For the union of a maiden—
CAPT. *and* SIR JOSEPH.   For her union with his lordship.
ALL.   Rend with songs the air above
      For the man who owns her love !

             [*Exit* JOS.

   CAPT. Sir Joseph, I cannot express to you my delight at the happy result of your eloquence. Your argument was unanswerable.

   SIR JOSEPH. Captain Corcoran, it is one of the happiest characteristics of this glorious country that official utterances are invariably regarded as unanswerable.

           [*Exit* SIR JOSEPH.

   CAPT. At last my fond hopes are to be crowned. My only daughter is to be the bride of a Cabinet Minister. The prospect is Elysian. (*During this speech* DICK DEADEYE *has entered.*)

   DICK. Captain.

   CAPT. Deadeye ! You here ? Don't ! (*Recoiling from him.*)

   DICK. Ah, don't shrink from me, Captain. I'm unpleasant to look at, and my name's agin me, but I ain't as bad as I seem.

   CAPT. What would you with me ?

   DICK (*mysteriously*). I'm come to give you warning.

   CAPT. Indeed ! do you propose to leave the Navy then?

   DICK. No, no, you misunderstand me ; listen !

DUET.

Captain *and* Dick Deadeye.

Dick. Kind Captain, I've important information,
     Sing hey, the kind commander that you are,
  About a certain intimate relation,
     Sing hey, the merry maiden and the tar.
Both.   The merry maiden and the tar.

Capt. Good fellow, in conundrums you are speaking,
     Sing hey, the mystic sailor that you are;
  The answer to them vainly I am seeking;
     Sing hey, the merry maiden and the tar.
Both.   The merry maiden and the tar.

Dick. Kind Captain, your young lady is a-sighing,
     Sing hey, the simple captain that you are,
  This very night with Rackstraw to be flying;
     Sing hey, the merry maiden and the tar.
Both.   The merry maiden and the tar.

Capt. Good fellow, you have given timely warning,
     Sing hey, the thoughtful sailor that you are,
  I'll talk to Master Rackstraw in the morning:
     Sing hey, the cat-o'-nine-tails and the tar.
                    (*Producing a " cat ".*)
Both.   The merry cat-o'-nine-tails and the tar!

Capt.   Dick Deadeye—I thank you for your warning—
I will at once take means to arrest their flight.   This boat
cloak will afford me ample disguise—So! (*Envelops
himself in a mysterious cloak, holding it before his face.*)
   Dick.   Ha, ha! They are foiled—foiled—foiled!

Enter Crew on tiptoe, with Ralph *and* Boatswain
   meeting Josephine, *who enters from cabin on tiptoe,
   with bundle of necessaries, and accompanied by* Little
   Buttercup.

ENSEMBLE.

Carefully on tiptoe stealing,
  Breathing gently as we may,
Every step with caution feeling,
  We will softly steal away.

(CAPTAIN *stamps*.)—*Chord*.

ALL (*much alarmed*). Goodness me—
            Why, what was that?
DICK.   Silent be,
            It was the cat!
ALL (*reassured*). It was—it was the cat!
CAPT. (*producing   cat-o'-nine-tails*). They're   right,   it
            was the cat!

ALL.   Pull ashore, in fashion steady,
            Hymen will defray the fare,
          For a clergyman is ready
            To unite the happy pair!

(*Stamp as before, and Chord.*)

ALL.   Goodness me,
            Why, what was that?
DICK.   Silent be,
            Again the cat!
ALL.   It was again that cat!
CAPT. (*aside*).   They're right, it was the cat!
CAPT. (*throwing off cloak*). Hold! (*All start.*)
        Pretty daughter of mine,
          I insist upon knowing
          Where you may be going
        With these sons of the brine,
          For my excellent crew,
        Though foes they could thump any,
        Are scarcely fit company,
          My daughter, for you.
CREW.   Now, hark at that, do!
        Though foes we could thump any,
        We are scarcely fit company
          For a lady like you!

RALPH.   Proud officer, that haughty lip uncurl!
        Vain man, suppress that supercilious sneer,
  For I have dared to love your matchless girl,
      A fact well known to all my messmates here!

CAPT.   Oh, horror!

RALPH *and* Jos. $\left\{ \begin{matrix} \text{I,} \\ \text{He,} \end{matrix} \right\}$ humble, poor, and lowly born,
      The meanest in the port division—
        The butt of epauletted scorn—
      The mark of quarter-deck derision—
      $\left.\begin{matrix}\text{Have} \\ \text{Has}\end{matrix}\right\}$ dared to raise $\left\{\begin{matrix}\text{my} \\ \text{his}\end{matrix}\right\}$ wormy eyes

    Above the dust to which you'd mould $\left\{\begin{matrix}\text{me} \\ \text{him}\end{matrix}\right.$

      In manhood's glorious pride to rise,
    $\left.\begin{matrix}\text{I am} \\ \text{He is}\end{matrix}\right\}$ an Englishman—behold $\left\{\begin{matrix}\text{me!} \\ \text{him!}\end{matrix}\right.$

ALL.   He is an Englishman!

BOAT.   He is an Englishman!
      For he himself has said it,
      And it's greatly to his credit,
      That he is an Englishman!

ALL.   That he is an Englishman!

BOAT.   For he might have been a Roosian,
      A French, or Turk, or Proosian,
      Or perhaps Itali-an!

ALL.   Or perhaps Itali-an!

BOAT.   But in spite of all temptations
    To belong to other nations,
      He remains an Englishman!

ALL.   For in spite of all temptations, etc.

CAPT. (*trying to repress his anger*).
      In uttering a reprobation
        To any British tar,
      I try to speak with moderation,
      But you have gone too far.

                    I'm very sorry to disparage
                       A humble foremast lad,
                 But to seek your captain's child in marriage,
                       Why, damme, it's too bad !

During this, COUSIN HEBE *and* FEMALE RELATIVES
                   have entered.

ALL (*shocked*).   Oh !
CAPT.   Yes, damme, it's too bad !
ALL.   Oh !
CAPT. *and* DICK DEADEYE.   Yes, damme, it's too bad.

   During this, SIR JOSEPH *has appeared on poop-deck.*
        He is horrified at the bad language.

HEBE.   Did you hear him—did you hear him ?
              Oh, the monster overbearing !
            Don't go near him—don't go near him—
              He is swearing—he is swearing !
SIR JOSEPH. My pain and my distress,
              I find it is not easy to express ;
            My amazement—my surprise—
          You may learn from the expression of my eyes !
CAPT.   My lord—one word—the facts are not before you
            The word was injudicious, I allow—
          But hear my explanation, I implore you,
            And you will be indignant too, I vow !
SIR JOSEPH. I will hear of no defence,
                Attempt none if you're sensible.
              That word of evil sense
                Is wholly indefensible.
              Go, ribald, get you hence
                To your cabin with celerity.
              This is the consequence
                Of ill-advised asperity !

    [*Exit* CAPTAIN, *disgraced, followed by* JOSEPHINE.

ALL.   This is the consequence,
                Of ill-advised asperity !
SIR JOSEPH. For I'll teach you all, ere long,
                To refrain from language strong.

For I haven't any sympathy for ill-bred taunts !

HEBE. No more have his sisters, nor his cousins, nor his aunts.

ALL. For he is an Englishman, etc.

SIR JOSEPH. Now, tell me, my fine fellow—for you *are* a fine fellow——

RALPH. Yes, your honour.

SIR JOSEPH. How came your captain so far to forget himself ? I am quite sure you had given him no cause for annoyance.

RALPH. Please your honour, it was thus-wise. You see I'm only a topman—a mere foremast hand——

SIR JOSEPH. Don't be ashamed of that. Your position as a topman is a very exalted one.

RALPH. Well, your honour, love burns as brightly in the fo'c'sle as it does on the quarter-deck, and Josephine is the fairest bud that ever blossomed upon the tree of a poor fellow's wildest hopes.

Enter JOSEPHINE ; *she rushes to* RALPH'S *arms.*

JOS. Darling ! (SIR JOSEPH *horrified.*)

RALPH. She is the figurehead of my ship of life—the bright beacon that guides me into my port of happiness— the rarest, the purest gem that ever sparkled on a poor but worthy fellow's trusting brow !

ALL. Very pretty, very pretty !

SIR JOSEPH. Insolent sailor, you shall repent this outrage. Seize him ! (*Two Marines seize him and handcuff him.*)

JOS. Oh, Sir Joseph, spare him, for I love him tenderly.

SIR JOSEPH. Pray, don't. I will teach this presumptuous mariner to discipline his affections. Have you such a thing as a dungeon on board ?

ALL. We have !

DICK. They have !

SIR JOSEPH. Then load him with chains and take him there at once !

E

OCTETTE.

RALPH.   Farewell, my own,
                  Light of my life, farewell !
              For crime unknown
                  I go to a dungeon cell.

JOS.   I will atone.
                  In the meantime farewell !
              And all alone
                  Rejoice in your dungeon cell !

SIR JOSEPH.   A bone, a bone
                  I'll pick with this sailor fell ;
              Let him be shown
                  At once to his dungeon cell.

BOATSWAIN, DICK DEADEYE, *and* COUSIN HEBE.

              He'll hear no tone
                  Of the maiden he loves so well !
              No telephone
                  Communicates with his cell !

BUT. (*mysteriously*).   But when is known
                  The secret I have to tell,
              Wide will be thrown
                  The door of his dungeon cell.

ALL.   For crime unknown
                  He goes to a dungeon cell !

                            [RALPH *is led off in custody.*

SIR JOSEPH.   My pain and my distress
              Again it is not easy to express.
              My amazement, my surprise,
              Again you may discover from my eyes.

ALL.   How terrible the aspect of his eyes !

BUT.   Hold !   Ere upon your loss
                  You lay much stress,
              A long-concealèd crime
                  I would confess.

SONG—BUTTERCUP.

A many years ago,
When I was young and charming,
As some of you may know,
I practised baby-farming.

ALL.   Now this is most alarming !
When she was young and charming,
She practised baby-farming,
A many years ago.

BUT.   Two tender babes I nussed :
One was of low condition,
The other, upper crust,
A regular patrician.

ALL (*explaining to each other*).
Now, this is the position :
One was of low condition,
The other a patrician,
A many years ago.

BUT.   Oh, bitter is my cup !
However could I do it ?
I mixed those children up,
And not a creature knew it !

ALL.   However could you do it ?
Some day, no doubt, you'll rue it,
Although no creature knew it,
So many years ago.

BUT.   In time each little waif
Forsook his foster-mother,
The well-born babe was Ralph—
Your captain was the other ! ! !

ALL.   They left their foster-mother,
The one was Ralph, our brother,
Our captain was the other,
A many years ago.

SIR JOSEPH.   Then I am to understand that Captain
Corcoran and Ralph were exchanged in childhood's happy

hour—that Ralph is really the Captain, and the Captain is Ralph ?

BUT.   That is the idea I intended to convey, officially !

SIR JOSEPH.   And very well you have conveyed it.

BUT.   Aye ! aye ! yer 'onour.

SIR JOSEPH.   Dear me ! Let them appear before me, at once !

> RALPH *enters as* CAPTAIN ; CAPTAIN *as a common sailor*. JOSEPHINE *rushes to his arms.*

JOS.   My father—a common sailor !

CAPT.   It is hard, is it not, my dear ?

SIR JOSEPH.   This is a very singular occurrence ; I congratulate you both. (*To* RALPH.) Desire that remarkably fine seaman to step forward.

RALPH.   Corcoran.   Three paces to the front—march !

CAPT.   If what ?

RALPH.   If what ?   I don't think I understand you.

CAPT.   If you please.

SIR JOSEPH.   The gentleman is quite right. If you *please.*

RALPH.   Oh ! If you *please.* (CAPTAIN *steps forward*).

SIR JOSEPH (*to* CAPTAIN).   You are an extremely fine fellow.

CAPT.   Yes, your honour.

SIR JOSEPH.   So it seems that you were Ralph, and Ralph was you.

CAPT.   So it seems, your honour.

SIR JOSEPH.   Well, I need not tell you that after this change in your condition, a marriage with your daughter will be out of the question.

CAPT.   Don't say that, your honour—love levels all ranks.

SIR JOSEPH.   It does to a considerable extent, but it does not level them as much as that. (*Handing* JOSEPHINE *to* RALPH.) Here—take her, sir, and mind you treat her kindly.

RALPH *and* JOS.   Oh bliss, oh rapture !

CAPT. *and* BUT.   Oh rapture, oh bliss !

SIR JOSEPH.   Sad my lot and sorry,
    What shall I do ? I cannot live alone !
HEBE. Fear nothing—while I live I'll not desert you.
    I'll soothe and comfort your declining days.
SIR JOSEPH. No, don't do that.
HEBE.   Yes, but indeed I'd rather—
SIR JOSEPH (*resigned*). To-morrow morn our vows shall
    all be plighted,
    Three loving pairs on the same day united !

QUARTETTE.

JOSEPHINE, HEBE, RALPH, *and* DEADEYE.

  Oh joy, oh rapture unforeseen,
  The clouded sky is now serene,
  The god of day—the orb of love,
  Has hung his ensign high above,
   The sky is all ablaze.

  With wooing words and loving song,
  We'll chase the lagging hours along,
  And if $\begin{Bmatrix} \text{he finds} \\ \text{I find} \end{Bmatrix}$ the maiden coy,
  We'll murmur forth decorous joy,
   In dreamy roundelay.

CAPT. For he's the Captain of the *Pinafore*.
ALL. And a right good captain too !
CAPT.   And though before my fall
    I was captain of you all,
  I'm a member of the crew.
ALL.   Although before his fall, etc.
CAPT. I shall marry with a wife,
   In my humble rank of life ! (*turning to* BUT.)
    And you, my own, are she—
  I must wander to and fro,
  But wherever I may go,
   I shall never be untrue to thee !
ALL.   What, never ?
CAPT.   No, never !

ALL.   What, *never* ?
CAPT.   Hardly ever !
ALL.   Hardly ever be untrue to thee.
                    Then give three cheers, and one cheer more
                    For the former Captain of the *Pinafore*.

BUT.   For he loves Little Buttercup, dear Little Buttercup,
              Though I could never tell why ;
          But still he loves Buttercup, poor Little Buttercup,
              Sweet Little Buttercup, aye !
ALL.   For he loves, etc.

SIR JOSEPH.   I'm the monarch of the sea,
                  And when I've married thee (*to* HEBE),
              I'll be true to the devotion that my love implants,
HEBE.   Then good-bye to his sisters, and his cousins, and
                  his aunts,
              Especially his cousins,
              Whom he reckons up by dozens,
              His sisters, and his cousins, and his aunts !

ALL.   For he is an Englishman,
              And he himself hath said it,
              And it's greatly to his credit
          That he is an Englishman !

CURTAIN.

THE PIRATES OF PENZANCE

OR

THE SLAVE OF DUTY

DRAMATIS PERSONÆ.

MAJOR-GENERAL STANLEY.

THE PIRATE KING.

SAMUEL (*his Lieutenant*).

FREDERIC (*the Pirate Apprentice*).

SERGEANT OF POLICE.

MABEL
EDITH
KATE } (*General Stanley's Daughters*).
ISABEL

RUTH (*a Pirate Maid of all Work*).

Chorus of Pirates, Police, and General Stanley's Daughters.

———

ACT I.—A Rocky Sea-shore on the Coast of Cornwall.

ACT II.—A Ruined Chapel by Moonlight.

First produced at the Opéra Comique on April 3, 1880.

THE PIRATES OF PENZANCE

OR

THE SLAVE OF DUTY

ACT I.

SCENE.—*A rocky sea-shore on the coast of Cornwall. In the distance is a calm sea, on which a schooner is lying at anchor. As the curtain rises groups of pirates are discovered—some drinking, some playing cards. SAMUEL, the Pirate Lieutenant, is going from one group to another, filling the cups from a flask. FREDERIC is seated in a despondent attitude at the back of the scene.*

OPENING CHORUS.

> Pour, oh, pour the pirate sherry ;
> Fill, oh, fill the pirate glass ;
> And, to make us more than merry,
> Let the pirate bumper pass.

SAM.   For to-day our pirate 'prentice
 Rises from indenture freed ;
Strong his arm and keen his scent is,
 He's a pirate now indeed !

ALL.   Here's good luck to Frederic's ventures !
Frederic's out of his indentures.

SAM.   Two-and-twenty now he's rising,
   And alone he's fit to fly,
  Which we're bent on signalizing
   With unusual revelry.

ALL.   Here's good luck to Frederic's ventures !
  Frederic's out of his indentures.
  Pour, oh, pour the pirate sherry, etc.

FREDERIC *rises and comes forward with* PIRATE KING,
who enters.

KING.   Yes, Frederic, from to-day you rank as a full-blown member of our band.

ALL.   Hurrah !

FRED.   My friends, I thank you all, from my heart, for your kindly wishes. Would that I could repay them as they deserve !

KING.   What do you mean ?

FRED.   To-day I am out of my indentures, and to-day I leave you for ever.

KING.   But this is quite unaccountable ; a keener hand at scuttling a Cunarder or cutting out a P. & O. never shipped a handspike.

FRED.   Yes, I have done my best for you.   And why ? It was my duty under my indentures, and I am the slave of duty.   As a child I was regularly apprenticed to your band.   It was through an error—no matter, the mistake was ours, not yours, and I was in honour bound by it.

SAM.   An error ?   What error ?

RUTH *enters.*

FRED.   I may not tell you ; it would reflect upon my well-loved Ruth.

RUTH.   Nay, dear master, my mind has long been gnawed by the cankering tooth of mystery.   Better have it out at once.

SONG—RUTH.

When Frederic was a little lad he proved so brave and
    daring,
His father thought he'd 'prentice him to some career sea-
    faring.
I was, alas! his nurserymaid, and so it fell to *my* lot
To take and bind the promising boy apprentice to a *pilot* —
A life not bad for a hardy lad, though surely not a high
    lot,
Though I'm a nurse, you might do worse than make your
    boy a pilot.

I was a stupid nurserymaid, on breakers always steering,
And I did not catch the word aright, through being hard
    of hearing;
Mistaking my instructions, which within my brain did
    gyrate,
I took and bound this promising boy apprentice to a *pirate*.
A sad mistake it was to make and doom him to a vile lot.
I bound him to a pirate—you—instead of to a pilot.

I soon found out, beyond all doubt, the scope of this
    disaster,
But I hadn't the face to return to my place, and break it
    to my master.
A nurserymaid is not afraid of what you people *call* work,
So I made up my mind to go as a kind of piratical maid-
    of-all-work.
And that is how you find me now, a member of your
    shy lot,
Which you wouldn't have found, had he been bound
    apprentice to a pilot.

RUTH. Oh, pardon! Frederic, pardon! (*Kneels.*)
FRED. Rise, sweet one, I have long pardoned you.
RUTH (*rises*). The two words were so much alike!
FRED. They were. They still are, though years have
rolled over their heads. But this afternoon my obligation
ceases. Individually, I love you all with affection un-

speakable, but, collectively, I look upon you with a disgust that amounts to absolute detestation. Oh ! pity me, my beloved friends, for such is my sense of duty that, once out of my indentures, I shall feel myself bound to devote myself heart and soul to your extermination !

ALL.   Poor lad—poor lad ! (*All weep.*)

KING.   Well, Frederic, if you conscientiously feel that it is your duty to destroy us, we cannot blame you for acting on that conviction.   Always act in accordance with the dictates of your conscience, my boy, and chance the consequences.

SAM.   Besides, we can offer you but little temptation to remain with us.   We don't seem to make piracy pay. I'm sure I don't know why, but we don't.

FRED.   *I* know why, but, alas ! I mustn't tell you ; it wouldn't be right.

KING.   Why not, my boy ?   It's only half-past eleven, and you are one of us until the clock strikes twelve.

SAM.   True, and until then you are bound to protect our interests.

ALL.   Hear, hear !

FRED.   Well, then, it is my duty, as a pirate, to tell you that you are too tender-hearted.   For instance, you make a point of never attacking a weaker party than yourselves, and when you attack a stronger party you invariably get thrashed.

KING.   There is some truth in that.

FRED.   Then, again, you make a point of never molesting an orphan !

SAM.   Of course : we are orphans ourselves, and know what it is.

FRED.   Yes, but it has got about, and what is the consequence ?   Every one we capture says he's an orphan. The last three ships we took proved to be manned entirely by orphans, and so we had to let them go.   One would think that Great Britain's mercantile navy was recruited solely from her orphan asylums—which we know is not the case.

SAM. But, hang it all! you wouldn't have us absolutely merciless?

FRED. There's my difficulty; until twelve o'clock I would, after twelve I wouldn't. Was ever a man placed in so delicate a situation?

RUTH. And Ruth, your own Ruth, whom you love so well, and who has won her middle-aged way into your boyish heart, what is to become of *her*?

KING. Oh, he will take you with him.

FRED. Well, Ruth, I feel some little difficulty about you. It is true that I admire you very much, but I have been constantly at sea since I was eight years old, and yours is the only woman's face I have seen during that time. I think it is a sweet face.

RUTH. It is—oh, it is!

FRED. I say I *think* it is; that is my impression. But as I have never had an opportunity of comparing you with other women, it is just possible I may be mistaken.

KING. True.

FRED. What a terrible thing it would be if I were to marry this innocent person, and then find out that she is, on the whole, plain!

KING. Oh, Ruth is very well, very well indeed.

SAM. Yes, there are the remains of a fine woman about Ruth.

FRED. Do you really think so?

SAM. I do.

FRED. Then I will not be so selfish as to take her from you. In justice to her, and in consideration for you, I will leave her behind. (*Hands* RUTH *to* KING.)

KING. No, Frederic, this must not be. We are rough men who lead a rough life, but we are not so utterly heartless as to deprive thee of thy love. I think I am right in saying that there is not one here who would rob thee of this inestimable treasure for all the world holds dear.

ALL (*loudly*). Not one!

KING. No, I thought there wasn't. Keep thy love, Frederic, keep thy love. (*Hands her back to* FREDERIC.)

FRED.   You're very good, I'm sure.   [*Exit* RUTH.

KING.   Well, it's the top of the tide, and we must be off. Farewell, Frederic. When your process of extermination begins, let our deaths be as swift and painless as you can conveniently make them.

FRED.   I will ! By the love I have for you, I swear it ! Would that you could render this extermination unnecessary by accompanying me back to civilization !

KING.   No, Frederic, it cannot be. I don't think much of our profession, but, contrasted with respectability, it is comparatively honest. No, Frederic, I shall live and die a Pirate King.

SONG—PIRATE KING.

Oh, better far to live and die
Under the brave black flag I fly,
Than play a sanctimonious part,
With a pirate head and a pirate heart.
Away to the cheating world go you,
Where pirates all are well-to-do ;
But I'll be true to the song I sing,
And live and die a Pirate King.
For I am a Pirate King.

ALL.   You are !
Hurrah for our Pirate King !

KING.   And it is, it is a glorious thing
To be a Pirate King.

ALL.   Hurrah !
Hurrah for our Pirate King !

KING.   When I sally forth to seek my prey
I help myself in a royal way :
I sink a few more ships, it's true,
Than a well-bred monarch ought to do ;
But many a king on a first-class throne,
If he wants to call his crown his own,
Must manage somehow to get through
More dirty work than ever *I* do,
Though I am a Pirate King.

ALL.   You are !
                        Hurrah for our Pirate King !

KING.   And it is, it is a glorious thing
                        To be a Pirate King !

ALL.   It is !
                        Hurrah for our Pirate King !

[Exeunt all except FREDERIC.

Enter RUTH.

RUTH.   Oh, take me with you ! I cannot live if I am left behind.

FRED.   Ruth, I will be quite candid with you. You are very dear to me, as you know, but I must be circumspect. You see, you are considerably older than I. A lad of twenty-one usually looks for a wife of seventeen.

RUTH.   A wife of seventeen ! You will find me a wife of a thousand !

FRED.   No, but I shall find you a wife of forty-seven, and that is quite enough. Ruth, tell me candidly, and without reserve : compared with other women—how are *you* ?

RUTH.   I will answer you truthfully, master—I have a slight cold, but otherwise I am quite well.

FRED.   I am sorry for your cold, but I was referring rather to your personal appearance. Compared with other women, are you beautiful ?

RUTH (*bashfully*).   I have been told so, dear master.

FRED.   Ah, but lately ?

RUTH.   Oh, no, years and years ago.

FRED.   What do you think of yourself ?

RUTH.   It is a delicate question to answer, but I think I am a fine woman.

FRED.   That is your candid opinion ?

RUTH.   Yes, I should be deceiving you if I told you otherwise.

FRED.   Thank you, Ruth, I believe you, for I am sure you would not practise on my inexperience ; I wish to do the right thing, and if—I say *if*—you are really a fine woman, your age shall be no obstacle to our union! (*Chorus of Girls heard in the distance.*) Hark! Surely I hear voices! Who has ventured to approach our all but inaccessible lair? Can it be Custom House? No, it does not sound like Custom House.

RUTH (*aside*). Confusion! it is the voices of young girls! If he should see them I am lost.

FRED. (*looking off*). By all that's marvellous, a bevy of beautiful maidens!

RUTH (*aside*). Lost! lost! lost!

FRED. How lovely! how surpassingly lovely is the plainest of them! What grace—what delicacy—what refinement! And Ruth—Ruth told me she was beautiful!

RECIT.

FRED.   Oh, false one, you have deceived me!
RUTH.   I have deceived you?
FRED.   Yes, deceived me!

(*Denouncing her.*)

DUET—FRED. *and* RUTH.

FRED.   You told me you were fair as gold!
RUTH (*wildly*). And, master, am I not so?
FRED.   And now I see you're plain and old.
RUTH.   I am sure I am not a jot so.
FRED.   Upon my innocence you play.
RUTH.   I'm not the one to plot so.
FRED.   Your face is lined, your hair is grey.
RUTH.   It's gradually got so.
FRED.   Faithless woman, to deceive me,
                I who trusted so!
RUTH.   Master, master, do not leave me!
                Hear me, ere you go!
            My love without reflecting,
            Oh, do not be rejecting.
    Take a maiden tender—her affection raw and green,
            At very highest rating,
            Has been accumulating
Summers seventeen—summers seventeen.

Don't, beloved master,
Crush me with disaster.
What is such a dower to the dower I have here ?
My love unabating
Has been accumulating
Forty-seven year—forty-seven year !

ENSEMBLE.

Ruth.	Fred.
Don't, beloved master,	Yes, your former master
Crush me with disaster.	Saves you from disaster.
What is such a dower to the dower	Your love would be uncomfortably
I have here ?	fervid, it is clear,
My love unabating	If, as you are stating,
Has been accumulating	It's been accumulating
Forty - seven year — forty - seven	Forty - seven year — forty - seven
year !	year !

[*At the end he renounces her, and she goes off in
despair.*

RECIT.—FRED.

What shall I do ?   Before these gentle maidens
I dare not show in this alarming costume.
No, no, I must remain in close concealment
Until I can appear in decent clothing !

(*Hides in cave as they enter climbing over the rocks.*)

GIRLS.   Climbing over rocky mountain,
Skipping rivulet and fountain,
Passing where the willows quiver
By the ever-rolling river,
    Swollen with the summer rain ;
Threading long and leafy mazes
Dotted with unnumbered daisies ;
Scaling rough and rugged passes,
Climb the hardy little lasses,
    Till the bright sea-shore they gain !

EDITH.   Let us gaily tread the measure,
              Make the most of fleeting leisure ;
              Hail it as a true ally,
              Though it perish by and by.

ALL.   Hail it as a true ally,
               Though it perish by and by.

EDITH.   Every moment brings a treasure
              Of its own especial pleasure,
              Though the moments quickly die,
              Greet them gaily as they fly.

KATE.   Far away from toil and care,
              Revelling in fresh sea air,
              Here we live and reign alone
              In a world that's all our own.
              Here in this our rocky den,
              Far away from mortal men,
              We'll be queens, and make decrees—
              They may honour them who please.

ALL.   Let us gaily tread the measure, etc.

KATE.   What a picturesque spot !   I wonder where we are !

EDITH.   And I wonder where papa is.   We have left him ever so far behind.

ISABEL.   Oh, he will be here presently !   Remember poor papa is not as young as we are, and we have come over a rather difficult country.

KATE.   But how thoroughly delightful it is to be so entirely alone !   Why, in all probability we are the first human beings who ever set foot on this enchanting spot.

ISABEL.   Except the mermaids—it's the very place for mermaids.

KATE.   Who are only human beings down to the waist !

EDITH.   And who can't be said strictly to set *foot* anywhere.   Tails they may, but feet they *cannot*.

KATE.   But what shall we do until papa and the servants arrive with the luncheon ?

EDITH.   We are quite alone, and the sea is as smooth as glass.   Suppose we take off our shoes and stockings and paddle ?

ALL.   Yes, yes !   The very thing !   (*They prepare to carry out the suggestion. They have all taken off one shoe, when* FREDERIC *comes forward from cave.*)

FRED. (*recitative*).   Stop, ladies, pray !

ALL (*hopping on one foot*).   A man !

FRED.   I had intended
    Not to intrude myself upon your notice
    In this effective but alarming costume,
    But under these peculiar circumstances
    It is my bounden duty to inform you
    That your proceedings will not be unwitnessed !

EDITH.   But who are you, sir ?   Speak !   (*All hopping.*)

FRED.   I am a pirate !

ALL (*recoiling, hopping*).   A pirate !   Horror !

FRED.   Ladies, do not shun me !
    This evening I renounce my wild profession ;
    And to that end, oh, pure and peerless maidens !
    Oh, blushing buds of ever-blooming beauty !
    I, sore at heart, implore your kind assistance.

EDITH.   How pitiful his tale !

KATE.   How rare his beauty !

ALL.   How pitiful his tale !   How rare his beauty !

SONG—FRED.

    Oh, is there not one maiden breast
      Which does not feel the moral beauty
    Of making worldly interest
      Subordinate to sense of duty ?
    Who would not give up willingly
      All matrimonial ambition,
    To rescue such a one as I
      From his unfortunate position ?

ALL.   Alas ! there's not one maiden breast
      Which seems to feel the moral beauty

Of making worldly interest
    Subordinate to sense of duty !

FRED.   Oh, is there not one maiden here
        Whose homely face and bad complexion
    Have caused all hopes to disappear
        Of ever winning man's affection ?
    To such a one, if such there be,
        I swear by Heaven's arch above you,
    If you will cast your eyes on me—
        However plain you be—I'll love you !

ALL.   Alas ! there's not one maiden here
        Whose homely face and bad complexion
    Have caused all hope to disappear
        Of ever winning man's affection !

FRED. (*in despair*).   Not one ?
ALL.   No, no—not one !
FRED.   Not one ?
ALL.   No, no !

MABEL *enters*.

MABEL.   Yes, one !
ALL.   'Tis Mabel !
MABEL.   Yes, 'tis Mabel !

RECIT.—MABEL.

Oh, sisters, deaf to pity's name,
        For shame !
It's true that he has gone astray,
        But pray
Is that a reason good and true
        Why you
Should all be deaf to pity's name ?

ALL (*aside*).   The question is, had he not been
        A thing of beauty,
    Would she be swayed by quite as keen
        A sense of duty ?

MABEL.   For shame, for shame, for shame !

SONG—MABEL.

Poor wandering one !
Though thou hast surely strayed,
　Take heart of grace,
　Thy steps retrace,
Poor wandering one !
Poor wandering one !
If such poor love as mine
　Can help thee find
　True peace of mind—
Why, take it, it is thine !
　Take heart, fair days will shine ;
　Take any heart—take mine !

ALL.　　　Take heart ; no danger lowers ;
　　　　Take any heart—but ours !

[*Exeunt* MABEL *and* FREDERIC.

(EDITH *beckons her sisters, who form in a semicircle
around her.*)

EDITH.

What ought we to do,
　Gentle sisters, say ?
Propriety, we know,
　Says we ought to stay ;
While sympathy exclaims,
　" Free them from your tether—
Play at other games—
　Leave them here together."

KATE.

Her case may, any day,
　Be yours, my dear, or mine.
Let her make her hay
　While the sun doth shine.
Let us compromise,
　(Our hearts are not of leather.)
Let us shut our eyes,
　And talk about the weather.

GIRLS.   Yes, yes, let's talk about the weather.

CHATTERING CHORUS.

How beautifully blue the sky,
The glass is rising very high,
Continue fine I hope it may,
And yet it rained but yesterday.
To-morrow it may pour again
(I hear the country wants some rain),
Yet people say, I know not why,
That we shall have a warm July.

Enter MABEL *and* FREDERIC.

(*During* MABEL'S *solo the Girls continue chatter pianissimo, but listening eagerly all the time.*)

SOLO—MABEL.

Did ever maiden wake
From dream of homely duty,
To find her daylight break
With such exceeding beauty?
Did ever maiden close
Her eyes on waking sadness,
To dream of such exceeding gladness?

FRED.   Oh, yes! ah, yes! this is exceeding gladness.

GIRLS.   How beautifully blue the sky, etc.

SOLO—FRED.

(*During this, Girls continue their chatter pianissimo as before, but listening intently all the time.*)

Did ever pirate roll
His soul in guilty dreaming,
And wake to find that soul
With peace and virtue beaming?

ENSEMBLE.

MABEL.	FRED.	GIRLS.
Did ever maiden wake, etc.	Did ever pirate roll, etc.	How beautifully blue the sky, etc.

RECIT.—FRED.

Stay, we must not lose our senses ;
  Men who stick at no offences
    Will anon be here.
Piracy their dreadful trade is ;
  Pray you, get you hence, young ladies,
    While the coast is clear.

[FREDERIC *and* MABEL *retire.*

GIRLS.   No, we must not lose our senses,
    If they stick at no offences
      We should not be here.
    Piracy their dreadful trade is—
    Nice companions for young ladies !
      Let us disappear.

*During this chorus the Pirates have entered stealthily,
  and formed in a semicircle behind the Girls.   As the
  Girls move to go off each Pirate seizes a girl.* KING
  seizes EDITH *and* ISABEL, SAMUEL *seizes* KATE.

ALL.   Too late !
PIRATES.   Ha !   Ha !
ALL.   Too late !
PIRATES.   Ha !   Ha !
    Ha ! ha ! ha ! ha !   Ha ! ha ! ha ! ha !

ENSEMBLE.

(*Pirates pass in front of Girls.*)   (*Girls pass in front of Pirates.*)

PIRATES.	GIRLS.
Here's a first-rate opportunity	We have missed our opportunity
To get married with impunity,	Of escaping with impunity ;
And indulge in the felicity	So farewell to the felicity
Of unbounded domesticity.	Of our maiden domesticity !
You shall quickly be parsonified,	We shall quickly be parsonified,
Conjugally matrimonified,	Conjugally matrimonified,
By a doctor of divinity,	By a doctor of divinity,
Who resides in this vicinity.	Who resides in this vicinity.

MABEL (*coming forward*).

RECIT.

Hold, monsters ! Ere your pirate caravanserai
Proceed, against our will, to wed us all,
Just bear in mind that we are Wards in Chancery,
And father is a Major-General !

SAM. (*cowed*). We'd better pause, or danger may befall,
Their father is a Major-General.

GIRLS. Yes, yes ; he is a Major-General !

The MAJOR-GENERAL *has entered unnoticed, on rock.*

GEN.   Yes, I am a Major-General !
SAM.   For he is a Major-General !
ALL.   He is ! Hurrah for the Major-General !
GEN.   And it is—it is a glorious thing
             To be a Major-General !
ALL.   It is ! Hurrah for the Major-General !

SONG—MAJOR-GENERAL.

I am the very model of a modern Major-General,
I've information vegetable, animal, and mineral,
I know the kings of England, and I quote the fights
    historical,
From Marathon to Waterloo, in order categorical ;
I'm very well acquainted too with matters mathe-
    matical,
I understand equations, both the simple and
    quadratical,
About binomial theorem I'm teeming with a lot o'
    news—
With many cheerful facts about the square of the
    hypotenuse.

ALL.   With many cheerful facts, etc.
GEN.   I'm very good at integral and differential calculus,
       I know the scientific names of beings animalculous ;
       In short, in matters vegetable, animal, and mineral,
       I am the very model of a modern Major-General.

ALL. In short, in matters vegetable, animal, and mineral,
      He is the very model of a modern Major-General.

GEN. I know our mythic history, King Arthur's and Sir
          Caradoc's,
          I answer hard acrostics, I've a pretty taste for
              paradox,
      I quote in elegiacs all the crimes of Heliogabalus,
      In conics I can floor peculiarities parabolous.
      I can tell undoubted Raphaels from Gerard Dows
          and Zoffanies,
      I know the croaking chorus from the *Frogs* of
          Aristophanes,
      Then I can hum a fugue of which I've heard the
          music's din afore,
      And whistle all the airs from that infernal nonsense
          Pinafore.

ALL. And whistle all the airs, etc.

GEN. Then I can write a washing bill in Babylonic
          cuneiform,
      And tell you every detail of Caractacus's uniform ;
      In short, in matters vegetable, animal, and mineral,
      I am the very model of a modern Major-General.

ALL. In short, in matters vegetable, animal, and mineral,
      He is the very model of a modern Major-General.

GEN. In fact, when I know what is meant by " mamelon "
          and " ravelin,"
      When I can tell at sight a chassepôt rifle from a
          javelin,
      When such affairs as sorties and surprises I'm more
          wary at,
      And when I know precisely what is meant by
          " commissariat ",
      When I have learnt what progress has been made
          in modern gunnery,
      When I know more of tactics than a novice in a
          nunnery :

> In short, when I've a smattering of elemental strategy,
> You'll say a better Major-Gener*al* has never *sat* a gee—

ALL.   You'll say a better, etc.

GEN.   For my military knowledge, though I'm plucky and adventury,
> Has only been brought down to the beginning of the century ;
> But still in matters vegetable, animal, and mineral,
> I am the very model of a modern Major-General.

ALL.   But still in matters vegetable, animal, and mineral,
> He is the very model of a modern Major-General.

GEN.   And now that I've introduced myself I should like to have some idea of what's going on.

KATE.   Oh, papa—we——

SAM.   Permit me, I'll explain in two words : we propose to marry your daughters.

GEN.   Dear me !

GIRLS.   Against our wills, papa—against our wills !

GEN.   Oh, but you mustn't do that ! May I ask—this is a picturesque uniform, but I'm not familiar with it. What are you ?

KING.   We are all single gentlemen.

GEN.   Yes, I gathered that—anything else ?

KING.   No, nothing else.

EDITH.   Papa, don't believe them ; they are pirates—the famous Pirates of Penzance !

GEN.   The Pirates of Penzance ! I have often heard of them.

MABEL.   All except this gentleman—(*indicating* FREDERIC)—who was a pirate once, but who is out of his indentures to-day, and who means to lead a blameless life evermore.

GEN.   But wait a bit. I object to pirates as sons-in-law.

KING.   We object to Major-Generals as fathers-in-law. But we waive that point.   We do not press it.   We look over it.

GEN. (*aside*).   Hah ! an idea !   (*Aloud.*)   And do you mean to say that you would deliberately rob me of these, the sole remaining props of my old age, and leave me to go through the remainder of my life unfriended, un-protected, and alone ?

KING.   Well, yes, that's the idea.

GEN.   Tell me, have you ever known what it is to be an orphan ?

PIRATES (*disgusted*).   Oh, dash it all !

KING.   Here we are again !

GEN.   I ask you, have you ever known what it is to be an orphan ?

KING.   Often !

GEN.   Yes, orphan.   Have you ever known what it is to be one ?

KING.   I say, often.

ALL (*disgusted*).   Often, often, often.   (*Turning away.*)

GEN.   I don't think we quite understand one another. I ask you, have you ever known what it is to be an orphan, and you say "orphan".   As I understand you, you are merely repeating the word "orphan" to show that you understand me.

KING.   I didn't repeat the word often.

GEN.   Pardon me, you did indeed

KING.   I only repeated it once.

GEN.   True, but you repeated it.

KING.   But not often.

GEN.   Stop : I think I see where we are getting confused.   When you said "orphan", did you mean "orphan"—a person who has lost his parents, or "often" —frequently ?

KING.   Ah ! I beg pardon—I see what you mean— frequently.

GEN.   Ah ! you said often—frequently.

KING.   No, only once.

GEN. (*irritated*). Exactly—you said often, frequently,
only once.

RECIT.—GENERAL.

Oh, men of dark and dismal fate,
   Forgo your cruel employ,
Have pity on my lonely state,
   I am an orphan boy !

KING *and* SAM.   An orphan boy ?
GEN.   An orphan boy !
PIRATES.   How sad—an orphan boy .

SOLO—GENERAL.

These children whom you see
Are all that I can call my own !
PIRATES.   Poor fellow !
GEN.   Take them away from me
And I shall be indeed alone.
PIRATES.   Poor fellow !
GEN.   If pity you can feel,
   Leave me my sole remaining joy—
   See, at your feet they kneel ;
   Your hearts you cannot steel
Against the sad, sad tale of the lonely orphan boy !
PIRATES (*sobbing*).   Poor fellow !
   See at our feet they kneel ;
   Our hearts we cannot steel
Against the sad, sad tale of the lonely orphan boy !
KING.   The orphan boy !
SAM.   The orphan boy !
ALL.   The lonely orphan boy !   Poor fellow !

ENSEMBLE.

GENERAL (*aside*).	GIRLS (*aside*).	PIRATES (*aside*).
I'm telling a terrible story,	He's telling a terrible story,	If he's telling a terrible story,
But it doesn't diminish my glory ;	Which will tend to diminish his glory ;	He shall die by a death that is gory,
For they would have taken my daughters	Though they would have taken his daughters	One of the cruellest slaughters
Over the billowy waters,	Over the billowy waters.	That ever were known in these waters ;

GENERAL (*aside*).	GIRLS (*aside*).	PIRATES (*aside*).
If I hadn't, in elegant diction, Indulged in an innocent fiction ; Which is not in the same category As a regular terrible story.	It's easy, in elegant diction, To call it an innocent fiction, But it comes in the same category As a regular terrible story.	And we'll finish his moral affliction By a very complete malediction, As a compliment valedictory, If he's telling a terrible story.

KING.

Although our dark career
    Sometimes involves the crime of stealing,
We rather think that we're
    Not altogether void of feeling.
Although we live by strife,
    We're always sorry to begin it,
For what, we ask, is life
    Without a touch of Poetry in it ?

ALL (*kneeling*).

Hail, Poetry, thou heaven-born maid !
Thou gildest e'en the pirate's trade :
Hail, flowing fount of sentiment !
All hail, Divine Emollient !   (*All rise.*)

KING.

You may go, for you're at liberty, our pirate rules
    protect you,
And honorary members of our band we do elect you !

SAM.   For he is an orphan boy.
CHORUS.   He is !   Hurrah for the orphan boy.

GEN.   And it sometimes is a useful thing
           To be an orphan boy.
CHORUS.   It is !   Hurrah for the orphan boy !

           Oh, happy day, with joyous glee
           They will away and married be ;
           Should it befall auspiciously,
           Our sisters all will bridesmaids be !

RUTH *enters and comes down·to* FREDERIC.

RUTH.   Oh, master, hear one word, I do implore you!
           Remember Ruth, your Ruth, who kneels before
           you!

CHORUS.   Yes, yes, remember Ruth, who kneels before
           you!

FRED.   (*Pirates threaten* RUTH.)   Away, you did de-
           ceive me!

CHORUS.   Away, you did deceive him!

RUTH.   Oh, do not leave me!

CHORUS.   Oh, do not leave her!

FRED.   Away, you grieve me!

CHORUS.   Away, you grieve him!

FRED.   I wish you'd leave me!

           (FREDERIC *casts* RUTH *from him.*)

CHORUS.   We wish you'd leave him!

ENSEMBLE.

Pray observe the magnanimity
We $\Big\}$ display to lace and dimity!
They
Never was such opportunity
To get married with impunity,
But $\Big\{$ we $\Big\}$ give up the felicity
        they
Of unbounded domesticity,
Though a doctor of divinity
Resides in this vicinity.

[*Girls and* GENERAL *go up rocks, while Pirates
      indulge in a wild dance of delight on
      stage. The* GENERAL *produces a British
      flag, and the* PIRATE KING *produces a
      black flag with skull and cross-bones.
      Enter* RUTH, *who makes a final appeal to*
      FREDERIC, *who casts her from him.*

END OF ACT I.

THE SAVOY OPERAS

ACT II.

SCENE.—*A Ruined Chapel by Moonlight. Ruined Gothic windows at back.* GENERAL STANLEY *discovered seated pensively, surrounded by his daughters.*

CHORUS.

Oh, dry the glistening tear
That dews that martial cheek ;
Thy loving children hear,
In them thy comfort seek.
With sympathetic care
Their arms around thee creep,
For oh, they cannot bear
To see their father weep !

Enter MABEL.

SOLO—MABEL.

Dear father, why leave your bed
At this untimely hour,
When happy daylight is dead,
And darksome dangers lower ?
See, heaven has lit her lamp,
The midnight hour is past,
The chilly night air is damp,
And the dews are falling fast !
Dear father, why leave your bed
When happy daylight is dead ?

FREDERIC *enters.*

127

MABEL.   Oh, Frederic, cannot you, in the calm excellence of your wisdom, reconcile it with your conscience to say something that will relieve my father's sorrow?

FRED.   I will try, dear Mabel.   But why does he sit, night after night, in this draughty old ruin?

GEN.   Why do I sit here?   To escape from the pirates' clutches, I described myself as an orphan, and, heaven help me, I am no orphan!   I come here to humble myself before the tombs of my ancestors, and to implore their pardon for having brought dishonour on the family escutcheon.

FRED.   But you forget, sir, you only bought the property a year ago, and the stucco in your baronial hall is scarcely dry.

GEN.   Frederic, in this chapel are ancestors: you cannot deny that.   With the estate, I bought the chapel and its contents.   I don't know whose ancestors they *were*, but I know whose ancestors they *are*, and I shudder to think that their descendant by purchase (if I may so describe myself) should have brought disgrace upon what, I have no doubt, was an unstained escutcheon.

FRED.   Be comforted.   Had you not acted as you did, these reckless men would assuredly have called in the nearest clergyman, and have married your large family on the spot.

GEN.   I thank you for your proffered solace, but it is unavailing.   I assure you, Frederic, that such is the anguish and remorse I feel at the abominable falsehood by which I escaped these easily deluded pirates, that I would go to their simple-minded chief this very night and confess all, did I not fear that the consequences would be most disastrous to myself.   At what time does your expedition march against these scoundrels?

FRED.   At eleven, and before midnight I hope to have atoned for my involuntary association with the pestilent scourges by sweeping them from the face of the earth—and then, dear Mabel, you will be mine!

GEN.   Are your devoted followers at hand?

FRED.   They are, they only wait my orders.

RECIT.—General.

Then, Frederic, let your escort lion-hearted
Be summoned to receive a General's blessing,
Ere they depart upon their dread adventure.

FRED.   Dear sir, they come.

*Enter Police, marching in single file.   They form in
line, facing audience.*

SONG—Sergeant.

When the foeman bares his steel,
Tarantara ! tarantara !
We uncomfortable feel,
Tarantara !
And we find the wisest thing,
Tarantara ! tarantara !
Is to slap our chests and sing
Tarantara !
For when threatened with emeutes,
Tarantara ! tarantara !
And your heart is in your boots,
Tarantara !
There is nothing brings it round,
Tarantara ! tarantara !
Like the trumpet's martial sound,
Tarantara ! tarantara !
Tarantara-ra-ra-ra-ra !

ALL.   Tarantara-ra-ra-ra-ra !

MABEL.   Go, ye heroes, go to glory,
Though you die in combat gory,
Ye shall live in song and story.
Go to immortality !
Go to death, and go to slaughter ;
Die, and every Cornish daughter
With her tears your grave shall water.
Go, ye heroes, go and die !

ALL.   Go, ye heroes, go and die !

F

POLICE.

    Though to us it's evident,
              Tarantara ! tarantara !
    These intentions are well meant,
              Tarantara !
    Such expressions don't appear,
              Tarantara ! tarantara !
    Calculated men to cheer,
              Tarantara !
    Who are going to meet their fate
    In a highly nervous state,
              Tarantara !
    Still to us it's evident
    These intentions are well meant.
              Tarantara !

EDITH.   Go and do your best endeavour,
         And before all links we sever,
         We will say farewell for ever.
              Go to glory and the grave !

GIRLS.   For your foes are fierce and ruthless,
         False, unmerciful, and truthless.
         Young and tender, old and toothless,
              All in vain their mercy crave.

SERG.   We observe too great a stress,
         On the risks that on us press,
         And of reference a lack
         To our chance of coming back.
         Still, perhaps it would be wise
         Not to carp or criticise,
         For it's very evident
         These attentions are well meant.

ALL.   Yes, to them it's evident
         Our attentions are well meant.
              Tarantara-ra-ra-ra-ra !
    Go, ye heroes, go to glory, etc.

ENSEMBLE.

Chorus of all but Police.   *Chorus of Police.*

Go and do your best endeavour,   Such expressions don't appear,
And before all links we sever   Tarantara, tarantara !
We will say farewell for ever.   Calculated men to cheer,
   Go to glory and the grave !   Tarantara !
For your foes are fierce and ruth-   Who are going to their fate,
   less,   Tarantara, tarantara !
False, unmerciful, and truth-   In a highly nervous state—
   less.   Tarantara !
Young and tender, old and tooth-   We observe too great a stress,
   less,   Tarantara, tarantara !
   All in vain their mercy crave.   On the risks that on us press,
                                                 Tarantara !
                                     And of reference a lack,
                                                 Tarantara, tarantara !
                                     To our chance of coming back,
                                                 Tarantara !

GEN.   Away, away !
POLICE (*without moving*).   Yes, yes, we go.
GEN.   These pirates slay.
POLICE.   Tarantara !
GEN.   Then do not stay.
POLICE.   Tarantara !
GEN.   Then why this delay ?
POLICE.   All right—we go.
            Yes, forward on the foe !
GEN.   Yes, but you *don't* go !
POLICE.   We go, we go !
            Yes, forward on the foe !
GEN.   Yes, but you *don't* go !
ALL.   At last they really go.

[MABEL *tears herself from* FREDERIC *and exit,
    followed by her sisters, consoling her.
    The* GENERAL *and others follow.* FRED-
    ERIC *remains.*

RECIT.—FRED.

Now for the pirates' lair !   Oh, joy unbounded !
Oh, sweet relief !   Oh, rapture unexampled !

At last I may atone, in some slight measure,
For the repeated acts of theft and pillage
Which, at a sense of duty's stern dictation,
I, circumstance's victim, have been guilty.

(KING *and* RUTH *appear at the window, armed.*)

KING.   Young Frederic ! (*Covering him with pistol.*)
FRED.   Who calls ?
KING.   Your late commander !
RUTH.   And I, your little Ruth ! (*Covering him with pistol.*)
FRED.   Oh, mad intruders,
         How dare ye face me ?   Know ye not, oh rash ones,
         That I have doomed you to extermination ?

(KING *and* RUTH *hold a pistol to each ear.*)

KING.   Have mercy on us, hear us, ere you slaughter.
FRED.   I do not think I ought to listen to you.
         Yet, mercy should alloy our stern resentment,
         And so I will be merciful—say on !

TRIO—RUTH, KING, *and* FRED.

RUTH.   When you had left our pirate fold
             We tried to raise our spirits faint,
         According to our customs old,
             With quips and quibbles quaint.
         But all in vain the quips we heard,
             We lay and sobbed upon the rocks,
         Until to somebody occurred
             A startling paradox.
FRED.   A paradox ?
KING (*laughing*).   A paradox !
RUTH.   A most ingenious paradox !
         We've quips and quibbles heard in flocks,
         But none to beat this paradox !
             Ha ! ha ! ha ! ha ! Ho ! ho ! ho ! ho !

KING.   We knew your taste for curious quips,
        For cranks and contradictions queer,
     And with the laughter on our lips,
     We wished you there to hear.
     We said, " If we could tell it him,
       How Frederic would the joke enjoy ! "
     And so we've risked both life and limb
      To tell it to our boy.

FRED. (*interested*). That paradox ? That paradox ?

KING
and }(*laughing*). That most ingenious paradox !
RUTH

     We've quips and quibbles heard in flocks,
     But none to beat that paradox !
      Ha ! ha ! ha ! ha ! Ho ! ho ! ho ! ho !

CHANT—KING.

For some ridiculous reason, to which, however, I've no
    desire to be disloyal,
Some person in authority, I don't know who, very likely
    the Astronomer Royal,
Has decided that, although for such a beastly month as
    February, twenty-eight days as a rule are plenty,
One year in every four his days shall be reckoned as nine-
    and-twenty.
Through some singular coincidence—I shouldn't be sur-
    prised if it were owing to the agency of an ill-natured
    fairy—
You are the victim of this clumsy arrangement, having
    been born in leap-year, on the twenty-ninth of
    February,
And so, by a simple arithmetical process, you'll easily
    discover,
That though you've lived twenty-one years, yet, if we go
    by birthdays, you're only five and a little bit over !

RUTH.   Ha ! ha ! ha ! ha !
KING.   Ho ! ho ! ho ! ho !

FRED. Dear me !
Let's see ! (*counting on fingers*).
Yes, yes ; with yours my figures do agree !

ALL. Ha ! ha ! ha ! ha ! Ho ! ho ! ho ! ho ! (FRED-
ERIC *more amused than any.*)

FRED. How quaint the ways of Paradox !
At common sense she gaily mocks !
Though counting in the usual way,
    Years twenty-one I've been alive,
Yet, reckoning by my natal day,
    I am a little boy of five !

ALL. He is a little boy of five ! Ha ! ha !
A paradox, a paradox,
A most ingenious paradox !
Ha ! ha ! ha ! ha ! Ho ! ho ! ho ! ho ! (RUTH
    and KING *throw themselves back on seats,
    exhausted with laughter.*)

FRED. Upon my word, this is most curious—most
absurdly whimsical. Five-and-a-quarter ! No one would
think it to look at me !

RUTH. You are glad now, I'll be bound, that you
spared us. You would never have forgiven yourself
when you discovered that you had killed *two of your
comrades.*

FRED. My comrades ?

KING (*rises*). I'm afraid you don't appreciate the
delicacy of your position. You were apprenticed to us——

FRED. Until I reached my twenty-first year.

KING. No, until you reached your twenty-first *birthday*
(*producing document*), and, going by birthdays, you are as
yet only five-and-a-quarter.

FRED. You don't mean to say you are going to hold
me to that ?

KING. No, we merely remind you of the fact, and leave
the rest to your sense of duty.

RUTH. Your sense of duty !

FRED. (*wildly*). Don't put it on that footing ! As I
was merciful to you just now, be merciful to me ! I

implore you not to insist on the letter of your bond just as the cup of happiness is at my lips !

RUTH. We insist on nothing ; we content ourselves with pointing out to you *your duty*.

KING. Your duty !

FRED. (*after a pause*). Well, you have appealed to my sense of duty, and my duty is only too clear. I abhor your infamous calling ; I shudder at the thought that I have ever been mixed up with it ; but duty is before all— at any price I will do my duty.

KING. Bravely spoken ! Come, you are one of us once more.

FRED. Lead on, I follow. (*Suddenly.*) Oh, horror !

KING. ⎱ What the matter ?
RUTH. ⎰

FRED. Ought I to tell you ? No, no, I cannot do it ; and yet, as one of your band——

KING. Speak out, I charge you by that sense of conscientiousness to which we have never yet appealed in vain.

FRED. General Stanley, the father of my Mabel——

KING. ⎱ Yes, yes !
RUTH. ⎰

FRED. He escaped from you on the plea that he was an orphan !

KING. He did !

FRED. It breaks my heart to betray the honoured father of the girl I adore, but as your apprentice I have no alternative. It is my duty to tell you that General Stanley is no orphan !

KING. ⎱ What !
RUTH. ⎰

FRED. More than that, he never was one !

KING. Am I to understand that, to save his contemptible life, he dared to practise on our credulous simplicity ? (FREDERIC *nods as he weeps*.) Our revenge shall be swift and terrible. We will go and collect our band and attack Tremorden Castle this very night.

FRED.   But—stay——

KING.   Not a word !   He is doomed !

TRIO.

KING *and* RUTH.   FRED.

Away, away ! my heart's on fire,   Away, away ! ere I expire—
   I burn this base deception to   I find my duty hard to do to-day!
     repay,   My heart is filled with anguish dire,
This very night my vengeance dire   It strikes me to the core.   Away,
   Shall glut itself in gore.   Away,   away !
     away !

KING.

With falsehood foul
He tricked us of our brides.
Let vengeance howl ;
The Pirate so decides.
Our nature stern
He softened with his lies,
And, in return,
To-night the traitor dies.

ALL.   Yes, yes ! to-night the traitor dies.

RUTH.   To-night he dies !

KING.   Yes, or early to-morrow.

FRED.   His girls likewise ?

RUTH.   They will welter in sorrow.

KING.   The one soft spot

FRED.   In their natures they cherish—

RUTH.   And all who plot

KING.   To abuse it shall perish !

ALL.   Yes, all who plot
To abuse it shall perish !
Away, away ! etc.

[*Exeunt* KING *and* RUTH.

Enter MABEL.

RECIT.—Mabel.

All is prepared, your gallant crew await you.
My Frederic in tears ?   It cannot be
That lion-heart quails at the coming conflict ?

FRED.   No, Mabel, no.   A terrible disclosure
Has just been made !   Mabel, my dearly-loved
    one,
I bound myself to serve the pirate captain
Until I reached my one-and-twentieth birthday—

MABEL.   But you *are* twenty-one ?

FRED.   I've just discovered
That I was born in leap-year, and that birthday
Will not be reached by me till 1940.

MABEL.   Oh, horrible ! catastrophe appalling !

FRED.   And so, farewell !

MABEL.   No, no !   Ah, Frederic, hear me.

DUET—Mabel *and* Fred.

MABEL.   Stay, Frederic, stay !
                They have no legal claim,
                No shadow of a shame
                Will fall upon thy name.
            Stay, Frederic, stay !

FRED.   Nay, Mabel, nay !
                To-night I quit these walls,
                The thought my soul appals,
                But when stern Duty calls,
            I must obey.

MABEL.   Stay, Frederic, stay !

FRED.   Nay, Mabel, nay !

MABEL.   They have no claim—

FRED.   But Duty's name !
                The thought my soul appals,
                But when stern Duty calls,
            I must obey.

F 2

BALLAD—Mabel.

Ah, leave me not to pine
    Alone and desolate ;
No fate seemed fair as mine,
    No happiness so great !
And nature, day by day,
    Has sung, in accents clear,
This joyous roundelay,
    " He loves thee—he is here.
        Fa-la, fa-la, fa-la."

FRED.   Ah, must I leave thee here
    In endless night to dream,
Where joy is dark and drear,
    And sorrow all supreme !
Where nature, day by day,
    Will sing, in altered tone,
This weary roundelay,
    " He loves thee—he is gone.
        Fa-la, fa-la, fa-la.

FRED.   In 1940 I of age shall be,
    I'll then return, and claim you—I declare it !
MABEL.   It seems so long !
FRED.   Swear that, till then, you will be true to me.
MABEL.   Yes, I'll be strong !
    By all the Stanleys dead and gone, I swear it !

ENSEMBLE.

Oh, here is love, and here is truth,
    And here is food for joyous laughter.
He }
She } will be faithful to { his }
                          { her } sooth
    Till we are wed, and even after.

[FREDERIC *rushes to window and leaps out.*

MABEL (*almost fainting*). No, I am brave! Oh, family
        descent,
      How great thy charm, thy sway how excellent!
      Come, one and all, undaunted men in blue,
      A crisis, now, affairs are coming to!

      Enter Police, marching in single file.

SERG.   Though in body and in mind,
             Tarantara, tarantara!
         We are timidly inclined,
             Tarantara!
         And anything but blind,
             Tarantara, tarantara!
         To the danger that's behind,
             Tarantara!
         Yet, when the danger's near,
             Tarantara, tarantara!
         We manage to appear,
             Tarantara!
         As insensible to fear
         As anybody here.
             Tarantara, tarantara-ra-ra-ra-ra!

MABEL. Sergeant, approach! Young Frederic was
to have led you to death and glory.

ALL. That is not a pleasant way of putting it.

MABEL. No matter; he will not so lead you, for he
has allied himself once more with his old associates.

ALL. He has acted shamefully!

MABEL. You speak falsely. You know nothing about
it. He has acted nobly.

ALL. He has acted nobly!

MABEL. Dearly as I loved him before, his heroic
sacrifice to his sense of duty has endeared him to me
tenfold. He has done his duty. I will do mine. Go ye
and do yours.   [*Exit* MABEL.

ALL. Right oh!

SERG. This is perplexing.

ALL. We cannot understand it at all.

SERG. Still, as he is actuated by a sense of duty——

ALL. That makes a difference, of course. At the same time we repeat, we cannot understand it at all.

SERG. No matter; our course is clear. We must do our best to capture these pirates alone. It is most distressing to us to be the agents whereby our erring fellow-creatures are deprived of that liberty which is so dear to all—but we should have thought of that before we joined the Force.

ALL. We should !

SERG. It is too late now !

ALL. It is !

SONG—SERGEANT.

SERG. When a felon's not engaged in his employment—

ALL.   His employment,

SERG. Or maturing his felonious little plans—

ALL.   Little plans,

SERG. His capacity for innocent enjoyment—

ALL.   'Cent enjoyment

SERG. Is just as great as any honest man's—

ALL.   Honest man's.

SERG. Our feelings we with difficulty smother—

ALL.   'Culty smother

SERG. When constabulary duty's to be done—

ALL.   To be done.

SERG. Ah, take one consideration with another—

ALL.   With another,

SERG. A policeman's lot is not a happy one.

ALL.   When constabulary duty's to be done—

                To be done,

      The policeman's lot is not a happy one.

SERG. When the enterprising burglar's not a-burgling—

ALL.   Not a-burgling,

SERG. When the cut-throat isn't occupied in crime—

ALL.   'Pied in crime,

SERG. He loves to hear the little brook a-gurgling—

ALL.   Brook a-gurgling,

SERG. And listen to the merry village chime—
ALL.   Village chime.
SERG. When the coster's finished jumping on his mother—
ALL.   On his mother,
SERG. He loves to lie a-basking in the sun—
ALL.   In the sun.
SERG. Ah, take one consideration with another—
ALL.   With another,
SERG. The policeman's lot is not a happy one.
ALL.   When constabulary duty's to be done—
                         To be done,
         The policeman's lot is not a happy one—
                         Happy one.

(Chorus of Pirates without, in the distance.)

         A rollicking band of pirates we,
         Who, tired of tossing on the sea,
         Are trying their hand at a burglaree,
                 With weapons grim and gory.

SERG. Hush, hush! I hear them on the manor poaching,
         With stealthy step the pirates are approaching.

(Chorus of Pirates, resumed nearer.)

         We are not coming for plate or gold—
         A story General Stanley's told—
         We seek a penalty fifty-fold,
                 For General Stanley's story.

POLICE.   They seek a penalty—
PIRATES *(without)*.   Fifty-fold,
         We seek a penalty—
POLICE.   Fifty-fold,
ALL.   We ⎫
         They ⎭ seek a penalty fifty-fold,
         For General Stanley's story.
SERG.   They come in force, with stealthy stride,
         Our obvious course is now—to hide.

*Police conceal themselves. As they do so, the Pirates
are seen appearing at ruined window. They enter
cautiously, and come down stage.* SAMUEL *is laden
with burglarious tools and pistols, etc.*

CHORUS—PIRATES (*very loud*).
    With cat-like tread,
      Upon our prey we steal,
    In silence dread
      Our cautious way we feel.
    No sound at all,
      We never speak a word,
    A fly's foot-fall
      Would be distinctly heard—

POLICE (*pianissimo*).   Tarantara, tarantara !

PIRATES. So stealthily the pirate creeps,
    While all the household soundly sleeps.
    Come, friends, who plough the sea,
      Truce to navigation,
      Take another station ;
    Let's vary piracee
    With a little burglaree !

POLICE (*pianissimo*).   Tarantara, tarantara !

SAM. (*distributing implements to various members of the
gang*).
    Here's your crowbar and your centrebit,
    Your life-preserver—you may want to hit ;
    Your silent matches, your dark lantern seize,
    Take your file and your skeletonic keys.

Enter KING, FREDERIC, *and* RUTH.

ALL (*fortissimo*).   With cat-like tread, etc.

RECIT.

FRED.   Hush, hush, not a word ! I see a light inside !
      The Major-General comes, so quickly hide !

PIRATES.   Yes, yes, the Major-General comes !

[*Exeunt* KING, FREDERIC, SAMUEL, *and* RUTH.

POLICE.   Yes, yes, the Major-General comes !
GEN. (*entering in dressing-gown, carrying a light*).
                Yes, yes, the Major-General comes !

SOLO—GENERAL.

Tormented with the anguish dread
    Of falsehood unatoned,
I lay upon my sleepless bed,
    And tossed and turned and groaned.
The man who finds his conscience ache
    No peace at all enjoys,
And as I lay in bed awake
    I though I heard a noise.

PIRATES. } He though he heard a noise—ha ! ha !
POLICE. } He thought he heard a noise—ha ! ha ! (*Very
                loud.*)

GEN.   No, all is still
                In dale, on hill ;
            My mind is set at ease.
            So still the scene—
                It must have been
            The sighing of the breeze.

BALLAD—GENERAL.

Sighing softly to the river
    Comes the loving breeze,
Setting nature all a-quiver,
    Rustling through the trees—

ALL.   Through the trees.
GEN.   And the brook, in rippling measure,
            Laughs for very love,
        While the poplars, in their pleasure,
            Wave their arms above.

POLICE } Yes, the trees, for very love,
  and } Wave their leafy arms above,
PIRATES.}   River, river, little river,
            May thy loving prosper ever.

Heaven speed thee, poplar tree,
May thy wooing happy be.

GEN. Yet, the breeze is but a rover ;
When he wings away,
Brook and poplar mourn a lover !
Sighing well-a-day !

ALL. Well-a-day !

GEN. Ah ! the doing and undoing,
That the rogue could tell !
When the breeze is out a-wooing,
Who can woo so well ?

POLICE   Shocking tales the rogue could tell,
and   Nobody can woo so well.
PIRATES.   Pretty brook, thy dream is over,
For thy love is but a rover !
Sad the lot of poplar trees,
Courted by the fickle breeze !

Enter the GENERAL'S *daughters, all in white peignoirs
and night-caps, and carrying lighted candles.*

GIRLS. Now what is this, and what is that, and why does
father leave his rest
At such a time of night as this, so very incom-
pletely dressed ?
Dear father is, and always was, the most
methodical of men !
It's his invariable rule to go to bed at half-past ten.
What strange occurrence can it be that calls dear
father from his rest
At such a time of night as this, so very incom-
pletely dressed ?

Enter KING, SAMUEL, *and* FREDERIC.

KING. Forward, my men, and seize that General there!
(*They seize the* GENERAL.)

GIRLS. The pirates ! the pirates ! Oh, despair !

PIRATES. Yes, we're the pirates, so despair !

GEN.   Frederic here ! Oh, joy ! Oh, rapture !
         Summon your men and effect their capture !
MABEL.   Frederic, save us !
FRED.   Beautiful Mabel,
         I would if I could, but I am not able.
PIRATES. He's telling the truth, he is not able.
KING.   With base deceit
                 You worked upon our feelings !
             Revenge is sweet,
                 And flavours all our dealings !
             With courage rare
                 And resolution manly,
             For death prepare,
                 Unhappy General Stanley.

MABEL (*wildly*).   Is he to die, unshriven—unannealed ?
GIRLS.   Oh, spare him !
MABEL.   Will no one in his cause a weapon wield ?
GIRLS.   Oh, spare him !
POLICE (*springing up*).   Yes, we are here, though hitherto
                                    concealed !
GIRLS.   Oh, rapture !
POLICE.   So to Constabulary, pirates, yield !
GIRLS.   Oh, rapture !

(*A struggle ensues between Pirates and Police. Eventually
    the Police are overcome, and fall prostrate, the Pirates
    standing over them with drawn swords.*)

CHORUS OF POLICE AND PIRATES.

         You ⎱ triumph now, for well we trow
         We ⎰
             Our mortal career's cut short,
         No pirate band will take its stand
             At the Central Criminal Court.
SERG.   To gain a brief advantage you've contrived,
        But your proud triumph will not be long-lived.

KING.   Don't say you are orphans, for we know that game.
SERG.   On your allegiance we've a stronger claim—
        We charge you yield, in Queen Victoria's name !
KING (*baffled*).   You do !
POLICE.   We do !
        We charge you yield, in Queen Victoria's name !

(*Pirates kneel, Police stand over them triumphantly.*)

KING.   We yield at once, with humbled mien,
        Because, with all our faults, we love our Queen.
POLICE. Yes, yes, with all their faults, they love their
        Queen.
GIRLS.   Yes, yes, with all, etc.

(*Police, holding Pirates by the collar, take out
            handkerchiefs and weep.*)

GEN.   Away with them, and place them at the bar !

Enter RUTH.

RUTH.   One moment ! let me tell you who they are.
        They are no members of the common throng ;
        They are all noblemen who have gone wrong !
GEN.   No Englishman unmoved that statement hears,
        Because, with all our faults, we love our House
        of Peers.

RECIT.—GENERAL.

I pray you, pardon me, ex-Pirate King,
Peers will be peers, and youth will have its fling.
Resume your ranks and legislative duties,
And take my daughters, all of whom are beauties.

FINALE.

Poor wandering ones !
Though ye have surely strayed,
Take heart of grace,
Your steps retrace,
Poor wandering ones !

Poor wandering ones !
  If such poor love as ours
  Can help you find
  True peace of mind,
Why, take it, it is yours !
  Poor wandering ones ! etc.

CURTAIN.

PATIENCE

OR

BUNTHORNE'S BRIDE

DRAMATIS PERSONÆ.

COLONEL CALVERLEY   *(Officers of*
MAJOR MURGATROYD   *Dragoon*
LIEUT. THE DUKE OF DUNSTABLE   *Guards).*
REGINALD BUNTHORNE (*a Fleshly Poet*).
ARCHIBALD GROSVENOR (*an Idyllic Poet*).
MR. BUNTHORNE'S SOLICITOR.
THE LADY ANGELA
THE LADY SAPHIR
THE LADY ELLA   *(Rapturous Maidens).*
THE LADY JANE
PATIENCE (*a Dairy Maid*).
Chorus of Rapturous Maidens and Officers of Dragoon Guards.

ACT I.—Exterior of Castle Bunthorne.

ACT II.—A Glade.

First produced at the Opéra Comique on April 23, 1881.

PATIENCE

OR

BUNTHORNE'S BRIDE

ACT I.

SCENE.—*Exterior of Castle Bunthorne. Entrance to Castle by drawbridge over moat. Young ladies dressed in æsthetic draperies are grouped about the stage. They play on lutes, mandolins, etc., as they sing, and all are in the last stage of despair.* ANGELA, ELLA, *and* SAPHIR *lead them.*

CHORUS.

Twenty love-sick maidens we,
　　Love-sick all against our will.
Twenty years hence we shall be
　　Twenty love-sick maidens still.
Twenty love-sick maidens we,
And we die for love of thee.

SOLO—ANGELA.

Love feeds on hope, they say, or love will die—

ALL.　　　　　　　　　Ah, miserie !

Yet my love lives, although no hope have I !

ALL.　　　　　　　　　Ah, miserie !

Alas, poor heart, go hide thyself away—
To weeping concords tune thy roundelay !

　　　　　　　　　　Ah, miserie !

CHORUS.

All our love is all for one,
    Yet that love he heedeth not,
He is coy and cares for none,
    Sad and sorry is our lot !
                        Ah, miserie !

SOLO—ELLA.

Go, breaking heart,
    Go, dream of love requited ;
Go, foolish heart,
    Go, dream of lovers plighted ;
Go, madcap heart,
    Go, dream of never waking ;
And in thy dream
    Forget that thou art breaking !

CHORUS.   Ah, miserie !
ELLA.   Forget that thou art breaking !
CHORUS.   Twenty love-sick maidens, etc.

ANG.   There is a strange magic in this love of ours !
Rivals as we all are in the affections of our Reginald, the
very hopelessness of our love is a bond that binds us to
one another !

SAPH.   Jealousy is merged in misery.   While he, the
very cynosure of our eyes and hearts, remains icy insensible—what have we to strive for ?

ELLA.   The love of maidens is, to him, as interesting
as the taxes !

SAPH.   Would that it were !   He pays his taxes.

ANG.   And cherishes the receipts !

Enter LADY JANE.

SAPH.   Happy receipts !

JANE (*suddenly*).   Fools !

ANG.   I beg your pardon ?

JANE.   Fools and blind !   The man loves—wildly loves !

ANG.   But whom ?   None of us !

JANE. No, none of us. His weird fancy has lighted, for the nonce, on Patience, the village milkmaid!

SAPH. On Patience? Oh, it cannot be!

JANE. Bah! But yesterday I caught him in her dairy, eating fresh butter with a tablespoon. To-day he is not well!

SAPH. But Patience boasts that she has never loved—that love is, to her, a sealed book! Oh, he cannot be serious!

JANE. 'Tis but a fleeting fancy—'twill quickly pass away. (*Aside.*) Oh, Reginald, if you but knew what a wealth of golden love is waiting for you, stored up in this rugged old bosom of mine, the milkmaid's triumph would be short indeed!

(PATIENCE *appears on an eminence. She looks down with pity on the despondent Ladies.*)

RECIT.—PATIENCE.

Still brooding on their mad infatuation!
I thank thee, Love, thou comest not to me!
Far happier I, free from thy ministration,
Than dukes or duchesses who love can be!

SAPH. (*looking up*). 'Tis Patience—happy girl! Loved by a Poet!

PA. Your pardon, ladies. I intrude upon you. (*Going.*)

ANG. Nay, pretty child, come hither. Is it true
That you have never loved?

PA. Most true indeed.

SOPRANOS. Most marvellous!

CONTRALTOS. And most deplorable!

SONG—PATIENCE.

I cannot tell what this love may be
That cometh to all, but not to me.
It cannot be kind as they'd imply,
Or why do these ladies sigh?

It cannot be joy and rapture deep,
Or why do these gentle ladies weep ?
It cannot be blissful as 'tis said,
Or why are their eyes so wondrous red ?

Though everywhere true love I see
A-coming to all, but not to me,
I cannot tell what this love may be !
For I am blithe and I am gay,
While they sit sighing night and day
Think of the gulf 'twixt them and me,
" Fal la la la ! "—and " Miserie ! "

CHORUS.   Yes, she is blithe, etc.

PA.   If love is a thorn, they show no wit
Who foolishly hug and foster it.
If love is a weed, how simple they
Who gather it, day by day !
If love is a nettle that makes you smart,
Then why do you wear it next your heart ?
And if it be none of these, say I,
Ah, why do you sit and sob and sigh ?
Though everywhere, etc.

CHORUS.   For she is blithe, etc.

ANG.   Ah, Patience, if you have never loved, you have
never known true happiness ! (*All sigh.*)

PA.   But the truly happy always seem to have so much
on their minds.   The truly happy never seem quite well.

JANE.   There is a transcendentality of delirium—an
acute accentuation of supremest ecstasy—which the earthy
might easily mistake for indigestion.   But it is *not* indigestion—it is æsthetic transfiguration ! (*To the others.*)
Enough of babble.   Come !

PA.   But stay, I have some news for you.   The 35th
Dragoon Guards have halted in the village, and are even
now on their way to this very spot.

ANG.   The 35th Dragoon Guards !

SAPH.   They are fleshly men, of full habit !

ELLA.   We care nothing for Dragoon Guards !

PA.   But, bless me, you were all engaged to them a year ago !

SAPH.   A year ago !

ANG.   My poor child, you don't understand these things. A year ago they were very well in our eyes, but since then our tastes have been etherealized, our perceptions exalted. (*To others.*)   Come, it is time to lift up our voices in morning carol to our Reginald.   Let us to his door.

> [*The Ladies go off, two and two, into the Castle, singing refrain of " Twenty love - sick maidens we", and accompanying themselves on harps and mandolins.* PATIENCE *watches them in surprise, as she climbs the rock by which she entered.*

March. Enter Officers of Dragoon Guards, led by MAJOR.

CHORUS OF DRAGOONS.

The soldiers of our Queen
Are linked in friendly tether ;
Upon the battle scene
They fight the foe together.
There every mother's son
Prepared to fight and fall is ;
The enemy of one
The enemy of all is !

Enter COLONEL.

SONG—COLONEL.

If you want a receipt for that popular mystery,
    Known to the world as a Heavy Dragoon,
Take all the remarkable people in history,
    Rattle them off to a popular tune.
The pluck of Lord Nelson on board of the *Victory*—
Genius of Bismarck devising a plan—
The humour of Fielding (which sounds contradictory)—
    Coolness of Paget about to trepan—

The science of Jullien, the eminent musico—
    Wit of Macaulay, who wrote of Queen Anne—
The pathos of Paddy, as rendered by Boucicault—
    Style of the Bishop of Sodor and Man—
The dash of a D'Orsay, divested of quackery—
Narrative powers of Dickens and Thackeray—
Victor Emmanuel—peak-haunting Peveril—
Thomas Aquinas, and Doctor Sacheverell—
Tupper and Tennyson—Daniel Defoe—
Anthony Trollope and Mr. Guizot !
        Take of these elements all that is fusible,
        Melt them all down in a pipkin or crucible,
        Set them to simmer and take off the scum,
        And a Heavy Dragoon is the residuum !

CHORUS.   Yes ! yes ! yes ! yes !
            A Heavy Dragoon is the residuum !

COL.   If you want a receipt for this soldier-like paragon,
        Get at the wealth of the Czar (if you can)—
The family pride of a Spaniard from Arragon—
    Force of Mephisto pronouncing a ban—
A smack of Lord Waterford, reckless and rollicky—
    Swagger of Roderick, heading his clan—
The keen penetration of Paddington Pollaky—
    Grace of an Odalisque on a divan—
The genius strategic of Cæsar or Hannibal—
Skill of Sir Garnet in thrashing a cannibal—
Flavour of Hamlet—the Stranger, a touch of him—
Little of Manfred (but not very much of him)—
Beadle of Burlington—Richardson's show—
Mr Micawber and Madame Tussaud !
        Take of these elements all that is fusible,
        Melt them all down in a pipkin or crucible,
        Set them to simmer and take off the scum,
        And a Heavy Dragoon is the residuum !

ALL.   Yes ! yes ! yes ! yes !
            A Heavy Dragoon is the residuum !

COL. Well, here we are once more on the scene of our former triumphs. But where's the Duke?

Enter DUKE, *listlessly, and in low spirits.*

DUKE. Here I am! (*Sighs.*)

COL. Come, cheer up, don't give way!

DUKE. Oh, for that, I'm as cheerful as a poor devil can be expected to be who has the misfortune to be a duke, with a thousand a day!

MAJ. Humph! Most men would envy you!

DUKE. Envy *me*? Tell me, Major, are you fond of toffee?

MAJ. Very!

COL. We are all fond of toffee.

ALL. We are!

DUKE. Yes, and toffee in moderation is a capital thing. But to *live* on toffee—toffee for breakfast, toffee for dinner, toffee for tea—to have it supposed that you care for nothing *but* toffee, and that you would consider yourself insulted if anything but toffee were offered to you—how would you like *that*?

COL. I can quite believe that, under those circumstances, even toffee would become monotonous.

DUKE. For " toffee " read flattery, adulation, and abject deference, carried to such a pitch that I began, at last, to think that man was born bent at an angle of forty-five degrees! Great Heavens, what is there to adulate in me! Am I particularly intelligent, or remarkably studious, or excruciatingly witty, or unusually accomplished, or exceptionally virtuous?

COL. You're about as commonplace a young man as ever I saw.

ALL. You are!

DUKE. Exactly! That's it exactly! That describes me to a T! Thank you all very much! Well, I couldn't stand it any longer, so I joined this second-class cavalry regiment. In the Army, thought I, I shall be occasionally snubbed, perhaps even bullied, who knows? The thought was rapture, and here I am.

Col. (*looking off*).   Yes, and here are the ladies !
Duke.   But who is the gentleman with the long hair ?
Col.   I don't know.
Duke.   He seems popular !
Col.   He *does* seem popular !

Bunthorne *enters, followed by Ladies, two and two, singing and playing on harps as before. He is composing a poem, and quite absorbed. He sees no one, but walks across the stage, followed by Ladies. They take no notice of Dragoons — to the surprise and indignation of those Officers.*

Chorus of Ladies.

In a doleful train
    Two and two we walk all day—
For we love in vain !
    None so sorrowful as they
        Who can only sigh and say,
        Woe is me, alackaday !

Chorus of Dragoons.

Now is not this ridiculous—and is not this preposterous ?
    A thorough-paced absurdity—explain it if you can.
Instead of rushing eagerly to cherish us and foster us,
    They all prefer this melancholy literary man.
        Instead of slyly peering at us,
        Casting looks endearing at us,
    Blushing at us, flushing at us—flirting with a fan ;
They're actually sneering at us, fleering at us, jeering at us !
        Pretty sort of treatment for a military man !
        Pretty sort of treatment for a military man !

Ang.   Mystic poet, hear our prayer,
        Twenty love-sick maidens we—
    Young and wealthy, dark and fair—
        All of county family.
            And we die for love of thee—
            Twenty love-sick maidens we !

CHORUS OF LADIES.   Yes, we die for love of thee—
                    Twenty love-sick maidens we !

BUN. (*aside—slyly*).   Though my book I seem to scan
                In a rapt ecstatic way,
            Like a literary man
                Who despises female clay,
            I hear plainly all they say,
            Twenty love-sick maidens they !

OFFICERS (*to each other*).   He hears plainly, etc.

SAPH.   Though so excellently wise,
            For a moment mortal be,
        Deign to raise thy purple eyes
            From thy heart-drawn poesy.
        Twenty love-sick maidens see—
        Each is kneeling on her knee !   (*All kneel.*)

CHORUS OF LADIES.   Twenty love-sick, etc.

BUN. (*aside*).   Though, as I remarked before,
            Any one convinced would be
        That some transcendental lore
            Is monopolizing me,
        Round the corner I can see
        Each is kneeling on her knee !

OFFICERS (*to each other*).   Round the corner, etc.

ENSEMBLE.

| OFFICERS. | LADIES. |
| Now is not this ridiculous, etc. | Mystic poet, hear our prayer, etc. |

COL.   Angela ! what is the meaning of this ?

ANG.   Oh, sir, leave us ; our minds are but ill-tuned
to light love-talk.

MAJ.   But what in the world has come over you all ?

JANE.   Bunthorne ! *He* has come over us. He has
come among us, and he has idealized us.

DUKE.   Has he succeeded in idealizing *you* ?

JANE.   He has !

DUKE.   Good old Bunthorne !

JANE.   My eyes are open ; I droop despairingly ; I am soulfully intense ; I am limp and I cling !

(*During this* BUNTHORNE *is seen in all the agonies of composition. The Ladies are watching him intently as he writhes. At last he hits on the word he wants and writes it down. A general sense of relief.*)

BUN.   Finished !   At last !   Finished !

(*He staggers, overcome with the mental strain, into arms of* COLONEL.)

COL.   Are you better now ?

BUN.   Yes—oh, it's you—I am better now.   The poem is finished, and my soul had gone out into it.   That was all.   It was nothing worth mentioning, it occurs three times a day.   (*Sees* PATIENCE, *who has entered during this scene.*)   Ah, Patience !   Dear Patience !   (*Holds her hand ; she seems frightened.*)

ANG.   Will it please you read it to us, sir ?

SAPH.   This we supplicate.   (*All kneel.*)

BUN.   Shall I ?

ALL THE DRAGOONS.   No !

BUN.   (*annoyed—to* PATIENCE).   I will read it if *you* bid me !

PA.   (*much frightened*).   You can if you like !

BUN.   It is a wild, weird, fleshly thing ; yet very tender, very yearning, very precious.   It is called, " Oh, Hollow !   Hollow !   Hollow ! "

PA.   Is it a hunting song ?

BUN.   A hunting song ?   No, it is *not* a hunting song. It is the wail of the poet's heart on discovering that everything is commonplace.   To understand it, cling passionately to one another and think of faint lilies.   (*They do so as he recites*)—

" OH, HOLLOW ! HOLLOW ! HOLLOW ! "

What time the poet hath hymned
The writhing maid, lithe-limbed,
　　Quivering on amaranthine asphodel,
How can he paint her woes,
Knowing, as well he knows,
　　That all can be set right with calomel ?

When from the poet's plinth
The amorous colocynth
　　Yearns for the aloe, faint with rapturous thrills,
How can he hymn their throes
Knowing, as well he knows,
　　That they are only uncompounded pills ?

Is it, and can it be,
Nature hath this decree,
　　Nothing poetic in the world shall dwell ?
Or that in all her works
Something poetic lurks,
　　Even in colocynth and calomel ?
　　　　　　　　　　　　I cannot tell.

　　　　　　　　　　　　　　　[*Exit* BUNTHORNE.

ANG.　How purely fragrant !

SAPH.　How earnestly precious !

PA.　Well, it seems to me to be nonsense.

SAPH.　Nonsense, yes, perhaps—but oh, what precious nonsense !

COL.　This is all very well, but you seem to forget that you are engaged to us.

SAPH.　It can never be.　You are not Empyrean.　You are not Della Cruscan.　You are not even Early English. Oh, be Early English ere it is too late ! (*Officers look at each other in astonishment.*)

JANE (*looking at uniform*).　Red and Yellow !　Primary colours !　Oh, South Kensington !

DUKE.　We didn't design our uniforms, but we don't see how they could be improved.

JANE.　No, you wouldn't.　Still, there *is* a cobwebby

grey velvet, with a tender bloom like cold gravy, which, made Florentine fourteenth - century, trimmed with Venetian leather and Spanish altar lace, and surmounted with something Japanese—it matters not what—would at least be Early English! Come, maidens.

> [*Exeunt Maidens, two and two, singing refrain*
> *of "Twenty love-sick maidens we". The*
> *Officers watch them off in astonishment.*

DUKE. Gentlemen, this is an insult to the British uniform——

COL. A uniform that has been as successful in the courts of Venus as on the field of Mars!

SONG—COLONEL.

When I first put this uniform on,
I said, as I looked in the glass,
" It's one to a million
That any civilian
My figure and form will surpass.
Gold lace has a charm for the fair,
And I've plenty of that, and to spare,
While a lover's professions,
When uttered in Hessians,
Are eloquent everywhere! "
A fact that I counted upon,
When I first put this uniform on!

CHORUS OF DRAGOONS.

By a simple coincidence, few
Could ever have counted upon,
The same thing occurred to me, too,
When I first put this uniform on!

COL. I said, when I first put it on,
" It is plain to the veriest dunce
That every beauty
Will feel it her duty
To yield to its glamour at once.

They will see that I'm freely gold-laced
In a uniform handsome and chaste "—
   But the peripatetics
   Of long-haired æsthetics
Are very much more to their taste—
   Which I never counted upon,
    When I first put this uniform on !

CHORUS.   By a simple coincidence, few
    Could ever have reckoned upon,
   I didn't anticipate that,
    When I first put this uniform on !

               [*The Dragoons go off angrily.*

Enter BUNTHORNE, *who changes his manner
and becomes intensely melodramatic.*

RECIT. AND SONG—BUNTHORNE.

   Am I alone,
      And unobserved ? I am !
   Then let me own
      I'm an æsthetic sham !
   This air severe
      Is but a mere
          Veneer !
   This cynic smile
      Is but a wile
          Of guile !
   This costume chaste
      Is but good taste
          Misplaced !

   Let me confess !
A languid love for lilies does *not* blight me !
Lank limbs and haggard cheeks do *not* delight me !
   I do *not* care for dirty greens
      By any means.

I do *not* long for all one sees
    That's Japanese.
I am *not* fond of uttering platitudes
    In stained-glass attitudes.
In short, my mediævalism's affectation,
Born of a morbid love of admiration !

SONG.

If you're anxious for to shine in the high æsthetic line as
    a man of culture rare,
You must get up all the germs of the transcendental terms,
    and plant them everywhere.
You must lie upon the daisies and discourse in novel
    phrases of your complicated state of mind,
The meaning doesn't matter if it's only idle chatter of a
    transcendental kind.
          And every one will say,
          As you walk your mystic way,
" If this young man expresses himself in terms too deep
    for *me*,
Why, what a very singularly deep young man this deep
    young man must be ! "

Be eloquent in praise of the very dull old days which have
    long since passed away,
And convince 'em, if you can, that the reign of good Queen
    Anne was Culture's palmiest day.
Of course you will pooh-pooh whatever's fresh and new,
    and declare it's crude and mean,
For Art stopped short in the cultivated court of the Empress
    Josephine.
          And every one will say,
          As you walk your mystic way,
" If that's not good enough for him which is good enough
    for *me*,
Why, what a very cultivated kind of youth this kind of
    youth must be ! "

Then a sentimental passion of a vegetable fashion must
    excite your languid spleen,
An attachment *à la* Plato for a bashful young potato, or
    a not-too-French French bean !
Though the Philistines may jostle, you will rank as an
    apostle in the high æsthetic band,
If you walk down Piccadilly with a poppy or a lily in
    your mediæval hand.
        And every one will say,
        As you walk your flowery way,
" If he's content with a vegetable love which would
    certainly not suit *me*,
Why, what a most particularly pure young man this pure
    young man must be ! "

At the end of his song PATIENCE *enters. He sees her.*

BUN. Ah ! Patience, come hither. I am pleased
with thee. The bitter-hearted one, who finds all else
hollow, is pleased with thee. For you are not hollow.
Are you ?

PA. No, thanks, I have dined ; but—I beg your
pardon—I interrupt you.

BUN. Life is made up of interruptions. The tortured
soul, yearning for solitude, writhes under them. Oh, but
my heart is a-weary ! Oh, I am a cursed thing ! Don't go.

PA. Really, I'm very sorry——

BUN. Tell me, girl, do you ever yearn ?

PA. (*misunderstanding him*). I earn my living.

BUN. (*impatiently*). No, no ! Do you know what it
is to be heart-hungry ? Do you know what it is to yearn
for the Indefinable, and yet to be brought face to face,
daily, with the Multiplication Table ? Do you know what
it is to seek oceans and to find puddles ?—to long for
whirlwinds and yet to have to do the best you can with
the bellows ? That's my case. Oh, I am a cursed thing !
Don't go.

PA. If you please, I don't understand you—you
frighten me !

Bun. Don't be frightened—it's only poetry.

Pa. Well, if that's poetry, I don't like poetry.

Bun. (*eagerly*). Don't you? (*Aside.*) Can I trust her? (*Aloud.*) Patience, you don't like poetry—well, between you and me, *I* don't like poetry. It's hollow, unsubstantial—unsatisfactory. What's the use of yearning for Elysian Fields when you know you can't get 'em, and would only let 'em out on building leases if you had 'em?

Pa. Sir, I——

Bun. Patience, I have long loved you. Let me tell you a secret. I am not as bilious as I look. If you like, I will cut my hair. There is more innocent fun within me than a casual spectator would imagine. You have never seen me frolicsome. Be a good girl—a very good girl—and one day you shall. If you are fond of touch-and-go jocularity—this is the shop for it.

Pa. Sir, I will speak plainly. In the matter of love I am untaught. I have never loved but my great-aunt. But I am quite certain that, under any circumstances, I couldn't possibly love *you*.

Bun. Oh, you think not?

Pa. I'm quite sure of it. Quite sure. Quite.

Bun. Very good. Life is henceforth a blank. I don't care what becomes of me. I have only to ask that you will not abuse my confidence; though *you* despise me, I am extremely popular with the other young ladies.

Pa. I only ask that you will leave me and never renew the subject.

Bun. Certainly. Broken-hearted and desolate, I go. (*Recites.*)

> " Oh, to be wafted away
>   From this black Aceldama of sorrow,
> Where the dust of an earthy to-day
>   Is the earth of a dusty to-morrow ! "

It is a little thing of my own. I call it " Heart Foam ". I shall not publish it. Farewell ! Patience, Patience, farewell !

[*Exit* Bunthorne.

PA. What on earth does it all mean ? Why does he love me ? Why does he expect me to love him ? He's not a relation ! It frightens me !

Enter ANGELA.

ANG. Why, Patience, what is the matter ?

PA. Lady Angela, tell me two things. Firstly, what on earth is this love that upsets everybody ; and, secondly, how is it to be distinguished from insanity ?

ANG. Poor blind child ! Oh, forgive her, Eros ! Why, love is of all passions the most essential ! It is the embodiment of purity, the abstraction of refinement ! It is the one unselfish emotion in this whirlpool of grasping greed !

PA. Oh, dear, oh ! (*Beginning to cry.*)

ANG. Why are you crying ?

PA. To think that I have lived all these years without having experienced this ennobling and unselfish passion ! Why, what a wicked girl I must be ! For it *is* unselfish, isn't it ?

ANG. Absolutely ! Love that is tainted with selfishness is no love. Oh, try, try, try to love ! It really isn't difficult if you give your whole mind to it.

PA. I'll set about it at once. I won't go to bed until I'm head over ears in love with somebody.

ANG. Noble girl ! But is it possible that you have never loved anybody ?

PA. Yes, one.

ANG. Ah ! Whom ?

PA. My great-aunt——

ANG. Great-aunts don't count.

PA. Then there's nobody. At least—no, nobody. Not since I was a baby. But *that* doesn't count, I suppose.

ANG. I don't know. Tell me all about it.

DUET—PATIENCE *and* ANGELA.

Long years ago—fourteen, maybe—
  When but a tiny babe of four,
Another baby played with me,
  My elder by a year or more ;

> A little child of beauty rare,
> With marvellous eyes and wondrous hair,
> Who, in my child-eyes, seemed to me
> All that a little child should be !
>   Ah, how we loved, that child and I !
>   How pure our baby joy !
> How true our love—and, by the by,
>   *He* was a little boy !

ANG.   Ah, old, old tale of Cupid's touch !
>   I thought as much—I thought as much !
>   He *was* a little boy !

PA. (*shocked*). Pray don't misconstrue what I say—
>   Remember, pray—remember, pray,
>   He was a *little* boy !

ANG.   No doubt ! Yet, spite of all your pains,
>   The interesting fact remains—
>   He was a little *boy* !

ENSEMBLE. { Ah, yes, in / No doubt ! Yet, } spite of all { my / your } pains, etc.

[*Exit* ANGELA.

PA. It's perfectly dreadful to think of the appalling state I must be in ! I had no idea that love was a duty. No wonder they all look so unhappy ! Upon my word, I hardly like to associate with myself. I don't think I'm respectable. I'll go at once and fall in love with—— (*Enter* GROSVENOR.) A stranger !

DUET—PATIENCE *and* GROSVENOR.

GROS. Prithee, pretty maiden—prithee, tell me true,
>   (Hey, but I'm doleful, willow willow waly !)
> Have you e'er a lover a-dangling after you ?
>   Hey willow waly O !
>   I would fain discover
>   If you have a lover ?
>   Hey willow waly O !

PA.   Gentle sir, my heart is frolicsome and free—
        (Hey, but he's doleful, willow willow waly !)
        Nobody I care for comes a-courting me—
            Hey willow waly O !
            Nobody I care for
            Comes a-courting—therefore,
            Hey willow waly O !

GROS. Prithee, pretty maiden, will you marry me ?
        (Hey, but I'm hopeful, willow willow waly !)
        I may say, at once, I'm a man of propertee—
            Hey willow waly O !
            Money, I despise it ;
            Many people prize it,
            Hey willow waly O !

PA.   Gentle sir, although to marry I design—
        (Hey, but he's hopeful, willow willow waly !)
        As yet I do not know you, and so I must decline.
            Hey willow waly O !
            To other maidens go you—
            As yet I do not know you,
            Hey willow waly O !

GROS. Patience ! Can it be that you don't recognise
me ?

PA.   Recognise you ? No, indeed I don't !

GROS. Have fifteen years so greatly changed me ?

PA.   Fifteen years ? What do you mean ?

GROS. Have you forgotten the friend of your youth,
your Archibald ?—your little playfellow ? Oh, Chronos,
Chronos, this is too bad of you !

PA.   Archibald ! Is it possible ? Why, let me look !
It is ! It is ! It must be ! Oh, how happy I am !
I thought we should never meet again ! And how you've
grown !

GROS. Yes, Patience, I am much taller and much
stouter than I was.

PA.   And how you've improved !

Gros. Yes, Patience, I am very beautiful! (*Sighs.*)

Pa. But surely *that* doesn't make you unhappy?

Gros. Yes, Patience. Gifted as I am with a beauty which probably has not its rival on earth, I am, nevertheless, utterly and completely miserable.

Pa. Oh—but why?

Gros. My child-love for you has never faded. Conceive, then, the horror of my situation when I tell you that it is my hideous destiny to be madly loved at first sight by every woman I come across!

Pa. But why do you make yourself so picturesque? Why not disguise yourself, disfigure yourself, anything to escape this persecution?

Gros. No, Patience, that may not be. These gifts—irksome as they are—were given to me for the enjoyment and delectation of my fellow-creatures. I am a trustee for Beauty, and it is my duty to see that the conditions of my trust are faithfully discharged.

Pa. And you, too, are a Poet?

Gros. Yes, I am the Apostle of Simplicity. I am called " Archibald the All-Right "—for I am infallible!

Pa. And is it possible that you condescend to love such a girl as I?

Gros. Yes, Patience, is it not strange? I have loved you with a Florentine fourteenth-century frenzy for full fifteen years!

Pa. Oh, marvellous! I have hitherto been deaf to the voice of love. I seem now to know what love is! It has been revealed to me—it is Archibald Grosvenor!

Gros. Yes, Patience, it is!

Pa. (*as in a trance*). We will never, never part!

Gros. We will live and die together!

Pa. I swear it!

Gros. We both swear it!

Pa. (*recoiling from him*). But—oh, horror!

Gros. What's the matter?

Pa. Why, you are perfection! A source of endless ecstasy to all who know you!

Gros.   I know I am.   Well ?

Pa.   Then, bless my heart, there can be nothing unselfish in loving *you* !

Gros.   Merciful powers !   I never thought of that !

Pa.   To monopolize those features on which all women love to linger !   It would be unpardonable !

Gros.   Why, so it would !   Oh, fatal perfection, again you interpose between me and my happiness !

Pa.   Oh, if you were but a thought less beautiful than you are !

Gros.   Would that I were ;   but candour compels me to admit that I'm not !

Pa.   Our duty is clear ; we must part, and for ever !

Gros.   Oh, misery !   And yet I cannot question the propriety of your decision.   Farewell, Patience !

Pa.   Farewell, Archibald !   But stay !

Gros.   Yes, Patience ?

Pa.   Although I may not love *you*—for you are perfection—there is nothing to prevent your loving *me*. I am plain, homely, unattractive !

Gros.   Why, that's true !

Pa.   The love of such a man as you for such a girl as I must be unselfish !

Gros.   Unselfishness itself !

DUET—Patience *and* Grosvenor.

Pa.   Though to marry you would very selfish be—
Gros.   Hey, but I'm doleful—willow willow waly !
Pa.   You may, all the same, continue loving me—
Gros.   Hey willow waly O !
Both.   All the world ignoring,
                You'll ⎫
                   I'll ⎭ go on adoring—
                Hey willow waly O !

[*At the end, exeunt despairingly, in opposite directions.*

FINALE—ACT I.

Enter BUNTHORNE, *crowned with roses and hung about with garlands, and looking very miserable. He is led by* ANGELA *and* SAPHIR (*each of whom holds an end of the rose-garland by which he is bound*), *and accompanied by procession of Maidens. They are dancing classically, and playing on cymbals, double pipes, and other archaic instruments.*

CHORUS.

Let the merry cymbals sound,
Gaily pipe Pandæan pleasure,
With a Daphnephoric bound
Tread a gay but classic measure.
Every heart with hope is beating,
For at this exciting meeting
Fickle Fortune will decide
Who shall be our Bunthorne's bride !

Enter Dragoons, led by COLONEL, MAJOR, *and* DUKE.
They are surprised at proceedings.

CHORUS OF DRAGOONS.

Now tell us, we pray you,
Why thus they array you—
Oh, poet, how say you—
What is it you've done ?

DUKE.   Of rite sacrificial,
By sentence judicial,
This seems the initial,
Then why don't you run ?

COL.   They cannot have led you
To hang or behead you,
Nor may they *all* wed you,
Unfortunate one !

CHORUS OF DRAGOONS.

Then tell us, we pray you,
Why thus they array you—
Oh, poet, how say you—
What is it you've done ?

RECIT.—BUNTHORNE.

Heart-broken at my Patience's barbarity,
By the advice of my solicitor (*introducing his Solicitor*),
In aid—in aid of a deserving charity,
I've put myself up to be raffled for !

MAIDENS. By the advice of his solicitor
He's put himself up to be raffled for !

DRAGOONS. Oh, horror ! urged by his solicitor,
He's put himself up to be raffled for !

MAIDENS. Oh, heaven's blessing on his solicitor !

DRAGOONS. A hideous curse on his solicitor !

[*The* SOLICITOR, *horrified at the Dragoons'*
curse, rushes off.

COL. Stay, we implore you,
Before our hopes are blighted ;
You see before you
The men to whom you're plighted !

CHORUS OF DRAGOONS.

Stay we implore you,
For we adore you ;
To us you're plighted
To be united—
Stay, we implore you !

SOLO—DUKE.

Your maiden hearts, ah, do not steel
To pity's eloquent appeal,
Such conduct British soldiers feel.
(*Aside to Dragoons.*) Sigh, sigh, all sigh !
(*They all sigh.*)

To foeman's steel we rarely see
A British soldier bend the knee,
Yet, one and all, they kneel to ye—
(*Aside to Dragoons.*)   Kneel, kneel, all kneel!

(*They all kneel.*)

Our soldiers very seldom cry,
And yet—I need not tell you why—
A tear-drop dews each martial eye!
(*Aside to Dragoons.*)   Weep, weep, all weep!

(*They all weep.*)

ENSEMBLE.

Our soldiers very seldom cry,
And yet—I need not tell you why—
A tear-drop dews each manly eye!
Weep, weep, all weep!

BUNTHORNE (*who has been impatient during this appeal*).

Come, walk up, and purchase with avidity,
Overcome your diffidence and natural timidity,
Tickets for the raffle should be purchased with avidity,
    Put in half a guinea and a husband you may gain—
Such a judge of blue-and-white and other kinds of pottery—
From early Oriental down to modern terra-cotta-ry—
Put in half a guinea—you may draw him in a lottery—
    Such an opportunity may not occur again.

CHORUS.   Such a judge of blue-and-white, etc.

(*Maidens crowd up to purchase tickets ; during this
    Dragoons dance in single file round stage, to express
    their indifference.*)

DRAGOONS.   We've been thrown over, we're aware,
    But we don't care—but we don't care!
    There's fish in the sea, no doubt of it,
    As good as ever came out of it,
    And some day we shall get our share,
    So we don't care—so we don't care!

During this the Maidens have been buying tickets. At last JANE *presents herself.* BUNTHORNE *looks at her with aversion.*

RECIT.

BUN.   And are *you* going a ticket for to buy ?

JANE (*surprised*). Most certainly I am ; why shouldn't I ?

BUN. (*aside*). Oh, Fortune, this is hard ! (*Aloud.*)
        Blindfold your eyes ;
        Two minutes will decide who wins the
        prize ! (*Maidens blindfold themselves.*)

CHORUS OF MAIDENS.

Oh, Fortune, to my aching heart be kind !

Like us, thou art blindfolded, but not blind ! (*Each
    uncovers one eye.*)

Just raise your bandage, thus, that you may see,

And give the prize, and give the prize to me ! (*They
    cover their eyes again.*)

BUN. Come, Lady Jane, I pray you draw the first !

JANE (*joyfully*). He loves me best !

BUN. (*aside*).   I want to know the worst !

JANE *puts hand in bag to draw ticket.* PATIENCE
    enters and prevents her doing so.

PA. Hold ! Stay your hand !

ALL (*uncovering their eyes*). What means this interfer-
    ence ?
    Of this bold girl I pray you make a clearance !

JANE. Away with you, and to your milk-pails go !

BUN. (*suddenly*). She wants a ticket ! Take a dozen !

PA.   No !

SOLO—PATIENCE (*kneeling to* BUNTHORNE).

    If there be pardon in your breast
      For this poor penitent,
    Who, with remorseful thought opprest,
      Sincerely doth repent ;

If you, with one so lowly, still
Desire to be allied,
Then you may take me, if you will,
For I will be your bride !

ALL.   Oh, shameless one !
           Oh, bold-faced thing !
        Away you run,
           Go, take you wing,
        You shameless one !
           You bold-faced thing !

BUN. How strong is love !   For many and many a week
She's loved me fondly and has feared to speak,
But Nature, for restraint too mighty far,
Has burst the bonds of Art—and here we are !

PA.   No, Mr. Bunthorne, no—you're wrong again ;
Permit me—I'll endeavour to explain !

SONG—PATIENCE.

PA.   True love must single-hearted be—
BUN.   Exactly so !
PA.   From every selfish fancy free—
BUN.   Exactly so !
PA.   No idle thought of gain or joy
        A maiden's fancy should employ—
        True love must be without alloy.
ALL.   Exactly so !

PA.   Imposture to contempt must lead—
COL.   Exactly so !
PA.   Blind vanity's dissension's seed—
MAJ.   Exactly so !
PA.   It follows, then, a maiden who
        Devotes herself to loving *you* (*indicating*
           BUNTHORNE)
        Is prompted by no selfish view—
ALL.   Exactly so !

SAPH.   Are you resolved to wed this shameless one ?
ANG.   Is there no chance for any other ?
BUN. (*decisively*).   None ! (*Embraces* PATIENCE.)
                    [*Exeunt* PATIENCE *and* BUNTHORNE.

(ANGELA, SAPHIR, *and* ELLA *take* COLONEL, DUKE, *and*
   MAJOR *down, while Girls gaze fondly at other Officers.*)

SESTETTE.

I hear the soft note of the echoing voice
    Of an old, old love, long dead—
It whispers my sorrowing heart " rejoice "—
    For the last sad tear is shed—
The pain that is all but a pleasure will change
    For the pleasure that's all but pain,
And never, oh never, this heart will range
    From that old, old love again !
                        (*Girls embrace Officers.*)

CHORUS.   Yes, the pain that is all, etc.   (*Embrace.*)

Enter PATIENCE *and* BUNTHORNE.

As the Dragoons and Girls are embracing, enter GROSVENOR,
   *reading. He takes no notice of them, but comes slowly
   down, still reading. The Girls are all strangely
   fascinated by him, and gradually withdraw from
   Dragoons.*

ANG.   But who is this, whose god-like grace
                Proclaims he comes of noble race ?
                And who is this, whose manly face
                Bears sorrow's interesting trace ?

ENSEMBLE—TUTTI.

            Yes, who is this, etc.

GROS.   I am a broken-hearted troubadour,
            Whose mind's æsthetic and whose tastes are pure !
ANG.   Æsthetic !   He is æsthetic !

GROS.   Yes, yes—I am æsthetic
                          And poetic !

ALL THE LADIES.   Then, we love you !

(*The Girls leave Dragoons and group, kneeling, around*
        GROSVENOR. *Fury of* BUNTHORNE, *who recognizes*
        a rival.)

DRAGOONS.   They love him !   Horror !
BUN. *and* PA.   They love him !   Horror !
GROS.   They love me !   Horror !   Horror !   Horror !

ENSEMBLE—TUTTI.

GIRLS.	GROSVENOR.
Oh, list while we a love confess	Again my cursed comeliness
That words imperfectly express.	Spreads hopeless anguish and
Those shell-like ears, ah, do not	distress !
close	Thine ears, oh Fortune, do not
To blighted love's distracting	close
woes !	To my intolerable woes.

PATIENCE.	BUNTHORNE.
List, Reginald, while I confess	My jealousy I can't express,
A love that's all unselfishness ;	Their love they openly confess ;
That it's unselfish, goodness	His shell-like ears he does not
knows,	close
You won't dispute it, I suppose ?	To their recital of their woes.

DRAGOONS.   Now is not this ridiculous, etc.

END OF ACT I.

ACT II.

SCENE.—*A glade. JANE is discovered leaning on a violoncello, upon which she presently accompanies herself. Chorus of Maidens are heard singing in the distance.*

JANE. The fickle crew have deserted Reginald and sworn allegiance to his rival, and all, forsooth, because he has glanced with passing favour on a puling milkmaid! Fools! of that fancy he will soon weary—and then I, who alone am faithful to him, shall reap my reward. But do not dally too long, Reginald, for my charms are ripe, Reginald, and already they are decaying. Better secure me ere I have gone too far!

RECIT.—JANE.

Sad is that woman's lot who, year by year,
Sees, one by one, her beauties disappear,
When Time, grown weary of her heart-drawn sighs,
Impatiently begins to " dim her eyes " !
Compelled, at last, in life's uncertain gloamings,
To wreathe her wrinkled brow with well - saved " combings ",
Reduced, with rouge, lip-salve, and pearly grey,
To " make up " for lost time as best she may !

SONG—JANE.

Silvered is the raven hair,
    Spreading is the parting straight,
Mottled the complexion fair,
    Halting is the youthful gait,

Hollow is the laughter free,
  Spectacled the limpid eye—
Little will be left of me
  In the coming by and by !

Fading is the taper waist,
  Shapeless grows the shapely limb,
And although severely laced,
  Spreading is the figure trim !
Stouter than I used to be,
  Still more corpulent grow I—
There will be too much of me
  In the coming by and by !

[*Exit* JANE.

Enter GROSVENOR, *followed by Maidens, two and two,
  each playing on an archaic instrument, as in Act I.
  He is reading abstractedly, as* BUNTHORNE *did in
  Act I., and pays no attention to them.*

CHORUS OF MAIDENS.

Turn, oh, turn in this direction,
  Shed, oh, shed a gentle smile,
With a glance of sad perfection
  Our poor fainting hearts beguile !
On such eyes as maidens cherish
  Let thy fond adorers gaze,
Or incontinently perish
  In their all-consuming rays !

(*He sits—they group around him.*)

GROS. (*aside*). The old, old tale. How rapturously
these maidens love me, and how hopelessly ! Oh, Patience,
Patience, with the love of thee in my heart, what have I
for these poor mad maidens but an unvalued pity ? Alas,
they will die of hopeless love for me, as I shall die of
hopeless love for thee !

ANG. Sir, will it please you read to us ?

GROS. (*sighing*). Yes, child, if you will. What shall I read?

ANG. One of your own poems.

GROS. One of my own poems? Better not, my child. *They* will not cure thee of thy love.

ELLA. Mr. Bunthorne used to read us a poem of his own every day.

SAPH. And, to do him justice, he read them extremely well.

GROS. Oh, did he so? Well, who am I that I should take upon myself to withhold my gifts from you? What am I but a trustee? Here is a decalet—a pure and simple thing, a very daisy—a babe might understand it. To appreciate it, it is not necessary to think of anything at all.

ANG. Let us think of nothing at all!

GROSVENOR *recites*.

Gentle Jane was good as gold,
She always did as she was told;
She never spoke when her mouth was full,
Or caught bluebottles their legs to pull,
Or spilt plum jam on her nice new frock,
Or put white mice in the eight-day clock,
Or vivisected her last new doll,
Or fostered a passion for alcohol.
And when she grew up she was given in marriage
To a first-class earl who keeps his carriage!

GROS. I believe I am right in saying that there is not one word in that decalet which is calculated to bring the blush of shame to the cheek of modesty.

ANG. Not one; it is purity itself.

GROS. Here's another.

Teasing Tom was a very bad boy,
A great big squirt was his favourite toy;
He put live shrimps in his father's boots,
And sewed up the sleeves of his Sunday suits;

> He punched his poor little sisters' heads,
> And cayenne-peppered their four-post beds ,
> He plastered their hair with cobbler's wax,
> And dropped hot halfpennies down their backs.
>   The consequence was he was lost tot*a*lly,
>   And married a girl in the *corps de bally* !

ANG.   Marked you how grandly—how relentlessly—the damning catalogue of crime strode on, till Retribution, like a poisèd hawk, came swooping down upon the Wrong-Doer ?   Oh, it was terrible !

ELLA.   Oh, sir, you are indeed a true poet, for you touch our hearts, and they go out to you !

GROS. (*aside*). This is simply cloying. (*Aloud.*) Ladies, I am sorry to appear ungallant, but this is Saturday, and you have been following me about ever since Monday.   I should like the usual half-holiday.   I shall take it as a personal favour if you will kindly allow me to close early to-day.

SAPH.   Oh, sir, do not send us from you !

GROS.   Poor, poor girls !   It is best to speak plainly. I know that I am loved by you, but I never can love you in return, for my heart is fixed elsewhere !   Remember the fable of the Magnet and the Churn.

ANG. (*wildly*).   But we don't know the fable of the Magnet and the Churn !

GROS.   Don't you ?   Then I will sing it to you.

SONG—GROSVENOR.

> A magnet hung in a hardware shop,
> And all around was a loving crop
> Of scissors and needles, nails and knives,
> Offering love for all their lives ;
> But for iron the magnet felt no whim,
> Though he charmed iron, it charmed not him ;
> From needles and nails and knives he'd turn,
> For he'd set his love on a Silver Churn !

ALL.   A Silver Churn ?

GROS.   A Silver Churn !

> His most æsthetic,
> Very magnetic
> Fancy took this turn—
> " If I can wheedle
> A knife or a needle,
> Why not a Silver Churn ? "

CHORUS.   His most æsthetic, etc.

GROS.   And Iron and Steel expressed surprise,
The needles opened their well-drilled eyes,
The penknives felt " shut up ", no doubt,
The scissors declared themselves " cut out ",
The kettles they boiled with rage, 'tis said,
While every nail went off its head,
And hither and thither began to roam,
Till a hammer came up—and drove them home.

ALL.   It drove them home ?
GROS.   It drove them home !

> While this magnetic,
> Peripatetic
> Lover he lived to learn,
> By no endeavour
> Can magnet ever
> Attract a Silver Churn !

ALL.   While this magnetic, etc.

[*They go off in low spirits, gazing back at him
from time to time.*

GROS.   At last they are gone !   What is this mysterious
fascination that I seem to exercise over all I come across ?
A curse on my fatal beauty, for I am sick of conquests !

PATIENCE *appears.*

PA.   Archibald !
GROS. (*turns and sees her*).   Patience !

PA. I have escaped with difficulty from my Reginald. I wanted to see you so much that I might ask you if you still love me as fondly as ever?

GROS. Love you? If the devotion of a lifetime—— (*Seizes her hand.*)

PA. (*indignantly*). Hold! Unhand me, or I scream! (*He releases her.*) If you are a gentleman, pray remember that I am another's! (*Very tenderly.*) But you *do* love me, don't you?

GROS. Madly, hopelessly, despairingly!

PA. That's right! I never can be yours; but that's right!

GROS. And you love this Bunthorne?

PA. With a heart-whole ecstasy that withers, and scorches, and burns, and stings! (*Sadly.*) It is my duty.

GROS. Admirable girl! But you are not happy with him?

PA. Happy? I am miserable beyond description!

GROS. That's right! I never can be yours; but that's right!

PA. But go now. I see dear Reginald approaching. Farewell, dear Archibald; I cannot tell you how happy it has made me to know that you still love me.

GROS. Ah, if I only dared—— (*Advances towards her.*)

PA. Sir! this language to one who is promised to another! (*Tenderly.*) Oh, Archibald, think of me sometimes, for my heart is breaking! He is so unkind to me, and you would be so loving!

GROS. Loving! (*Advances towards her.*)

PA. Advance one step, and as I am a good and pure woman, I scream! (*Tenderly.*) Farewell, Archibald! (*Sternly.*) Stop there! (*Tenderly.*) Think of me sometimes! (*Angrily.*) Advance at your peril! Once more, adieu!

> [GROSVENOR *sighs, gazes sorrowfully at her,*
> *sighs deeply, and exit. She bursts into*
> *tears.*

Enter BUNTHORNE, *followed by* JANE. *He is moody and preoccupied.*

JANE *sings.*

In a doleful train,
One and one I walk all day ;
For I love in vain—
None so sorrowful as they
Who can only sigh and say,
Woe is me, alackaday !

BUN. (*seeing* PATIENCE). Crying, eh ? What are you crying about ?

PA. I've only been thinking how dearly I love you !

BUN. Love me ! Bah !

JANE. Love him ! Bah !

BUN. (*to* JANE). Don't you interfere.

JANE. He always crushes me !

PA. (*going to him*). What is the matter, dear Reginald? If you have any sorrow, tell it to me, that I may share it with you. (*Sighing.*) It is my duty !

BUN. (*snappishly*). Whom were you talking with just now ?

PA. With dear Archibald.

BUN. (*furiously*). With dear Archibald ! Upon my honour, this is too much !

JANE. A great deal too much !

BUN. (*angrily to* JANE). Do be quiet !

JANE. Crushed again !

PA. I think he is the noblest, purest, and most perfect being I have ever met. But I don't love him. It is true that he is devotedly attached to me, but indeed I don't love *him*. Whenever he grows affectionate, I scream. It is my duty ! (*Sighing.*)

BUN. I dare say !

JANE. So do I ! *I* dare say !

PA. Why, how could I love him and love you too ? You can't love two people at once !

BUN.   Oh, can't you, though !

PA.   No, you can't ; I only wish you could.

BUN.   I don't believe you know what love is !

PA. (*sighing*).   Yes, I do.   There was a happy time when I didn't, but a bitter experience has taught me.

[*Exeunt* BUNTHORNE *and* JANE.

BALLAD—PATIENCE.

Love is a plaintive song,
   Sung by a suffering maid,
Telling a tale of wrong,
   Telling of hope betrayed ;
Tuned to each changing note,
   Sorry when *he* is sad,
Blind to his every mote,
   Merry when he is glad !
      Love that no wrong can cure,
       Love that is always new,
     That is the love that's pure,
     That is the love that's true !

Rendering good for ill,
   Smiling at every frown,
Yielding your own self-will,
   Laughing your tear-drops down ;
Never a selfish whim,
   Trouble, or pain to stir ;
Everything for him,
   Nothing at all for her !
      Love that will aye endure,
       Though the rewards be few,
     That is the love that's pure,
     That is the love that's true !

[*At the end of ballad exit* PATIENCE, *weeping.*

Enter BUNTHORNE *and* JANE.

BUN.   Everything has gone wrong with me since that

smug-faced idiot came here. Before that I was admired—
I may say, loved.

JANE. Too mild—adored !

BUN. Do let a poet soliloquize ! The damozels used
to follow me wherever I went ; now they all follow him !

JANE. Not all ! *I* am still faithful to you.

BUN. Yes, and a pretty damozel *you* are !

JANE. No, not pretty. Massive. Cheer up ! I will
never leave you, I swear it !

BUN. Oh, thank you ! I know what it is ; it's his
confounded mildness. They find me too highly spiced,
if you please ! And no doubt I *am* highly spiced.

JANE. Not for my taste !

BUN. (*savagely*). No, but I am for theirs. But I will
show the world I can be as mild as he. If they want
insipidity, they shall have it. I'll meet this fellow on his
own ground and beat him on it.

JANE. You shall. And I will help you.

BUN. You will ? Jane, there's a good deal of good
in you, after all !

DUET—BUNTHORNE *and* JANE.

JANE. So go to him and say to him, with compliment
        ironical—

BUN.   Sing " Hey to you—
        Good day to you "—
        And that's what I shall say !

JANE. " Your style is much too sanctified—your cut is
        too canonical "—

BUN.   Sing " Bah to you—
        Ha ! ha ! to you "—
        And that's what I shall say !

JANE. " I was the beau ideal of the morbid young
        æsthetical—
        To doubt my inspiration was regarded as
        heretical—
        Until you cut me out with your placidity
        emetical."—

BUN.   Sing " Booh to you—
                   Pooh, pooh to you "—
          And that's what I shall say !

BOTH.   Sing " Hey to you—good day to you "—
          Sing " Bah to you—ha ! ha ! to you "—
          Sing " Booh to you—pooh, pooh to you "—
          And that's what $\left\{\begin{array}{c} \text{you} \\ \text{I} \end{array}\right\}$ shall say !

BUN.   I'll tell him that unless he will consent to be more
                        jocular—
JANE.   Sing " Booh to you—
                   Pooh, pooh to you "—
          And that's what you should say !

BUN.   To cut his curly hair, and stick an eyeglass in his
                        ocular—
JANE.   Sing " Bah to you—
                   Ha ! ha ! to you "—
          And that's what you should say !

BUN.   To stuff his conversation full of quibble and of
                        quiddity—
       To dine on chops and roly-poly pudding with
                        avidity—
       He'd better clear away with all convenient
                        rapidity.
JANE.   Sing " Hey to you—
                   Good day to you "—
          And that's what you should say !

BOTH.   Sing " Booh to you—pooh, pooh to you "—
          Sing " Bah to you—ha ! ha ! to you "—
          Sing " Hey to you—good day to you "—
          And that's what $\left\{\begin{array}{c} \text{I} \\ \text{you} \end{array}\right\}$ shall say !

[*Exeunt* JANE *and* BUNTHORNE *together.*

Enter DUKE, COLONEL, *and* MAJOR. *They have aban-*
doned their uniforms, and are dressed and made up
in imitation of Æsthetics. They have long hair, and
other outward signs of attachment to the brotherhood.
As they sing they walk in stiff, constrained, and
angular attitudes—a grotesque exaggeration of the
attitudes adopted by BUNTHORNE *and the young Ladies*
in Act I.

TRIO—DUKE, COLONEL, *and* MAJOR.

It's clear that mediæval art alone retains its zest,
To charm and please its devotees we've done our little best.
We're not quite sure if all we do has the Early English ring;
But, as far as we can judge, it's something like this sort
of thing :
You hold yourself like this (*attitude*),
You hold yourself like that (*attitude*),
By hook and crook you try to look both angular and flat
(*attitude*).
We venture to expect
That what we recollect,
Though but a part of true High Art, will have its due effect.

If this is not exactly right, we hope you won't upbraid ;
You can't get high Æsthetic tastes, like trousers, ready
made.
True views on Mediævalism Time alone will bring,
But, as far as we can judge, it's something like this sort
of thing :
You hold yourself like this (*attitude*),
You hold yourself like that (*attitude*),
By hook and crook you try to look both angular and flat
(*attitude*).
To cultivate the trim
Rigidity of limb,
You ought to get a Marionette, and form your style on
him (*attitude*).

COL. (*attitude*). Yes, it's quite clear that our only chance of making a lasting impression on these young ladies is to become as æsthetic as they are.

MAJ. (*attitude*). No doubt. The only question is how far we've succeeded in doing so. I don't know why, but I've an idea that this is not quite right.

DUKE. (*attitude*). *I* don't like it. I never did. I don't see what it means. I do it, but I don't like it.

COL. My good friend, the question is not whether we like it, but whether they do. They understand these things—we don't. Now I shouldn't be surprised if this is effective enough—at a distance.

MAJ. I can't help thinking we're a little stiff at it. It would be extremely awkward if we were to be " struck " so !

COL. I don't think we shall be struck so. Perhaps we're a little awkward at first—but everything must have a beginning. Oh, here they come ! 'Tention !

They strike fresh attitudes, as ANGELA *and* SAPHIR *enter.*

ANG. (*seeing them*). Oh, Saphir—see—see ! The immortal fire has descended on them, and they are of the Inner Brotherhood—perceptively intense and consummately utter. (*The Officers have some difficulty in maintaining their constrained attitudes.*)

SAPH. (*in admiration*). How Botticellian ! How Fra Angelican ! Oh, Art, we thank thee for this boon !

COL. (*apologetically*). I'm afraid we're not quite right.

ANG. Not supremely, perhaps, but oh, so all-but ! (*To* SAPHIR.) Oh, Saphir, are they not quite too all-but ?

SAPHIR. They are indeed jolly utter !

MAJ. (*in agony*). I wonder what the Inner Brotherhood usually recommend for cramp ?

COL. Ladies, we will not deceive you. We are doing this at some personal inconvenience with a view of expressing the extremity of our devotion to you. We trust that it is not without its effect.

ANG. We will not deny that we are much moved by this proof of your attachment.

SAPH. Yes, your conversion to the principles of Æsthetic Art in its highest development has touched us deeply.

ANG. And if Mr. Grosvenor should remain obdurate—

SAPH. Which we have every reason to believe he will—

MAJ. (*aside, in agony*). I wish they'd make haste.

ANG. We are not prepared to say that our yearning hearts will not go out to you.

COL. (*as giving a word of command*). By sections of threes—Rapture! (*All strike a fresh attitude, expressive of æsthetic rapture.*)

SAPH. Oh, it's extremely good—for beginners it's admirable.

MAJ. The only question is, who will take who?

COL. Oh, the Duke chooses first, as a matter of course.

DUKE. Oh, I couldn't think of it—you are really too good!

COL. Nothing of the kind. You are a great matrimonial fish, and it's only fair that each of these ladies should have a chance of hooking you. It's perfectly simple. Observe, suppose you choose Angela, I take Saphir, Major takes nobody. Suppose you choose Saphir, Major takes Angela, I take nobody. Suppose you choose neither, I take Angela, Major takes Saphir. Clear as day!

QUINTET.

DUKE, COLONEL, MAJOR, ANGELA, *and* SAPHIR.

DUKE (*taking* SAPHIR).

If Saphir I choose to marry,
    I shall be fixed up for life;
Then the Colonel need not tarry,
    Angela can be his wife.

(DUKE *dances with* SAPHIR, COLONEL *with* ANGELA, MAJOR *dances alone.*)

MAJOR (*dancing alone*).

In that case unprecedented,
    Single I shall live and die—
I shall have to be contented
    With their heartfelt sympathy !

ALL (*dancing as before*).

He will have to be contented
    With our heartfelt sympathy !

DUKE (*taking* ANGELA).

If on Angy I determine,
    At my wedding she'll appear
Decked in diamonds and in ermine,
    Major then can take Saphir !

(DUKE *dances with* ANGELA, MAJOR *with* SAPHIR,
    COLONEL *dances alone*.)

COLONEL (*dancing*).

In that case unprecedented,
    Single I shall live and die—
I shall have to be contented
    With their heartfelt sympathy !

ALL (*dancing as before*).

He will have to be contented
    With our heartfelt sympathy !

DUKE (*taking both* ANGELA *and* SAPHIR).

After some debate internal,
    If on neither I decide,
Saphir then can take the Colonel,
        (*Handing* SAPHIR *to* COLONEL.)
    Angy be the Major's bride !
        (*Handing* ANGELA *to* MAJOR.)

(COLONEL *dances with* SAPHIR, MAJOR *with* ANGELA,
DUKE *dances alone.*)

DUKE (*dancing*).

In that case unprecedented,
    Single I must live and die—
I shall have to be contented
    With their heartfelt sympathy !

ALL (*dancing as before*).

He will have to be contented
    With our heartfelt sympathy.

[*At the end*, DUKE, COLONEL, *and* MAJOR,
and two girls dance off arm-in-arm.

Enter GROSVENOR.

GROS. It is very pleasant to be alone. It is pleasant
to be able to gaze at leisure upon those features which
all others may gaze upon at their good will ! (*Looking
at his reflection in hand-mirror.*) Ah, I am a very
Narcissus !

Enter BUNTHORNE, *moodily.*

BUN. It's no use ; I can't live without admiration.
Since Grosvenor came here, insipidity has been at a
premium. Ah, he is there !
GROS. Ah, Bunthorne ! come here — look ! Very
graceful, isn't it !
BUN. (*taking hand-mirror*). Allow me ; I haven't
seen it. Yes, it is graceful.
GROS. (*re-taking hand-mirror*). Oh, good gracious !
not that—this——
BUN. You don't mean that ! Bah ! I am in no
mood for trifling.
GROS.   And what is amiss ?

H

Bun. Ever since you came here, you have entirely monopolized the attentions of the young ladies. I don't like it, sir !

Gros. My dear sir, how can I help it ? They are the plague of my life. My dear Mr. Bunthorne, with your personal disadvantages, you can have no idea of the inconvenience of being madly loved, at first sight, by every woman you meet.

Bun. Sir, until you came here I was adored !

Gros. Exactly—until I came here. That's my grievance. I cut everybody out ! I assure you, if you could only suggest some means whereby, consistently with my duty to society, I could escape these inconvenient attentions, you would earn my everlasting gratitude.

Bun. I will do so at once. However popular it may be with the world at large, your personal appearance is highly objectionable to *me*.

Gros. It is ? (*Shaking his hand.*) Oh, thank you ! thank you ! How can I express my gratitude ?

Bun. By making a complete change at once. Your conversation must henceforth be perfectly matter-of-fact. You must cut your hair, and have a back parting. In appearance and costume you must be absolutely commonplace.

Gros. (*decidedly*). No. Pardon me, that's impossible.

Bun. Take care ! When I am thwarted I am very terrible.

Gros. I can't help that. I am a man with a mission. And that mission must be fulfilled.

Bun. I don't think you quite appreciate the consequences of thwarting me.

Gros. I don't care what they are.

Bun. Suppose—I won't go so far as to say that I will do it—but suppose for one moment I were to curse you ? (Grosvenor *quails*.) Ah ! Very well. Take care.

Gros. But surely you would never do that ? (*In great alarm.*)

BUN. I don't know. It would be an extreme measure, no doubt. Still——

GROS. (*wildly*). But you would not do it—I am sure you would not. (*Throwing himself at* BUNTHORNE'S *knees, and clinging to him.*) Oh, reflect, reflect! You had a mother once.

BUN. Never!

GROS. Then you had an aunt! (BUNTHORNE *affected.*) Ah! I see you had! By the memory of that aunt, I implore you to pause ere you resort to this last fearful expedient. Oh, Mr. Bunthorne, reflect, reflect! (*Weeping.*)

BUN. (*aside, after a struggle with himself*). I must not allow myself to be unmanned! (*Aloud.*) It is useless. Consent at once, or may a nephew's curse——

GROS. Hold! Are you absolutely resolved?

BUN. Absolutely.

GROS. Will nothing shake you?

BUN. Nothing. I am adamant.

GROS. Very good. (*Rising.*) Then I yield.

BUN. Ha! You swear it?

GROS. I do, cheerfully. I have long wished for a reasonable pretext for such a change as you suggest. It has come at last. I do it on compulsion!

BUN. Victory! I triumph!

DUET—BUNTHORNE *and* GROSVENOR.

BUN.
        When I go out of door,
          Of damozels a score
            (All sighing and burning,
            And clinging and yearning)
          Will follow me as before.
          I shall, with cultured taste,
          Distinguish gems from paste,
            And " High diddle diddle "
            Will rank as an idyll,
          If I pronounce it chaste!

BOTH. A most intense young man,
      A soulful-eyed young man,
An ultra-poetical, super-æsthetical,
      Out-of-the-way young man !

GROS. Conceive me, if you can,
      An every-day young man :
      A commonplace type,
      With a stick and a pipe,
And a half-bred black-and-tan ;
      Who thinks suburban " hops "
      More fun than " Monday Pops ",
Who's fond of his dinner,
      And doesn't get thinner
      On bottled beer and chops.

BOTH. A commonplace young man,
      A matter-of-fact young man,
A steady and stolid-y, jolly Bank-holiday
      Every-day young man !

BUN. A Japanese young man,
      A blue-and-white young man,
Francesca di Rimini, miminy, piminy,
Je-ne-sais-quoi young man !

GROS. A Chancery Lane young man,
      A Somerset House young man,
A very delectable, highly respectable,
      Threepenny-bus young man !

BUN. A pallid and thin young man,
      A haggard and lank young man,
A greenery-yallery, Grosvenor Gallery,
      Foot-in-the-grave young man !

GROS. A Sewell & Cross young man,
      A Howell & James young man,
A pushing young particle—" What's the next
      article ? "—
      Waterloo House young man !

ENSEMBLE.

Bun.	Gros.
Conceive me, if you can,	Conceive me, if you can,
A crotchety, cracked young man,	A matter-of-fact young man,
An ultra-poetical, super-æsthetical,	An alphabetical, arithmetical,
Out-of-the-way young man !	Every-day young man !

[*At the end*, GROSVENOR *dances off.* BUN-
THORNE *remains.*

BUN. It is all right ! I have committed my last act of ill-nature, and henceforth I'm a changed character. (*Dances about stage, humming refrain of last air.*)

Enter PATIENCE. *She gazes in astonishment at him.*

PA. Reginald ! Dancing ! And—what in the world is the matter with you ?

BUN. Patience, I'm a changed man. Hitherto I've been gloomy, moody, fitful—uncertain in temper and selfish in disposition—

PA. You have, indeed ! (*Sighing.*)

BUN. All that is changed. I have reformed. I have modelled myself upon Mr. Grosvenor. Henceforth I am mildly cheerful. My conversation will blend amusement with instruction. I shall still be æsthetic ; but my æstheticism will be of the most pastoral kind.

PA. Oh, Reginald ! Is all this true ?

BUN. Quite true. Observe how amiable I am. (*Assuming a fixed smile.*)

PA. But, Reginald, how long will this last ?

BUN. With occasional intervals for rest and refreshment, as long as I do.

PA. Oh, Reginald, I'm so happy ! (*In his arms.*) Oh, dear, dear Reginald, I cannot express the joy I feel at this change. It will no longer be a duty to love you, but a pleasure—a rapture—an ecstasy !

BUN. My darling !

PA. But—oh, horror ! (*Recoiling from him.*)

BUN. What's the matter ?

PA. Is it quite certain that you have absolutely reformed—that you are henceforth a perfect being—utterly free from defect of any kind ?

BUN. It is quite certain. I have sworn it.

PA. Then I never can be yours !

BUN. Why not ?

PA. Love, to be pure, must be absolutely unselfish, and there can be nothing unselfish in loving so perfect a being as you have now become !

BUN. But, stop a bit ! I don't want to change—I'll relapse—I'll be as I was—interrupted !

Enter GROSVENOR, *followed by all the young Ladies, who are followed by Chorus of Dragoons. He has had his hair cut, and is dressed in an ordinary suit of dittoes and a pot hat. They all dance cheerfully round the stage in marked contrast to their former languor.*

CHORUS—GROSVENOR *and* GIRLS.

GROS.	GIRLS.
I'm a Waterloo House young man,	We're Swears & Wells young girls,
A Sewell & Cross young man,	We're Madame Louise young girls,
A steady and stolid-y, jolly Bank-holiday,	We're prettily pattering, cheerily chattering,
Every-day young man !	Every-day young girls !

BUN. Angela—Ella—Saphir—what—what does this mean ?

ANG. It means that Archibald the All-Right cannot be all-wrong ; and if the All-Right chooses to discard æstheticism, it proves that æstheticism ought to be discarded.

PA. Oh, Archibald ! Archibald ! I'm shocked—surprised—horrified !

GROS. I can't help it. I'm not a free agent. I do it on compulsion.

PA. This is terrible. Go ! I shall never set eyes on you again. But—oh, joy !

Gros. What is the matter?

Pa. Is it quite, quite certain that you will always be a commonplace young man?

Gros. Always—I've sworn it.

Pa. Why, then, there's nothing to prevent my loving you with all the fervour at my command!

Gros. Why, that's true.

Pa. My Archibald!

Gros. My Patience! (*They embrace.*)

Bun. Crushed again!

Enter JANE.

JANE (*who is still æsthetic*). Cheer up! I am still here. I have never left you, and I never will!

Bun. Thank you, Jane. After all, there is no denying it, you're a fine figure of a woman!

JANE. My Reginald!

Bun. My Jane!

Flourish. Enter COLONEL, DUKE, *and* MAJOR.

Col. Ladies, the Duke has at length determined to select a bride! (*General excitement.*)

Duke. I have a great gift to bestow. Approach, such of you as are truly lovely. (*All come forward, bashfully, except* JANE *and* PATIENCE.) In personal appearance you have all that is necessary to make a woman happy. In common fairness, I think I ought to choose the only one among you who has the misfortune to be distinctly plain. (*Girls retire disappointed.*) Jane!

JANE (*leaving* BUNTHORNE'S *arms*). Duke! (JANE *and* DUKE *embrace.* BUNTHORNE *is utterly disgusted.*)

Bun. Crushed again!

FINALE.

Duke.   After much debate internal,
            I on Lady Jane decide,
        Saphir now may take the Colonel,
            Angy be the Major's bride!

(SAPHIR *pairs off with* COLONEL, ANGELA *with* MAJOR,
ELLA *with* SOLICITOR.)

BUN. In that case unprecedented,
    Single I must live and die—
  I shall have to be contented
    With a tulip or li*ly* !

(*Takes a lily from button-hole and gazes affectionately at it.*)

ALL. He will have to be contented
    With a tulip or li*ly* !

  Greatly pleased with one another,
    To get married we decide.
  Each of us will wed the other,
    Nobody be Bunthorne's Bride !

DANCE.

CURTAIN

IOLANTHE

OR

THE PEER AND THE PERI

DRAMATIS PERSONÆ.

THE LORD CHANCELLOR.

EARL OF MOUNTARARAT

EARL TOLLOLLER.

PRIVATE WILLIS (*of the Grenadier Guards*).

STREPHON (*an Arcadian Shepherd*).

QUEEN OF THE FAIRIES.

IOLANTHE (*a Fairy, Strephon's Mother*).

CELIA ⎫

LEILA ⎬ *Fairies*.

FLETA ⎭

PHYLLIS (*an Arcadian Shepnerdess and Ward in Chancery*).

Chorus of Dukes, Marquises, Earls, Viscounts, Barons, and Fairies.

ACT I.—An Arcadian Landscape.

ACT II.—Palace Yard, Westminster.

First produced at the Savoy Theatre, November 25, 1882.

IOLANTHE

OR

THE PEER AND THE PERI

ACT I.

Scene.—*An Arcadian Landscape. A river runs around the back of the stage. A rustic bridge crosses the river.*

Enter Fairies, led by Leila, Celia, *and* Fleta. *They trip around the stage, singing as they dance.*

Chorus.

Tripping hither, tripping thither,
Nobody knows why or whither;
We must dance and we must sing
Round about our fairy ring!

SOLO—Celia.

We are dainty little fairies,
    Ever singing, ever dancing;
We indulge in our vagaries
    In a fashion most entrancing.
If you ask the special function
    Of our never-ceasing motion,
We reply, without compunction,
    That we haven't any notion!

CHORUS.

No, we haven't any notion !
Tripping hither, etc.

SOLO—LEILA.

If you ask us how we live,
Lovers all essentials give—
　　We can ride on lovers' sighs,
　　Warm ourselves in lovers' eyes,
　　Bathe ourselves in lovers' tears,
　　Clothe ourselves with lovers' fears,
　　Arm ourselves with lovers' darts,
　　Hide ourselves in lovers' hearts.
When you know us, you'll discover
That we almost live on lover !

CHORUS.

Tripping hither, etc.

(*At the end of Chorus, all sigh wearily.*)

CELIA.　Ah, it's all very well, but since our Queen
banished Iolanthe, fairy revels have not been what they
were !

LEILA.　Iolanthe was the life and soul of Fairyland.
Why, she wrote all our songs and arranged all our dances !
We sing her songs and we trip her measures, but we don't
enjoy ourselves !

FLETA.　To think that five-and-twenty years have
elapsed since she was banished !　What could she have
done to have deserved so terrible a punishment ?

LEILA.　Something awful !　She married a mortal !

FLETA.　Oh !　Is it injudicious to marry a mortal ?

LEILA.　Injudicious ?　It strikes at the root of the
whole fairy system !　By our laws, the fairy who marries
a mortal dies !

CELIA.　But Iolanthe didn't die !

Enter FAIRY QUEEN.

QUEEN. No, because your Queen, who loved her with a surpassing love, commuted her sentence to penal servitude for life, on condition that she left her husband and never communicated with him again !

LEILA. That sentence of penal servitude she is now working out, on her head, at the bottom of that stream !

QUEEN. Yes, but when I banished her, I gave her all the pleasant places of the earth to dwell in. I'm sure I never intended that she should go and live at the bottom of a stream ! It makes me perfectly wretched to think of the discomfort she must have undergone !

LEILA. Think of the damp ! And her chest was always delicate.

QUEEN. And the frogs ! Ugh ! I never shall enjoy any peace of mind until I know why Iolanthe went to live among the frogs !

FLETA. Then why not summon her and ask her ?

QUEEN. Why ? Because if I set eyes on her I should forgive her at once !

CELIA. Then why not forgive her ? Twenty-five years —it's a long time !

LEILA. Think how we loved her !

QUEEN. Loved her ? What was your love to mine ? Why, she was invaluable to me ! Who taught me to curl myself inside a buttercup ? Iolanthe ! Who taught me to swing upon a cobweb ? Iolanthe ! Who taught me to dive into a dewdrop—to nestle in a nutshell—to gambol upon gossamer ? Iolanthe !

LEILA. She certainly did surprising things !

FLETA. Oh, give her back to us, great Queen, for your sake if not for ours ! (*All kneel in supplication.*)

QUEEN (*irresolute*). Oh, I should be strong, but I am weak ! I should be marble, but I am clay ! Her punishment has been heavier than I intended. I did not mean that she should live among the frogs—and—well, well, it shall be as you wish—it shall be as you wish !

INVOCATION—Queen.

Iolanthe !
From thy dark exile thou art summoned !
Come to our call—
Come, Iolanthe !

CELIA.	Iolanthe !
LEILA.	Iolanthe !
ALL.	Come to our call,
	Come, Iolanthe !

IOLANTHE *rises from the water. She is clad in water-*
weeds. She approaches the QUEEN *with head bent*
and arms crossed.

IOLANTHE.   With humbled breast
And every hope laid low,
To thy behest,
Offended Queen, I bow !

QUEEN. For a dark sin against our fairy laws
We sent thee into life-long banishment ;
But mercy holds her sway within our hearts—
Rise—thou art pardoned !

IOL.   Pardoned !
ALL.   Pardoned !

(*Her weeds fall from her, and she appears clothed as a*
fairy. The QUEEN *places a diamond coronet on her*
head, and embraces her. The others also embrace her.)

CHORUS.

Welcome to our hearts again,
Iolanthe ! Iolanthe !
We have shared thy bitter pain,
Iolanthe ! Iolanthe !

> Every heart and every hand
> In our loving little band
> Welcomes thee to Fairyland,
>   Iolanthe !

QUEEN. And now, tell me, with all the world to choose from, why on earth did you decide to live at the bottom of that stream ?

IOL. To be near my son, Strephon.

QUEEN. Bless my heart, I didn't know you had a son.

IOL. He was born soon after I left my husband by your royal command—but he does not even know of his father's existence.

FLETA. How old is he ?

IOL. Twenty-four.

LEILA. Twenty-four ! No one, to look at you, would think you had a son of twenty-four ! But that's one of the advantages of being immortal. We never grow old ! Is he pretty ?

IOL. He's extremely pretty, but he's inclined to be stout.

ALL (*disappointed*). Oh !

QUEEN. I see no objection to stoutness, in moderation.

CELIA. And what is he ?

IOL. He's an Arcadian shepherd — and he loves Phyllis, a Ward in Chancery.

CELIA. A mere shepherd ! and he half a fairy !

IOL. He's a fairy down to the waist—but his legs are mortal.

ALL. Dear me !

QUEEN. I have no reason to suppose that I am more curious than other people, but I confess I should like to see a person who is a fairy down to the waist, but whose legs are mortal.

IOL. Nothing easier, for here he comes !

Enter STREPHON, *singing and dancing and playing on a flageolet. He does not see the Fairies, who retire up stage as he enters.*

SONG—STREPHON.

Good morrow, good mother !
    Good mother, good morrow !
By some means or other,
    Pray banish your sorrow !
        With joy beyond telling
        My bosom is swelling,
        So join in a measure
        Expressive of pleasure,
For I'm to be married to-day—to-day—
    Yes, I'm to be married to-day !

CHORUS (*aside*). Yes, he's to be married to-day—to-day—
        Yes, he's to be married to-day !

IOL. Then the Lord Chancellor has at last given his consent to your marriage with his beautiful ward, Phyllis ?

STREPH. Not he, indeed. To all my tearful prayers he answers me, " A shepherd lad is no fit helpmate for a Ward of Chancery." I stood in court, and there I sang him songs of Arcadee, with flageolet accompaniment—in vain. At first he seemed amused, so did the Bar ; but quickly wearying of my song and pipe, bade me get out. A servile usher then, in crumpled bands and rusty bombazine, led me, still singing, into Chancery Lane ! I'll go no more ; I'll marry her to-day, and brave the upshot, be it what it may ! (*Sees Fairies.*) But who are these ?

IOL. Oh, Strephon ! rejoice with me, my Queen has pardoned me !

STREPH. Pardoned you, mother ? This is good news indeed.

IOL. And these ladies are my beloved sisters.

STREPH. Your sisters ! Then they are—my aunts !

QUEEN. A pleasant piece of news for your bride on her wedding day !

STREPH. Hush ! My bride knows nothing of my

fairyhood. I dare not tell her, lest it frighten her. She thinks me mortal, and prefers me so.

LEILA. Your fairyhood doesn't seem to have done you much good.

STREPH. Much good ! My dear aunt ! it's the curse of my existence ! What's the use of being half a fairy ? My body can creep through a keyhole, but what's the good of that when my legs are left kicking behind ? I can make myself invisible down to the waist, but that's of no use when my legs remain exposed to view ? My brain is a fairy brain, but from the waist downwards I'm a gibbering idiot. My upper half is immortal, but my lower half grows older every day, and some day or other must die of old age. What's to become of my upper half when I've buried my lower half I really don't know !

FAIRIES. Poor fellow !

QUEEN. I see your difficulty, but with a fairy brain you should seek an intellectual sphere of action. Let me see. I've a borough or two at my disposal. Would you like to go into Parliament ?

IOL. A fairy Member ! That would be delightful !

STREPH. I'm afraid I should do no good there—you see, down to the waist, I'm a Tory of the most determined description, but my legs are a couple of confounded Radicals, and, on a division, they'd be sure to take me into the wrong lobby. You see, they're two to one, which is a strong working majority.

QUEEN. Don't let that distress you ; you shall be returned as a Liberal-Unionist, and your legs shall be our peculiar care.

STREPH. (*bowing*). I see your Majesty does not do things by halves.

QUEEN. No, we are fairies down to the feet.

ENSEMBLE.

QUEEN.   Fare thee well, attractive stranger.
FAIRIES.   Fare thee well, attractive stranger.
QUEEN.   Shouldst thou be in doubt or danger,

Peril or perplexitee,
Call us, and we'll come to thee !

FAIRIES.   Call us, and we'll come to thee !
Tripping hither, tripping thither,
Nobody knows why or whither ;
We must now be taking wing
To another fairy ring !

[*Fairies and* QUEEN *trip off,* IOLANTHE, *who
takes an affectionate farewell of her son,
going off last.*

Enter PHYLLIS, *singing and dancing, and accompanying
herself on a flageolet.*

SONG—PHYLLIS.

Good morrow, good lover !
Good lover, good morrow !
I prithee discover,
Steal, purchase, or borrow
Some means of concealing
The care you are feeling,
And join in a measure
Expressive of pleasure,
For we're to be married to-day—to-day !
For we're to be married to-day !

BOTH.   Yes, we're to be married, etc.

STREPH. (*embracing her*). My Phyllis ! And to-day
we are to be made happy for ever.

PHYL. Well, we're to be married.

STREPH. It's the same thing.

PHYL. I suppose it is. But oh, Strephon, I tremble
at the step I'm taking ! I believe it's penal servitude for
life to marry a Ward of Court without the Lord Chancellor's
consent ! I shall be of age in two years. Don't you
think you could wait two years ?

STREPH. Two years. Have you ever looked in the glass ?

PHYL. No, never.

STREPH. Here, look at that (*showing her a pocket mirror*), and tell me if you think it rational to expect me to wait two years ?

PHYL. (*looking at herself*). No. You're quite right— it's asking too much. One must be reasonable.

STREPH. Besides, who knows what will happen in two years ? Why, you might fall in love with the Lord Chancellor himself by that time !

PHYL. Yes. He's a clean old gentleman.

STREPH. As it is, half the House of Lords are sighing at your feet.

PHYL. The House of Lords are certainly extremely attentive.

STREPH. Attentive ? I should think they were ! Why did five-and-twenty Liberal Peers come down to shoot over your grass-plot last autumn ? It couldn't have been the sparrows. Why did five-and-twenty Conservative Peers come down to fish your pond ? Don't tell me it was the gold-fish ! No, no—delays are dangerous, and if we are to marry, the sooner the better.

DUET—STREPHON *and* PHYLLIS.

PHYLLIS.   None shall part us from each other,
      One in life and death are we :
  All in all to one another—
      I to thee and thou to me !

BOTH.   Thou the tree and I the flower—
      Thou the idol ; I the throng—
  Thou the day and I the hour—
      Thou the singer ; I the song !

STREPH.   All in all since that fond meeting
      When, in joy, I woke to find
  Mine the heart within thee beating,
      Mine the love that heart enshrined !

BOTH.   Thou the stream and I the willow—
                   Thou the sculptor ; I the clay—
                   Thou the ocean ; I the billow—
                       Thou the sunrise ; I the day !

                       [*Exeunt* STREPHON *and* PHYLLIS *together.*

March.   Enter Procession of Peers.

CHORUS.

Loudly let the trumpet bray !
                   Tantantara !
   Proudly bang the sounding brasses !
                       Tzing !   Boom !
As upon its lordly way
   This unique procession passes,
           Tantantara !   Tzing !   Boom !
Bow, bow, ye lower middle classes !
Bow, bow, ye tradesmen, bow, ye masses !
Blow the trumpets, bang the brasses !
           Tantantara !   Tzing !   Boom !
We are peers of highest station,
Paragons of legislation,
Pillars of the British nation !
           Tantantara !   Tzing !   Boom !

Enter the LORD CHANCELLOR, *followed by his train-bearer.*

SONG—LORD CHANCELLOR.

The Law is the true embodiment
Of everything that's excellent.
It has no kind of fault or flaw,
And I, my Lords, embody the Law.
The constitutional guardian I
Of pretty young Wards in Chancery,
All very agreeable girls—and none
Are over the age of twenty-one.
       A pleasant occupation for
       A rather susceptible Chancellor !

ALL.   A pleasant, etc.

But though the compliment implied
Inflates me with legitimate pride,
It nevertheless can't be denied
That it has its inconvenient side.
For I'm not so old, and not so plain,
And I'm quite prepared to marry again,
But there'd be the deuce to pay in the Lords
If I fell in love with one of my Wards!
    Which rather tries my temper, for
    I'm *such* a susceptible Chancellor!

ALL.   Which rather, etc.

And every one who'd marry a Ward
Must come to me for my accord,
And in my court I sit all day,
Giving agreeable girls away,
With one for him—and one for he—
And one for you—and one for ye—
And one for thou—and one for thee—
But never, oh, never a one for me!
    Which is exasperating for
    A highly susceptible Chancellor!

ALL.   Which is, etc.

Enter LORD TOLLOLLER.

LORD TOLL. And now, my Lords, to the business of the day.

LORD CH. By all means. Phyllis, who is a Ward of Court, has so powerfully affected your Lordships, that you have appealed to me in a body to give her to whichever one of you she may think proper to select, and a noble Lord has just gone to her cottage to request her immediate attendance. It would be idle to deny that I, myself, have the misfortune to be singularly attracted by this young person. My regard for her is rapidly undermining my constitution. Three months ago I was a stout man. I need say no more. If I could reconcile it with my duty,

I should unhesitatingly award her to myself, for I can conscientiously say that I know no man who is so well fitted to render her exceptionally happy. (*Peers* : Hear, hear !) But such an award would be open to misconstruction, and therefore, at whatever personal inconvenience, I waive my claim.

LORD TOLL. My Lord, I desire, on the part of this House, to express its sincere sympathy with your Lordship's most painful position.

LORD CH. I thank your Lordships. The feelings of a Lord Chancellor who is in love with a Ward of Court are not to be envied. What is his position ? Can he give his own consent to his own marriage with his own Ward ? Can he marry his own Ward without his own consent ? And if he marries his own Ward without his own consent, can he commit himself for contempt of his own Court ? And if he commit himself for contempt of his own Court, can he appear by counsel before himself, to move for arrest of his own judgement ? Ah, my Lords, it is indeed painful to have to sit upon a woolsack which is stuffed with such thorns as these !

Enter LORD MOUNTARARAT.

LORD MOUNT. My Lords, I have much pleasure in announcing that I have succeeded in inducing the young person to present herself at the Bar of this House.

Enter PHYLLIS.

RECIT.—PHYLLIS.

My well-loved Lord and Guardian dear,
You summoned me, and I am here !

CHORUS OF PEERS.

Oh, rapture, how beautiful !
How gentle—how dutiful !

SOLO—Lord Tolloller.

Of all the young ladies I know
   This pretty young lady's the fairest ;
Her lips have the rosiest show,
   Her eyes are the richest and rarest.
Her origin's lowly, it's true,
   But of birth and position I've plenty ;
I've grammar and spelling for two,
   And blood and behaviour for twenty !
     Her origin's lowly, it's true,
     I've grammar and spelling for two ;

Chorus.   Of birth and position he's plenty,
     With blood and behaviour for twenty !

SOLO—Lord Mountararat.

Though the views of the House have diverged
   On every conceivable motion,
All questions of Party are merged
   In a frenzy of love and devotion ;
If you ask us distinctly to say
   What Party we claim to belong to,
We reply, without doubt or delay,
   The Party I'm singing this song to !

SOLO—Phyllis.

I'm very much pained to refuse,
   But I'll stick to my pipes and my tabors ;
I can spell all the words that I use,
   And my grammar's as good as my neighbours'.
As for birth—I was born like the rest,
   My behaviour is rustic but hearty,
And I know where to turn for the best,
   When I want a particular Party !

CHORUS.   Though her station is none of the best,
           I suppose she was born like the rest ;
           And she knows where to look for her hearty,
           When she wants a particular Party !

                    RECIT.—PHYLLIS.
              Nay, tempt me not.
                 To rank I'll not be bound ;
              In lowly cot
                 Alone is virtue found !

CHORUS.   No, no ; indeed high rank will never hurt you,
          The Peerage is not destitute of virtue.

                BALLAD—LORD TOLLOLLER.
              Spurn not the nobly born
                 With love affected,
              Nor treat with virtuous scorn
                 The well-connected.
              High rank involves no shame—
              We boast an equal claim
              With him of humble name
                 To be respected !
              Blue blood ! blue blood !
                 When virtuous love is sought
                 Thy power is naught,
              Though dating from the Flood,
                 Blue blood !

CHORUS.   Blue blood ! blue blood ! etc.

              Spare us the bitter pain
                 Of stern denials,
              Nor with low-born disdain
                 Augment our trials.
              Hearts just as pure and fair
              May beat in Belgrave Square
              As in the lowly air
                 Of Seven Dials !

Blue blood ! Blue blood !
Of what avail art thou
To serve us now ?
Though dating from the Flood,
Blue blood !

CHORUS. Blue blood ! blue blood ! etc.

RECIT.—PHYLLIS.

My Lords, it may not be.
With grief my heart is riven !
You waste your time on me,
For ah ! my heart is given !

ALL.	Given !
PHYL.	Yes, given !
ALL.	Oh, horror ! ! !

RECIT.—LORD CHANCELLOR.

And who has dared to brave our high displeasure,
And thus defy our definite command ?

Enter STREPHON.

STREPH. 'Tis I—young Strephon ! mine this priceless
treasure !
Against the world I claim my darling's hand !

(PHYLLIS *rushes to his arms.*)

A shepherd I—

ALL.	A shepherd he !
STREPH.	Of Arcady—
ALL.	Of Arcadee !
STREPH.	Betrothed are we !
ALL.	Betrothed are they—
STREPH.	And mean to be—
ALL.	Espoused to-day !

ENSEMBLE.

STREPH.	THE OTHERS.
A shepherd I	A shepherd he
Of Arcady,	Of Arcadee,
Betrothed are we,	Betrothed is he,
And mean to be	And means to be
Espoused to-day!	Espoused to-day!

DUET—LORD MOUNTARARAT *and* LORD TOLLOLLER
(*aside to each other*).

'Neath this blow,
Worse than stab of dagger—
Though we mo-
Mentarily stagger,
In each heart
Proud are we innately—
Let's depart,
Dignified and stately!

ALL.   Let's depart,
Dignified and stately!

CHORUS OF PEERS.

Though our hearts she's badly bruising,
In another suitor choosing,
Let's pretend it's most amusing.
Ha! ha! ha! Tan-ta-ra!

[*Exeunt all the Peers, marching round stage
with much dignity*. LORD CHANCELLOR
separates PHYLLIS *from* STREPHON *and
orders her off. She follows Peers. Manent*
LORD CHANCELLOR *and* STREPHON.

LORD CH. Now, sir, what excuse have you to offer
for having disobeyed an order of the Court of Chancery?
STREPH. My Lord, I know no Courts of Chancery;
I go by Nature's Acts of Parliament. The bees—the

breeze—the seas—the rooks—the brooks—the gales—the vales—the fountains and the mountains cry, " You love this maiden—take her, we command you ! " 'Tis writ in heaven by the bright barbèd dart that leaps forth into lurid light from each grim thundercloud. The very rain pours forth her sad and sodden sympathy ! When chorused Nature bids me take my love, shall I reply, " Nay, but a certain Chancellor forbids it " ? Sir, you are England's Lord High Chancellor, but are you Chancellor of birds and trees, King of the winds and Prince of thunderclouds ?

LORD CH. No. It's a nice point. I don't know that I ever met it before. But my difficulty is that at present there's no evidence before the Court that chorused Nature has interested herself in the matter.

STREPH. No evidence ! You have my word for it. I tell you that she bade me take my love.

LORD CH. Ah ! but, my good sir, you mustn't tell us what she told you—it's not evidence. Now an affidavit from a thunderstorm, or a few words on oath from a heavy shower, would meet with all the attention they deserve.

STREPH. And have you the heart to apply the prosaic rules of evidence to a case which bubbles over with poetical emotion ?

LORD CH. Distinctly. I have always kept my duty strictly before my eyes, and it is to that fact that I owe my advancement to my present distinguished position.

SONG—LORD CHANCELLOR.

When I went to the Bar as a very young man,
    (Said I to myself—said I),
I'll work on a new and original plan
    (Said I to myself—said I),
I'll never assume that a rogue or a thief
Is a gentleman worthy implicit belief,
Because his attorney has sent me a brief
    (Said I to myself—said I !).

Ere I go into court I will read my brief through
    (Said I to myself—said I).
And I'll never take work I'm unable to do
    (Said I to myself—said I),
My learned profession I'll never disgrace
By taking a fee with a grin on my face,
When I haven't been there to attend to the case
    (Said I to myself—said I !).

I'll never throw dust in a juryman's eyes
    (Said I to myself—said I),
Or hoodwink a judge who is not over-wise
    (Said I to myself—said I),
Or assume that the witnesses summoned in force
In Exchequer, Queen's Bench, Common Pleas, or Divorce,
Have perjured themselves as a matter of course
    (Said I to myself—said I !).

In other professions in which men engage
    (Said I to myself—said I),
The Army, the Navy, the Church, and the Stage
    (Said I to myself—said I),
Professional licence, if carried too far,
Your chance of promotion will certainly mar—
And I fancy the rule might apply to the Bar
    (Said I to myself—said I !).

                        [*Exit* LORD CHANCELLOR.

Enter IOLANTHE.

STREPH. Oh, Phyllis, Phyllis ! To be taken from you just as I was on the point of making you my own ! Oh, it's too much—it's too much !

IOL. (*to* STREPHON, *who is in tears*). My son in tears— and on his wedding day !

STREPH. My wedding day ! Oh, mother, weep with me, for the Law has interposed between us, and the Lord Chancellor has separated us for ever !

Iol. The Lord Chancellor ! (*Aside.*) Oh, if he did but know !

Streph. (*overhearing her*). If he did but know what ?

Iol. No matter ! The Lord Chancellor has no power over you. Remember you are half a fairy. You can defy him—down to the waist.

Streph. Yes, but from the waist downwards he can commit me to prison for years ! Of what avail is it that my body is free, if my legs are working out seven years' penal servitude ?

Iol. True. But take heart—our Queen has promised you her special protection. I'll go to her and lay your peculiar case before her.

Streph. My beloved mother ! how can I repay the debt I owe you ?

FINALE—Quartet.

As it commences, the Peers appear at the back, advancing unseen and on tiptoe. Lord Mountararat *and* Lord Tolloller *lead* Phyllis *between them, who listens in horror to what she hears.*

Streph. (*to* Iolanthe). When darkly looms the day,
   And all is dull and grey,
    To chase the gloom away,
     On thee I'll call !

Phyl. (*speaking aside to* Lord Mountararat). What was that ?

Lord Mount. (*aside to* Phyllis).
   I think I heard him say,
   That on a rainy day,
   To while the time away,
    On her he'd call !

Chorus. We think we heard him say, etc.
  (Phyllis *much agitated at her lover's supposed faithlessness.*)

Iol. (*to* Strephon). When tempests wreck thy bark,
   And all is drear and dark,
    If thou shouldst need an Ark,
     I'll give thee one !

PHYL. (*speaking aside to* LORD TOLLOLLER). What was that?

LORD TOLL. (*aside to* PHYLLIS).
I heard the minx remark,
She'd meet him after dark,
Inside St. James's Park,
And give him one!

PHYL.
The prospect's very bad,
My heart so sore and sad
Will never more be glad
As summer's sun.

IOL., LORD TOLL., STREPH., LORD MOUNT.
The prospect's not so bad,
$\left. \begin{array}{l} My \\ Thy \end{array} \right\}$ heart so sore and sad
May very soon be glad
As summer's sun;

PHYL., IOL., LORD TOLL., STREPH., LORD MOUNT.
For when the sky is dark
And tempests wreck $\left\{ \begin{array}{l} my \\ thy \\ his \end{array} \right\}$ bark,

If $\left\{ \begin{array}{l} he\ should \\ I\ should \\ thou\ shouldst \end{array} \right\}$ need an Ark,

$\left. \begin{array}{l} She'll \\ I'll \end{array} \right\}$ give $\left\{ \begin{array}{l} him \\ me \\ thee \end{array} \right\}$ one!

PHYL. (*revealing herself*). Ah!

(IOLANTHE *and* STREPHON *much confused.*)

PHYL.
Oh, shameless one, tremble!
Nay, do not endeavour
Thy fault to dissemble,
We part—and for ever!
I worshipped him blindly,
He worships another—

STREPH.	Attend to me kindly,
	This lady's my mother!
TOLL.	This lady's his *what*?
STREPH.	This lady's my mother!
TENORS.	This lady's his *what*?
BASSES.	He says she's his mother!

(*They point derisively to* IOLANTHE, *laughing heartily at her. She goes for protection to* STREPHON.)

Enter LORD CHANCELLOR. IOLANTHE *veils herself.*

LORD CH. What means this mirth unseemly,
  That shakes the listening earth?

LORD TOLL. The joke is good extremely,
  And justifies our mirth.

LORD MOUNT. This gentleman is seen,
  With a maid of seventeen,
A-taking of his *dolce far niente*;
  And wonders he'd achieve,
  For he asks us to believe
She's his mother—and he's nearly five-and-twenty!

LORD CH. (*sternly*). Recollect yourself, I pray,
  And be careful what you say—
As the ancient Romans said, *festina lente*.
  For I really do not see
  How so young a girl could be
The mother of a man of five-and-twenty.

ALL. Ha! ha! ha! ha! ha!

STREPH. My Lord, of evidence I have no dearth—
  She is—has been—my mother from my birth!

BALLAD.

In babyhood
Upon her lap I lay,
With infant food
She moistenèd my clay;

     Had she withheld
    The succour she supplied,
     By hunger quelled,
    Your Strephon might have died !

LORD CH. (*much moved*).
    Had that refreshment been denied,
    Indeed our Strephon might have died !

ALL (*much affected*).
    Had that refreshment been denied,
    Indeed our Strephon might have died !

LORD MOUNT. But as she's not
    His mother, it appears,
     Why weep these hot
    Unnecessary tears ?
     And by what laws
    Should we so joyously
     Rejoice, because
    Our Strephon did not die ?
   Oh, rather let us pipe our eye
   Because our Strephon did not die !

ALL.   That's very true—let's pipe our eye
   Because our Strephon did not die !

   [*All weep.* IOLANTHE, *who has succeeded in
    hiding her face from* LORD CHANCELLOR,
    escapes unnoticed.*

PHYL. Go, traitorous one—for ever we must part :
    To one of you, my Lords, I give my heart !
ALL.   Oh, rapture !
STREPH. Hear me, Phyllis, ere you leave me.
PHYL. Not a word—you did deceive me.
ALL.   Not a word—you did deceive her.

          [*Exit* STREPHON.

BALLAD—Phyllis.

For riches and rank I do not long—
    Their pleasures are false and vain ;
I gave up the love of a lordly throng
    For the love of a simple swain.
But now that simple swain's untrue,
With sorrowful heart I turn to you—
      A heart that's aching,
      Quaking, breaking,
As sorrowful hearts are wont to do !

The riches and rank that you befall
    Are the only baits you use,
So the richest and rankiest of you all
    My sorrowful heart shall choose.
As none are so noble—none so rich
As this couple of lords, I'll find a niche
      In my heart that's aching,
      Quaking, breaking,
For one of you two—and I don't care which !

ENSEMBLE.

PHYL. (*to* LORD MOUNTARARAT *and* LORD TOLLOLLER).
    To you I give my heart so rich !
ALL (*puzzled*).   To which ?
PHYL.   I do not care !
    To you I yield—it is my doom !
ALL.   To whom ?
PHYL.   I'm not aware !
    I'm yours for life if you but choose.
ALL.   She's whose ?
PHYL.   That's your affair !
    I'll be a countess, shall I not ?
ALL.   Of what ?
PHYL.   I do not care !

I

ALL.   Lucky little lady !
                Strephon's lot is shady ;
                Rank, it seems, is vital,
                " Countess " is the title,
                But of what I'm not aware !

                        Enter STREPHON.

STREPH.   Can I inactive see my fortunes fade ?
                        No, no !
            Mighty protectress, hasten to my aid !

Enter Fairies, tripping, headed by CELIA, LEILA, *and*
    FLETA, *and followed by* QUEEN.

                CHORUS OF FAIRIES.
            Tripping hither, tripping thither,
            Nobody knows why or whither ;
            Why you want us we don't know,
            But you've summoned us, and so
                    Enter all the little fairies
                        To their usual tripping measure !
                    To oblige you all our care is—
                        Tell us, pray, what is your pleasure !

STREPH.   The lady of my love has caught me talking to
                        another—
PEERS.   Oh, fie ! our Strephon is a rogue !
STREPH.   I tell her very plainly that the lady is my
                        mother—
PEERS.   Taradiddle, taradiddle, tol lol lay !
STREPH.   She won't believe my statement, and declares we
                        must be parted,
            Because on a career of double-dealing I have
                        started,
            Then gives her hand to one of these, and leaves
                        me broken-hearted—
PEERS.   Taradiddle, taradiddle, tol lol lay !

QUEEN. Ah, cruel ones, to separate two lovers from each other !

FAIRIES. Oh, fie ! our Strephon's not a rogue !

QUEEN. You've done him an injustice, for the lady *is* his mother !

FAIRIES. Taradiddle, taradiddle, tol lol lay !

LORD CH. That fable perhaps may serve his turn as well as any other.

(*Aside.*) I didn't see her face, but if they fondled one another,
And she's but seventeen—I don't believe it was his mother !
Taradiddle, taradiddle.

ALL. Tol lol lay !

LORD TOLL. I have often had a use
For a thorough-bred excuse
Of a sudden (which is English for " *repente* "),
But of all I ever heard
This is much the most absurd,
For she's seventeen, and he is five-and-twenty !

ALL. Though she is seventeen, and he's four or five-and-twenty !
Oh, fie ! our Strephon is a rogue !

LORD MOUNT. Now, listen, pray, to me,
For this paradox will be
Carried, nobody at all *contradicente.*
Her age, upon the date
Of his birth, was *minus* eight,
If she's seventeen, and he is five-and-twenty !

ALL. To say she is his mother is an utter bit of folly !
Oh, fie ! our Strephon is a rogue !
Perhaps his brain is addled, and it's very melancholy !
Taradiddle, taradiddle, tol lol lay !

>   I wouldn't say a word that could be reckoned as
>   injurious,
>   But to find a mother younger than her son is very
>   curious,
>   And that's a kind of mother that is usually spurious.
>   Taradiddle, taradiddle, tol lol lay!

LORD CH.   Go away, madam;
               I should say, madam,
               You display, madam,
                   Shocking taste.

               It is rude, madam,
               To intrude, madam,
               With your brood, madam,
                   Brazen-faced!

               You come here, madam,
               Interfere, madam,
               With a peer, madam.
                   (I am one.)

               You're aware, madam,
               What you dare, madam,
               So take care, madam,
                   And begone!

ENSEMBLE.

FAIRIES (*to* QUEEN).

Let us stay, madam;
I should say, madam,
They display, madam,
    Shocking taste.

It is rude, madam,
To allude, madam,
To your brood, madam,
    Brazen-faced!

PEERS.

Go away, madam;
I should say, madam,
You display, madam,
    Shocking taste.

It is rude, madam,
To intrude, madam,
With your brood, madam,
    Brazen-faced!

We don't fear, madam,
Any peer, madam,
Though, my dear madam,
    This is one.

You come here, madam,
Interfere, madam,
With a peer, madam,
    (I am one.)

They will stare, madam,
When aware, madam,
What they dare, madam—
    What they've done !

You're aware, madam,
What you dare, madam,
So take care, madam,
    And begone !

QUEEN
(*furious*).

Bearded by these puny mortals !
I will launch from fairy portals
All the most terrific thunders
In my armoury of wonders !

PHYL. (*aside*).

Should they launch terrific wonders,
All would then repent their blunders.
Surely these must be immortals.

                               [*Exit* PHYLLIS.

QUEEN.

Oh ! Chancellor unwary
It's highly necessary
    Your tongue to teach
    Respectful speech—
Your attitude to vary !

Your badinage so airy,
Your manner arbitrary,
    Are out of place
    When face to face
With an influential Fairy.

ALL THE PEERS
(*aside*).

We never knew
    We were talking to
An influential Fairy !

LORD CH.

A plague on this vagary,
I'm in a nice quandary !
    Of hasty tone
    With dames unknown

I ought to be more chary ;
It seems that she's a fairy
From Andersen's library,
And I took her for
The proprietor
Of a Ladies' Seminary !

PEERS.   We took her for
The proprietor
Of a Ladies' Seminary !

QUEEN.   When next your Houses do assemble,
You may tremble !

CELIA.   Our wrath, when gentlemen offend us,
Is tremendous !

LEILA.   They meet, who underrate our calling,
Doom appalling !

QUEEN.   Take down our sentence as we speak it,
And *he* shall wreak it !

(*Indicating* STREPHON)

PEERS.   Oh, spare us !

QUEEN.   Henceforth, Strephon, cast away
Crooks and pipes and ribbons so gay—
Flocks and herds that bleat and low ;
Into Parliament you shall go !

ALL.   Into Parliament he shall go !
Backed by our supreme authority,
He'll command a large majority ;
Into Parliament he shall go !

QUEEN.   In the Parliamentary hive,
Liberal or Conservative—
Whig or Tory—I don't know—
But into Parliament you shall go !

FAIRIES.   Into Parliament, etc.

IOLANTHE 231

QUEEN (*speaking through music*).

Every bill and every measure
That may gratify his pleasure,
Though your fury it arouses,
Shall be passed by both your Houses!

PEERS.   Oh!

You shall sit, if he sees reason,
Through the grouse and salmon season;

PEERS.   No!

He shall end the cherished rights
You enjoy on Friday nights:

PEERS.   No!

He shall prick that annual blister,
Marriage with deceased wife's sister:

PEERS.   Mercy!

Titles shall ennoble, then,
All the Common Councilmen:

PEERS.   Spare us!

Peers shall teem in Christendom,
And a Duke's exalted station
Be attainable by Com-
Petitive Examination!

PEERS.   FAIRIES *and* PHYLLIS.

Oh, horror!   Their horror
                        They can't dissemble
              Nor hide the fear that makes them
                              tremble!

ENSEMBLE.

PEERS.	FAIRIES, PHYLLIS, *and* STREPHON.
Young Strephon is the kind of lout	With Strephon for your foe, no doubt,
We do not care a fig about!	A fearful prospect opens out,
We cannot say	And who shall say
What evils may	What evils may
Result in consequence.	Result in consequence?

But lordly vengeance will pursue
All kinds of common people who
   Oppose our views,
   Or boldly choose
  To offer us offence.

A hideous vengeance will pursue
All noblemen who venture to
   Oppose his views,
   Or boldly choose
  To offer him offence.

He'd better fly at humbler
   game,
Or our forbearance he must
   claim,
   If he'd escape
   In any shape
  A very painful wrench !

'Twill plunge them into grief and
   shame ;
His kind forbearance they must
   claim,
   If they'd escape
   In any shape
  A very painful wrench.

Your powers we dauntlessly pooh-
   pooh :
A dire revenge will fall on you,
   If you besiege
   Our high *prestige*
(The word " *prestige* " is French).

Although our threats you now
   pooh-pooh,
A dire revenge will fall on you,
   Should he besiege
   Your high *prestige*—
(The word " *prestige* " is French).

PEERS.   Our lordly style
           You shall not quench
       With base *canaille* !
FAIRIES.   (That word is French.)
PEERS.   Distinction ebbs
           Before a herd
           Of vulgar *plebs* !
FAIRIES.   (A Latin word.)
PEERS.   'Twould fill with joy,
           And madness stark
       The οἱ πολλοί !
FAIRIES.   (A Greek remark.)

PEERS.   One Latin word, one Greek remark,
       And one that's French.

FAIRIES.   Your lordly style
           We'll quickly quench
       With base *canaille* !

IOLANTHE

PEERS.	(That word is French.)
FAIRIES.	Distinction ebbs
	Before a herd
	Of vulgar *plebs* !
PEERS.	(A Latin word.)
FAIRIES.	'Twill fill with joy
	And madness stark
	The οἱ πολλοί !
PEERS.	(A Greek remark.)

FAIRIES.   One Latin word, one Greek remark,
            And one that's French.

PEERS.	FAIRIES.
You needn't wait :	We will not wait :
Away you fly !	We go sky-high !
Your threatened hate	Our threatened hate
We won't defy !	You won't defy !

(*Fairies threaten Peers with their wands. Peers kneel as begging for mercy.* PHYLLIS *implores* STREPHON *to relent. He casts her from him, and she falls fainting into the arms of* LORD MOUNTARARAT *and* LORD TOLLOLLER.)

END OF ACT I.

ACT II.

SCENE.—*Palace Yard, Westminster. Westminster Hall,*
L. *Clock tower up,* R.C. PRIVATE WILLIS *discovered on sentry,* R. *Moonlight.*

SONG—PRIVATE WILLIS.

When all night long a chap remains
    On sentry-go, to chase monotony
He exercises of his brains,
    That is, assuming that he's got any.
Though never nurtured in the lap
    Of luxury, yet I admonish you,
I am an intellectual chap,
    And think of things that would astonish you.
      I often think it's comical—Fal, lal, la !
      How Nature always does contrive—Fal, lal, la !
      That every boy and every gal
        That's born into the world alive
      Is either a little Liberal
        Or else a little Conservative !
          Fal, lal, la !

When in that House M.P.'s divide,
    If they've a brain and cerebellum, too,
They've got to leave that brain outside,
    And vote just as their leaders tell 'em to.

But then the prospect of a lot
  Of dull M.P.'s in close proximity,
All thinking for themselves, is what
  No man can face with equanimity.
          Then let's rejoice with loud Fal la—Fal lal la !
          That Nature always does contrive—Fal lal la !
            That every boy and every gal
              That's born into the world alive
              Is either a little Liberal
                Or else a little Conservative !
                  Fal lal la !

Enter Fairies, with CELIA, LEILA, *and* FLETA.
        They trip round stage.

CHORUS OF FAIRIES.

Strephon's a Member of Parliament !
Carries every Bill he chooses.
To his measures all assent—
    Showing that fairies have their uses.
        Whigs and Tories
        Dim their glories,
Giving an ear to all his stories—
Lords and Commons are both in the blues !
Strephon makes them shake in their shoes !
    Shake in their shoes !
    Shake in their shoes !
Strephon makes them shake in their shoes !

Enter Peers from Westminster Hall.

CHORUS OF PEERS.

Strephon's a Member of Parliament !
    Running a-muck of all abuses.
His unqualified assent
    Somehow nobody now refuses.
        Whigs and Tories
        Dim their glories,

Giving an ear to all his stories—
Carrying every Bill he may wish :
Here's a pretty kettle of fish !
Kettle of fish !
Kettle of fish !
Here's a pretty kettle of fish !

Enter LORD MOUNTARARAT *and* LORD TOLLOLLER
from Westminster Hall.

CELIA.   You seem annoyed.

LORD MOUNT.   Annoyed !   I should think so !   Why, this ridiculous *protégé* of yours is playing the deuce with everything !   To-night is the second reading of his Bill to throw the Peerage open to Competitive Examination !

LORD TOLL.   And he'll carry it, too !

LORD MOUNT.   Carry it ?   Of course he will !   He's a Parliamentary Pickford—he carries everything !

LEILA.   Yes.   If you please, that's our fault !

LORD MOUNT.   The deuce it is !

CELIA.   Yes ; we influence the members, and compel them to vote just as he wishes them to.

LEILA.   It's our system.   It shortens the debates.

LORD TOLL.   Well, but think what it all means.   I don't so much mind for myself, but with a House of Peers with no grandfathers worth mentioning, the country must go to the dogs !

LEILA.   I suppose it must !

LORD MOUNT.   I don't want to say a word against brains—I've a great respect for brains—I often wish I had some myself—but with a House of Peers composed exclusively of people of intellect, what's to become of the House of Commons ?

LEILA.   I never thought of that !

LORD MOUNT.   This comes of women interfering in politics.   It so happens that if there is an institution in Great Britain which is not susceptible of any improvement at all, it is the House of Peers !

SONG—LORD MOUNTARARAT.

When Britain really ruled the waves—
   (In good Queen Bess's time)
The House of Peers made no pretence
To intellectual eminence,
   Or scholarship sublime ;
Yet Britain won her proudest bays
In good Queen Bess's glorious days !

CHORUS.   Yes, Britain won, etc.

When Wellington thrashed Bonaparte,
   As every child can tell,
The House of Peers, throughout the war,
Did nothing in particular,
   And did it very well :
Yet Britain set the world ablaze
In good King George's glorious days !

CHORUS.   Yes, Britain set, etc.

And while the House of Peers withholds
   Its legislative hand,
And noble statesmen do not itch
To interfere with matters which
   They do not understand,
As bright will shine Great Britain's rays
As in King George's glorious days !

CHORUS.   As bright will shine, etc.

LEILA (*who has been much attracted by the Peers during this song*). Charming persons, are they not ?

CELIA. Distinctly. For self-contained dignity, combined with airy condescension, give me a British Representative Peer !

LORD TOLL. Then pray stop this *protégé* of yours before it's too late. Think of the mischief you're doing !

LEILA (*crying*). But we *can't* stop him now. (*Aside to* CELIA.) Aren't they lovely ! (*Aloud.*) Oh, why did you go and defy us, you great geese !

DUET—LEILA *and* CELIA.

LEILA.   In vain to us you plead—
                        Don't go !
                Your prayers we do not heed—
                        Don't go !
                It's true we sigh,
                        But don't suppose
                A tearful eye
                        Forgiveness shows.
                                Oh, no !
                We're very cross indeed—
                        Don't go !

FAIRIES.   It's true we sigh, etc.

CELIA.   Your disrespectful sneers—
                        Don't go !
                Call forth indignant tears—
                        Don't go !
                You break our laws—
                        You are our foe :
                We cry because
                        We hate you so !
                                You know !
                You very wicked Peers !
                        Don't go !

FAIRIES.	LORDS MOUNT. *and* TOLL.
You break our laws—	Our disrespectful sneers,
You are our foe :	Ha, ha !
We cry because	Call forth indignant tears,
We hate you so !	Ha, ha !
You know !	If that's the case, my dears—
You very wicked peers !	FAIRIES. Don't go !
Don't go !	PEERS. We'll go !

[*Exeunt* LORD MOUNTARARAT, LORD TOL-
        LOLLER, *and Peers. Fairies gaze wist-
        fully after them.*

Enter FAIRY QUEEN.

QUEEN. Oh, shame—shame upon you! Is this your fidelity to the laws you are bound to obey? Know ye not that it is death to marry a mortal?

LEILA. Yes, but it's not death to *wish* to marry a mortal!

FLETA. If it were, you'd have to execute us all!

QUEEN. Oh, this is weakness! Subdue it!

CELIA. We know it's weakness, but the weakness is so strong!

LEILA. We are not all as tough as you are!

QUEEN. Tough! Do you suppose that I am insensible to the effect of manly beauty? Look at that man! (*Referring to Sentry.*) A perfect picture! (*To Sentry.*) Who are you, sir?

WILLIS (*coming to " attention "*). Private Willis, B Company, 1st Grenadier Guards.

QUEEN. You're a very fine fellow, sir.

WILLIS. I am generally admired.

QUEEN. I can quite understand it. (*To Fairies.*) Now here is a man whose physical attributes are simply godlike. That man has a most extraordinary effect upon me. If I yielded to a natural impulse, I should fall down and worship that man. But I mortify this inclination; I wrestle with it, and it lies beneath my feet! That is how I treat my regard for that man!

SONG—FAIRY QUEEN.

Oh, foolish fay,
    Think you, because
His brave array
    My bosom thaws,
I'd disobey
    Our fairy laws?
Because I fly
    In realms above,
In tendency
    To fall in love,
Resemble I
    The amorous dove?

(*Aside.*)   Oh, amorous dove !
                          Type of Ovidius Naso !
                             This heart of mine
                             Is soft as thine,
                          Although I dare not say so !

CHORUS.   Oh, amorous dove, etc.

                   On fire that glows
                       With heat intense
                   I turn the hose
                       Of common sense,
                   And out it goes
                       At small expense !
                   We must maintain
                       Our fairy law ;
                   That is the main
                       On which to draw—
                   In that we gain
                       A Captain Shaw !
(*Aside.*)   Oh, Captain Shaw !
                          Type of true love kept under !
                             Could thy Brigade
                             With cold cascade
                          Quench my great love, I wonder !

CHORUS.   Oh, Captain Shaw ! etc.

[*Exeunt Fairies and* FAIRY QUEEN, *sorrowfully.*

Enter PHYLLIS.

PHYL. (*half crying*). I can't think why I'm not in
better spirits. I'm engaged to two noblemen at once.
That ought to be enough to make any girl happy. But
I'm miserable ! Don't suppose it's because I care for
Strephon, for I hate him ! No girl *could* care for a man
who goes about with a mother considerably younger than
himself !

Enter LORD MOUNTARARAT *and* LORD TOLLOLLER.

LORD MOUNT. Phyllis! My darling!

LORD TOLL. Phyllis! My own!

PHYL. Don't! How dare you? Oh, but perhaps you're the two noblemen I'm engaged to?

LORD MOUNT. I am one of them.

LORD TOLL. I am the other.

PHYL. Oh, then, my darling! (*to* LORD MOUNT-ARARAT). My own! (*to* LORD TOLLOLLER). Well, have you settled which it's to be?

LORD TOLL. Not altogether. It's a difficult position. It would be hardly delicate to toss up. On the whole we would rather leave it to you.

PHYL. How can it possibly concern me? You are both Earls, and you are both rich, and you are both plain.

LORD MOUNT. So we are. At least I am.

LORD TOLL. So am I.

LORD MOUNT. No, no!

LORD TOLL. I am indeed. Very plain.

LORD MOUNT. Well, well—perhaps you are.

PHYL. There's really nothing to choose between you. If one of you would forgo his title, and distribute his estates among his Irish tenantry, why, then, I should then see a reason for accepting the other.

LORD MOUNT. Tolloller, are you prepared to make this sacrifice?

LORD TOLL. No!

LORD MOUNT. Not even to oblige a lady?

LORD TOLL. No! not even to oblige a lady.

LORD MOUNT. Then, the only question is, which of us shall give way to the other? Perhaps, on the whole, she would be happier with me. I don't know. I may be wrong.

LORD TOLL. No. I don't know that you are. I really believe she would. But the awkward part of the thing is that if you rob me of the girl of my heart, we must fight, and one of us must die. It's a family tradition that I have sworn to respect. It's a painful position, for I have a very strong regard for you, George.

LORD MOUNT. (*much affected*). My dear Thomas!

LORD TOLL. You are very dear to me, George. We were boys together—at least *I* was. If I were to survive you, my existence would be hopelessly embittered.

LORD MOUNT. Then, my dear Thomas, you must not do it. I say it again and again—if it will have this effect upon you, you must not do it. No, no. If one of us is to destroy the other, let it be me!

LORD TOLL. No, no!

LORD MOUNT. Ah, yes!—by our boyish friendship I implore you!

LORD TOLL. (*much moved*). Well, well, be it so. But, no—no!—I cannot consent to an act which would crush you with unavailing remorse.

LORD MOUNT. But it would not do so. I should be very sad at first—oh, who would not be?—but it would wear off. I like you *very much*—but not, perhaps, as much as you like me.

LORD TOLL. George, you're a noble fellow, but that tell-tale tear betrays you. No, George; you are very fond of me, and I cannot consent to give you a week's uneasiness on my account.

LORD MOUNT. But, dear Thomas, it would not last a week! Remember, you lead the House of Lords! on your demise I shall take your place! Oh, Thomas, it would not last a day!

PHYL. (*coming down*). Now, I do hope you're not going to fight about me, because it's really not worth while.

LORD TOLL. (*looking at her*). Well, I don't believe it is!

LORD MOUNT. Nor I. The sacred ties of Friendship are paramount.

QUARTETTE—LORD MOUNTARARAT,
LORD TOLLOLLER, PHYLLIS, *and* PRIVATE WILLIS.

LORD TOLL. Though p'r'aps I may incur your blame,
The things are few
I would not do
In Friendship's name!

LORD MOUNT.   And I may say I think the same ;
              Not even love
              Should rank above
              True Friendship's name !

PHYL.   Then free me, pray ; be mine the blame ;
              Forget your craze
              And go your ways
              In Friendship's name !

ALL.   Oh, many a man, in Friendship's name,
              Has yielded fortune, rank, and fame !
              But no one yet, in the world so wide,
              Has yielded up a promised bride !

WILLIS.   Accept, O Friendship, all the same,

ALL.   This sacrifice to thy dear name !

[*Exeunt* LORD MOUNTARARAT *and* LORD
TOLLOLLER, *lovingly, in one direction,
and* PHYLLIS *in another. Exit Sentry.*

Enter LORD CHANCELLOR, *very miserable.*

RECIT.—LORD CHANCELLOR.

Love, unrequited, robs me of my rest :
  Love, hopeless love, my ardent soul encumbers :
Love, nightmare-like, lies heavy on my chest,
  And weaves itself into my midnight slumbers !

SONG—LORD CHANCELLOR.

When you're lying awake with a dismal headache, and
  repose is taboo'd by anxiety,
I conceive you may use any language you choose to
  indulge in, without impropriety ;
For your brain is on fire—the bedclothes conspire of usual
  slumber to plunder you :
First your counterpane goes, and uncovers your toes, and
  your sheet slips demurely from under you ;

Then the blanketing tickles—you feel like mixed pickles—
    so terribly sharp is the pricking,
And you're hot, and you're cross, and you tumble and toss
    till there's nothing 'twixt you and the ticking.
Then the bedclothes all creep to the ground in a heap, and
    you pick 'em all up in a tangle ;
Next your pillow resigns and politely declines to remain
    at its usual angle !
Well, you get some repose in the form of a doze, with hot
    eye-balls and head ever aching,
But your slumbering teems with such horrible dreams that
    you'd very much better be waking ;
For you dream you are crossing the Channel, and tossing
    about in a steamer from Harwich—
Which is sometimes between a large bathing machine and
    a very small second-class carriage—
And you're giving a treat (penny ice and cold meat) to a
    party of friends and relations—
They're a ravenous horde—and they all came on board
    at Sloane Square and South Kensington Stations.
And bound on that journey you find your attorney (who
    started that morning from Devon) ;
He's a bit undersized, and you don't feel surprised when
    he tells you he's only eleven.
Well, you're driving like mad with this singular lad
    (by the by, the ship's now a four-wheeler),
And you're playing round games, and he calls you bad
    names when you tell him that " ties pay the dealer " ;
But this you can't stand, so you throw up your hand, and
    you find you're as cold as an icicle,
In your shirt and your socks (the black silk with gold
    clocks), crossing Salisbury Plain on a bicycle :
And he and the crew are on bicycles too—which they've
    somehow or other invested in—
And he's telling the tars all the particulars of a company
    he's interested in—
It's a scheme of devices, to get at low prices all goods
    from cough mixtures to cables

(Which tickled the sailors), by treating retailers as though
    they were all vege*t*ables—
You get a good spadesman to plant a small tradesman
    (first take off his boots with a boot-tree),
And his legs will take root, and his fingers will shoot, and
    they'll blossom and bud like a fruit-tree—
From the greengrocer tree you get grapes and green pea,
    cauliflower, pineapple, and cranberries,
While the pastrycook plant cherry brandy will grant, apple
    puffs, and three-corners, and Banburys—
The shares are a penny, and ever so many are taken by
    Rothschild and Baring,
And just as a few are allotted to you, you awake with a
    shudder despairing—
You're a regular wreck, with a crick in your neck, and no
    wonder you snore, for your head's on the floor, and
    you've needles and pins from your soles to your shins,
    and your flesh is a-creep, for your left leg's asleep,
    and you've cramp in your toes, and a fly on your
    nose, and some fluff in your lung, and a feverish
    tongue, and a thirst that's intense, and a general
    sense that you haven't been sleeping in clover ;
But the darkness has passed, and it's daylight at last, and
    the night has been long—ditto ditto my song—and
    thank goodness they're both of them over !

(LORD CHANCELLOR *falls exhausted on a seat*.)

LORDS MOUNTARARAT *and* TOLLOLLER *come forward*.

LORD MOUNT. I am much distressed to see your
Lordship in this condition.

LORD CH. Ah, my Lords, it is seldom that a Lord
Chancellor has reason to envy the position of another,
but I am free to confess that I would rather be two Earls
engaged to Phyllis than any other half-dozen noblemen
upon the face of the globe.

LORD TOLL. (*without enthusiasm*). Yes. It's an
enviable position when you're the only one.

LORD MOUNT. Oh yes, no doubt—most enviable. At

the same time, seeing you thus, we naturally say to ourselves, " This is very sad. His Lordship is constitutionally as blithe as a bird—he trills upon the bench like a thing of song and gladness. His series of judgements in F sharp minor, given *andante* in six-eight time, are among the most remarkable effects ever produced in a Court of Chancery. He is, perhaps, the only living instance of a judge whose decrees have received the honour of a double *encore*. How can we bring ourselves to do that which will deprive the Court of Chancery of one of its most attractive features ? "

Lord Ch. I feel the force of your remarks, but I am here in two capacities, and they clash, my Lord, they clash ! I deeply grieve to say that in declining to entertain my last application to myself, I presumed to address myself in terms which render it impossible for me ever to apply to myself again. It was a most painful scene, my Lord—most painful !

Lord Toll. This is what it is to have two capacities ! Let us be thankful that we are persons of no capacity whatever.

Lord Mount. Come, come. Remember you are a very just and kindly old gentleman, and you need have no hesitation in approaching yourself, so that you do so respectfully and with a proper show of deference.

Lord Ch. Do you really think so ?

Lord Mount. I do.

Lord Ch. Well, I will nerve myself to another effort, and, if that fails, I resign myself to my fate !

TRIO—Lord Chancellor, Lords Mountararat
and Tolloller.

Lord Mount.   If you go in
                You're sure to win—
        Yours will be the charming maidie :
                Be your law
                The ancient saw,
    " Faint heart never won fair lady ! "

ALL.   Faint heart never won fair lady !
       Every journey has an end—
       When at the worst affairs will mend—
       Dark the dawn when day is nigh—
       Hustle your horse and don't say die !

LORD TOLL.   He who shies
             At such a prize
       Is not worth a maravedi,
             Be so kind
             To bear in mind—
       Faint heart never won fair lady !

ALL.   Faint heart never won fair lady !
       While the sun shines make your hay—
       Where a will is, there's a way—
       Beard the lion in his lair—
       None but the brave deserve the fair !

LORD CH.   I'll take heart
           And make a start—
       Though I fear the prospect's shady—
             Much I'd spend
             To gain my end—
       Faint heart never won fair lady !

ALL.   Faint heart never won fair lady !
       Nothing venture, nothing win—
       Blood is thick, but water's thin—
       In for a penny, in for a pound—
       It's Love that makes the world go round !

       [*Dance, and exeunt arm-in-arm together.*

Enter STREPHON, *in very low spirits.*

STREPH.   I suppose one ought to enjoy oneself in Parliament, when one leads both Parties, as I do ! But I'm miserable, poor, broken-hearted fool that I am ! Oh, Phyllis, Phyllis !——

Enter PHYLLIS.

PHYL.   Yes.

STREPH. (*surprised*).   Phyllis !   But I suppose I should say " My Lady ".   I have not yet been informed which title your ladyship has pleased to select ?

PHYL.   I—I haven't quite decided.   You see *I* have no *mother* to advise *me* !

STREPH.   No.   I have.

PHYL.   Yes ; a *young* mother.

STREPH.   Not very—a couple of centuries or so.

PHYL.   Oh !   She wears well.

STREPH.   She does.   She's a fairy.

PHYL.   I beg your pardon—a what ?

STREPH.   Oh, I've no longer any reason to conceal the fact—she's a fairy.

PHYL.   A fairy !   Well, but—that would account for a good many things !   Then—I suppose *you're* a fairy ?

STREPH.   I'm half a fairy.

PHYL.   Which half ?

STREPH.   The upper half—down to the waistcoat.

PHYL.   Dear me !   (*Prodding him with her fingers.*) There is nothing to show it !

STREPH.   Don't do that.

PHYL.   But why didn't you tell me this before ?

STREPH.   I thought you would take a dislike to me. But as it's all off, you may as well know the truth—I'm only half a mortal !

PHYL. (*crying*).   But I'd rather have half a mortal I do love, than half a dozen I don't !

STREPH.   Oh, I think not—go to your half-dozen.

PHYL. (*crying*).   It's only two !   and I hate 'em ! Please forgive me !

STREPH.   I don't think I ought to.   Besides, all sorts of difficulties will arise.   You know, my grandmother looks quite as young as my mother.   So do all my aunts.

PHYL.   I quite understand.   Whenever I see you kissing a very young lady, I shall know it's an elderly relative.

STREPH. You will? Then, Phyllis, I think we shall
be very happy! (*Embracing her.*)

PHYL. We won't wait long.

STREPH. No. We might change our minds. We'll
get married first.

PHYL. And change our minds afterwards?

STREPH. That's the usual course.

DUET—STREPHON *and* PHYLLIS.

STREPH.
　　If we're weak enough to tarry
　　　　Ere we marry,
　　　　　　You and I,
　　Of the feeling I inspire
　　　　You may tire
　　　　　　By and by.
　　For peers with flowing coffers
　　　　Press their offers—
　　　　　　That is why
　　I am sure we should not tarry
　　　　Ere we marry,
　　　　　　You and I!

PHYL.
　　If we're weak enough to tarry
　　　　Ere we marry,
　　　　　　You and I,
　　With a more attractive maiden,
　　　　Jewel-laden,
　　　　　　You may fly.
　　If by chance we should be parted,
　　　　Broken-hearted
　　　　　　I should die—
　　So I think we will not tarry
　　　　Ere we marry,
　　　　　　You and I.

PHYL. But does your mother know you're—　I mean,
is she aware of our engagement?

Enter IOLANTHE.

IOL. She is ; and thus she welcomes her daughter-in-law ! (*Kisses her.*)

PHYL. She kisses just like other people ! But the Lord Chancellor ?

STREPH. I forgot him ! Mother, none can resist your fairy eloquence ; you will go to him and plead for us ?

IOL. (*much agitated*). No, no ; impossible !

STREPH. But our happiness—our very lives—depend upon our obtaining his consent !

PHYL. Oh, madam, you cannot refuse to do this !

IOL. You know not what you ask ! The Lord Chancellor is—my husband !

STREPH. *and* PHYL. Your husband !

IOL. My husband and your father ! (*Addressing* STREPHON, *who is much moved.*)

PHYL. Then our course is plain ; on his learning that Strephon is his son, all objection to our marriage will be at once removed !

IOL. No ; he must never know ! He believes me to have died childless, and, dearly as I love him, I am bound, under penalty of death, not to undeceive him. But see— he comes ! Quick—my veil !

> [IOLANTHE *veils herself.* STREPHON *and*
>   PHYLLIS *go off on tiptoe.*

Enter LORD CHANCELLOR.

LORD CH. Victory ! Victory ! Success has crowned my efforts, and I may consider myself engaged to Phyllis ! At first I wouldn't hear of it—it was out of the question. But I took heart. I pointed out to myself that I was no stranger to myself ; that, in point of fact, I had been personally acquainted with myself for some years. This had its effect. I admitted that I had watched my professional advancement with considerable interest, and I handsomely added that I yielded to no one in admiration for my private and professional virtues. This was a great point gained. I then endeavoured to work upon my feelings. Conceive my joy when I distinctly perceived a tear glistening in my own eye! Eventually, after a severe struggle with myself, I reluctantly—most reluctantly—consented.

(IOLANTHE *comes down veiled.*)

RECIT.—IOLANTHE.

My lord, a suppliant at your feet I kneel,
Oh, listen to a mother's fond appeal!
Hear me to-night! I come in urgent need—
'Tis for my son, young Strephon, that I plead!

BALLAD—IOLANTHE.

He loves! If in the bygone years
    Thine eyes have ever shed
Tears—bitter, unavailing tears,
    For one untimely dead—
If, in the eventide of life,
    Sad thoughts of her arise,
Then let the memory of thy wife
    Plead for my boy—he dies!

He dies! If fondly laid aside
    In some old cabinet,
Memorials of thy long-dead bride
    Lie, dearly treasured yet,
Then let her hallowed bridal dress—
    Her little dainty gloves—
Her withered flowers—her faded tress—
    Plead for my boy—he loves!

(*The* LORD CHANCELLOR *is moved by this appeal.*
After a pause.)

LORD CH. It may not be—for so the fates decide!
    Learn thou that Phyllis is my promised bride.

IOL. (*in horror*).			Thy bride ! No ! no !

LORD CH.			It shall be so !
				Those who would separate us woe betide !

IOL.			My doom thy lips have spoken—
					I plead in vain !

CHORUS OF FAIRIES (*without*).		Forbear ! forbear !

IOL.			A vow already broken
					I break again !

CHORUS OF FAIRIES (*without*).		Forbear ! forbear !

IOL.			For him—for her—for thee
					I yield my life.
				Behold—it may not be !
					I am thy wife.

CHORUS OF FAIRIES (*without*).   Aiaiah! Aiaiah! Willaloo!

LORD CH. (*recognizing her*).   Iolanthe ! thou livest ?

IOL.						Aye !
					I live ! Now let me die !

Enter FAIRY QUEEN *and Fairies.* IOLANTHE *kneels
					to her.*

QUEEN.	Once again thy vows are broken :
		Thou thyself thy doom hast spoken !

CHORUS OF FAIRIES.		Aiaiah ! Aiaiah !
					Willahalah ! Willaloo !
					Willahalah ! Willaloo !

QUEEN.	Bow thy head to Destiny :
		Death thy doom, and thou shalt die !

CHORUS OF FAIRIES.		Aiaiah ! Aiaiah ! etc.

Peers and Sentry enter. The QUEEN *raises her spear.*

LEILA.   Hold !   If Iolanthe must die, so must we all ;
for, as she has sinned, so have we !

QUEEN. What?

CELIA. We are all fairy duchesses, marchionesses, countesses, viscountesses, and baronesses.

LORD MOUNT. It's our fault. They couldn't help themselves.

QUEEN. It seems they *have* helped themselves, and pretty freely, too! (*After a pause.*) You have all incurred death; but I can't slaughter the whole company! And yet (*unfolding a scroll*) the law is clear—every fairy must die who marries a mortal!

LORD CH. Allow me, as an old Equity draftsman, to make a suggestion. The subtleties of the legal mind are equal to the emergency. The thing is really quite simple—the insertion of a single word will do it. Let it stand that every fairy shall die who *doesn't* marry a mortal, and there you are, out of your difficulty at once!

QUEEN. We like your humour. Very well! (*Altering the MS. in pencil.*) Private Willis!

SENTRY (*coming forward*). Ma'am!

QUEEN. To save my life, it is necessary that I marry at once. How should you like to be a fairy guardsman?

SENTRY. Well, ma'am, I don't think much of the British soldier who wouldn't ill-convenience himself to save a female in distress.

QUEEN. You are a brave fellow. You're a fairy from this moment. (*Wings spring from Sentry's shoulders.*) And you, my Lords, how say you, will you join our ranks?

(*Fairies kneel to Peers and implore them to do so.*)

PHYLLIS *and* STREPHON *enter.*

LORD MOUNT. (*to* LORD TOLLOLLER). Well, now that the Peers are to be recruited entirely from persons of intelligence, I really don't see what use *we* are, down here, do you, Tolloller?

LORD TOLL. None whatever.

QUEEN. Good! (*Wings spring from shoulders of Peers.*) Then away we go to Fairyland.

FINALE.

PHYL.	Soon as we may,
	Off and away !
	We'll commence our journey airy—
	Happy are we—
	As you can see,
	Every one is now a fairy !
ALL.	Every one is now a fairy !
IOL., QUEEN,	Though as a general rule we know
and PHYL.	Two strings go to every bow,
	Make up your minds that grief 'twill bring,
	If you've two beaux to every string.
ALL.	Though as a general rule, etc.
LORD CH.	Up in the sky,
	Ever so high,
	Pleasures come in endless series ;
	We will arrange
	Happy exchange—
	House of Peers for House of Peris !
ALL.	House of Peers for House of Peris !
LORDS CH.,	Up in the air, sky-high, sky-high,
MOUNT.,	Free from Wards in Chancery,
and TOLL.	I }
	He } will be surely happier, for
	I'm }
	He's } such a susceptible Chancellor.
ALL.	Up in the air, etc.

CURTAIN.

PRINCESS IDA

OR

CASTLE ADAMANT

DRAMATIS PERSONÆ.

KING HILDEBRAND.

HILARION (*his Son*).

CYRIL
FLORIAN } (*Hilarion's Friends*).

KING GAMA.

ARAC
GURON } (*his Sons*).
SCYNTHIUS

PRINCESS IDA (*Gama's Daughter*).

LADY BLANCHE (*Professor of Abstract Science*).

LADY PSYCHE (*Professor of Humanities*).

MELISSA (*Lady Blanche's Daughter*).

SACHARISSA
CHLOE } (*Girl Graduates*).
ADA

Soldiers, Courtiers, " Girl Graduates ", " Daughters of the Plough ",
etc.

ACT I.—Pavilion in King Hildebrand's Palace.

ACT II.—Gardens of Castle Adamant.

ACT III.—Courtyard of Castle Adamant.

First produced at the Savoy Theatre, January 5, 1884.

PRINCESS IDA

OR

CASTLE ADAMANT

ACT I.

SCENE.—*Pavilion attached to* KING HILDEBRAND'S *Palace. Soldiers and Courtiers discovered looking out through opera-glasses, telescopes, etc.,* FLORIAN *leading.*

CHORUS.

> Search throughout the panorama
> For a sign of royal Gama,
>   Who to-day should cross the water
>   With his fascinating daughter—
>   Ida is her name.
>
> Some misfortune evidently
> Has detained them—consequently
>   Search throughout the panorama
>   For the daughter of King Gama,
>   Prince Hilarion's flame!

SOLO.

FLOR.   Will Prince Hilarion's hopes be sadly blighted?
ALL.   Who can tell?
FLOR.   Will Ida break the vows that she has plighted?
ALL.   Who can tell?

FLOR. Will she back out, and say she did not mean them ?
ALL.   Who can tell ?
FLOR. If so, there'll be the deuce to pay between them !

ALL.   No, no—we'll not despair,
                  For Gama would not dare
                  To make a deadly foe
                  Of Hildebrand, and so,
                      Search throughout, etc.

Enter KING HILDEBRAND, *with* CYRIL.

HILD. See you no sign of Gama ?
FLOR.   None, my liege !
HILD. It's very odd indeed.   If Gama fail
       To put in an appearance at our Court
       Before the sun has set in yonder west,
       And fail to bring the Princess Ida here
       To whom our son Hilarion was betrothed
       At the extremely early age of one,
       There's war between King Gama and ourselves !
       (*Aside to* CYRIL.)   Oh, Cyril, how I dread this
           interview
       It's twenty years since he and I have met.
       He was a twisted monster—all awry—
       As though Dame Nature, angry with her work,
       Had crumpled it in fitful petulance !
CYR.   But, sir, a twisted and ungainly trunk
       Often bears goodly fruit.   Perhaps he was
       A kind, well-spoken gentleman ?
HILD.   Oh, no !
       For, adder-like, his sting lay in his tongue.
       (His " sting " is present, though his " stung " is
           past.)
FLOR. (*looking through glass*).   But stay, my liege ; o'er
           yonder mountain's brow
       Comes a small body, bearing Gama's arms ;

And now I look more closely at it, sir,
I see attached to it King Gama's legs;
From which I gather this corollary
That that small body must be Gama's own!

HILD.   Ha! Is the Princess with him?

FLOR.   Well, my liege,
Unless her highness is full six feet high,
And wears mustachios too—and smokes cigars—
And rides *en cavalier* in coat of steel—
I do not think she is.

HILD.   One never knows.
She's a strange girl, I've heard, and does odd
      things!
Come, bustle there!
For Gama place the richest robes we own—
For Gama place the coarsest prison dress—
For Gama let our best spare bed be aired—
For Gama let our deepest dungeon yawn—
For Gama lay the costliest banquet out—
For Gama place cold water and dry bread!
For as King Gama brings the Princess here,
Or brings her not, so shall King Gama have
Much more than everything—much less than
      nothing!

SONG AND CHORUS.

HILD.   Now hearken to my strict command
           On every hand, on every hand—

CHORUS.

           To your command,
           On every hand,
           We dutifully bow!

HILD.   If Gama bring the Princess here,
           Give him good cheer, give him good cheer.

CHORUS.

If she come here
We'll give him a cheer,
And we will show you how.
Hip, hip, hurrah ! hip, hip, hurrah !
Hip, hip, hurrah ! hurrah ! hurrah !
We'll shout and sing
Long live the King,
And his daughter, too, I trow !
Then shout ha ! ha ! hip, hip, hurrah !
Hip, hip, hip, hip, hurrah !
For the fair Princess and her good papa,
Hurrah ! hurrah !

HILD. But if he fail to keep his troth,
Upon our oath, we'll trounce them both !

CHORUS.

He'll trounce them both,
Upon his oath,
As sure as quarter-day !

HILD. We'll shut him up in a dungeon cell,
And toll his knell on a funeral bell.

CHORUS.

From dungeon cell,
His funeral knell
Shall strike him with dismay !
Hip, hip, hurrah ! hip, hip, hurrah !
Hip, hip, hurrah ! hurrah ! hurrah !
As up we string
The faithless King,
In the old familiar way !
We'll shout ha ! ha ! hip, hip, hurrah !
Hip, hip, hip, hip, hurrah !
As we make an end of her false papa,
Hurrah ! hurrah !

[*Exeunt all.*

Enter HILARION.

RECIT.—HILARION.

To-day we meet, my baby bride and I—
   But ah, my hopes are balanced by my fears !
What transmutations have been conjured by
   The silent alchemy of twenty years !

BALLAD—HILARION.

   Ida was a twelvemonth old,
      Twenty years ago !
   I was twice her age, I'm told,
      Twenty years ago !
   Husband twice as old as wife
   Argues ill for married life
   Baleful prophecies were rife,
      Twenty years ago !

   Still, I was a tiny prince
      Twenty years ago.
   She has gained upon me, since
      Twenty years ago.
   Though she's twenty-one, it's true,
   I am barely twenty-two—
   False and foolish prophets you,
      Twenty years ago !

Enter HILDEBRAND.

HIL.   Well, father, is there news for me at last ?
HILD. King Gama is in sight, but much I fear
      With no Princess !
HIL.   Alas, my liege, I've heard
      That Princess Ida has forsworn the world,
      And, with a band of women, shut herself
      Within a lonely country house, and there
      Devotes herself to stern philosophies !

HILD.   Then I should say the loss of such a wife
         Is one to which a reasonable man
         Would easily be reconciled.

HIL.   Oh, no !
         Or I am not a reasonable man.
         She *is* my wife—has been for twenty years !
         (*Holding glass.*)   I think I see her now.

HILD.   Ha ! let me look !

HIL.   In my mind's eye, I mean—a blushing bride,
         All bib and tucker, frill and furbelow !
         How exquisite she looked as she was borne,
         Recumbent, in her foster-mother's arms !
         How the bride wept—nor would be comforted
         Until the hireling mother-for-the-nonce
         Administered refreshment in the vestry.
         And I remember feeling much annoyed
         That she should weep at marrying with me.
         But then I thought, " These brides are all alike.
         You cry at marrying me ?   How much more cause
         You'd have to cry if it were broken off ! "
         These were my thoughts ; I kept them to myself,
         For at that age I had not learnt to speak.

                                       [*Exeunt.*

Enter Courtiers.

CHORUS.

From the distant panorama
Come the sons of royal Gama.
     They are heralds evidently,
     And are sacred consequently,
         Sons of Gama, hail ! oh, hail !

Enter ARAC, GURON, *and* SCYNTHIUS.

SONG—ARAC.

We are warriors three,
     Sons of Gama, Rex.
Like most sons are we,
     Masculine in sex.

ALL THREE. Yes, yes, yes,
Masculine in sex.

ARAC. Politics we bar,
They are not our bent ;
On the whole we are
Not intelligent.

ALL THREE. No, no, no,
Not intelligent.

ARAC. But with doughty heart,
And with trusty blade
We can play our part—
Fighting is our trade.

ALL THREE. Yes, yes, yes,
Fighting is our trade.

ALL THREE. Bold, and fierce, and strong, ha ! ha !
For a war we burn,
With its right or wrong, ha ! ha !
We have no concern.
Order comes to fight, ha ! ha !
Order is obeyed,
We are men of might, ha ! ha !
Fighting is our trade.
Yes, yes, yes,
Fighting is our trade, ha ! ha !

CHORUS.

They are men of might, ha ! ha !
Fighting is their trade.
Order comes to fight, ha ! ha !
Order is obeyed, ha ! ha !
Fighting is their trade !

Enter KING GAMA.

SONG—Gama.

If you give me your attention, I will tell you what I am :
I'm a genuine philanthropist—all other kinds are sham.
Each little fault of temper and each social defect
In my erring fellow-creatures I endeavour to correct.
To all their little weaknesses I open people's eyes ;
And little plans to snub the self-sufficient I devise ;
I love my fellow-creatures—I do all the good I can—
Yet everybody says I'm such a disagreeable man !
        And I can't think why !

To compliments inflated I've a withering reply ;
And vanity I always do my best to mortify ;
A charitable action I can skilfully dissect ;
And interested motives I'm delighted to detect ;
I know everybody's income and what everybody earns ;
And I carefully compare it with the income-tax returns ;
But to benefit humanity however much I plan,
Yet everybody says I'm such a disagreeable man !
        And I can't think why !

I'm sure I'm no ascetic ; I'm as pleasant as can be ;
You'll always find me ready with a crushing repartee,
I've an irritating chuckle, I've a celebrated sneer,
I've an entertaining snigger, I've a fascinating leer.
To everybody's prejudice I know a thing or two ;
I can tell a woman's age in half a minute—and I do.
But although I try to make myself as pleasant as I can,
Yet everybody says I am a disagreeable man !
        And I can't think why !

Enter Hildebrand, Hilarion, Cyril, *and* Florian.

Gama. So this is Castle Hildebrand ? Well, well !
        Dame Rumour whispered that the place was grand ;
        She told me that your taste was exquisite,
        Superb, unparalleled !

HILD. (*gratified*).   Oh, really, King!

GAMA. But she's a liar! Why, how old you've grown!
      Is this Hilarion? Why, you've changed too—
      You were a singularly handsome child!
(*To* FLOR.) Are you a courtier? Come, then, ply your
          trade,
      Tell me some lies. How do you like your King?
      Vile rumour says he's all but imbecile.
      Now, that's not true?

FLOR.   My lord, we love our King.
      His wise remarks are valued by his court
      As precious stones.

GAMA.   And for the self-same cause.
      Like precious stones, his sensible remarks
      Derive their value from their scarcity!
      Come now, be honest, tell the truth for once!
      Tell it of me. Come, come, I'll harm you not.
      This leg is crooked—this foot is ill-designed—
      This shoulder wears a hump! Come, out with it!
      Look, here's my face! Now, am I not the worst
      Of Nature's blunders?

CYR.   Nature never errs.
      To those who know the workings of your mind,
      Your face and figure, sir, suggest a book
      Appropriately bound.

GAMA (*enraged*).   Why, harkye, sir,
      How dare you bandy words with me?

CYR.   No need
      To bandy aught that appertains to you.

GAMA (*furiously*). Do you permit this, King?

HILD.   We are in doubt
      Whether to treat you as an honoured guest,
      Or as a traitor knave who plights his word
      And breaks it.

GAMA (*quickly*).   If the casting vote's with me,
      I give it for the former!

HILD.   We shall see.
      By the terms of our contract, signed and sealed,

You're bound to bring the Princess here to-day :
Why is she not with you ?

GAMA.   Answer me this :
What think you of a wealthy purse-proud man,
Who, when he calls upon a starving friend,
Pulls out his gold and flourishes his notes,
And flashes diamonds in the pauper's eyes ?
What name have you for such an one ?

HILD.   A snob.

GAMA. Just so.   The girl has beauty, virtue, wit,
Grace, humour, wisdom, charity, and pluck.
Would it be kindly, think you, to parade
These brilliant qualities before *your* eyes ?
Oh no, King Hildebrand, I am no snob !

HILD. (*furiously*). Stop that tongue,
Or you shall lose the monkey head that holds it !

GAMA. Bravo ! your King deprives me of my head,
That he and I may meet on equal terms !

HILD. Where is she now ?

GAMA.   In Castle Adamant,
One of my many country houses. There
She rules a woman's University,
With full a hundred girls, who learn of her.

CYR. A hundred girls ! A hundred ecstasies !

GAMA. But no mere girls, my good young gentleman ;
With all the college learning that you boast,
The youngest there will prove a match for *you.*

CYR. With all my heart, if she's the prettiest !
(*To* FLOR.) Fancy, a hundred matches—all alight !—
That's if I strike them as I hope to do !

GAMA. Despair your hope ; their hearts are dead to
        men.
He who desires to gain their favour must
Be qualified to strike their teeming brains,
And not their hearts. They're safety matches, sir,
And they light only on the knowledge box—
So *you've* no chance !

FLOR. Are there no males whatever in those walls ?

GAMA. None, gentlemen, excepting letter mails—
      And they are driven (as males often are
      In other large communities) by women.
      Why, bless my heart, she's so particular
      She'll scarcely suffer Dr. Watts's hymns—
      And all the animals she owns are " hers " !
      The ladies rise at cockcrow every morn—
CYR. Ah, then they have male poultry ?
GAMA.   Not at all,
(*Confidentially*.) The crowing's done by an accomplished
           hen !

DUET—GAMA *and* HILDEBRAND.

GAMA.   Perhaps if you address the lady
           Most politely, most politely—
       Flatter and impress the lady,
           Most politely, most politely—
       Humbly beg and humbly sue—
       She may deign to look on you,
       But your doing you must do
           Most politely, most politely !

ALL.   Humbly beg and humbly sue, etc.

HILD.   Go you, and inform the lady,
           Most politely, most politely,
       If she don't, we'll storm the lady
           Most politely, most politely !
(*To* GAMA.) You'll remain as hostage here ;
       Should Hilarion disappear,
       We will hang you, never fear,
           Most politely, most politely !

             He'll ⎫
ALL.   I'll ⎬ remain as hostage here, etc.
            You'll ⎭

        [GAMA, ARAC, GURON, *and* SCYNTHIUS *are
           marched off in custody*, HILDEBRAND
           following.

RECIT.—HILARION.

Come, Cyril, Florian, our course is plain,
To-morrow morn fair Ida we'll engage ;
But we will use no force her love to gain,
Nature has armed us for the war we wage !

TRIO—HILARION, CYRIL, *and* FLORIAN.

HIL.
Expressive glances
Shall be our lances,
And pops of Sillery
Our light artillery.
We'll storm their bowers
With scented showers
Of fairest flowers
That we can buy !

CHORUS.
Oh, dainty triolet !
Oh, fragrant violet !
Oh, gentle heigho-let
(Or little sigh).
On sweet urbanity,
Though mere inanity,
To touch their vanity
We will rely !

CYR.
When day is fading,
With serenading
And such frivolity
We'll prove our quality.
A sweet profusion
Of soft allusion
This bold intrusion
Shall justify.

CHORUS.
Oh, dainty triolet, etc.

FLOR.
  We'll charm their senses
  With verbal fences,
   With ballads amatory
   And declamatory.
  Little heeding
  Their pretty pleading,
  Our love exceeding
   We'll justify !

CHORUS.   Oh, dainty triolet, etc.

 Re-enter GAMA, ARAC, GURON, *and* SCYNTHIUS
    heavily ironed.

RECIT.

GAMA. Must we, till then, in prison cell be thrust ?
HILD.   You must !
GAMA. This seems unnecessarily severe !
ARAC, GURON, and SCYNTHIUS. Hear, hear !

TRIO—ARAC, GURON, *and* SCYNTHIUS.

  For a month to dwell
  In a dungeon cell ;
   Growing thin and wizen
   In a solitary prison,
  Is a poor look-out
  For a soldier stout,
   Who is longing for the rattle
   Of a complicated battle—
  For the rum-tum-tum
  Of the military drum,
   And the guns that go boom ! boom !

ALL.
  The rum-tum-tum
  Of the military drum, etc.

HILD.
When Hilarion's bride
Has at length complied
    With the just conditions
    Of our requisitions,
You may go in haste
And indulge your taste
    For the fascinating rattle
    Of a complicated battle—
For the rum-tum-tum,
Of the military drum,
    And the guns that go boom ! boom !

ALL.
For the rum-tum-tum
Of the military drum, etc.

ALL.
But till that time $\left\{ \begin{array}{l} \text{we'll} \\ \text{you'll} \end{array} \right\}$ here remain,

And bail $\left\{ \begin{array}{l} \text{they} \\ \text{we} \end{array} \right\}$ will not entertain,

Should she $\left\{ \begin{array}{l} \text{his} \\ \text{our} \end{array} \right\}$ mandate disobey,

$\left. \begin{array}{l} \text{Our} \\ \text{Your} \end{array} \right\}$ lives the penalty will pay !

[GAMA, ARAC, GURON, *and* SCYNTHIUS *are
marched off.*

END OF ACT I.

ACT II.

Gardens in Castle Adamant. A river runs across the back of the stage, crossed by a rustic bridge. Castle Adamant in the distance.

Girl graduates discovered seated at the feet of LADY PSYCHE.

CHORUS.

Towards the empyrean heights
    Of every kind of lore,
We've taken several easy flights,
    And mean to take some more.
In trying to achieve success
    No envy racks our heart,
And all the knowledge we possess,
    We mutually impart.

SONG—MELISSA.

Pray, what authors should she read
Who in Classics would succeed ?

PSYCHE.

If you'd climb the Helicon,
You should read Anacreon,
Ovid's *Metamorphoses*,
Likewise Aristophanes,
And the works of Juvenal :

These are worth attention, all ;
But, if you will be advised,
You will get them Bowdlerized !

CHORUS.

Ah ! we will get them Bowdlerized !

SOLO—SACHARISSA.

Pray you, tell us, if you can,
What's the thing that's known as Man ?

PSYCHE.

Man will swear and Man will storm—
Man is not at all good form—
Man is of no kind of use—
Man's a donkey—Man's a goose—
Man is coarse and Man is plain—
Man is more or less insane—
Man's a ribald—Man's a rake,
Man is Nature's sole mistake !

CHORUS.

We'll a memorandum make—
Man is Nature's sole mistake !

And thus to empyrean height
    Of every kind of lore,
In search of wisdom's pure delight,
    Ambitiously we soar.
In trying to achieve success
    No envy racks our heart,
For all we know and all we guess,
    We mutually impart !

Enter LADY BLANCHE.   *All stand up demurely.*

BLA.   Attention, ladies, while I read to you
       The Princess Ida's list of punishments.
       The first is Sacharissa.   She's expelled !

ALL. Expelled !

BLA.   Expelled, because although she knew
      No man of any kind may pass our walls,
      She dared to bring a set of chessmen here !

SACH. (*crying*).   I meant no harm ; they're only men of
        wood !

BLA.   They're men with whom you give each other mate,
      And that's enough !   The next is Chloe.

CHLOE.   Ah !

BLA.   Chloe will lose three terms, for yesterday,
      When looking through her drawing-book, I found
      A sketch of a perambulator !

ALL (*horrified*).   Oh !

BLA.   *Double* perambulator, shameless girl !
      That's all at present.   Now, attention, pray ;
      Your Principal the Princess comes to give
      Her usual inaugural address
      To those young ladies who joined yesterday.

CHORUS.

     Mighty maiden with a mission,
         Paragon of common sense,
    Running fount of erudition,
         Miracle of eloquence,
      We are blind, and we would see ;
      We are bound, and would be free ;
      We are dumb, and we would talk ;
      We are lame, and we would walk.

Enter the PRINCESS.

     Mighty maiden with a mission—
         Paragon of common sense ;
    Running fount of erudition—
         Miracle of eloquence !

PRIN. (*Recit.*).   Minerva, oh, hear me !

ARIA.

Oh, goddess wise
  That lovest light,
  Endow with sight
Their unillumined eyes.

At this my call,
  A fervent few
  Have come to woo
The rays that from thee fall.
Let fervent words and fervent thoughts be mine,
That I may lead them to thy sacred shrine !

Women of Adamant, fair Neophytes—
Who thirst for such instruction as we give,
Attend, while I unfold a parable.
The elephant is mightier than Man,
Yet Man subdues him.   Why ?   The elephant
Is elephantine everywhere but here (*tapping her
  forehead*),
And Man, whose brain is to the elephant's
As Woman's brain to Man's—(that's rule of three),—
Conquers the foolish giant of the woods,
As Woman, in her turn, shall conquer Man.
In Mathematics, Woman leads the way :
The narrow-minded pedant still believes
That two and two make four !   Why, we can prove,
We women—household drudges as we are—
That two and two make five—or three—or seven ;
Or five-and-twenty, if the case demands !
Diplomacy ?   The wiliest diplomat
Is absolutely helpless in our hands,
He wheedles monarchs—woman wheedles him !
Logic ?   Why, tyrant Man himself admits
It's waste of time to argue with a woman !
Then we excel in social qualities :
Though Man professes that he holds our sex
In utter scorn, I venture to believe

He'd rather pass the day with one of you,
Than with five hundred of his fellow-men !
In all things we excel.   Believing this,
A hundred maidens here have sworn to place
Their feet upon his neck.   If we succeed,
We'll treat him better than he treated us :
But if we fail, why, then let hope fail too !
Let no one care a penny how she looks—
Let red be worn with yellow—blue with green—
Crimson with scarlet—violet with blue !
Let all your things misfit, and you yourselves
At inconvenient moments come undone !
Let hair-pins lose their virtue : let the hook
Disdain the fascination of the eye—
The bashful button modestly evade
The soft embraces of the button-hole !
Let old associations all dissolve,
Let Swan secede from Edgar—Gask from Gask,
Sewell from Cross—Lewis from Allenby !
In other words—let Chaos come again !
(*Coming down.*)   Who lectures in the Hall of Arts to-day ?

BLA. I, madam, on Abstract Philosophy.
There I propose considering, at length,
Three points—The Is, the Might Be, and the Must.
Whether the Is, from being actual fact,
Is more important than the vague Might Be,
Or the Might Be, from taking wider scope,
Is for that reason greater than the Is :
And lastly, how the Is and Might Be stand
Compared with the inevitable Must !

PRIN. The subject's deep—how do you treat it, pray ?

BLA. Madam, I take three possibilities,
And strike a balance, then, between the three :
As thus : The Princess Ida Is our head,
The Lady Psyche Might Be,—Lady Blanche,
Neglected Blanche, inevitably Must.
Given these three hypotheses—to find
The actual betting against each of them !

PRIN. Your theme's ambitious : pray you, bear in mind
       Who highest soar fall farthest.   Fare you well,
       You and your pupils !   Maidens, follow me.

> [*Exeunt* PRINCESS *and Maidens singing re-*
> *frain of chorus, " And thus to empyrean*
> *heights* ", *etc.   Manet* LADY BLANCHE.

BLA.   I should command here—I was born to rule,
       But do I rule ?   I don't.   Why ?   I don't know.
       I shall some day.   Not yet.   I bide my time.
       I once was Some One—and the Was Will Be.
       The Present as we speak becomes the Past,
       The Past repeats itself, and so is Future !
       This sounds involved.   It's not.   It's right enough.

SONG—LADY BLANCHE.

Come, mighty Must !
  Inevitable Shall !
In thee I trust.
  Time weaves my coronal !
Go, mocking Is !
  Go, disappointing Was !
That I am this
  Ye are the cursed cause !
Yet humble second shall be first,
    I ween ;
And dead and buried be the curst
    Has Been !

Oh, weak Might Be !
  Oh, May, Might, Could, Would, Should !
How powerless ye
  For evil or for good !
In every sense
  Your moods I cheerless call,
Whate'er your tense
  Ye are Imperfect, all !

Ye have deceived the trust I've shown
> In ye !
Away !   The Mighty Must alone
> Shall be !

[*Exit* LADY BLANCHE.

Enter HILARION, CYRIL, *and* FLORIAN, *climbing over wall,
and creeping cautiously among the trees and rocks at
the back of the stage.*

TRIO—HILARION, CYRIL, FLORIAN.

> Gently, gently,
> Evidently
>> We are safe so far,
> After scaling
> Fence and paling,
>> Here, at last, we are !
> In this college
> Useful knowledge
>> Everywhere one finds,
> And already,
> Growing steady,
>> We've enlarged our minds.

CYR.   We've learnt that prickly cactus
Has the power to attract us
> When we fall.

ALL.   When we fall !

HIL.   That nothing man unsettles
Like a bed of stinging nettles,
> Short or tall.

ALL.   Short or tall !

FLOR.   That bull-dogs feed on throttles—
That we don't like broken bottles
> On a wall.

ALL.   On a wall !

HIL.   That spring-guns breathe defiance !
            And that burglary's a science

                                   After all !

ALL.   After all !

RECIT.—FLORIAN.

A Woman's college ! maddest folly going !
What can girls learn within its walls worth knowing ?
I'll lay a crown (the Princess shall decide it)
I'll teach them twice as much in half-an-hour outside it.

HILARION.

Hush, scoffer ; ere you sound your puny thunder,
List to their aims, and bow your head in wonder !

            They intend to send a wire
                To the moon—to the moon ;
            And they'll set the Thames on fire
                Very soon—very soon ;
            Then they learn to make silk purses
                With their rigs—with their rigs,
            From the ears of Lady Circe's
                Piggy-wigs—piggy-wigs.
            And weasels at their slumbers
                They trepan—they trepan ;
            To get sunbeams from cu*cum*bers,
                They've a plan—they've a plan.
            They've a firmly rooted notion
            They can cross the Polar Ocean,
            And they'll find Perpetual Motion,
                If they can—if they can.

ALL.   These are the phenomena
                That every pretty domina
                    Is hoping we shall see
                    At her Universitee !

CYR.
As for fashion, they forswear it,
　　So they say—so they say ;
And the circle—they will square it
　　Some fine day—some fine day ;
Then the little pigs they're teaching
　　For to fly—for to fly ;
And the niggers they'll be bleaching,
　　By and by—by and by !
Each newly-joined aspirant
　　To the clan—to the clan—
Must repudiate the tyrant
　　Known as Man—known as Man.
They mock at him and flout him,
For they do not care about him,
And they're " going to do without him "
　　If they can—if they can !

ALL.
　　These are the phenomena, etc.

　　　In this college
　　　Useful knowledge
　　　Ev'rywhere one finds,
　　　And already growing steady
　　　We've enlarg'd our minds.

HIL.
So that's the Princess Ida's castle !　Well,
They must be lovely girls, indeed, if it requires
Such walls as those to keep intruders off !

CYR.
To keep men off is only half their charge,
And that the easier half.　I much suspect
The object of these walls is not so much
To keep men off as keep the maidens in !

FLOR.
But what are these ?　(*Examining some Collegiate
　　robes.*)

HIL. (*looking at them*).　Why, Academic robes,
Worn by the lady undergraduates
When they matriculate.　Let's try them on.　(*They
　　do so.*)
Why, see,—we're covered to the very toes.

Three lovely lady undergraduates
Who, weary of the world and all its wooing—
FLOR.   And penitent for deeds there's no undoing—
CYR.   Looked at askance by well-conducted maids—
ALL.   Seek sanctuary in these classic shades !

TRIO—HILARION, CYRIL, FLORIAN.
HIL.   I am a maiden, cold and stately,
    Heartless I, with a face divine.
    What do I want with a heart, innately ?
    Every heart I meet is mine !

ALL.   Haughty, humble, coy, or free,
      Little care I what maid may be.
    So that a maid is fair to see,
      Every maid is the maid for me !
                      (*Dance.*)

CYR.   I am a maiden frank and simple,
    Brimming with joyous roguery ;
    Merriment lurks in every dimple,
    Nobody breaks more hearts than I !

ALL.   Haughty, humble, coy, or free,
      Little care I what maid may be.
    So that a maid is fair to see,
      Every maid is the maid for me !
                      (*Dance.*)

FLOR.   I am a maiden coyly blushing,
    Timid am I as a startled hind ;
    Every suitor sets me flushing :
    I am the maid that wins mankind !

ALL.   Haughty, humble, coy, or free,
      Little care I what maid may be.
    So that a maid is fair to see,
      Every maid is the maid for me !

Enter the PRINCESS *reading.   She does not see them.*

FLOR.   But who comes here ?   The Princess, as I live !
    What shall we do ?

HIL. (*aside*).   Why, we must brave it out !
(*Aloud.*)   Madam, accept our humblest reverence.

(*They bow, then, suddenly recollecting themselves, curtsey.*)

PRIN. (*surprised*).   We greet you, ladies.   What would
        you with us ?
HIL. (*aside*).   What shall I say ?   (*Aloud.*)   We are three
        students, ma'am,
            Three well-born maids of liberal estate,
            Who wish to join this University.

(HILARION *and* FLORIAN *curtsey again.* CYRIL *bows
    extravagantly, then, being recalled to himself by*
    FLORIAN, *curtseys.*)

PRIN.   If, as you say, you wish to join our ranks,
            And will subscribe to all our rules, 'tis well.
FLOR.   To all your rules we cheerfully subscribe.
PRIN.   You say you're noblewomen.   Well, you'll find
            No sham degrees for noblewomen here.
            You'll find no sizars here, or servitors,
            Or other cruel distinctions, meant to draw
            A line 'twixt rich and poor : you'll find no tufts
            To mark nobility, except such tufts
            As indicate nobility of brain.
            As for your fellow-students, mark me well :
            There are a hundred maids within these walls,
            All good, all learned, and all beautiful :
            They are prepared to love you : will you swear
            To give the fullness of your love to them ?
HIL.   Upon our words and honours, ma'am, we will !
PRIN.   But we go further : will you undertake
            That you will never marry any man ?
FLOR.   Indeed we never will !
PRIN.   Consider well,
            You must prefer our maids to all mankind !
HIL.   To all mankind we much prefer your maids !
CYR.   We should be dolts indeed, if we did not,
            Seeing how fair——

HIL. (*aside to* CYRIL).   Take care—that's rather strong !

PRIN.   But have you left no lovers at your home
    Who may pursue you here ?

HIL.   No, madam, none.
    We're homely ladies, as no doubt you see,
    And we have never fished for lover's love.
    We smile at girls who deck themselves with gems,
    False hair, and meretricious ornament,
    To chain the fleeting fancy of a man,
    But do not imitate them.   What we have
    Of hair, is all our own.   Our colour, too,
    Unladylike, but not unwomanly,
    Is Nature's handiwork, and man has learnt
    To reckon Nature an impertinence.

PRIN.   Well, beauty counts for naught within these walls ;
    If all you say is true, you'll pass with us
    A happy, happy time !

CYR.   If, as you say,
    A hundred lovely maidens wait within,
    To welcome us with smiles and open arms,
    I think there's very little doubt we shall !

QUARTETTE—PRINCESS, HILARION, CYRIL, FLORIAN

PRIN.   The world is but a broken toy,
          Its pleasure hollow—false its joy,
            Unreal its loveliest hue,
                Alas !
          Its pains alone are true,
                Alas !
          Its pains alone are true.

HIL.   The world is everything you say,
          The world we think has had its day.
          Its merriment is slow,
                Alas !
          We've tried it, and we know,
                Alas !
          We've tried it and we know.

TUTTI.

PRINCESS.	HILARION, CYRIL, FLORIAN.
The world is but a broken toy,	The world is but a broken toy,
Its pleasure hollow—false its joy,	We freely give it up with joy,
Unreal its loveliest hue,	Unreal its loveliest hue,
Alas !	Alas !
Its pains alone are true,	Its pains alone are true,
Alas !	Alas !
Its pains alone are true !	Its pains alone are true !

[*Exit* PRINCESS. *The three gentlemen watch
her off.* LADY PSYCHE *enters, and regards
them with amazement.*

HIL.   I'faith, the plunge is taken, gentlemen !
For, willy-nilly, we are maidens now,
And maids against our will we must remain !
                              (*All laugh heartily.*)

PSY. (*aside*).   These ladies are unseemly in their mirth.

(*The gentlemen see her, and, in confusion, resume
their modest demeanour.*)

FLOR. (*aside*).   Here's a catastrophe, Hilarion !
This is my sister !   She'll remember me,
Though years have passed since she and I have
met !

HIL. (*aside to* FLORIAN).   Then make a virtue of necessity,
And trust our secret to her gentle care.

FLOR. (*to* PSYCHE, *who has watched* CYRIL *in amazement*).
              Psyche !
Why, don't you know me ?   Florian !

PSY. (*amazed*).   Why, Florian !

FLOR.   My sister ! (*embraces her*).

PSY.   Oh, my dear !
What are you doing here—and who are these ?

HIL.   I am that Prince Hilarion to whom
Your Princess is betrothed.   I come to claim
Her plighted love.   Your brother Florian
And Cyril come to see me safely through.

PSY.   The Prince Hilarion ?   Cyril too ?   How strange !
My earliest playfellows !

HIL.   Why, let me look !
Are you that learned little Psyche who
At school alarmed her mates because she called
A buttercup " ranunculus bulbosus " ?

CYR.   Are you indeed that Lady Psyche, who
At children's parties drove the conjuror wild,
Explaining all his tricks before he did them ?

HIL.   Are you that learned little Psyche, who
At dinner parties, brought in to dessert,
Would tackle visitors with " You don't know
Who first determined longitude—I do—
Hipparchus 'twas—B.C. one sixty-three ! "
Are you indeed that small phenomenon ?

PSY.   That small phenomenon indeed am I !
But, gentlemen, 'tis death to enter here :
We have all promised to renounce mankind !

FLOR.   Renounce mankind ? On what ground do you base
This senseless resolution ?

PSY.   Senseless ? No.
We are all taught, and, being taught, believe
That Man, sprung from an Ape, is Ape at heart.

CYR.   That's rather strong.

PSY.   The truth is always strong !

SONG—LADY PSYCHE.

A Lady fair, of lineage high,
Was loved by an Ape, in the days gone by.
The Maid was radiant as the sun,
The Ape was a most unsightly one—
       So it would not do—
       His scheme fell through,
For the Maid, when his love took formal shape,
       Expressed such terror
       At his monstrous error,
That he stammered an apology and made his 'scape,
The picture of a disconcerted Ape.

With a view to rise in the social scale,
He shaved his bristles, and he docked his tail,
He grew moustachios, and he took his tub,
And he paid a guinea to a toilet club—
　　　But it would not do,
　　　The scheme fell through—
For the Maid was Beauty's fairest Queen,
　　　With golden tresses,
　　　Like a real princess's,
While the Ape, despite his razor keen,
Was the apiest Ape that ever was seen !

He bought white ties, and he bought dress suits,
He crammed his feet into bright tight boots—
And to start in life on a brand-new plan,
He christened himself Darwinian Man !
　　　But it would not do,
　　　The scheme fell through—
For the Maiden fair, whom the monkey craved,
　　　Was a radiant Being,
　　　With a brain far-seeing—
While Darwinian Man, though well-behaved,
At best is only a monkey shaved !

ALL.　　　　While Darwinian Man, etc.

During this MELISSA *has entered unobserved ; she
　　　looks on in amazement.*

MEL. (*coming down*).　Oh, Lady Psyche !
PSY. (*terrified*).　　　　　　What ! you heard us then ?
　　　Oh, all is lost !
MEL.　　　　　　　　Not so ! I'll breathe no word !
　　　　　　(*Advancing in astonishment to* FLORIAN.)
　　　How marvellously strange ! and are you then
　　　Indeed young men ?
FLOR.　　　　　　　　Well, yes, just now we are—
　　　But hope by dint of study to become,
　　　In course of time, young women.
MEL. (*eagerly*).　　　　　　　No, no, no—
　　　Oh, don't do that ! Is this indeed a man ?

I've often heard of them, but, till to-day,
Never set eyes on one.   They told me men
Were hideous, idiotic, and deformed !
They're quite as beautiful as women are !
As beautiful, they're infinitely more so !
Their cheeks have not that pulpy softness which
One gets so weary of in womankind :
Their features are more marked—and—oh, their
    chins !
How curious !   (*Feeling his chin.*)

FLOR.   I fear it's rather rough.
MEL. (*eagerly*).   Oh, don't apologize—I like it so !

QUINTETTE—PSYCHE, MELISSA, HILARION,
        CYRIL, FLORIAN.

PSY.   The woman of the wisest wit
                May sometimes be mistaken, O !
            In Ida's views, I must admit,
                My faith is somewhat shaken, O !

CYR.   On every other point than this
                Her learning is untainted, O !
            But Man's a theme with which she is
                Entirely unacquainted, O !
                —acquainted, O !
                —acquainted, O !
                Entirely unacquainted, O !

ALL.   Then jump for joy and gaily bound,
            The truth is found—the truth is found !
            Set bells a-ringing through the air—
            Ring here and there and everywhere—
            And echo forth the joyous sound,
            The truth is found—the truth is found !
                                        (*Dance.*)

MEL.   My natural instinct teaches me
                (And instinct is important, O !)
            You're everything you ought to be,
                And nothing that you oughtn't, O !

HIL.   That fact was seen at once by you
     In casual conversation, O !
    Which is most creditable to
     Your powers of observation, O !
        —servation, O !
        —servation, O !
     Your powers of observation, O !

ALL.   Then jump for joy, etc.

    [*Exeunt* PSYCHE, HILARION, CYRIL, *and*
     FLORIAN. MELISSA *going*.

     Enter LADY BLANCHE.

BLA. Melissa !
MEL. (*returning*). Mother !
BLA.   Here—a word with you.
   Those are the three new students ?
MEL. (*confused*).   Yes, they are.
   They're charming girls.
BLA.   Particularly so.
   So graceful, and so very womanly !
   So skilled in all a girl's accomplishments !
MEL (*confused*). Yes—very skilled.
BLA.   They sing so nicely too !
MEL. They *do* sing nicely !
BLA.   Humph ! It's very odd.
   Two are tenors, one is a baritone !
MEL. (*much agitated*). They've all got colds !
BLA.   Colds ! Bah ! D'ye think I'm blind ?
   These " girls " are men disguised !
MEL.   Oh no—indeed !
   You wrong these gentlemen—I mean—why, see,
   Here is an *étui* dropped by one of them (*picking
    up an étui*).
   Containing scissors, needles, and——
BLA. (*opening it*).   Cigars !
   Why, these *are* men ! And you knew this, you
    minx !

MEL.   Oh, spare them—they are gentlemen indeed.
    The Prince Hilarion (married years ago
    To Princess Ida) with two trusted friends !
    Consider, mother, he's her husband now,
    And has been, twenty years !   Consider, too,
    You're only second here—you should be first.
    Assist the Prince's plan, and when he gains
    The Princess Ida, why, you *will* be first.
    You will design the fashions—think of that—
    And always serve out all the punishments !
    The scheme is harmless, mother—wink at it !

BLA. (*aside*).   The prospect's tempting !   Well, well, well,
        I'll try—
    Though I've not winked at anything for years !
    'Tis but one step towards my destiny—
    The mighty Must ! the inevitable Shall !

DUET—MELISSA *and* LADY BLANCHE.

MEL.   Now wouldn't you like to rule the roast,
        And guide this University ?

BLA.   I must agree
        'Twould pleasant be.
        (Sing hey, a Proper Pride !)

MEL.   And wouldn't you like to clear the coast
        Of malice and perversity ?

BLA.   Without a doubt
        I'll bundle 'em out,
        Sing hey, when I preside !

BOTH. Sing, hoity, toity !   Sorry for some !

    Sing, marry come up and $\begin{Bmatrix} my \\ her \end{Bmatrix}$ day will come !

        Sing, Proper Pride
        Is the horse to ride,
    And Happy-go-lucky, my Lady, O !

BLA.   For years I've writhed beneath her sneers,
   Although a born Plantagenet !

MEL.   You're much too meek,
      Or you would speak.
      (Sing hey, I'll say no more !)

BLA.   Her elder I, by several years,
   Although you'd ne'er imagine it.

MEL.   Sing, so I've heard
     But never a word
      Have I e'er believed before !

BOTH. Sing, hoity toity !   Sorry for some !

 Sing, marry come up and $\left\{ {my \atop her} \right\}$ day will come !

    Sing, she shall learn
    That a worm will turn.
   Sing Happy-go-lucky, my Lady, O !

       [*Exit* LADY BLANCHE.

MEL.   Saved for a time, at least !

    Enter FLORIAN, *on tiptoe.*

FLOR. (*whispering*).   Melissa—come !
MEL.   Oh, sir ! you must away from this at once—
   My mother guessed your sex !   It was my fault—
   I blushed and stammered so that she exclaimed,
   " Can these be men ? "   Then, seeing this, " Why
    these——"
   " *Are men* ", she would have added, but "*are men*"
   Stuck in her throat !   She keeps your secret, sir,
   For reasons of her own—but fly from this
   And take me with you—that is—no—not that !
FLOR. I'll go, but not without you !   (*Bell.*)   Why, what's
   that ?
MEL.   The luncheon bell.
FLOR.   I'll wait for luncheon then !

           L

Enter HILARION *with* PRINCESS, CYRIL *with* PSYCHE, LADY BLANCHE *and* LADIES. *Also " Daughters of the Plough " bearing luncheon.*

CHORUS.

Merrily ring the luncheon bell !
Here in meadow of asphodel,
Feast we body and mind as well,
So merrily ring the luncheon bell !

SOLO—BLANCHE.

Hunger, I beg to state,
Is highly indelicate,
This is a fact profoundly true,
So learn your appetites to subdue.

ALL   Yes, yes,
We'll learn our appetites to subdue !

SOLO—CYRIL (*eating*).

Madam, your words so wise,
Nobody should despise,
Cursed with an appetite keen I am
And I'll subdue it—
And I'll subdue it—
And I'll subdue it with cold roast lamb !

ALL.   Yes—yes—
We'll subdue it with cold roast lamb !

CHORUS.   Merrily ring, etc.

PRIN.   You say you know the court of Hildebrand ?
        There is a Prince there—I forget his name—
HIL.   Hilarion ?
PRIN.   Exactly—is he well ?
HIL.   If it be well to droop and pine and mope,
        To sigh " Oh, Ida ! Ida ! " all day long,

ACT II.

(The Next Morning.)

SCENE.—*Entrance Hall of the Grand Ducal Palace.*

Enter a procession of the members of the theatrical company (now dressed in the costumes of Troilus *and* Cressida*), carrying garlands, playing on pipes, cithæ, and cymbals, and heralding the return of* LUDWIG *and* JULIA *from the marriage ceremony, which has just taken place.*

CHORUS.

As before you we defile,
  Eloia ! Eloia !
Pray you, gentles, do not smile
If we shout, in classic style,
  Eloia !
Ludwig and his Julia true
Wedded are each other to—
So we sing, till all is blue,
  Eloia ! Eloia !
    Opoponax ! Eloia !

Wreaths of bay and ivy twine,
  Eloia ! Eloia !
Fill the bowl with Lesbian wine,
And to revelry incline—
  Eloia !

672

For as gaily we pass on
Probably we shall, anon,
Sing a Diergeticon—
        Eloia ! Eloia !
       Opoponax ! Eloia !

RECIT.—LUDWIG.

Your loyalty our Ducal heartstrings touches :
Allow me to present your new Grand Duchess.
Should she offend, you'll graciously excuse her—
And kindly recollect *I* didn't choose her !

SONG—LUDWIG.

At the outset I may mention it's my sovereign intention
   To revive the classic memories of Athens at its best,
For the company possesses all the necessary dresses
   And a course of quiet cramming will supply us with
      the rest.
We've a choir hyporchematic (that is, ballet-operatic)
   Who respond to the *choreutæ* of that cultivated age,
And our clever chorus-master, all but captious criticaster
   Would accept as the *choregus* of the early Attic stage.
This return to classic ages is considered in their wages,
   Which are always calculated by the day or by the week—
And I'll pay 'em (if they'll back me) all in *oboloi* and
    drachmæ,
   Which they'll get (if they prefer it) at the Kalends that
      are Greek !

(*Confidentially to audience.*)
        At this juncture I may mention
          That this erudition sham
      Is but classical pretension,
          The result of steady " cram." :
      Periphrastic methods spurning,
      To this audience discerning
      I admit this show of learning
          Is the fruit of steady " cram." !

CHORUS.   Periphrastic methods, etc.

z

In the period Socratic every dining-room was Attic
 (Which suggests an architecture of a topsy-turvy kind),
There they'd satisfy their thirst on a *recherché* cold ἄριστον,
  Which is what they called their lunch—and so may you,
   if you're inclined.
As they gradually got on, they'd τρέπεσθαι πρὸς τὸν πότον
 (Which is Attic for a steady and a conscientious drink).
But they mixed their wine with water—which I'm sure
  they didn't oughter—
  And we modern Saxons know a trick worth two of that,
   I think !
Then came rather risky dances (under certain circumstances)
  Which would shock that worthy gentleman, the Licenser
   of Plays,
Corybantian mani*ac* kick—Dionysiac or Bacchic—
  And the Dithyrambic revels of those undecorous days.
(*Confidentially to audience.*)
      And perhaps I'd better mention,
       Lest alarming you I am,
      That it isn't our intention
       To perform a Dithyramb—
      It displays a lot of stocking,
      Which is always very shocking,
      And of course I'm only mocking
       At the prevalence of " cram " !
CHORUS.   It displays a lot, etc.
Yes, on reconsideration, there are customs of that nation
 Which are not in strict accordance with the habits of
  our day,
And when I come to codify, their rules I mean to modify,
 Or Mrs. Grundy, p'r'aps, may have a word or two to say.
For they hadn't macintoshes or umbrellas or goloshes—
  And a shower with their dresses must have played the
   very deuce,
And it must have been unpleasing when they caught a
  fit of sneezing,
  For, it seems, of pocket-handkerchiefs they didn't know
   the use.

They wore little underclothing—scarcely anything—or no-
    thing—
  And their dress of Coan silk was quite transparent in
    design—
Well, in fact, in summer weather, something like the
    " altogether ".
  And it's *there*, I rather fancy, I shall have to draw the
    line !

(*Confidentially to audience.*)

        And again I wish to mention
          That this erudition sham
        Is but classical pretension,
          The result of steady " cram."
        Yet my classic lore aggressive
        (If you'll pardon the possessive)
        Is exceedingly impressive
          When you're passing an exam.

CHORUS.   Yet his classic lore, etc.

    [*Exeunt Chorus. Manent* LUDWIG, JULIA,
      and LISA.

LUD. (*recit.*).
  Yes, Ludwig and his Julia are mated !
For when an obscure comedian, whom the law backs,
  To sovereign rank is promptly elevated,
He takes it with its incidental drawbacks !
  So Julia and I are duly mated !

(LISA, *through this, has expressed intense distress at
    having to surrender* LUDWIG.)

SONG—LISA.

  Take care of him—he's much too good to live,
    With him you must be very gentle :
  Poor fellow, he's so highly sensitive,
    And O, so sentimental !

z 2

Be sure you never let him sit up late
  In chilly open air conversing—
Poor darling, he's extremely delicate,
  And wants a deal of nursing !

LUD.   I want a deal of nursing !

LISA.   And O, remember this—
       When he is cross with pain,
     A flower and a kiss—
     A simple flower—a tender kiss
       Will bring him round again !

His moods you must assiduously watch :
     When he succumbs to sorrow tragic,
Some hardbake or a bit of butter-scotch
     Will work on him like magic.
To contradict a character so rich
     In trusting love were simple blindness—
He's one of those exalted natures which
     Will only yield to kindness !

LUD.   I only yield to kindness !

LISA.   And O, the bygone bliss !
      And O, the present pain !
     That flower and that kiss—
     That simple flower—that tender kiss
      I ne'er shall give again !

             [*Exit, weeping.*

JULIA. And now that everybody has gone, and we're happily and comfortably married, I want to have a few words with my new-born husband.

LUD. (*aside*). Yes, I expect you'll often have a few words with your new-born husband ! (*Aloud.*) Well, what is it ?

JULIA. Why, I've been thinking that as you and I have to play our parts for life, it is most essential that we should come to a definite understanding as to how they

shall be rendered. Now, I've been considering how I can make the most of the Grand Duchess.

LUD. Have you ? Well, if you'll take my advice, you'll make a very fine part of it.

JULIA. Why, that's quite *my* idea.

LUD. I shouldn't make it one of your hoity-toity vixenish viragoes.

JULIA. You think not ?

LUD. Oh, I'm quite clear about that. I should make her a tender, gentle, submissive, affectionate (but not too affectionate) child-wife—timidly anxious to coil herself into her husband's heart, but kept in check by an awestruck reverence for his exalted intellectual qualities and his majestic personal appearance.

JULIA. Oh, that is your idea of a good part ?

LUD. Yes—a wife who regards her husband's slightest wish as an inflexible law, and who ventures but rarely into his august presence, unless (which would happen seldom) he should summon her to appear before him. A crushed, despairing violet, whose blighted existence would culminate (all too soon) in a lonely and pathetic death-scene ! A fine part, my dear.

JULIA. Yes. There's a good deal to be said for your view of it. Now there are some actresses whom it would fit like a glove.

LUD. (*aside*). I wish I'd married one of 'em !

JULIA. But, you see, I *must* consider my temperament. For instance, my temperament would demand some strong scenes of justifiable jealousy.

LUD. Oh, there's no difficulty about that. You shall have *them*.

JULIA. With a lovely but detested rival——

LUD. Oh, *I'll* provide the rival.

JULIA. Whom I should stab—stab—stab !

LUD. Oh, I wouldn't stab her. It's been done to death. I should treat her with a silent and contemptuous disdain, and delicately withdraw from a position which, to one of your sensitive nature, would be absolutely

untenable. Dear me, I can see you delicately withdrawing, up centre and off!

JULIA. *Can* you?

LUD. Yes. It's a fine situation—and in your hands, full of quiet pathos!

DUET—LUDWIG *and* JULIA.

LUD.
Now Julia, come,
Consider it from
    This dainty point of view—
A timid tender
Feminine gender,
    Prompt to coyly coo—
Yet silence seeking,
Seldom speaking
    Till she's spoken to—
A comfy, cosy,
Rosy-posy
    Innocent *ingenoo*!
    The part you're suited to—
    (To give the deuce her due)
A sweet (O, jiminy!)
Miminy-piminy,
    Innocent inge*noo*!

ENSEMBLE.

LUD.	JULIA.
The part you're suited to—	I'm much obliged to you,
(To give the deuce her due)	I don't think that would do—
A sweet (O, jiminy!)	To play (O, jiminy!)
Miminy-piminy,	Miminy-piminy,
Innocent inge*noo*!	Innocent inge*noo*!

JULIA. You forget my special magic
    (In a high dramatic sense)
Lies in situations tragic—
    Undeniably intense.

As I've justified promotion
  In the histrionic art,
I'll submit to you my notion
  Of a first-rate part.

LUD. Well, let us see your notion
    Of a first-rate part.

JULIA (*dramatically*).
  I have a rival !   Frenzy-thrilled,
    I find you both together !
  My heart stands still—with horror chilled—
    Hard as the millstone nether !
  Then softly, slyly, snaily, snaky—
  Crawly, creepy, quaily, quaky—
    I track her on her homeward way,
    As panther tracks her fated prey !

(*Furiously.*)   I fly at her soft white throat—
    The lily-white laughing leman !
  On her agonized gaze I gloat
    With the glee of a dancing demon !
  My rival she—I have no doubt of her—
  So I hold on—till the breath is out of her !
    —till the breath is out of her !

And then—Remorse !   Remorse !
O cold unpleasant corse,
    Avaunt !   Avaunt !
  That lifeless form
    I gaze upon—
  That face, still warm
    But weirdly wan—
  Those eyes of glass
    I contemplate—
  And then, alas,
    Too late—too late !
  I find she is—your Aunt !
(*Shuddering.*) Remorse !   Remorse !

          z 3

Then, mad—mad—mad !
With fancies wild—chimerical—
Now sorrowful—silent—sad—
Now hullaballoo hysterical !
Ha ! ha ! ha ! ha !
But whether I'm sad or whether I'm glad,
Mad ! mad ! mad ! mad !

This calls for the resources of a high-class art,
And satisfies my notion of a first-rate part !

[*Exit* JULIA.

Enter all the Chorus, hurriedly, and in great excitement.

CHORUS.

Your Highness, there's a party at the door—
Your Highness, at the door there is a party—
She says that we expect her,
But we do not recollect her,
For we never saw her countenance before !

With rage and indignation she is rife,
Because our welcome wasn't very hearty—
She's as sulky as a super,
And she's swearing like a trooper,
O, you never heard such language in your life !

Enter BARONESS VON KRAKENFELDT, *in a fury.*

BAR.   With fury indescribable I burn !
With rage I'm nearly ready to explode !
There'll be grief and tribulation when I learn
To whom this slight unbearable is owed !
For whatever may be due I'll pay it double—
There'll be terror indescribable and trouble !
With a hurly-burly and a hubble-bubble
I'll pay you for this pretty episode !

ALL.   Oh, whatever may be due she'll pay it double!—
            It's very good of her to take the trouble—
            But we don't know what she means by "hubble-
               bubble "—
        No doubt it's an expression *à la mode.*

BAR. (*to* LUDWIG).
        Do you know who I am ?

LUD. (*examining her*).   I don't ;
        Your countenance I can't fix, my dear.

BAR.   This proves I'm not a sham.
          (*Showing pocket-handkerchief.*)

LUD. (*examining it*).   It won't ;
        It only says " Krakenfeldt, Six," my dear.

BAR.   Express your grief profound !

LUD.   I shan't !
        This tone I never allow, my love.

BAR.   Rudolph at once produce !

LUD.   I can't ;
        He isn't at home just now, my love.

BAR. (*astonished*).   He isn't at home just now !

ALL.   He isn't at home just now,
(*Dancing derisively.*)   He has an appointment particular,
               very—
        You'll find him, I think, in the town cemetery ;
        And that's how we come to be making so merry,
        For he isn't at home just now !

BAR.   But bless my heart and soul alive, it's impudence
          personified !
        I've come here to be matrimonially matrimonified !

LUD.   For any disappointment I am sorry unaffectedly,
        But yesterday that nobleman expired quite un-
          expectedly—

ALL (*sobbing*).   Tol the riddle lol !
Tol the riddle lol !
Tol the riddle, lol the riddle, lol lol lay !
(*Then laughing wildly*.)   Tol the riddle, lol the riddle,
lol lol lay !

BAR.   But this is most unexpected.   He was well enough at a quarter to twelve yesterday.

LUD.   Yes.   He died at half-past eleven.

BAR.   Bless me, how very sudden !

LUD.   It *was* sudden.

BAR.   But what in the world am I to do ?   I was to have been married to him to-day !

ALL (*singing and dancing*).
For any disappointment we are sorry unaffectedly,
But yesterday that nobleman expired quite un-
expectedly—
Tol the riddle lol !

BAR.   Is this Court Mourning or a Fancy Ball ?

LUD.   Well, it's a delicate combination of both effects. It is intended to express inconsolable grief for the decease of the late Duke and ebullient joy at the accession of his successor.   *I* am his successor.   Permit me to present you to my Grand Duchess.   (*Indicating* JULIA.)

BAR.   Your Grand Duchess ?   Oh, your Highness ! (*Curtseying profoundly*.)

JULIA (*sneering at her*).   Old frump !

BAR.   Humph !   A recent creation, probably ?

LUD.   We were married only half an hour ago.

BAR.   Exactly.   I thought she seemed new to the position.

JULIA.   Ma'am, I don't know who you are, but I flatter myself I can do justice to *any* part on the very shortest notice.

BAR.   My dear, under the circumstances you are doing admirably—and you'll improve with practice.   It's so difficult to be a lady when one isn't born to it.

JULIA (*in a rage, to* LUDWIG). Am I to stand this? Am I not to be allowed to pull her to pieces?

LUD. (*aside to* JULIA). No, no—it isn't Greek. Be a violet, I beg.

BAR. And now tell me all about this distressing circumstance. How did the Grand Duke die?

LUD. He perished nobly—in a Statutory Duel.

BAR. In a Statutory Duel? But that's only a civil death!—and the Act expires to-night, and then he will come to life again!

LUD. Well, no. Anxious to inaugurate my reign by conferring some inestimable boon on my people, I signalized this occasion by reviving the law for another hundred years.

BAR. For another hundred years? Then set the merry joybells ringing! Let festive epithalamia resound through these ancient halls! Cut the satisfying sandwich —broach the exhilarating Marsala—and let us rejoice to-day, if we never rejoice again!

LUD. But I don't think I quite understand. We have already rejoiced a good deal.

BAR. Happy man, you little reck of the extent of the good things you are in for. When you killed Rudolph you adopted all his overwhelming responsibilities. Know then that I, Caroline von Krakenfeldt, am the most overwhelming of them all!

LUD. But stop, stop—I've just been married to somebody else!

JULIA. Yes, ma'am, to somebody else, ma'am! Do you understand, ma'am? To somebody else!

BAR. Do keep this young woman quiet; she fidgets me!

JULIA. Fidgets you!

LUD. (*aside to* JULIA). Be a violet—a crushed, despairing violet.

JULIA. Do you suppose I intend to give up a magnificent part without a struggle?

LUD. My good girl, she has the law on her side.

Let us both bear this calamity with resignation. If you must struggle, go away and struggle in the seclusion of your chamber.

SONG—Baroness *and* Chorus.

Now away to the wedding we go,
  So summon the charioteers—
No kind of reluctance they show
  To embark on their married careers.
Though Julia's emotion may flow
  For the rest of her maidenly years,
All.   To the wedding we eagerly go,
  So summon the charioteers !

Now away, etc.

(*All dance off to wedding except* Julia.)

RECIT.—Julia.

So ends my dream—so fades my vision fair !
Of hope no gleam—distraction and despair !
My cherished dream, the Ducal throne to share,
That aim supreme has vanished into air !

SONG—Julia.

Broken every promise plighted—
  All is darksome—all is dreary.
Every new-born hope is blighted !
  Sad and sorry—weak and weary !
Death the Friend or Death the Foe,
Shall I call upon thee ?   No !
I will go on living, though
  Sad and sorry—weak and weary !

No, no !   Let the bygone go by !
  No good ever came of repining :
If to-day there are clouds o'er the sky,
  To-morrow the sun may be shining !

> To-morrow, be kind,
> To-morrow, to me !
> With loyalty blind
> I curtsey to thee !
> To-day is a day of illusion and sorrow,
> So *viva* To-morrow, To-morrow, To-morrow !
> God save you, To-morrow !
> Your servant, To-morrow !
> God save you, To-morrow, To-morrow, To-morrow !

[*Exit* JULIA.

Enter ERNEST.

ERN. It's of no use—I can't wait any longer. At any risk I must gratify my urgent desire to know what is going on. (*Looking off.*) Why, what's that ? Surely I see a wedding procession winding down the hill, dressed in my *Troilus and Cressida* costumes ! That's Ludwig's doing ! I see how it is—he found the time hang heavy on his hands, and is amusing himself by getting married to Lisa. No—it can't be to Lisa, for here she is !

Enter LISA.

LISA (*not seeing him*). I really cannot stand seeing my Ludwig married twice in one day to somebody else !

ERN. Lisa !

(LISA *sees him, and stands as if transfixed with horror.*)

ERN. Come here—don't be a little fool—I want you.

(LISA *suddenly turns and bolts off.*)

ERN. Why, what's the matter with the little donkey ? One would think she saw a ghost ! But if he's not marrying Lisa, whom *is* he marrying ? (*Suddenly.*) Julia ! (*Much overcome.*) I see it all ! The scoundrel ! He had to adopt all my responsibilities, and he's shabbily taken advantage of the situation to marry the girl I'm engaged to ! But no, it can't be Julia, for here *she* is !

Enter JULIA.

JULIA (*not seeing him*). I've made up my mind. I won't stand it ! I'll send in my notice at once !

Ern. Julia! Oh, what a relief!

(Julia *gazes at him as if transfixed.*)

Ern. Then you've not married Ludwig? You are still true to me?

(Julia *turns and bolts in grotesque horror.*
Ernest *follows and stops her.*)

Ern. Don't run away! Listen to me. Are you all crazy?

Julia (*in affected terror*). What would you with me, spectre? Oh, ain't his eyes sepulchral! And ain't his voice hollow! What are you doing out of your tomb at this time of day—apparition?

Ern. I do wish I could make you girls understand that I'm only technically dead, and that physically I'm as much alive as ever I was in my life!

Julia. Oh, but it's an awful thing to be haunted by a technical bogy!

Ern. You won't be haunted much longer. The law must be on its last legs, and in a few hours I shall come to life again—resume all my social and civil functions, and claim my darling as my blushing bride!

Julia. Oh—then you haven't heard?

Ern. My love, I've heard nothing. How could I? There are no daily papers where I come from.

Julia. Why, Ludwig challenged Rudolph and won, and now *he's* Grand Duke, and he's revived the law for another century!

Ern. What! But you're not serious—you're only joking!

Julia. My good sir, I'm a light-hearted girl, but I don't chaff bogies.

Ern. Well, that's the meanest dodge I ever heard of!

Julia. Shabby trick, *I* call it.

Ern. But you don't mean to say that you're going to cry off!

Julia. I really can't afford to wait until your time

is up. You know, I've always set my face against long engagements.

ERN. Then defy the law and marry me now. We will fly to your native country, and I'll play broken-English in London as you play broken-German here !

JULIA. No. These legal technicalities cannot be defied. Situated as you are, you have no power to make me your wife. At best you could only make me your widow.

ERN. Then be my widow—my little, dainty, winning, winsome widow !

JULIA. Now what would be the good of that ? Why, you goose, I should marry again within a month !

DUET—ERNEST *and* JULIA.

ERN.
    If the light of love's lingering ember
        Has faded in gloom,
    You cannot neglect, O remember,
        A voice from the tomb !
    That stern supernatural diction
    Should act as a solemn restriction,
    Although by a mere legal fiction
        A voice from the tomb !

JULIA (*in affected terror*).
    I own that that utterance chills me—
        It withers my bloom !
    With awful emotion it thrills me—
        That voice from the tomb !
    Oh, spectre, won't anything lay thee ?
    Though pained to deny or gainsay thee,
    In this case I cannot obey thee,
        Thou voice from the tomb !

(*Dancing.*)
    So, spectre appalling,
        I bid you good-day—
    Perhaps you'll be calling
        When passing this way.

Your bogydom scorning,
And all your love-lorning,
I bid you good-morning,
I bid you good-day.

ERN. (*furious*).   My offer recalling,
Your words I obey—
Your fate is appalling,
And full of dismay.
To pay for this scorning
I give you fair warning
I'll haunt you each morning,
Each night, and each day !

(*Repeat Ensemble, and exeunt in opposite directions.*)

Re-enter the Wedding Procession dancing.

CHORUS.

Now bridegroom and bride let us toast
In a magnum of merry champagne—
Let us make of this moment the most,
We may not be so lucky again.
So drink to our sovereign host
And his highly intelligent reign—
His health and his bride's let us toast
In a magnum of merry champagne !

SONG—BARONESS *with* CHORUS.

I once gave an evening party
(A sandwich and cut-orange ball),
But my guests had such appetites hearty
That I couldn't enjoy it, enjoy it at all !
I made a heroic endeavour
To look unconcerned, but in vain,
And I vow'd that I never—oh never–
Would ask anybody again !
But there's a distinction decided—
A difference truly immense—

When the wine that you drink is provided, provided,
 At somebody else's expense.
So bumpers—aye, ever so many—
 The cost we may safely ignore !
For the wine doesn't cost us a penny,
 Tho' it's Pomméry seventy-four !

CHORUS. So bumpers—aye, ever so many—etc.

 Come, bumpers—aye, ever so many—
  And then, if you will, many more !
 This wine doesn't cost us a penny,
  Tho' it's Pomméry, Pomméry seventy-four !
 Old wine is a true panacea
  For ev'ry conceivable ill,
 When you cherish the soothing idea
  That somebody else pays the bill !
 Old wine is a pleasure that's hollow
  When at your own table you sit,
 For you're thinking each mouthful you swallow
  Has cost you, has cost you a threepenny-bit !
 So bumpers—aye, ever so many—
  And then, if you will, many more !
 This wine doesn't cost us a penny,
  Tho' it's Pomméry seventy-four !

CHORUS. So, bumpers—aye, ever so many—etc.

     (*March heard.*)

LUD. (*recit.*). Why, who is this approaching,
     Upon our joy encroaching ?
     Some rascal come a-poaching
     Who's heard that wine we're broaching ?

ALL.   Who may this be ?
      Who may this be ?
   Who is he ? Who is he ? Who is he ?

     Enter HERALD.

HER.   The Prince of Monte Car*lo*,
      From Mediterranean water,
    Has come here to bestow
      On you his beautiful daughter.
    They've paid off all they owe,
      As every statesman oughter—
    That Prince of Monte Car*lo*
      And his be-eautiful daughter !

CHORUS.   The Prince of Monte Car*lo*, etc.

HER.   The Prince of Monte Car*lo*,
      Who is so very partickler,
    Has heard that you're also
      For ceremony a stickler—
    Therefore he lets you know
      By word of mouth auric'lar—
    (That Prince of Monte Car*lo*
      Who is so very particklar)—

CHORUS.   The Prince of Monte Car*lo*, etc.

HER.   That Prince of Monte Car*lo*,
      From Mediterranean water,
    Has come here to bestow
      On you his be-eautiful daughter !

LUD. (*recit.*). His Highness we know not—nor the locality
    In which is situate his Principality ;
    But, as he guesses by some odd fatality,
    This *is* the shop for cut and dried formality !
      Let him appear—
      He'll find that we're
    Remarkable for cut and dried formality.

    (*Reprise of March. Exit* HERALD.
     LUDWIG *beckons his Court.*)

LUD. I have a plan—I'll tell you all the plot of it—
   He wants formality—he shall have a lot of it !
    (*Whispers to them, through symphony.*)
   Conceal yourselves, and when I give the cue,
   Spring out on him—you all know what to do !

(All conceal themselves behind the draperies that enclose the stage.)

Pompous March. Enter the PRINCE *and* PRINCESS OF MONTE CARLO, *attended by six theatrical-looking nobles and the Court Costumier.*

DUET—PRINCE *and* PRINCESS.

PRINCE. We're rigged out in magnificent array
       (Our own clothes are much gloomier)
In costumes which we've hired by the day
       From a very well-known costumier.

COST. *(bowing).* *I* am the well-known costumier.

PRINCESS. With a brilliant staff a Prince should make a show
       (It's a rule that never varies),
So we've engaged from the Theatre Monaco
       Six supernumeraries.

NOBLES.   We're the supernumeraries.

ALL.   At a salary immense,
         Quite regardless of expense,
       Six supernumeraries !

PRINCE. They do not speak, for they break our grammar's laws,
       And their language is lamentable—
And they never take off their gloves, because
       Their nails are not presentable.

NOBLES.   Our nails are not presentable !

PRINCESS. To account for their shortcomings manifest
       We explain, in a whisper bated,
They are wealthy members of the brewing interest
       To the Peerage elevated.

NOBLES.   To the Peerage elevated.

ALL.   They're ⎱ very, very rich,
            We're ⎰
                And accordingly, as sich,
            To the Peerage elevated.

PRINCE.   Well, my dear, here we are at last—just in
time to compel Duke Rudolph to fulfil the terms of his
marriage contract. Another hour and we should have
been too late.

PRINCESS.   Yes, papa, and if you hadn't fortunately
discovered a means of making an income by honest
industry, we should never have got here at all.

PRINCE.   Very true. Confined for the last two years
within the precincts of my palace by an obdurate bootmaker
who held a warrant for my arrest, I devoted my enforced
leisure to a study of the doctrine of chances—mainly with
the view of ascertaining whether there was the remotest
chance of my ever going out for a walk again—and this
led to the discovery of a singularly fascinating little round
game which I have called Roulette, and by which, in
one sitting, I won no less than five thousand francs ! My
first act was to pay my bootmaker—my second, to engage
a good useful working set of second-hand nobles—and
my third, to hurry you off to Pfennig Halbpfennig as fast
as a *train de luxe* could carry us !

PRINCESS.   Yes, and a pretty job-lot of second-hand
nobles you've scraped together !

PRINCE (*doubtfully*).   Pretty, you think ? Humph !
I don't know. I should say tol - lol, my love — only
tol-lol. They are not wholly satisfactory. There is
a certain air of unreality about them — they are not
convincing.

COST.   But, my goot friend, vhat can you expect for
eighteenpence a day !

PRINCE.   Now take this Peer, for instance. What the
deuce do you call *him* ?

COST.   Him ? Oh, he's a swell—he's the Duke of
Riviera.

PRINCE. Oh, he's a Duke, is he? Well, that's no reason why he should look so confoundedly haughty. (*To Noble.*) Be affable, sir! (*Noble takes attitude of affability.*) That's better. (*Passing to another.*) Now, who's this with his moustache coming off?

COST. Vhy, you're Viscount Mentone, ain't you?

NOBLE. Blest if I know. (*Turning up sword-belt.*) It's wrote here—yes, Viscount Mentone.

COST. Then vhy don't you say so? 'Old yerself up— you ain't carryin' sandwich boards now. (*Adjusts his moustache.*)

PRINCE. Now, once for all, you Peers—when His Highness arrives, don't stand like sticks, but appear to take an intelligent and sympathetic interest in what is going on. You needn't say anything, but let your gestures be in accordance with the spirit of the conversation. Now take the word from me. Affability! (*attitude*). Submission! (*attitude*). Surprise! (*attitude*). Shame! (*attitude*). Grief! (*attitude*). Joy! (*attitude*). That's better! You can do it if you like!

PRINCESS. But, papa, where in the world is the Court? There is positively no one here to receive us! I can't help feeling that Rudolph wants to get out of it because I'm poor. He's a miserly little wretch—that's what he is.

PRINCE. Well, I shouldn't go so far as to say that. I should rather describe him as an enthusiastic collector of coins—of the realm—and we must not be too hard upon a numismatist if he feels a certain disinclination to part with some of his really very valuable specimens. It's a pretty hobby: I've often thought I should like to collect some coins myself.

PRINCESS. Papa, I'm sure there's some one behind that curtain. I saw it move!

PRINCE. Then no doubt they are coming. Now mind, you Peers—haughty affability combined with a sense of what is due to your exalted ranks, or I'll fine you half a franc each—upon my soul I will!

(Gong. The curtains fly back and the Court are discovered. They give a wild yell and rush on to the stage dancing wildly, with Prince, Princess, *and Nobles, who are taken by surprise at first, but eventually join in a reckless dance. At the end all fall down exhausted.)*

Lud. There, what do you think of that ? That's our official ceremonial for the reception of visitors of the very highest distinction.

Prince (*puzzled*). It's very quaint—very curious indeed. Prettily footed, too. Prettily footed.

Lud. Would you like to see how we say " good-bye " to visitors of distinction ? That ceremony is also performed with the foot.

Prince. Really, this tone—ah, but perhaps you have not completely grasped the situation ?

Lud. Not altogether.

Prince. Ah, then I'll give you a lead over. (*Significantly.*) I am the father of the Princess of Monte Carlo. Doesn't that convey any idea to the Grand Ducal mind ?

Lud. (*stolidly*). Nothing definite.

Prince (*aside*). H'm—very odd ! Never mind—try again ! (*Aloud.*) This is the daughter of the Prince of Monte Carlo. Do you take ?

Lud. (*still puzzled*). No—not yet. Go on—don't give it up—I daresay it will come presently.

Prince. Very odd—never mind—try again. (*With sly significance.*) Twenty years ago ! Little doddle doddle ! *Two* little doddle doddles ! Happy father—hers and yours. Proud mother—yours and hers ! Hah ! *Now* you take ? I see you do ! I see you do !

Lud. Nothing is more annoying than to feel that you're not equal to the intellectual pressure of the conversation. I wish he'd say something intelligible.

Prince. You didn't expect me ?

Lud. (*jumping at it*). No, no. I grasp that—thank you very much. (*Shaking hands with him.*) No, I did *not* expect you !

PRINCE. I thought not. But ha! ha! at last I have escaped from my enforced restraint. (*General movement of alarm.*) (*To crowd who are stealing off.*) No, no—you misunderstand me. I mean I've paid my debts!

ALL. Oh! (*They return.*)

PRINCESS (*affectionately*). But, my darling, I'm afraid that even now you don't quite realize who I am! (*Embracing him.*)

BARONESS. Why, you forward little hussy, how dare you? (*Takes her away from* LUDWIG.)

LUD. You mustn't do that, my dear—never in the presence of the Grand Duchess, I beg!

PRINCESS (*weeping*). Oh, papa, he's got a Grand Duchess!

LUD. *A* Grand Duchess! My good girl, I've got three Grand Duchesses!

PRINCESS. Well, I'm sure! Papa, let's go away—this is not a respectable Court.

PRINCE. All these Grand Dukes have their little fancies, my love. This potentate appears to be collecting wives. It's a pretty hobby—I should like to collect a few myself. This (*admiring* BARONESS) is a charming specimen—an antique, I should say—of the early Merovingian period, if I'm not mistaken ; and here's another—a Scotch lady, I think (*alluding to* JULIA), and (*alluding to* LISA) a little one thrown in. Two half-quarterns and a makeweight! (*To* LUDWIG.) Have you such a thing as a catalogue of the Museum?

PRINCESS. But I cannot permit Rudolph to keep a museum——

LUD. Rudolph? Get along with you, I'm not Rudolph! Rudolph died yesterday!

PRINCE *and* PRINCESS. What!

LUD. Quite suddenly—of—of—a cardiac affection.

PRINCE *and* PRINCESS. Of a cardiac affection?

LUD. Yes, a pack-of-cardiac affection. He fought a Statutory Duel with me and lost, and I took over all his engagements—including this imperfectly preserved old

lady, to whom he has been engaged for the last three
weeks.

PRINCESS. Three weeks! But I've been engaged to
him for the last twenty years!

BARONESS, LISA, *and* JULIA. Twenty years!

PRINCE (*aside*). It's all right, my love—they can't
get over that. (*Aloud.*) He's yours—take him, and hold
him as tight as you can!

PRINCESS. My own! (*Embracing* LUDWIG.)

LUD. Here's another!—the fourth in four-and-twenty
hours! Would anybody else like to marry me? You,
ma'am—or you—anybody! I'm getting used to it!

BARONESS. But let me tell you, ma'am——

JULIA. Why, you impudent little hussy——

LISA. Oh, here's another—here's another! (*Weeping.*)

PRINCESS. Poor ladies, I'm very sorry for you all;
but, you see, I've a prior claim. Come, away we go—
there's not a moment to be lost!

CHORUS (*as they dance towards exit*).

Away to the wedding we'll go
    To summon the charioteers,
No kind of reluctance we show
    To embark on our married careers—

(*At this moment* RUDOLPH, ERNEST, *and* NOTARY *appear.
All kneel in astonishment.*)

RECITATIVE.

RUD., ERN., *and* NOT.

Forbear! This may not be!
    Frustrated are your plans!
With paramount decree
    The Law forbids the banns!

ALL. The Law forbids the banns!

LUD. Not a bit of it! I've revived the law for another
century!

RUD.   You didn't revive it !   You couldn't revive it !
You—you are an impostor, sir—a tuppenny rogue, sir !
You—you never were, and in all human probability never
will be—Grand Duke of Pfennig Anything !

ALL.   What ! ! !

RUD.   Never—never, never !   (*Aside.*)   Oh, my internal economy !

LUD.   That's absurd, you know.   I fought the Grand
Duke.   He drew a King, and I drew an Ace.   He
perished in inconceivable agonies on the spot.   Now, as
that's settled, we'll go on with the wedding.

RUD.   It—it isn't settled.   You—you can't.   I—I—
(*to* NOTARY).   Oh, tell him—tell him !   I can't !

NOT.   Well, the fact is, there's been a little mistake
here.   On reference to the Act that regulates Statutory
Duels, I find it is expressly laid down that the Ace shall
count invariably as lowest !

ALL.   As lowest !

RUD.   (*breathlessly*).   As lowest—lowest—lowest !   So
you're the ghoest—ghoest—ghoest !   (*Aside.*)   Oh, what
is the matter with me inside here !

ERN.   Well, Julia, as it seems that the law hasn't
been revived—and as, consequently, I shall come to life
in about three minutes—(*consulting his watch*)——

JULIA.   My objection falls to the ground.   (*Resignedly.*)
Very well !

PRINCESS.   And am I to understand that I was on
the point of marrying a dead man without knowing it ?
(*To* RUDOLPH, *who revives.*)   Oh, my love, what a
narrow escape I've had !

RUD.   Oh—you are the Princess of Monte Carlo, and
you've turned up just in time !   Well, you're an attractive
little girl, you know, but you're as poor as a rat !   (*They
retire up together.*)

LISA.   That's all very well, but what is to become of
me ?   (*To* LUDWIG.)   If you're a dead man——(*Clock
strikes three.*)

LUD.   But I'm not.   Time's up—the Act has expired

—I've come to life—the parson is still in attendance, and we'll all be married directly.

ALL.　Hurrah !

FINALE.

Happy couples, lightly treading,
　　Castle chapel will be quite full !
Each shall have a pretty wedding,
　　As, of course, is only rightful,
　　Though the brides be fair or frightful.
Contradiction little dreading,
　　This will be a day delightful—
Each shall have a pretty wedding !
　　Such a pretty, pretty wedding !
　　　Such a pretty wedding !

(*All dance off to get married as the curtain falls.*)

THE END

Printed in Great Britain by R. & R. CLARK, LIMITED, *Edinburgh.*

" Ida ! my love ! my life !   Oh, come to me ! "
If it be well, I say, to do all this,
Then Prince Hilarion is very well.

PRIN. He breathes *our* name ?   Well, it's a common
       one !
      And is the booby comely ?

HIL.   Pretty well.
      I've heard it said that if I dressed myself
      In Prince Hilarion's clothes (supposing this
      Consisted with my maiden modesty),
      I might be taken for Hilarion's self.
      But what is this to you or me, who think
      Of all mankind with undisguised contempt ?

PRIN. Contempt ?   Why, damsel, when I think of man,
      Contempt is not the word.

CYR. (*getting tipsy*).   I'm sure of that,
      Or if it is, it surely should not be !

HIL. (*aside to* CYRIL). Be quiet, idiot, or they'll find us out.

CYR. The Prince Hilarion's a goodly lad !

PRIN. *You* know him then ?

CYR. (*tipsily*).   I rather think I do !
      We are inseparables !

PRIN.   Why, what's this ?
      You love him then ?

CYR.   We do indeed—all three !

HIL. Madam, she jests ! (*Aside to* CYRIL.)   Remember
      where you are !

CYR. Jests ?   Not at all !   Why, bless my heart alive,
      You and Hilarion, when at the Court,
      Rode the same horse !

PRIN. (*horrified*).   Astride ?

CYR.   Of course !   Why not ?
      Wore the same clothes—and once or twice, I think,
      Got tipsy in the same good company !

PRIN. Well, these are nice young ladies, on my word !

CYR. (*tipsy*). Don't you remember that old kissing-song
      He'd sing to blushing Mistress Lalage,
      The hostess of the Pigeons ?   Thus it ran :

SONG—CYRIL.

(*During symphony* HILARION *and* FLORIAN *try to stop* CYRIL. *He shakes them off angrily.*)

Would you know the kind of maid
    Sets my heart aflame-a ?
Eyes must be downcast and staid,
    Cheeks must flush for shame-a !
        She may neither dance nor sing,
        But, demure in everything,
        Hang her head in modest way,
        With pouting lips that seem to say,
" Oh, kiss me, kiss me, kiss me, kiss me,
        Though I die of shame-a ! "
    Please you, that's the kind of maid
        Sets my heart aflame-a !

When a maid is bold and gay
    With a tongue goes clang-a,
Flaunting it in brave array,
    Maiden may go hang-a !
        Sunflower gay and hollyhock
        Never shall my garden stock ;
        Mine the blushing rose of May,
        With pouting lips that seem to say,
" Oh, kiss me, kiss me, kiss me, kiss me,
        Though I die for shame-a ! "
    Please you, that's the kind of maid
        Sets my heart aflame-a !

PRIN.   Infamous creature, get you hence away !

(HILARION, *who has been with difficulty restrained by* FLORIAN *during this song, breaks from him and strikes* CYRIL *furiously on the breast.*)

HIL.   Dog ! there is something more to sing about !
CYR. (*sobered*).   Hilarion, are you mad ?

PRIN. (*horrified*).   Hilarion ?   Help !
    Why, these are men ! Lost ! lost ! betrayed ! un-
        done !   (*Running on to bridge.*)
    Girls, get you hence ! Man-monsters, if you dare
    Approach one step, I—— Ah !
      (*Loses her balance, and falls into the stream.*)

PSY.   Oh ! save her, sir !

BLA.   It's useless, sir,—you'll only catch your death !
                    (HILARION *springs in.*)

SACH. He catches her !

MEL.   And now he lets her go !
  Again she's in his grasp——

PSY.   And now she's not.
  He seizes her back hair !

BLA. (*not looking*).   And it comes off !

PSY.   No, no ! She's saved !—she's saved !—she's saved !
    —she's saved !

FINALE.

CHORUS OF LADIES.

Oh ! joy, our chief is saved,
   And by Hilarion's hand ;
The torrent fierce he braved,
   And brought her safe to land !
     For his intrusion we must own
     This doughty deed may well atone !

PRIN.   Stand forth ye three,
        Whoe'er ye be,
   And hearken to our stern decree !

HIL., CYR., *and* FLOR. Have mercy, lady,—disregard your
    oaths !

PRIN. I know not mercy, men in women's clothes !
    The man whose sacrilegious eyes
    Invade our strict seclusion, dies.
    Arrest these coarse intruding spies !

(*They are arrested by the " Daughters of the Plough ".*)

FLOR., CYR., *and* LADIES.   Have mercy, lady—disregard
          your oaths !
PRIN.   I know not mercy, men in women's clothes !

(CYRIL *and* FLORIAN *are bound.*)

SONG—HILARION.

Whom thou hast chained must wear his chain,
    Thou canst not set him free,
He wrestles with his bonds in vain
    Who lives by loving thee !
If heart of stone for heart of fire,
    Be all thou hast to give,
If dead to me my heart's desire,
    Why should I wish to live ?

FLOR., CYR., *and* LADIES.   Have mercy, O lady !

No word of thine—no stern command
    Can teach my heart to rove,
Then rather perish by thy hand,
    Than live without thy love !
A loveless life apart from thee
    Were hopeless slavery,
If kindly death will set me free,
    Why should I fear to die ?

[*He is bound by two of the attendants, and the
    three gentlemen are marched off.*

Enter MELISSA.

MEL.   Madam, without the castle walls
                  An armed band
              Demand admittance to our halls
                  For Hildebrand !

ALL.   Oh, horror !

PRIN.   Deny them !
                  We will defy them !

ALL.   Too late—too late !
                        The castle gate
                    Is battered by them !

(The gate yields. SOLDIERS *rush in.* ARAC, GURON,
and SCYNTHIUS *are with them, but with their hands
handcuffed.)*

ENSEMBLE.

GIRLS.	MEN.
Rend the air with wailing,	Walls and fences scaling,
Shed the shameful tear !	Promptly we appear ;
Walls are unavailing,	Walls are unavailing,
Man has entered here !	We have entered here.
Shame and desecration	Female execration
Are his staunch allies,	Stifle if you're wise,
Let your lamentation	Stop your lamentation,
Echo to the skies !	Dry your pretty eyes !

Enter HILDEBRAND.

RECIT.

PRIN   Audacious tyrant, do you dare
            To beard a maiden in her lair ?

HILD.   Since you inquire,
                 We've no desire
            To beard a maiden here, or anywhere !

SOL.   No, no—we've no desire
            To beard a maiden here, or anywhere !

SOLO—HILDEBRAND.

Some years ago
No doubt you know
(And if you don't I'll tell you so)
You gave your troth
Upon your oath
To Hilarion my son.
A vow you make
You must not break,
(If you think you may, it's a great mistake),

> For a bride's a bride
> Though the knot were tied
> At the early age of one !
> And I'm a peppery kind of King,
> Who's indisposed for parleying
> To fit the wit of a bit of a chit,
> And that's the long and the short of it !

Sol.　　For he's a peppery kind of King, etc.

> If you decide
> To pocket your pride
> And let Hilarion claim his bride,
> Why, well and good,
> It's understood
> We'll let bygones go by—
> But if you choose
> To sulk in the blues
> I'll make the whole of you shake in your shoes.
> I'll storm your walls,
> And level your halls,
> In the twinkling of an eye !
> For I'm a peppery Potentate,
> Who's little inclined his claim to bate,
> To fit the wit of a bit of a chit,
> And that's the long and the short of it !

Sol　　For he's a peppery kind of King, etc.

TRIO—Arac, Guron, *and* Scynthius.

> We may remark. though nothing can
> Dismay us,
> That if you thwart this gentleman,
> He'll slay us.
> We don't fear death, of course—we're taught
> To shame it ;
> But still upon the whole we thought
> We'd name it.

(*To each other.*)　　Yes, yes, yes, better perhaps to name it.

> Our interests we would not press
>> With chatter,
> Three hulking brothers more or less
>> Don't matter ;
> If you'd pooh-pooh this monarch's plan,
>> Pooh-pooh it,
> But when he says he'll hang a man,
>> He'll do it.

(*To each other.*)   Yes, yes, yes, devil doubt he'll do it.

PRIN.   (*Recit.*)   Be reassured, nor fear his anger blind,
His menaces are idle as the wind.
He dares not kill you—vengeance lurks behind !

AR., GUR., SCYN.   *We* rather think he dares, but never mind !

No, no,—never, never mind !

HILD.   I rather think I dare, but never, never mind !
Enough of parley—as a special boon,
We give you till to-morrow afternoon ;
Release Hilarion, then, and be his bride,
Or you'll incur the guilt of fratricide !

ENSEMBLE.

PRINCESS.	THE OTHERS.
To yield at once to such a foe With shame were rife ; So quick! away with him, although He saved my life ! That he is fair, and strong, and tall, Is very evident to all, Yet I will die before I call Myself his wife !	Oh! yield at once, 'twere better so Than risk a strife ! And let the Prince Hilarion go— He saved thy life ! Hilarion's fair, and strong, and tall— A worse misfortune might befall— It's not so dreadful, after all, To be his wife !

SOLO—PRINCESS.

> Though I am but a girl,
> Defiance thus I hurl,
>> Our banners all
>> On outer wall
> We fearlessly unfurl.

ALL.   Though she is but a girl, etc.

PRINCESS.   THE OTHERS.

That he is fair, etc.   Hilarion's fair, etc.

(*The* PRINCESS *stands, surrounded by girls kneeling.*
HILDEBRAND *and soldiers stand on built rocks at
back and sides of stage.   Picture.*)

CURTAIN.

END OF ACT II.

ACT III.

SCENE.—*Outer Walls and Courtyard of Castle Adamant.*
MELISSA, SACHARISSA, *and ladies discovered, armed
with battleaxes.*

CHORUS.

Death to the invader !
  Strike a deadly blow,
As an old Crusader
  Struck his Paynim foe !
Let our martial thunder
Fill his soul with wonder,
Tear his ranks asunder,
  Lay the tyrant low !

SOLO—MELISSA.

Thus our courage, all untarnished,
  We're instructed to display :
But to tell the truth unvarnished,
  We are more inclined to say,
" Please you, do not hurt us."

ALL.	" Do not hurt us, if it please you ! "
MEL.	" Please you let us be."
ALL.	" Let us be—let us be ! "
MEL.	" Soldiers disconcert us."
ALL.	" Disconcert us, if it please you ! "
MEL.	" Frightened maids are we."
ALL.	" Maids are we—maids are we ! "

MELISSA.

But 'twould be an error
To confess our terror,
So, in Ida's name,
Boldly we exclaim :

CHORUS.

Death to the invader !
  Strike a deadly blow,
As an old Crusader
  Struck his Paynim foe !

Flourish. Enter PRINCESS, *armed, attended by*
BLANCHE *and* PSYCHE.

PRIN. I like your spirit, girls ! We have to meet
       Stern bearded warriors in fight to-day :
       Wear naught but what is necessary to
       Preserve your dignity before their eyes,
       And give your limbs full play.
BLA.   One moment, ma'am,
       Here is a paradox we should not pass
       Without inquiry. We are prone to say,
       " This thing is Needful—that, Superfluous "—
       Yet they invariably co-exist !
       We find the Needful comprehended in
       The circle of the grand Superfluous,
       Yet the Superfluous cannot be bought
       Unless you're amply furnished with the Needful.
       These singular considerations are—
PRIN. Superfluous, yet not Needful—so you see
       The terms may independently exist.
(*To Ladies.*) Women of Adamant, we have to show
       That Woman, educated to the task,
       Can meet Man, face to face, on his own ground,
       And beat him there. Now let us set to work :
       Where is our lady surgeon ?
SAC.   Madam, here !

PRIN.   We shall require your skill to heal the wounds
       Of those that fall.

SAC. (*alarmed*).   What, heal the wounded ?

PRIN.   Yes !

SAC.   And cut off real live legs and arms ?

PRIN.   Of course !

SAC.   I wouldn't do it for a thousand pounds !

PRIN.   Why, how is this ? Are you faint-hearted, girl ?
       You've often cut them off in theory !

SAC.   In theory I'll cut them off again
       With pleasure, and as often as you like,
       But not in practice.

PRIN.   Coward ! get you hence,
       I've craft enough for that, and courage too,
       I'll do your work ! My fusiliers, advance !
       Why, you are armed with axes ! Gilded toys !
       Where are your rifles, pray ?

CHLOE.   Why, please you, ma'am,
       We left them in the armoury, for fear
       That in the heat and turmoil of the fight,
       They might go off !

PRIN.   " They might ! " Oh, craven souls !
       Go off yourselves ! Thank heaven, I have a heart
       That quails not at the thought of meeting men ;
       I will discharge your rifles ! Off with you !
       Where's my bandmistress ?

ADA.   Please you, ma'am, the band
       Do not feel well, and can't come out to-day !

PRIN.   Why, this is flat rebellion ! I've no time
       To talk to them just now. But, happily,
       I can play several instruments at once,
       And I will drown the shrieks of those that fall
       With trumpet music, such as soldiers love !
       How stand we with respect to gunpowder ?
       My Lady Psyche—you who superintend
       Our lab'ratory—are you well prepared
       To blow these bearded rascals into shreds ?

Psy.   Why, madam—

Prin.   Well ?

Psy.   Let us try gentler means.
        We can dispense with fulminating grains
        While we have eyes with which to flash our
            rage !
        We can dispense with villainous saltpetre
        While we have tongues with which to blow them
            up !
        We can dispense, in short, with all the arts
        That brutalize the practical polemist !

Prin. (*contemptuously*).   I never knew a more dispensing
            chemist !
        Away, away—I'll meet these men alone
        Since all my women have deserted me !

        [*Exeunt all but* Princess, *singing refrain of
        "Please you, do not hurt us", pianissimo.*

Prin.   So fail my cherished plans—so fails my faith—
        And with it hope, and all that comes of hope !

            SONG—Princess.

        I built upon a rock,
            But ere Destruction's hand
                Dealt equal lot
                To Court and cot,
            My rock had turned to sand !
        I leant upon an oak,
            But in the hour of need,
                Alack-a-day,
                My trusted stay
            Was but a bruisèd reed !
        Ah, faithless rock,
            My simple faith to mock !
        Ah, trait'rous oak,
            Thy worthlessness to cloak.

                I drew a sword of steel,
                    But when to home and hearth
                        The battle's breath
                        Bore fire and death,
                    My sword was but a lath !
            I lit a beacon fire,
                    But on a stormy day
                        Of frost and rime,
                        In wintertime,
            My fire had died away !
                        Ah, coward steel,
                        That fear can unanneal !
                        False fire indeed,
                        To fail me in my need !

She sinks on a seat.   Enter CHLOE *and all the ladies.*

CHLOE. Madam, your father and your brothers claim
        An audience !
PRIN.   What do they do here ?
CHLOE.   They come
        To fight for you !
PRIN.   Admit them !
BLA.   Infamous !
        One's brothers, ma'am, are men !
PRIN.   So I have heard.
        But all my women seem to fail me when
        I need them most.   In this emergency,
        Even one's brothers may be turned to use.

        Enter GAMA, *quite pale and unnerved.*

GAMA.   My daughter !
PRIN.   Father ! thou art free !
GAMA.   Aye, free !
        Free as a tethered ass !   I come to thee
        With words from Hildebrand.   Those duly given
        I must return to blank captivity.
        I'm free so far.

PRIN. Your message.

GAMA. Hildebrand
Is loth to war with women. Pit my sons,
My three brave sons, against these popinjays,
These tufted jack-a-dandy featherheads,
And on the issue let thy hand depend !

PRIN. Insult on insult's head ! Are we a stake
For fighting men ? What fiend possesses thee,
That thou hast come with offers such as these
From such as he to such an one as I ?

GAMA. I am possessed
By the pale devil of a shaking heart !
My stubborn will is bent. I dare not face
That devilish monarch's black malignity !
He tortures me with torments worse than death,
I haven't anything to grumble at !
He finds out what particular meats I love,
And gives me them. The very choicest wines,
The costliest robes—the richest rooms are mine :
He suffers none to thwart my simplest plan,
And gives strict orders none should contradict me!
He's made my life a curse ! (*weeps*).

PRIN. My tortured father !

SONG—GAMA.

Whene'er I poke
Sarcastic joke
　　Replete with malice spiteful,
This people mild
Politely smiled,
　　And voted me delightful !
Now when a wight
Sits up all night
　　Ill-natured jokes devising,
And all his wiles
Are met with smiles,
　　It's hard, there's no disguising !

Oh, don't the days seem lank and long
When all goes right and nothing goes wrong,
And isn't your life extremely flat
With nothing whatever to grumble at !

When German bands
From music stands
Played Wagner imper*fect*ly—
I bade them go—
They didn't say no,
But off they went directly !
The organ boys
They stopped their noise
With readiness surprising,
And grinning herds
Of hurdy-gurds
Retired apologising !
Oh, don't the days seem lank and long, etc.

I offered gold
In sums untold
To all who'd contradict me—
I said I'd pay
A pound a day
To any one who kicked me—
I bribed with toys
Great vulgar boys
To utter something spiteful,
But, bless you, no !
They *would* be so
Confoundedly politeful !

In short, these aggravating lads,
They tickle my tastes, they feed my fads,
They give me this and they give me that,
And I've nothing whatever to grumble at !

He bursts into tears, and falls sobbing on a seat.

PRIN.   My poor old father !   How he must have suffered !
         Well, well, I yield !

GAMA (*hysterically*).   She yields !   I'm saved, I'm saved !
                                                    [*Exit.*

PRIN.   Open the gates—admit these warriors,
         Then get you all within the castle walls.   [*Exit.*

*The gates are opened, and the girls mount the battle-
    ments as soldiers enter. Also* ARAC, GURON, *and*
    SCYNTHIUS.

CHORUS OF SOLDIERS.

When anger spreads his wing,
    And all seems dark as night for it,
    There's nothing but to fight for it,
But ere you pitch your ring,
    Select a pretty site for it,
    (This spot is suited quite for it),
And then you gaily sing,

" Oh, I love the jolly rattle
Of an ordeal by battle,
There's an end of tittle-tattle,
        When your enemy is dead.
It's an arrant molly-coddle
Fears a crack upon his noddle
And he's only fit to swaddle
        In a downy feather-bed ! "—

ALL.   For a fight's a kind of thing
          That I love to look upon,
              So let us sing,
              Long live the King,
          And his son Hilarion !

During this, HILARION, FLORIAN, *and* CYRIL *are brought
    out by the* " *Daughters of the Plough* ". *They are
    still bound and wear the robes. Enter* GAMA.

GAMA.   Hilarion ! Cyril ! Florian ! dressed as women !
         Is this indeed Hilarion ?

HIL.   Yes, it is !

GAMA.   Why, you look handsome in your women's clothes!
           Stick to 'em ! men's attire becomes you not !

(*To* CYRIL *and* FLORIAN). And you, young ladies, will
           you please to pray
           King Hildebrand to set me free again ?
           Hang on his neck and gaze into his eyes,
           He never could resist a pretty face !

HIL.   You dog, you'll find, though I wear woman's garb,
           My sword is long and sharp !

GAMA.   Hush, pretty one !
           Here's a virago !   Here's a termagant !
           If length and sharpness go for anything,
           You'll want no sword while you can wag your
                tongue !

CYR.   What need to waste your words on such as he ?
           He's old and crippled.

GAMA.   Aye, but I've three sons,
           Fine fellows, young, and muscular, and brave,
           They're well worth talking to ! Come, what
                d'ye say ?

ARAC.   Aye, pretty ones, engage yourselves with us,
           If three rude warriors affright you not !

HIL.   Old as you are, I'd wring your shrivelled neck
           If you were not the Princess Ida's father.

GAMA.   If I were not the Princess Ida's father,
           And so had not her brothers for my sons,
           No doubt you'd wring my neck—in safety too !
           Come, come, Hilarion, begin, begin !
           Give them no quarter—they will give you none.
           You've this advantage over warriors
           Who kill their country's enemies for pay,—
           You know what you are fighting for—look there !

(*Pointing to Ladies on the battlements.*)

[*Exit* GAMA. HILARION, FLORIAN, *and* CYRIL
    are led off.

SONG—Arac.

This helmet, I suppose,
Was meant to ward off blows,
    It's very hot,
    And weighs a lot,
As many a guardsman knows,
So off that helmet goes.

All.   Yes, yes, yes,
        So off that helmet goes !

            (*Giving their helmets to attendants.*)

Arac.   This tight-fitting cuirass
        Is but a useless mass,
            It's made of steel,
            And weighs a deal,
        A man is but an ass
        Who fights in a cuirass,
        So off goes that cuirass.

All.   Yes, yes, yes,
        So off goes that cuirass !

            (*Removing cuirasses.*)

Arac.   These brassets, truth to tell,
        May look uncommon well,
            But in a fight
            They're much too tight,
        They're like a lobster shell !

All.   Yes, yes, yes,
        They're like a lobster shell.

            (*Removing their brassets.*)

Arac.   These things I treat the same (*indicating
        leg pieces*).
        (I quite forget their name)
            They turn one's legs
            To cribbage pegs—
        Their aid I thus disclaim,
        Though I forget their name !

ALL.   Yes, yes, yes,
              Their aid $\left\{\begin{array}{l}\text{we}\\\text{they}\end{array}\right\}$ thus disclaim !

(*They remove their leg pieces and wear close-fitting
                    shape suits.*)

            Enter HILARION, FLORIAN, *and* CYRIL.

*Desperate fight between the three Princes and the three
    Knights, during which the Ladies on the battlements
    and the Soldiers on the stage sing the following
    chorus.*)

            This is our duty plain towards
                Our Princess all immaculate,
            We ought to bless her brothers' swords
                And piously ejaculate :
                    Oh, Hungary !
                    Oh, Hungary !
            Oh, doughty sons of Hungary !
                    May all success
                    Attend and bless
            Your warlike ironmongery !
            Hilarion !   Hilarion !   Hilarion !

By this time, ARAC, GURON, *and* SCYNTHIUS *are on the
    ground, wounded*—HILARION, CYRIL, *and* FLORIAN
    stand over them.)

PRIN. (*entering through gate and followed by Ladies*,
HILDEBRAND, *and* GAMA).   Hold ! stay your hands !—
we yield ourselves to you !
            Ladies, my brothers all lie bleeding there !
            Bind up their wounds—but look the other way.
(*Coming down.*) Is this the end ? (*bitterly to* LADY
            BLANCHE).   How say you, Lady Blanche—
            Can I with dignity my post resign ?
            And if I do, will you then take my place ?

BLA.   To answer this, it's meet that we consult
        The great Potential Mysteries ; I mean
        The five Subjunctive Possibilities—
        The May, the Might, the Would, the Could, the
            Should.
        Can you resign ?   The prince May claim you; if
        He Might, you Could—and if you Should, I
            Would !

PRIN.   I thought as much !   Then, to my fate I yield—
        So ends my cherished scheme !   Oh, I had hoped
        To band all women with my maiden throng,
        And make them all abjure tyrannic Man !

HILD.   A noble aim !

PRIN.   You ridicule it now ;
        But if I carried out this glorious scheme,
        At my exalted name Posterity
        Would bow in gratitude !

HILD.   But pray reflect—
        If you enlist all women in your cause,
        And make them all abjure tyrannic Man,
        The obvious question then arises, " How
        Is this Posterity to be provided ? "

PRIN.   I never thought of that !   My Lady Blanche,
        How do you solve the riddle ?

BLA.   Don't ask me—
        Abstract Philosophy won't answer it.
        Take him—he is your Shall.   Give in to Fate !

PRIN.   And you desert me.   I alone am staunch !

HIL.   Madam, you placed your trust in Woman—well,
        Woman has failed you utterly—try Man,
        Give him one chance, it's only fair—besides,
        Women are far too precious, too divine,
        To try unproven theories upon.
        Experiments, the proverb says, are made
        On humble subjects—try our grosser clay,
        And mould it as you will !

CYR.   Remember, too,
        Dear Madam, if at any time you feel

A-weary of the Prince, you can return
To Castle Adamant, and rule your girls
As heretofore, you know.

PRIN.   And shall I find
The Lady Psyche here ?

PSY.   If Cyril, ma'am,
Does not behave himself, I think you will.

PRIN. And you, Melissa, shall I find *you* here ?

MEL. Madam, however Florian turns out,
Unhesitatingly I answer, No !

GAMA. Consider this, my love, if your mamma
Had looked on matters from your point of view
(I wish she had), why where would you have been ?

BLA. There's an unbounded field of speculation,
On which I could discourse for hours !

PRIN.   No doubt !
We will not trouble you.   Hilarion,
I have been wrong—I see my error now.
Take me, Hilarion—" We will walk the world
Yoked in all exercise of noble end !
And so through those dark gates across the wild
That no man knows !   Indeed, I love thee—
      Come ! "

FINALE.

PRIN.   With joy abiding,
                  Together gliding
                      Through life's variety,
                      In sweet society,
                  And thus enthroning
                  The love I'm owning,
                  On this atoning
                      I will rely !

CHORUS.   It were profanity
                  For poor humanity
                  To treat as vanity
                      The sway of Love.

In no locality
Or principality
Is our mortality
  Its sway above !

HILARION.   When day is fading,
With serenading
  And such frivolity
    Of tender quality—
With scented showers
Of fairest flowers,
The happy hours
  Will gaily fly !

CHORUS.   It were profanity, etc.

CURTAIN.

THE MIKADO

OR

THE TOWN OF TITIPU

DRAMATIS PERSONÆ.

THE MIKADO OF JAPAN.

NANKI-POO (*his Son, disguised as a wandering minstrel, and in love with* YUM-YUM).

KO-KO (*Lord High Executioner of Titipu*).

POOH-BAH (*Lord High Everything Else*).

PISH-TUSH (*a Noble Lord*).

YUM-YUM
PITTI-SING   } *Three Sisters—Wards of* KO-KO.
PEEP-BO

KATISHA (*an elderly Lady, in love with* NANKI-POO).

Chorus of School-girls, Nobles, Guards, and Coolies.

ACT I.—Courtyard of Ko-Ko's Official Residence.

ACT II.—Ko-Ko's Garden.

First produced at the Savoy Theatre on March 14, 1885

THE MIKADO

OR

THE TOWN OF TITIPU

ACT I.

SCENE.—*Courtyard of* KO-KO'S *Palace in Titipu.*
Japanese nobles discovered standing and sitting in
attitudes suggested by native drawings.

CHORUS OF NOBLES.

If you want to know who we are,
    We are gentlemen of Japan :
On many a vase and jar—
    On many a screen and fan,
        We figure in lively paint :
        Our attitude's queer and quaint—
        You're wrong if you think it ain't, oh !

If you think we are worked by strings,
    Like a Japanese marionette,
You don't understand these things :
    It is simply Court etiquette.
        Perhaps you suppose this throng
        Can't keep it up all day long ?
        If that's your idea, you're wrong, oh !

Enter NANKI-POO *in great excitement. He carries a native guitar on his back and a bundle of ballads in his hand.*

RECIT.—NANKI-POO.

Gentlemen, I pray you tell me
Where a gentle maiden dwelleth,
Named Yum-Yum, the ward of Ko-Ko ?
In pity speak—oh, speak, I pray you !

A NOBLE. Why, who are you who ask this question ?
NANK. Come gather round me, and I'll tell you.

SONG AND CHORUS—NANKI-POO.

A wandering minstrel I—
   A thing of shreds and patches,
   Of ballads, songs and snatches,
And dreamy lullaby !

My catalogue is long,
   Through every passion ranging,
   And to your humours changing
I tune my supple song !

Are you in sentimental mood ?
  I'll sigh with you,
    Oh, sorrow, sorrow !
On maiden's coldness do you brood ?
  I'll do so, too—
    Oh, sorrow, sorrow !
I'll charm your willing ears
With songs of lovers' fears,
While sympathetic tears
  My cheeks bedew—
    Oh, sorrow, sorrow !

But if patriotic sentiment is wanted,
   I've patriotic ballads cut and dried ;
For where'er our country's banner may be
    planted,
   All other local banners are defied !
Our warriors, in serried ranks assembled,
   Never quail—or they conceal it if they do—
And I shouldn't be surprised if nations trembled
   Before the mighty troops of Titipu !

CHORUS. We shouldn't be surprised, etc.

NANK.   And if you call for a song of the sea,
    We'll heave the capstan round,
With a yeo heave ho, for the wind is free,
Her anchor's a-trip and her helm's a-lee,
   Hurrah for the homeward bound !

CHORUS.   Yeo-ho—heave ho—
     Hurrah for the homeward bound !

To lay aloft in a howling breeze
   May tickle a landsman's taste,
But the happiest hour a sailor sees
    Is when he's down
    At an inland town,
With his Nancy on his knees, yeo ho !
   And his arm around her waist !

CHORUS.   Then man the capstan—off we go,
     As the fiddler swings us round,
    With a yeo heave ho,
    And a rumbelow,
     Hurrah for the homeward bound !

    A wandering minstrel I, etc.

Enter PISH-TUSH.

PISH. And what may be your business with Yum-Yum?

NANK. I'll tell you. A year ago I was a member of the Titipu town band. It was my duty to take the cap round for contributions. While discharging this delicate office, I saw Yum-Yum. We loved each other at once, but she was betrothed to her guardian Ko-Ko, a cheap tailor, and I saw that my suit was hopeless. Overwhelmed with despair, I quitted the town. Judge of my delight when I heard, a month ago, that Ko-Ko had been condemned to death for flirting ! I hurried back at once, in the hope of finding Yum-Yum at liberty to listen to my protestations.

PISH. It is true that Ko-Ko was condemned to death for flirting, but he was reprieved at the last moment, and raised to the exalted rank of Lord High Executioner under the following remarkable circumstances :

SONG—PISH-TUSH *and* CHORUS.

Our great Mikado, virtuous man,
When he to rule our land began,
Resolved to try
A plan whereby
Young men might best be steadied.
So he decreed, in words succinct,
That all who flirted, leered or winked
(Unless connubially linked),
Should forthwith be beheaded.

And I expect you'll all agree
That he was right to so decree.
And I am right,
And you are right,
And all is right as right can be !

CHORUS.　　　　　　And you are right,
　　　　　　　　　 And we are right, etc

This stern decree, you'll understand,
Caused great dismay throughout the land !
    For young and old
    And shy and bold
    Were equally affected.
The youth who winked a roving eye,
Or breathed a non-connubial sigh,
Was thereupon condemned to die—
    He usually objected.

    And you'll allow, as I expect,
    That he was right to so object.
      And I am right,
      And you are right,
    And everything is quite correct !

CHORUS.   And you are right,
      And we are right, etc.

And so we straight let out on bail
A convict from the county jail,
    Whose head was next
      On some pretext
    Condemnëd to be mown off,
And made *him* Headsman, for we said,
" Who's next to be decapited
Cannot cut off another's head
    Until he's cut his own off."

    And we are right, I think you'll say,
    To argue in this kind of way ;
      And I am right,
      And you are right,
    And all is right—too-looral-lay !

CHORUS.   And you are right,
      And we are right, etc.

[*Exeunt* CHORUS.

Enter POOH-BAH.

NANK. Ko-Ko, the cheap tailor, Lord High Executioner of Titipu ! Why, that's the highest rank a citizen can attain !

POOH. It is. Our logical Mikado, seeing no moral difference between the dignified judge who condemns a criminal to die, and the industrious mechanic who carries out the sentence, has rolled the two offices into one, and every judge is now his own executioner.

NANK. But how good of you (for I see that you are a nobleman of the highest rank) to condescend to tell all this to me, a mere strolling minstrel !

POOH. Don't mention it. I am, in point of fact, a particularly haughty and exclusive person, of pre-Adamite ancestral descent. You will understand this when I tell you that I can trace my ancestry back to a protoplasmal primordial atomic globule. Consequently, my family pride is something inconceivable. I can't help it. I was born sneering. But I struggle hard to overcome this defect. I mortify my pride continually. When all the great officers of State resigned in a body, because they were too proud to serve under an ex-tailor, did I not unhesitatingly accept all their posts at once ?

PISH. And the salaries attached to them ? You did.

POOH. It is consequently my degrading duty to serve this upstart as First Lord of the Treasury, Lord Chief Justice, Commander-in-Chief, Lord High Admiral, Master of the Buckhounds, Groom of the Back Stairs, Archbishop of Titipu, and Lord Mayor, both acting and elect, all rolled into one. And at a salary ! A Pooh-Bah paid for his services ! I a salaried minion ! But I do it ! It revolts me, but I do it !

NANK. And it does you credit.

POOH. But I don't stop at that. I go and dine with middle - class people on reasonable terms. I dance at cheap suburban parties for a moderate fee. I accept refreshment at any hands, however lowly. I also retail State secrets at a very low figure. For instance, any

further information about Yum-Yum would come under the head of a State secret. (NANKI-POO *takes the hint, and gives him money*.) (*Aside*.) Another insult, and, I think, a light one !

SONG—POOH-BAH *with* NANKI-POO *and* PISH-TUSH.

Young man, despair,
Likewise go to,
Yum-Yum the fair
You must not woo.
It will not do :
I'm sorry for you,
You very imperfect ablutioner !
This very day
From school Yum-Yum
Will wend her way,
And homeward come,
With beat of drum
And a rum-tum-tum,
To wed the Lord High Executioner !
And the brass will crash,
And the trumpets bray,
And they'll cut a dash
On their wedding day.
She'll toddle away, as all aver,
With the Lord High Executioner !

NANK. *and* POOH.   And the brass will crash, etc.

It's a hopeless case,
As you may see,
And in your place
Away I'd flee ;
But don't blame me—
I'm sorry to be
Of your pleasure a diminutioner.

M

> They'll vow their pact
>   Extremely soon,
> In point of fact
>   This afternoon.
>   Her honeymoon
>   With that buffoon
> At seven commences, so *you* shun her !

ALL.   And the brass will crash, etc.

>   [*Exit* PISH-TUSH.

RECIT.—NANKI-POO *and* POOH-BAH.

NANK.   And I have journeyed for a month, or nearly,
         To learn that Yum-Yum, whom I love so dearly,
         This day to Ko-Ko is to be united !

POOH.   The fact appears to be as you've recited :
         But here he comes, equipped as suits his station ;
         He'll give you any further information.

>   [*Exeunt* POOH-BAH *and* NANKI-POO.

Enter CHORUS OF NOBLES.

> Behold the Lord High Executioner !
>   A personage of noble rank and title—
> A dignified and potent officer,
>   Whose functions are particularly vital !
>   Defer, defer,
>   To the Lord High Executioner !

Enter KO-KO *attended*.

SOLO—KO-KO.

> Taken from the county jail
>   By a set of curious chances ;
> Liberated then on bail,
>   On my own recognizances ;
> Wafted by a favouring gale
>   As one sometimes is in trances,

> To a height that few can scale,
>> Save by long and weary dances ;
> Surely, never had a male
>> Under such like circumstances
> So adventurous a tale,
>> Which may rank with most romances.

CHORUS.   Defer, defer,
>> To the Lord High Executioner, etc.

KO. Gentlemen, I'm much touched by this reception. I can only trust that by strict attention to duty I shall ensure a continuance of those favours which it will ever be my study to deserve. If I should ever be called upon to act professionally, I am happy to think that there will be no difficulty in finding plenty of people whose loss will be a distinct gain to society at large.

SONG—KO-KO *with* CHORUS OF MEN.

As some day it may happen that a victim must be found,
> I've got a little list—I've got a little list
Of society offenders who might well be underground,
> And who never would be missed—who never would be missed !
There's the pestilential nuisances who write for auto-
> graphs—
All people who have flabby hands and irritating laughs—
All children who are up in dates, and floor you with 'em
> flat—
All persons who in shaking hands, shake hands with you
> like *that*—
And all third persons who on spoiling *tête-à-têtes* insist—
> They'd none of 'em be missed—they'd none of 'em be
> missed !

CHORUS.   He's got 'em on the list—he's got 'em on the
>> list ;
>>> And they'll none of 'em be missed—they'll
>>> none of 'em be missed.

There's the nigger serenader, and the others of his race,
    And the piano-organist—I've got him on the list !
And the people who eat peppermint and puff it in your face,
    They never would be missed—they never would be missed !
Then the idiot who praises, with enthusiastic tone,
All centuries but this, and every country but his own ;
And the lady from the provinces, who dresses like a guy,
And who " doesn't think she waltzes, but would rather like to try " ;
And that singular anomaly, the lady novelist—
    I don't think she'd be missed—I'm *sure* she'd not be missed !

CHORUS.   He's got her on the list—he's got her on the list ;
        And I don't think she'll be missed—I'm *sure* she'll not be missed !

And that *Nisi Prius* nuisance, who just now is rather rife,
    The Judicial humorist—I've got *him* on the list !
All funny fellows, comic men, and clowns of private life—
    They'd none of 'em be missed—they'd none of 'em be missed.
And apologetic statesmen of a compromising kind,
Such as—What d'ye call him—Thing'em-bob, and likewise —Never-mind,
And 'St—'st—'st—and What's-his-name, and also You-know-who—
The task of filling up the blanks I'd rather leave to *you*.
But it really doesn't matter whom you put upon the list,
    For they'd none of 'em be missed—they'd none of 'em be missed !

CHORUS.   You may put 'em on the list—you may put 'em on the list ;
        And they'll none of 'em be missed—they'll none of 'em be missed !

Enter POOH-BAH.

KO. Pooh-Bah, it seems that the festivities in connection with my approaching marriage must last a week. I should like to do it handsomely, and I want to consult you as to the amount I ought to spend upon them.

POOH. Certainly. In which of my capacities? As First Lord of the Treasury, Lord Chamberlain, Attorney-General, Chancellor of the Exchequer, Privy Purse, or Private Secretary?

KO. Suppose we say as Private Secretary.

POOH. Speaking as your Private Secretary, I should say that, as the city will have to pay for it, don't stint yourself, do it well.

KO. Exactly—as the city will have to pay for it. That is your advice.

POOH. As Private Secretary. Of course you will understand that, as Chancellor of the Exchequer, I am bound to see that due economy is observed.

KO. Oh! But you said just now " Don't stint yourself, do it well ".

POOH. As Private Secretary.

KO. And now you say that due economy must be observed.

POOH. As Chancellor of the Exchequer.

KO. I see. Come over here, where the Chancellor can't hear us. (*They cross the stage.*) Now, as my Solicitor, how do you advise me to deal with this difficulty?

POOH. Oh, as your Solicitor, I should have no hesitation in saying " Chance it——"

KO. Thank you. (*Shaking his hand.*) I will.

POOH. If it were not that, as Lord Chief Justice, I am bound to see that the law isn't violated.

KO. I see. Come over here where the Chief Justice can't hear us. (*They cross the stage.*) Now, then, as First Lord of the Treasury?

POOH. Of course, as First Lord of the Treasury, I could propose a special vote that would cover all expenses,

if it were not that, as Leader of the Opposition, it would be my duty to resist it, tooth and nail. Or, as Paymaster-General, I could so cook the accounts that, as Lord High Auditor, I should never discover the fraud. But then, as Archbishop of Titipu, it would be my duty to denounce my dishonesty and give myself into my own custody as First Commissioner of Police.

Ko. That's extremely awkward.

Pooh. I don't say that all these distinguished people couldn't be squared ; but it is right to tell you that they wouldn't be sufficiently degraded in their own estimation unless they were insulted with a very considerable bribe.

Ko. The matter shall have my careful consideration. But my bride and her sisters approach, and any little compliment on your part, such as an abject grovel in a characteristic Japanese attitude, would be esteemed a favour.   [*Exeunt together.*

Enter procession of Yum-Yum's *schoolfellows, heralding* Yum-Yum, Peep-Bo, *and* Pitti-Sing.

Chorus of Girls.

Comes a train of little ladies
　　From scholastic trammels free,
Each a little bit afraid is,
　　Wondering what the world can be !

Is it but a world of trouble—
　　Sadness set to song ?
Is its beauty but a bubble
　　Bound to break ere long ?

Are its palaces and pleasures
　　Fantasies that fade ?
And the glory of its treasures
　　Shadow of a shade ?

Schoolgirls we, eighteen and under,
From scholastic trammels free,
And we wonder—how we wonder!—
What on earth the world can be!

TRIO.

Yum-Yum, Peep-Bo, *and* Pitti-Sing,
with Chorus of Girls.

The Three. Three little maids from school are we,
 Pert as a school-girl well can be,
 Filled to the brim with girlish glee,
  Three little maids from school!

Yum-Yum. Everything is a source of fun. (*Chuckle.*)
Peep-Bo. Nobody's safe, for we care for none!
 (*Chuckle.*)
Pitti-Sing. Life is a joke that's just begun! (*Chuckle.*)
The Three.   Three little maids from school!
All (*dancing*). Three little maids who, all unwary,
 Come from a ladies' seminary,
 Freed from its genius tutelary—
The Three (*suddenly demure*). Three little maids from
  school!

Yum-Yum. One little maid is a bride, Yum-Yum—
Peep-Bo. Two little maids in attendance come—
Pitti-Sing. Three little maids is the total sum.
The Three.   Three little maids from school!
Yum-Yum. From three little maids take one away.
Peep-Bo. Two little maids remain, and they—
Pitti-Sing. Won't have to wait very long, they say—
The Three.   Three little maids from school!
All (*dancing*). Three little maids who, all unwary,
 Come from a ladies' seminary,
 Freed from its genius tutelary—
The Three (*suddenly demure*). Three little maids from
  school!

Enter Ko-Ko *and* Pooh-Bah.

Ko.   At last, my bride that is to be ! (*About to embrace her.*)

Yum.   You're not going to kiss me before all these people ?

Ko.   Well, that was the idea.

Yum (*aside to* Peep-Bo).   It seems odd, doesn't it ?

Peep.   It's rather peculiar.

Pitti.   Oh, I expect it's all right.   Must have a beginning, you know.

Yum.   Well, of course I know nothing about these things ; but I've no objection if it's usual.

Ko.   Oh, it's quite usual, I think.   Eh, Lord Chamberlain ?   (*Appealing to* Pooh-Bah.)

Pooh.   I have known it done.   (Ko-Ko *embraces her.*)

Yum.   Thank goodness that's over ! (*Sees* Nanki-Poo, *and rushes to him.*)   Why, that's never you ?   (*The Three Girls rush to him and shake his hands, all speaking at once.*)

Yum.   Oh, I'm so glad !   I haven't seen you for ever so long, and I'm right at the top of the school, and I've got three prizes, and I've come home for good, and I'm not going back any more !

Peep.   And have you got an engagement ?—Yum-Yum's got one, but she doesn't like it, and she'd ever so much rather it was you !   I've come home for good, and I'm not going back any more !

Pitti.   Now tell us all the news, because you go about everywhere, and we've been at school, but, thank goodness, that's all over now, and we've come home for good, and we're not going back any more !

(*These three speeches are spoken together in one breath.*)

Ko.   I beg your pardon.   Will you present me ?

Yum.   ⎧ Oh, this is the musician who used—

Peep.   ⎨ Oh, this is the gentleman who used—

Pitti.   ⎩ Oh, it is only Nanki-Poo who used—

Ko.   One at a time, if you please.

Yum.   Oh, if you please he's the gentleman who used to play so beautifully on the—on the——

PITTI. On the Marine Parade.

YUM. Yes, I think that was the name of the instrument.

NANK. Sir, I have the misfortune to love your ward, Yum-Yum—oh, I know I deserve your anger!

KO. Anger! not a bit, my boy. Why, I love her myself. Charming little girl, isn't she? Pretty eyes, nice hair. Taking little thing, altogether. Very glad to hear my opinion backed by a competent authority. Thank you very much. Good-bye. (*To* PISH-TUSH.) Take him away. (PISH-TUSH *removes him.*)

PITTI (*who has been examining* POOH-BAH). I beg your pardon, but what is this? Customer come to try on?

KO. That is a Tremendous Swell.

PITTI. Oh, it's alive. (*She starts back in alarm.*)

POOH. Go away, little girls. Can't talk to little girls like you. Go away, there's dears.

KO. Allow me to present you, Pooh-Bah. These are my three wards. The one in the middle is my bride elect.

POOH. What do you want me to do to them? Mind, I *will not* kiss them.

KO. No, no, you shan't kiss them; a little bow—a mere nothing—you needn't mean it, you know.

POOH. It goes against the grain. They are not young ladies, they are young persons.

KO. Come, come, make an effort, there's a good nobleman.

POOH. (*aside to* KO-KO). Well, I shan't mean it. (*With a great effort.*) How de do, little girls, how de do? (*Aside.*) Oh, my protoplasmal ancestor!

KO. That's very good. (*Girls indulge in suppressed laughter.*)

POOH. I see nothing to laugh at. It is very painful to me to have to say "How de do, little girls, how de do?" to young persons. I'm not in the habit of saying "How de do, little girls, how de do?" to anybody under the rank of a Stockbroker.

KO. (*aside to girls*). Don't laugh at him, he can't help it—he's under treatment for it. (*Aside to* POOH-BAH.)

M 2

Never mind them, they don't understand the delicacy of your position.

POOH.   We know how delicate it is, don't we ?

KO.   I should think we did ! How a nobleman of your importance can do it at all is a thing I never can, never shall understand.   [KO-KO *retires up and goes off.*

QUARTET AND CHORUS OF GIRLS.
YUM-YUM, PEEP-BO, PITTI-SING, *and* POOH-BAH.

YUM., PEEP.   So please you, Sir, we much regret
and PITTI.   If we have failed in etiquette
            Towards a man of rank so high—
            We shall know better by and by.

YUM.   But youth, of course, must have its fling,
                So pardon us,
                So pardon us,

PITTI.   And don't, in girlhood's happy spring,
                Be hard on us,
                Be hard on us,
            If we're inclined to dance and sing.
                Tra la la, etc. (*Dancing.*)

CHORUS OF GIRLS.   But youth, of course, etc.

POOH.   I think you ought to recollect
            You cannot show too much respect
            Towards the highly titled few ;
            But nobody does, and why should you ?
            That youth at us should have its fling,
                Is hard on us,
                Is hard on us ;
            To our prerogative we cling—
                So pardon us,
                So pardon us,
            If we decline to dance and sing.
                Tra la la, etc. (*Dancing.*)

CHORUS OF GIRLS.   But youth, of course, must have its
                fling, etc.
                        [*Exeunt all but* YUM-YUM.

Enter NANKI-POO.

NANK. Yum-Yum, at last we are alone! I have sought you night and day for three weeks, in the belief that your guardian was beheaded, and I find that you are about to be married to him this afternoon!

YUM. Alas, yes!

NANK. But you do not love him?

YUM. Alas, no!

NANK. Modified rapture! But why do you not refuse him?

YUM. What good would that do? He's my guardian, and he wouldn't let me marry you!

NANK. But I would wait until you were of age!

YUM. You forget that in Japan girls do not arrive at years of discretion until they are fifty.

NANK. True; from seventeen to forty-nine are considered years of indiscretion.

YUM. Besides—a wandering minstrel, who plays a wind instrument outside tea-houses, is hardly a fitting husband for the ward of a Lord High Executioner.

NANK. But—— (*Aside*.) Shall I tell her? Yes! She will not betray me! (*Aloud*.) What if it should prove that, after all, I am no musician?

YUM. There! I was certain of it, directly I heard you play!

NANK. What if it should prove that I am no other than the son of his Majesty the Mikado?

YUM. The son of the Mikado! But why is your Highness disguised? And what has your Highness done? And will your Highness promise never to do it again?

NANK. Some years ago I had the misfortune to captivate Katisha, an elderly lady of my father's Court. She misconstrued my customary affability into expressions of affection, and claimed me in marriage, under my father's law. My father, the Lucius Junius Brutus of his race, ordered me to marry her within a week, or perish ignominiously on the scaffold. That night I fled his Court, and, assuming the disguise of a Second Trombone, I

joined the band in which you found me when I had the happiness of seeing you ! (*Approaching her.*)

YUM (*retreating*). If you please, I think your Highness had better not come too near. The laws against flirting are excessively severe.

NANK. But we are quite alone, and nobody can see us.

YUM. Still, that doesn't make it right. To flirt is capital.

NANK. It *is* capital !

YUM. And we must obey the law.

NANK. Deuce take the law !

YUM. I wish it would, but it won't !

NANK. If it were not for that, how happy we might be !

YUM. Happy indeed !

NANK. If it were not for the law, we should now be sitting side by side, like that. (*Sits by her.*)

YUM. Instead of being obliged to sit half a mile off, like that. (*Crosses and sits at other side of stage.*)

NANK. We should be gazing into each other's eyes, like that. (*Gazing at her sentimentally.*)

YUM. Breathing sighs of unutterable love—like that. (*Sighing and gazing lovingly at him.*)

NANK. With our arms round each other's waists, like that. (*Embracing her.*)

YUM. Yes, if it wasn't for the law.

NANK. If it wasn't for the law.

YUM. As it is, of course we couldn't do anything of the kind.

NANK. Not for worlds !

YUM. Being engaged to Ko-Ko, you know !

NANK. Being engaged to Ko-Ko !

DUET—YUM-YUM *and* NANKI-POO.

NANK.　　Were you not to Ko-Ko plighted,
　　　　　　I would say in tender tone,
　　　　　" Loved one, let us be united—
　　　　　　Let us be each other's own ! "

I would merge all rank and station,
 Worldly sneers are nought to us,
And, to mark my admiration,
 I would kiss you fondly thus— (*Kisses her.*)

BOTH. $\left.\begin{array}{l}\text{I}\\\text{He}\end{array}\right\}$ would kiss $\left\{\begin{array}{l}\text{you}\\\text{me}\end{array}\right\}$ fondly thus— (*Kiss.*)

YUM. But as I'm engaged to Ko-Ko,
 To embrace you thus, *con fuoco*,
 Would distinctly be no *giuoco*,
And for jam I should get toko—

BOTH. Toko, toko, toko, toko!

NANK. So, in spite of all temptation,
 Such a theme I'll not discuss,
And on no consideration
 Will I kiss you fondly thus— (*Kissing her.*)
Let me make it clear to you,
This is what I'll never do!
 This, oh, this, oh, this, oh, this— (*Kissing her.*)

TOGETHER. This, oh, this, etc.

       [*Exeunt in opposite directions.*

Enter KO-KO.

Ko. (*looking after* YUM-YUM). There she goes! To think how entirely my future happiness is wrapped up in that little parcel! Really, it hardly seems worth while! Oh, matrimony!— (*Enter* POOH-BAH *and* PISH-TUSH.) Now then, what is it? Can't you see I'm soliloquizing? You have interrupted an apostrophe, sir!

PISH. I am the bearer of a letter from his Majesty the Mikado.

Ko. (*taking it from him reverentially*). A letter from the Mikado! What in the world can he have to say to me? (*Reads letter.*) Ah, here it is at last! I thought it would come sooner or later! The Mikado is struck by the fact that no executions have taken place in Titipu

for a year, and decrees that unless somebody is beheaded within one month the post of Lord High Executioner shall be abolished, and the city reduced to the rank of a village !

PISH. But that will involve us all in irretrievable ruin !

Ko. Yes. There is no help for it, I shall have to execute somebody at once. The only question is, who shall it be ?

POOH. Well, it seems unkind to say so, but as you're already under sentence of death for flirting, everything seems to point to *you*.

Ko. To me ? What are you talking about ? I can't execute myself.

POOH. Why not ?

Ko. Why not ? Because, in the first place, self-decapitation is an extremely difficult, not to say dangerous, thing to attempt ; and, in the second, it's suicide, and suicide is a capital offence.

POOH. That is so, no doubt.

PISH. We might reserve that point.

POOH. True, it could be argued six months hence, before the full Court.

Ko. Besides, I don't see how a man *can* cut off his own head.

POOH. A man might try.

PISH. Even if you only succeeded in cutting it half off, that would be something.

POOH. It would be taken as an earnest of your desire to comply with the Imperial will.

Ko. No. Pardon me, but there I am adamant. As official Headsman, my reputation is at stake, and I can't consent to embark on a professional operation unless I see my way to a successful result.

POOH. This professional conscientiousness is highly creditable to *you*, but it places us in a very awkward position.

Ko. My good sir, the awkwardness of your position

is grace itself compared with that of a man engaged in the act of cutting off his own head.

Pish. I am afraid that, unless you can obtain a substitute——

Ko. A substitute ? Oh, certainly—nothing easier. (*To* Pooh-Bah.) Pooh-Bah, I appoint you Lord High Substitute.

Pooh. I should be delighted. Such an appointment would realize my fondest dreams. But no, at any sacrifice. I must set bounds to my insatiable ambition !

TRIO.

Kŏ-Kŏ.	Pooh-Bah.	Pish-Tush.
My brain it teems	I am so proud,	I heard one day
With endless schemes	If I allowed	A gentleman say
Both good and new	My family pride	That criminals who
For Titipu ;	To be my guide,	Are cut in two
But if I flit,	I'd volunteer	Can hardly feel
The benefit	To quit this sphere	The fatal steel,
That I'd diffuse	Instead of you,	And so are slain
The town would lose !	In a minute or two.	Without much pain.
Now every man	But family pride	If this is true,
To aid his clan	Must be denied,	It's jolly for you ;
Should plot and plan	And set aside,	Your courage screw
As best he can,	And mortified.	To bid us adieu,
And so,	And so,	And go
Although	Although	And show
I'm ready to go,	I wish to go,	Both friend and foe
Yet recollect	And greatly pine	How much you dare.
'Twere disrespect	To brightly shine,	I'm quite aware
Did I neglect	And take the line	It's your affair,
To thus effect	Of a hero fine,	Yet I declare
This aim direct,	With grief condign	I'd take your share,
So I object—	I must decline—	But I don't much care—
So I object—	I must decline—	I don't much care—
So I object—	I must decline—	I don't much care—

All. To sit in solemn silence in a dull, dark dock,
　　　In a pestilential prison, with a life-long lock,
　　　Awaiting the sensation of a short, sharp shock,
　　　From a cheap and chippy chopper on a big black
　　　　　block ! [*Exeunt* Pooh. *and* Pish.

Ko. This is simply appalling ! I, who allowed myself to be respited at the last moment, simply in order to benefit my native town, am now required to die within a month, and that by a man whom I have loaded with honours ! Is this public gratitude ? Is this—— (*Enter* NANKI-POO, *with a rope in his hands.*) Go away, sir ! How dare you ? Am I never to be permitted to soliloquize ?

NANK. Oh, go on—don't mind me.

Ko. What are you going to do with that rope ?

NANK. I am about to terminate an unendurable existence.

Ko. Terminate your existence ? Oh, nonsense ! What for ?

NANK. Because you are going to marry the girl I adore.

Ko. Nonsense, sir. I won't permit it. I am a humane man, and if you attempt anything of the kind I shall order your instant arrest. Come, sir, desist at once, or I summon my guard.

NANK. That's absurd. If you attempt to raise an alarm, I instantly perform the Happy Despatch with this dagger.

Ko. No, no, don't do that. This is horrible ! (*Suddenly.*) Why, you cold-blooded scoundrel, are you aware that, in taking your life, you are committing a crime which—which—which is—— Oh ! (*Struck by an idea.*) Substitute !

NANK. What's the matter ?

Ko. Is it *absolutely certain* that you are resolved to die ?

NANK. Absolutely !

Ko. Will *nothing* shake your resolution ?

NANK. Nothing.

Ko. Threats, entreaties, prayers—all useless ?

NANK. All ! My mind is made up.

Ko. Then, if you really mean what you say, and if you are absolutely resolved to die, and if nothing whatever will shake your determination—don't spoil yourself by

committing suicide, but be beheaded handsomely at the hands of the Public Executioner !

NANK.   I don't see how that would benefit me.

KO.   You don't ?   Observe :   you'll have a month to live, and you'll live like a fighting-cock at my expense. When the day comes there'll be a grand public ceremonial —you'll be the central figure—no one will attempt to deprive you of that distinction.   There'll be a procession— bands—dead march—bells tolling—all the girls in tears— Yum-Yum distracted—then, when it's all over, general rejoicings, and a display of fireworks in the evening.   *You* won't see them, but they'll be there all the same.

NANK.   Do you think Yum-Yum would really be distracted at my death ?

KO.   I am convinced of it.   Bless you, she's the most tender-hearted little creature alive.

NANK.   I should be sorry to cause her pain.   Perhaps, after all, if I were to withdraw from Japan, and travel in Europe for a couple of years, I might contrive to forget her.

KO.   Oh, I don't think you could forget Yum-Yum so easily ; and, after all, what is more miserable than a love-blighted life ?

NANK.   True.

KO.   Life without Yum-Yum—why, it seems absurd !

NANK.   And yet there are a good many people in the world who have to endure it.

KO.   Poor devils, yes !   You are quite right not to be of their number.

NANK. (*suddenly*).   I *won't* be of their number !

KO.   Noble fellow !

NANK.   I'll tell you how we'll manage it.   Let me marry Yum-Yum to-morrow, and in a month you may behead me.

KO.   No, no.   I draw the line at Yum-Yum.

NANK.   Very good.   If you can draw the line, so can I. (*Preparing rope.*)

KO.   Stop, stop—listen one moment—be reasonable.

How can I consent to your marrying Yum-Yum if I'm going to marry her myself?

NANK. My good friend, she'll be a widow in a month, and you can marry her then.

KO. That's true, of course. I quite see that. But, dear me! my position during the next month will be most unpleasant—most unpleasant.

NANK. Not half so unpleasant as my position at the end of it.

KO. But—dear me!—well—I agree—after all, it's only putting off my wedding for a month. But you won't prejudice her against me, will you? You see, I've educated her to be my wife; she's been taught to regard me as a wise and good man. Now I shouldn't like her views on that point disturbed.

NANK. Trust me, she shall never learn the truth from me.

FINALE.

Enter CHORUS, POOH-BAH, *and* PISH-TUSH.

CHORUS.

With aspect stern
And gloomy stride,
We come to learn
How you decide.

Don't hesitate
Your choice to name,
A dreadful fate
You'll suffer all the same.

POOH. To ask you what you mean to do we punctually appear.

KO. Congratulate me, gentlemen, I've found a Volunteer!

ALL. The Japanese equivalent for Hear, Hear, Hear!

Ko. (*presenting him*).   'Tis Nanki-Poo !
ALL.   Hail, Nanki-Poo !
Ko.   I think he'll do ?
ALL.   Yes, yes, he'll do !

Ko.   He yields his life if I'll Yum-Yum surrender.
      Now I adore that girl with passion tender,
      And could not yield her with a ready will,
                  Or her allot,
            If I did not
      Adore myself with passion tenderer still !

      Enter YUM-YUM, PEEP-BO, *and* PITTI-SING.

ALL.   Ah, yes !
      He loves himself with passion tenderer still !
Ko. (*to* NANKI-POO).   Take her—she's yours !
                                      [*Exit* KO-KO.

ENSEMBLE.

NANKI-POO. The threatened cloud has passed away,
YUM-YUM.   And brightly shines the dawning day ;
NANKI-POO. What though the night may come too soon,
YUM-YUM.   There's yet a month of afternoon !

      NANKI-POO, POOH-BAH, YUM-YUM, PITTI-SING,
                  and PEEP-BO.

            Then let the throng
            Our joy advance,
            With laughing song
            And merry dance,

CHORUS.   With joyous shout and ringing cheer,
           Inaugurate our brief career !

PITTI-SING. A day, a week, a month, a year——
YUM.   Or far or near, or far or near,
POOH.   Life's eventime comes much too soon,
PITTI-SING. You'll live at least a honeymoon !

ALL.   Then let the throng, etc.

CHORUS.   With joyous shout, etc.

SOLO—POOH-BAH.

As in a month you've got to die,
   If Ko-Ko tells us true,
'Twere empty compliment to cry
   " Long life to Nanki-Poo ! "
But as one month you have to live
   As fellow-citizen,
This toast with three times three we'll give—
   " Long life to you—till then ! "

                                [*Exit* POOH-BAH.

CHORUS.   May all good fortune prosper you,
                 May you have health and riches too,
                 May you succeed in all you do !
                    Long life to you—till then !

(*Dance.*)

Enter KATISHA *melodramatically.*

KAT.   Your revels cease !   Assist me, all of you !
CHORUS.   Why, who is this whose evil eyes
             Rain blight on our festivities ?
KAT.   I claim my perjured lover, Nanki-Poo !
       Oh, fool ! to shun delights that never cloy !
CHORUS. Go, leave thy deadly work undone !
KAT.   Come back, oh, shallow fool ! come back to joy !
CHORUS. Away, away ! ill-favoured one !
NANK. (*aside to* YUM-YUM).   Ah !
       'Tis Katisha !
       The maid of whom I told you. (*About to go.*)
KAT. (*detaining him*).   No !
       You shall not go,
       These arms shall thus enfold you !

SONG—KATISHA.

KAT. (*addressing* NANKI-POO).
Oh fool, that fleest
My hallowed joys !
Oh blind, that seest
No equipoise !
Oh rash, that judgest
From half, the whole !
Oh base, that grudgest
Love's lightest dole !
Thy heart unbind,
Oh fool, oh blind !
Give me my place,
Oh rash, oh base !

CHORUS.   If she's thy bride, restore her place,
Oh fool, oh blind, oh rash, oh base !

KAT. (*addressing* YUM-YUM).
Pink cheek, that rulest
Where wisdom serves !
Bright eye, that foolest
Heroic nerves !
Rose lip, that scornest
Lore-laden years !
Smooth tongue, that warnest
Who rightly hears !
Thy doom is nigh,
Pink cheek, bright eye !
Thy knell is rung,
Rose lip, smooth tongue !

CHORUS.   If true her tale, thy knell is rung,
Pink cheek, bright eye, rose lip, smooth tongue !

PITTI-SING.   Away, nor prosecute your quest—
From our intention, well expressed,
You cannot turn us !

The state of your connubial views
Towards the person you accuse
Does not concern us !
For he's going to marry Yum-Yum—

ALL.   Yum-Yum !
PITTI.   Your anger pray bury,
For all will be merry,
I think you had better succumb—

ALL.   Cumb—cumb !
PITTI.   And join our expressions of glee.
On this subject I pray you be dumb—

ALL.   Dumb—dumb.
PITTI.   You'll find there are many
Who'll wed for a penny—
The word for your guidance is " Mum "—

ALL.   Mum—mum !
PITTI.   There's lots of good fish in the sea !

ALL.   On this subject we pray you be dumb, etc.

SOLO—KATISHA.

The hour of gladness
Is dead and gone ;
In silent sadness
I live alone !
The hope I cherished
All lifeless lies,
And all has perished
Save love, which never dies !
Oh, faithless one, this insult you shall rue !
In vain for mercy on your knees you'll sue.
I'll tear the mask from your disguising !

NANK. (*aside*).   Now comes the blow !
KAT.   Prepare yourselves for new surprising !
NANK. (*aside*).   How foil my foe ?
KAT.   No minstrel he, despite bravado !
YUM. (*aside, struck by an idea*).   Ha ! ha ! I know !
KAT.   He is the son of your——

(NANKI-POO, YUM-YUM, *and* CHORUS, *interrupting,*
sing Japanese words, to drown her voice.)

O ni ! bikkuri shakkuri to !

KAT.   In vain you interrupt with this tornado !
He is the only son of your——

ALL.   O ni ! bikkuri shakkuri to !

KAT.   I'll spoil——

ALL.   O ni ! bikkuri shakkuri to !

KAT.   Your gay gambado !
He is the son——

ALL.   O ni ! bikkuri shakkuri to !

KAT.   Of your——

ALL.   O ni ! bikkuri shakkuri to !

KAT.   The son of your——

ALL.   O ni ! bikkuri shakkuri to ! oya ! oya !

ENSEMBLE.

KATISHA.	THE OTHERS.
Ye torrents roar !	We'll hear no more,
Ye tempests howl !	Ill-omened owl,
Your wrath outpour	To joy we soar,
With angry growl !	Despite your scowl !
Do ye your worst, my vengeance call	The echoes of our festival
Shall rise triumphant over all !	Shall rise triumphant over all !
Prepare for woe,	Away you go,
Ye haughty lords,	Collect your hordes ;
At once I go	Proclaim your woe
Mikado-wards,	In dismal chords ;
My wrongs with vengeance shall be crowned !	We do not heed their dismal sound,
My wrongs with vengeance shall be crowned !	For joy reigns everywhere around.

(KATISHA *rushes furiously up stage, clearing the crowd
away right and left, finishing on steps at the back
of stage.*)

END OF ACT I.

ACT II.

SCENE.—KO-KO's *Garden.*

YUM-YUM *discovered seated at her bridal toilet, surrounded by maidens, who are dressing her hair and painting her face and lips, as she judges of the effect in a mirror.*

SOLO—PITTI-SING *and* CHORUS OF GIRLS.

CHORUS.

Braid the raven hair—
Weave the supple tress—
Deck the maiden fair
In her loveliness—
Paint the pretty face—
Dye the coral lip—
Emphasize the grace
Of her ladyship !
Art and nature, thus allied,
Go to make a pretty bride.

SOLO—PITTI-SING.

Sit with downcast eye—
Let it brim with dew—
Try if you can cry—
We will do so, too.

344

When you're summoned, start
  Like a frightened roe—
Flutter, little heart,
  Colour, come and go !
Modesty at marriage-tide
Well becomes a pretty bride !

CHORUS.
Braid the raven hair, etc.

[*Exeunt* PITTI-SING, PEEP-BO, *and* CHORUS.

YUM. Yes, I am indeed beautiful ! Sometimes I sit and wonder, in my artless Japanese way, why it is that I am so much more attractive than anybody else in the whole world. Can this be vanity ? No ! Nature is lovely and rejoices in her loveliness. I am a child of Nature, and take after my mother.

SONG—YUM-YUM.

The sun, whose rays
Are all ablaze
  With ever-living glory,
Does not deny
His majesty—
  He scorns to tell a story !
He don't exclaim,
  " I blush for shame,
  So kindly be indulgent."
But, fierce and bold,
In fiery gold,
  He glories all effulgent !

I mean to rule the earth,
  As he the sky—
We really know our worth,
  The sun and I !

Observe his flame,
That placid dame,
　The moon's Celestial Highness ;
There's not a trace
Upon her face
　Of diffidence or shyness :
She borrows light
That, through the night,
　Mankind may all acclaim her !
And, truth to tell,
She lights up well,
　So I, for one, don't blame her !

　　Ah, pray make no mistake,
　　　We are not shy ;
　　We're very wide awake,
　　　The moon and I !

Enter PITTI-SING *and* PEEP-BO.

YUM.　Yes, everything seems to smile upon me.　I am to be married to-day to the man I love best, and I believe I am the very happiest girl in Japan !

PEEP.　The happiest girl indeed, for she is indeed to be envied who has attained happiness in all but perfection.

YUM.　In " all but " perfection ?

PEEP.　Well, dear, it can't be denied that the fact that your husband is to be beheaded in a month is, in its way, a drawback.　It does seem to take the top off it, you know.

PITTI.　I don't know about that.　It all depends !

PEEP.　At all events, *he* will find it a drawback.

PITTI.　Not necessarily.　Bless you, it all depends !

YUM. (*in tears*).　I think it very indelicate of you to refer to such a subject on such a day.　If my married happiness *is* to be—to be——

PEEP.　Cut short.

YUM.   Well, cut short—in a month, can't you let me forget it ?   (*Weeping*.)

Enter NANKI-POO, *followed by* PISH-TUSH.

NANK.   Yum-Yum in tears—and on her wedding morn !

YUM. (*sobbing*).   They've been reminding me that in a month you're to be beheaded !   (*Bursts into tears*.)

PITTI.   Yes, we've been reminding her that you're to be beheaded.   (*Bursts into tears*.)

PEEP.   It's quite true, you know, you *are* to be beheaded !   (*Bursts into tears*.)

NANK. (*aside*).   Humph !   Now, some bridegrooms would be depressed by this sort of thing !   (*Aloud*.) A month ?   Well, what's a month ?   Bah !   These divisions of time are purely arbitrary.   Who says twenty-four hours make a day ?

PITTI.   There's a popular impression to that effect.

NANK.   Then we'll efface it.   We'll call each second a minute—each minute an hour—each hour a day—and each day a year.   At that rate we've about thirty years of married happiness before us !

PEEP.   And, at that rate, this interview has already lasted four hours and three-quarters !

[*Exit* PEEP-BO.

YUM. (*still sobbing*).   Yes.   How time flies when one is thoroughly enjoying oneself !

NANK.   That's the way to look at it !   Don't let's be downhearted !   There's a silver lining to every cloud.

YUM.   Certainly.   Let's — let's be perfectly happy ! (*Almost in tears*.)

GO-TO.   By all means.   Let's—let's thoroughly enjoy ourselves.

PITTI.   It's—it's absurd to cry !   (*Trying to force a laugh*.)

YUM.   Quite ridiculous !   (*Trying to laugh*.)

(*All break into a forced and melancholy laugh*.)

MADRIGAL.

YUM-YUM, PITTI-SING, NANKI-POO, *and* PISH-TUSH.

Brightly dawns our wedding day ;
  Joyous hour, we give thee greeting !
  Whither, whither art thou fleeting ?
Fickle moment, prithee stay !
  What though mortal joys be hollow ?
  Pleasures come, if sorrows follow :
Though the tocsin sound, ere long,
  Ding dong !   Ding dong !
Yet until the shadows fall
Over one and over all,
Sing a merry madrigal—
          A madrigal !

Fal-la—fal-la ! etc.   (*Ending in tears.*)

Let us dry the ready tear,
  Though the hours are surely creeping
  Little need for woeful weeping,
Till the sad sundown is near.
  All must sip the cup of sorrow—
  I to-day and thou to-morrow ;
This the close of every song—
  Ding dong !   Ding dong !
What, though solemn shadows fall,
Sooner, later, over all ?
Sing a merry madrigal—
          A madrigal !

Fal-la—fal-la ! etc.   (*Ending in tears.*)

[*Exeunt* PITTI-SING *and* PISH-TUSH.

(NANKI-POO *embraces* YUM-YUM.   *Enter* KO-KO.
NANKI-POO *releases* YUM-YUM.)

KO.   Go on—don't mind me.
NANK.   I'm afraid we're distressing you.
KO.   Never mind, I must get used to it.   Only please

do it by degrees. Begin by putting your arm round her waist. (NANKI-POO *does so*.) There; let me get used to that first.

YUM. Oh, wouldn't you like to retire? It must pain you to see us so affectionate together!

KO. No, I must learn to bear it! Now oblige me by allowing her head to rest on your shoulder.

NANK. Like that? (*He does so*. KO-KO *much affected*.)

KO. I am much obliged to you. Now—kiss her! (*He does so*. KO-KO *writhes with anguish*.) Thank you—it's simple torture!

YUM. Come, come, bear up. After all, it's only for a month.

KO. No. It's no use deluding oneself with false hopes.

NANK.
YUM.   } What do you mean?

KO. (*to* YUM-YUM). My child—my poor child! (*Aside*.) How shall I break it to her? (*Aloud*.) My little bride that was to have been——

YUM. (*delighted*). *Was* to have been?

KO. Yes, you never can be mine!

NANK.
YUM.   } (*in ecstasy*). { What!
                              { I'm so glad!

KO. I've just ascertained that, by the Mikado's law, when a married man is beheaded his wife is buried alive.

NANK.
YUM.   } Buried alive!

KO. Buried alive. It's a most unpleasant death.

NANK. But whom did you get that from?

KO. Oh, from Pooh-Bah. He's my Solicitor.

YUM. But he may be mistaken!

KO. So I thought; so I consulted the Attorney-General, the Lord Chief Justice, the Master of the Rolls, the Judge Ordinary, and the Lord Chancellor. They're all of the same opinion. Never knew such unanimity on a point of law in my life!

Nank. But stop a bit! This law has never been put in force.

Ko. Not yet. You see, flirting is the only crime punishable with decapitation, and married men never flirt.

Nank. Of course, they don't. I quite forgot that! Well, I suppose I may take it that my dream of happiness is at an end!

Yum. Darling—I don't want to appear selfish, and I love you with all my heart——I don't suppose I shall ever love anybody else half as much—but when I agreed to marry you—my own—I had no idea—pet—that I should have to be buried alive in a month!

Nank. Nor I! It's the very first I've heard of it!

Yum. It—it makes a difference, doesn't it?

Nank. It *does* make a difference, of course.

Yum. You see—burial alive—it's such a stuffy death!

Nank. I call it a beast of a death.

Yum. You see my difficulty, don't you?

Nank. Yes, and I see my own. If I insist on your carrying out your promise, I doom you to a hideous death; if I release you, you marry Ko-Ko at once!

TRIO.—Yum-Yum, Nanki-Poo, *and* Ko-Ko.

Yum.   Here's a how-de-do!
         If I marry you,
      When your time has come to perish,
      Then the maiden whom you cherish
         Must be slaughtered, too!
         Here's a how-de-do!

Nank.   Here's a pretty mess!
         In a month, or less,
      I must die without a wedding!
      Let the bitter tears I'm shedding
         Witness my distress,
         Here's a pretty mess!

Ko.
> Here's a state of things !
> To her life she clings !
> Matrimonial devotion
> Doesn't seem to suit her notion—
> Burial it brings !
> Here's a state of things !

ENSEMBLE.

Yum-Yum *and* Nanki-Poo.	Ko-Ko.
With a passion that's intense I worship and adore, But the laws of common sense We oughtn't to ignore. If what he says is true, 'Tis death to marry you ! Here's a pretty state of things ! Here's a pretty how-de-do !	With a passion that's intense You worship and adore, But the laws of common sense You oughtn't to ignore. If what I say is true, 'Tis death to marry you ! Here's a pretty state of things ! Here's a pretty how-de-do !

[*Exit* Yum-Yum.

Ko. (*going up to* Nanki-Poo). My poor boy, I'm really very sorry for you.

Nank. Thanks, old fellow. I'm sure you are.

Ko. You see I'm quite helpless.

Nank. I quite see that.

Ko. I can't conceive anything more distressing than to have one's marriage broken off at the last moment. But you shan't be disappointed of a wedding—you shall come to mine.

Nank. It's awfully kind of you, but that's impossible.

Ko. Why so ?

Nank. To-day I die.

Ko. What do you mean ?

Nank. I can't live without Yum-Yum. This afternoon I perform the Happy Despatch.

Ko. No, no—pardon me—I can't allow that.

Nank. Why not ?

Ko. Why, hang it all, you're under contract to die

by the hand of the Public Executioner in a month's time !
If you kill yourself, what's to become of me ? Why, I
shall have to be executed in your place !

NANK.   It would certainly seem so !

Enter POOH-BAH.

KO.   Now then, Lord Mayor, what is it ?

POOH.   The Mikado and his suite are approaching
the city, and will be here in ten minutes.

KO.   The Mikado ! He's coming to see whether his
orders have been carried out ! (*To* NANKI-POO.) Now
look here, you know—this is getting serious—a bargain's
a bargain, and you really mustn't frustrate the ends of
justice by committing suicide. As a man of honour and
a gentleman, you are bound to die ignominiously by the
hands of the Public Executioner.

NANK.   Very well, then—behead me.

KO.   What, now ?

NANK.   Certainly ; at once.

POOH.   Chop it off ! Chop it off !

KO.   My good sir, I don't go about prepared to
execute gentlemen at a moment's notice. Why, I never
even killed a blue-bottle !

POOH.   Still, as Lord High Executioner——

KO.   My good sir, as Lord High Executioner, I've
got to behead him in a month. I'm not ready yet. I
don't know how it's done. I'm going to take lessons.
I mean to begin with a guinea pig, and work my way
through the animal kingdom till I come to a Second
Trombone. Why, you don't suppose that, as a humane
man, I'd have accepted the post of Lord High Executioner
if I hadn't thought the duties were purely nominal ?
I *can't* kill you—I can't kill anything ! I can't kill
anybody ! (*Weeps*.)

NANK.   Come, my poor fellow, we all have unpleasant
duties to discharge at times ; after all, what is it ? If
I don't mind, why should you ? Remember, sooner or
later it must be done.

Ko. (*springing up suddenly*). *Must it?* I'm not so sure about that!

Nank. What do you mean?

Ko. Why should I kill you when making an affidavit that you've been executed will do just as well? Here are plenty of witnesses—the Lord Chief Justice, Lord High Admiral, Commander-in-Chief, Secretary of State for the Home Department, First Lord of the Treasury, and Chief Commissioner of Police.

Nank. But where are they?

Ko. There they are. They'll all swear to it—won't you? (*To* Pooh-Bah.)

Pooh. Am I to understand that all of us high Officers of State are required to perjure ourselves to ensure your safety?

Ko. Why not? You'll be grossly insulted, as usual.

Pooh. Will the insult be cash down, or at a date?

Ko. It will be a ready-money transaction.

Pooh. (*Aside.*) Well, it will be a useful discipline. (*Aloud.*) Very good. Choose your fiction, and I'll endorse it! (*Aside.*) Ha! ha! Family Pride, how do you like *that*, my buck?

Nank. But I tell you that life without Yum-Yum——

Ko. Oh, Yum-Yum, Yum-Yum! Bother Yum-Yum! Here, Commissionaire (*to* Pooh-Bah), go and fetch Yum-Yum. (*Exit* Pooh-Bah.) Take Yum-Yum and marry Yum-Yum, only go away and never come back again. (*Enter* Pooh-Bah *with* Yum-Yum.) Here she is. Yum-Yum, are you particularly busy?

Yum. Not particularly.

Ko. You've five minutes to spare?

Yum. Yes.

Ko. Then go along with his Grace the Archbishop of Titipu; he'll marry you at once.

Yum. But if I'm to be buried alive?

Ko. Now, don't ask any questions, but do as I tell you, and Nanki-Poo will explain all.

Nank. But one moment——

N

Ko. Not for worlds. Here comes the Mikado, no doubt to ascertain whether I've obeyed his decree, and if he finds you alive I shall have the greatest difficulty in persuading him that I've beheaded you. (*Exeunt* NANKI-POO *and* YUM-YUM, *followed by* POOH-BAH.) Close thing that, for here he comes!

[*Exit* KO-KO.

March.—Enter procession, heralding MIKADO, *with* KATISHA.

Entrance of MIKADO *and* KATISHA.

("*March of the Mikado's troops.*")

CHORUS.　Miya sama, miya sama,
　　　　On n'm-ma no mayé ni
　　　　Pira-Pira suru no wa
　　　　Nan gia na
　　　　Toko tonyaré tonyaré na?

DUET—MIKADO *and* KATISHA.

MIK.　From every kind of man
　　　　Obedience I expect;
　　　　I'm the Emperor of Japan—

KAT.　And I'm his daughter-in-law elect!
　　　　He'll marry his son
　　　　(He's only got one)
　　　　To his daughter-in-law elect.

MIK.　My morals have been declared
　　　　Particularly correct;

KAT.　But they're nothing at all, compared
　　　　With those of his daughter-in-law elect!
　　　　Bow—Bow—
　　　　To his daughter-in-law elect!

ALL.　　Bow—Bow—
　　　　To his daughter-in-law elect.

MIK.	In a fatherly kind of way
	I govern each tribe and sect,
	All cheerfully own my sway—

KAT.	Except his daughter-in-law elect !
	As tough as a bone,
	With a will of her own,
	Is his daughter-in-law elect !

| MIK. | My nature is love and light— |
| | My freedom from all defect— |

KAT.	Is insignificant quite,
	Compared with his daughter-in-law elect !
	Bow—Bow—
	To his daughter-in-law elect !

| ALL. | Bow—Bow— |
| | To his daughter-in-law elect ! |

SONG—MIKADO *and* CHORUS.

A more humane Mikado never
    Did in Japan exist,
        To nobody second,
        I'm certainly reckoned
    A true philanthropist.
It is my very humane endeavour
    To make, to some extent,
        Each evil liver
        A running river
    Of harmless merriment.

        My object all sublime
        I shall achieve in time—
    To let the punishment fit the crime—
        The punishment fit the crime ;
        And make each prisoner pent
        Unwillingly represent
    A source of innocent merriment !
        Of innocent merriment !

All prosy dull society sinners,
Who chatter and bleat and bore,
Are sent to hear sermons
From mystical Germans
Who preach from ten till four.
The amateur tenor, whose vocal villainies
All desire to shirk,
Shall, during off-hours,
Exhibit his powers
To Madame Tussaud's waxwork.

The lady who dies a chemical yellow,
Or stains her grey hair puce,
Or pinches her figger,
Is blacked like a nigger
With permanent walnut juice.
The idiot who, in railway carriages,
Scribbles on window-panes,
We only suffer
To ride on a buffer
In Parliamentary trains.

My object all sublime, etc.

CHORUS.   His object all sublime, etc.

The advertising quack who wearies
With tales of countless cures,
His teeth, I've enacted,
Shall all be extracted
By terrified amateurs.
The music-hall singer attends a series
Of masses and fugues and " ops "
By Bach, interwoven
With Spohr and Beethoven,
At classical Monday Pops.

The billiard sharp whom any one catches,
His doom's extremely hard—

He's made to dwell—
In a dungeon cell
On a spot that's always barred.
And there he plays extravagant matches
In fitless finger-stalls
On a cloth untrue,
With a twisted cue
And elliptical billiard balls !

My object all sublime, etc.

CHORUS.   His object all sublime, etc.

Enter POOH-BAH, KO-KO, *and* PITTI-SING.   *All kneel.*

(POOH-BAH *hands a paper to* KO-KO.)

KO.   I am honoured in being permitted to welcome
your Majesty.   I guess the object of your Majesty's visit—
your wishes have been attended to.   The execution has
taken place.

MIK.   Oh, you've had an execution, have you ?

KO. Yes.   The Coroner has just handed me his
certificate.

POOH.   I am the Coroner.   (KO-KO *hands certificate
to* MIKADO.)

MIK.   And this is the certificate of his death.   (*Reads.*)
" At Titipu, in the presence of the Lord Chancellor, Lord
Chief Justice, Attorney-General, Secretary of State for
the Home Department, Lord Mayor, and Groom of the
Second Floor Front——"

POOH.   They were all present, your Majesty.   I
counted them myself.

MIK.   Very good house.   I wish I'd been in time for
the performance.

KO.   A tough fellow he was, too—a man of gigantic
strength.   His struggles were terrific.   It was really a
remarkable scene.

MIK.   Describe it.

TRIO AND CHORUS.

KO-KO, PITTI-SING, POOH-BAH, *and* CHORUS.

Ko.   The criminal cried, as he dropped him down,
     In a state of wild alarm—
With a frightful, frantic, fearful frown,
     I bared my big right arm.
I seized him by his little pig-tail,
     And on his knees fell he,
       As he squirmed and struggled,
       And gurgled and guggled,
I drew my snickersnee!
       Oh, never shall I
       Forget the cry,
Or the shriek that shriekèd he,
       As I gnashed my teeth,
       When from its sheath
I drew my snickersnee!

CHORUS.

     We know him well,
     He cannot tell
Untrue or groundless tales—
     He always tries
     To utter lies,
And every time he fails.

PITTI.   He shivered and shook as he gave the sign
     For the stroke he didn't deserve;
When all of a sudden his eye met mine,
     And it seemed to brace his nerve;
For he nodded his head and kissed his hand,
     And he whistled an air, did he,
       As the sabre true
       Cut cleanly through
His cervical vertebræ!

When a man's afraid,
A beautiful maid
Is a cheering sight to see ;
And it's oh, I'm glad
That moment sad
Was soothed by sight of me !

CHORUS.

Her terrible tale
You can't assail,
With truth it quite agrees :
Her taste exact
For faultless fact
Amounts to a disease.

POOH. Now though you'd have said that head was dead
(For its owner dead was he),
It stood on its neck, with a smile well-bred,
And bowed three times to me !
It was none of your impudent off-hand nods,
But as humble as could be ;
For it clearly knew
The deference due
To a man of pedigree !
And it's oh, I vow,
This deathly bow
Was a touching sight to see ;
Though trunkless, yet
It couldn't forget
The deference due to me !

CHORUS.

This haughty youth,
He speaks the truth
Whenever he finds it pays :
And in this case
It all took place
Exactly as he says !

[*Exeunt* CHORUS.

MIK. All this is very interesting, and I should like to have seen it. But we came about a totally different matter. A year ago my son, the heir to the throne of Japan, bolted from our Imperial Court.

Ko. Indeed! Had he any reason to be dissatisfied with his position?

KAT. None whatever. On the contrary, I was going to marry him—yet he fled!

POOH. I am surprised that he should have fled from one so lovely!

KAT. That's not true.

POOH. No!

KAT. You hold that I am not beautiful because my face is plain. But you know nothing; you are still unenlightened. Learn, then, that it is not in the face alone that beauty is to be sought. My face is unattractive!

POOH. It is.

KAT. But I have a left shoulder-blade that is a miracle of loveliness. People come miles to see it. My right elbow has a fascination that few can resist.

POOH. Allow me!

KAT. It is on view Tuesdays and Fridays, on presentation of visiting card. As for my circulation, it is the largest in the world.

Ko. And yet he fled!

MIK. And is now masquerading in this town, disguised as a Second Trombone.

Ko. ⎫
POOH. ⎬ A Second Trombone!
PITTI. ⎭

MIK. Yes; would it be troubling you too much if I asked you to produce him? He goes by the name of——

KAT. Nanki-Poo.

MIK. Nanki-Poo.

Ko. It's quite easy. That is, it's rather difficult. In point of fact, he's gone abroad!

MIK. Gone abroad ! His address.

KO. Knightsbridge !

KAT. (*who is reading certificate of death*). Ha !

MIK. What's the matter ?

KAT. See here—his name—Nanki-Poo—beheaded this morning. Oh, where shall I find another ? Where shall I find another ?

(KO-KO, POOH-BAH, *and* PITTI-SING *fall on their knees.*)

MIK. (*looking at paper*). Dear, dear, dear ! this is very tiresome. (*To* KO-KO.) My poor fellow, in your anxiety to carry out my wishes you have beheaded the heir to the throne of Japan !

KO. I beg to offer an unqualified apology.

POOH. I desire to associate myself with that expression of regret.

PITTI. We really hadn't the least notion——

MIK. Of course you hadn't. How could you ? Come, come, my good fellow, don't distress yourself—it was no fault of yours. If a man of exalted rank chooses to disguise himself as a Second Trombone, he must take the consequences. It really distresses me to see you take on so. I've no doubt he thoroughly deserved all he got. (*They rise.*)

KO. We are infinitely obliged to your Majesty——

PITTI. Much obliged, your Majesty.

POOH. Very much obliged, your Majesty.

MIK. Obliged ? not a bit. Don't mention it. How *could* you tell ?

POOH. No, of course we couldn't tell who the gentleman really was.

PITTI. It wasn't written on his forehead, you know.

KO. It might have been on his pocket-handkerchief, but Japanese don't use pocket-handkerchiefs ! Ha ! ha ! ha !

MIK. Ha ! ha ! ha ! (*To* KATISHA.) I forget the punishment for compassing the death of the Heir Apparent.

Ko. ⎫
Pooh. ⎬   Punishment.   (*They drop down on their knees*
Pitti. ⎭   *again.*)

Mik.   Yes.   Something lingering, with boiling oil in
it, I fancy.   Something of that sort.   I think boiling oil
occurs in it, but I'm not sure.   I know it's something
humorous, but lingering, with either boiling oil or melted
lead.   Come, come, don't fret—I'm not a bit angry.

Ko. (*in abject terror*).   If your Majesty will accept our
assurance, we had no idea——

Mik.   Of course——

Pitti.   I knew nothing about it.

Pooh.   I wasn't there.

Mik.   That's the pathetic part of it.   Unfortunately,
the fool of an Act says " compassing the death of the Heir
Apparent."   There's not a word about a mistake——

Ko., Pitti., *and* Pooh.   No !

Mik.   Or not knowing——

Ko.   No !

Mik.   Or having no notion——

Pitti.   No !

Mik.   Or not being there——

Pooh.   No !

Mik.   There should be, of course——

Ko., Pitti., *and* Pooh.   Yes !

Mik.   But there isn't.

Ko., Pitti., *and* Pooh.   Oh !

Mik.   That's the slovenly way in which these Acts
are always drawn.   However, cheer up, it'll be all right.
I'll have it altered next session.   Now, let's see about
your execution—will after luncheon suit you ?   Can you
wait till then ?

Ko., Pitti., *and* Pooh.   Oh, yes—we can wait till then !

Mik.   Then we'll make it after luncheon.

Pooh.   I don't want any lunch.

Mik.   I'm really very sorry for you all, but it's an unjust world, and virtue is triumphant only in theatrical
performances.

THE MIKADO

GLEE.

Pitti-Sing, Katisha, Ko-Ko, Pooh-Bah, *and* Mikado.

Mik.   See how the Fates their gifts allot,
                For A is happy—B is not.
                Yet B is worthy, I dare say,
                Of more prosperity than A !

Ko., Pooh., *and* Pitti.   *Is* B more worthy ?

Kat.   I should say
              He's worth a great deal more than A

Ensemble.

> Yet A is happy !
> Oh, so happy !
> Laughing, Ha ! ha !
> Chaffing, Ha ! ha !
> Nectar quaffing, Ha ! ha ! ha !
> Ever joyous, ever gay,
> Happy, undeserving A !

Ko., Pooh., *and* Pitti.

              If I were Fortune—which I'm not—
              B should enjoy A's happy lot,
              And A should die in miserie—
              That is, assuming I am B.

Mik. *and* Kat.   But *should* A perish ?

Ko., Pooh., *and* Pitti.   That should he
              (Of course, assuming I am B).
              B should be happy !
                Oh, so happy !
              Laughing, Ha ! ha !
              Chaffing, Ha ! ha !
              Nectar quaffing, Ha ! ha ! ha !
              But condemned to die is he,
              Wretched meritorious B !

                      [Exeunt Mikado *and* Katisha.

Ko.   Well, a nice mess you've got us into, with your nodding head and the deference due to a man of pedigree !

Pooh.   Merely corroborative detail, intended to give

artistic verisimilitude to an otherwise bald and unconvincing narrative.

PITTI.   Corroborative detail indeed ! Corroborative fiddlestick !

KO.   And you're just as bad as he is with your cock-and-a-bull stories about catching his eye and his whistling an air.   But that's so like you !   You must put in your oar !

POOH.   But how about your big right arm ?

PITTI.   Yes, and your snickersnee !

KO.   Well, well, never mind that now.   There's only one thing to be done.   Nanki-Poo hasn't started yet—he must come to life again at once.   (*Enter* NANKI-POO *and* YUM-YUM *prepared for journey*.)   Here he comes. Here, Nanki-Poo, I've good news for you—you're reprieved.

NANK.   Oh, but it's too late.   I'm a dead man, and I'm off for my honeymoon.

KO.   Nonsense !   A terrible thing has just happened. It seems you're the son of the Mikado.

NANK.   Yes, but that happened some time ago.

KO.   Is this a time for airy persiflage ?   Your father is here, and with Katisha !

NANK.   My father !   And with Katisha !

KO.   Yes, he wants you particularly.

POOH.   So does she.

YUM.   Oh, but he's married now.

KO.   But, bless my heart ! what has that to do with it ?

NANK.   Katisha claims me in marriage, but I can't marry her because I'm married already—consequently she will insist on my execution, and if I'm executed, my wife will have to be buried alive.

YUM.   You see our difficulty.

KO.   Yes.   I don't know what's to be done.

NANK.   There's one chance for you.   If you could persuade Katisha to marry you, she would have no further claim on me, and in that case I could come to life without any fear of being put to death.

KO.   I marry Katisha !

YUM.   I really think it's the only course.

Ko. But, my good girl, have you seen her? She's something appalling!

Pitti. Ah! that's only her face. She has a left elbow which people come miles to see!

Pooh. I am told that her right heel is much admired by connoisseurs.

Ko. My good sir, I decline to pin my heart upon any lady's right heel.

Nank. It comes to this: While Katisha is single, I prefer to be a disembodied spirit. When Katisha is married, existence will be as welcome as the flowers in spring.

DUET—Nanki-Poo *and* Ko-Ko.

(*With* Yum-Yum, Pitti-Sing, *and* Pooh-Bah.)

Nank.   The flowers that bloom in the spring,
                    Tra la,
              Breathe promise of merry sunshine—
         As we merrily dance and we sing,
                    Tra la,
         We welcome the hope that they bring,
                    Tra la,
              Of a summer of roses and wine.
                   And that's what we mean when we say that
                        a thing
                   Is welcome as flowers that bloom in the spring.
                        Tra la la la la la la, etc.

All.   Tra la la la la, etc.

Ko.   The flowers that bloom in the spring,
                    Tra la,
              Have nothing to do with the case.
         I've got to take under my wing,
                    Tra la,
         A most unattractive old thing,
                    Tra la,
              With a caricature of a face.

And that's what I mean when I say, or
　　I sing,
" Oh, bother the flowers that bloom in the
　　spring."
　　　　　　　　Tra la la la la la, etc.

ALL.　　　　Tra la la la, Tra la la la, etc.

[*Dance and exeunt* NANKI-POO, YUM-YUM,
　　POOH-BAH, PITTI-SING, *and* KO-KO.

Enter KATISHA.

RECITATIVE AND SONG.—KATISHA.

Alone, and yet alive !　Oh, sepulchre !
My soul is still my body's prisoner !
Remote the peace that Death alone can give—
My doom, to wait ! my punishment, to live !

SONG.

Hearts do not break !
They sting and ache
For old love's sake,
　　But do not die,
Though with each breath
They long for death
As witnesseth
　　The living I !
　　　　Oh, living I !
　　　　Come, tell me why,
　　　　When hope is gone,
　　　　Dost thou stay on ?
　　　　Why linger here,
　　　　Where all is drear ?
　　　　Oh, living I !
　　　　Come, tell me why,
　　　　When hope is gone,
　　　　Dost thou stay on ?
　　　　May not a cheated maiden die ?

KO. (*entering and approaching her timidly*). Katisha!

KAT. The miscreant who robbed me of my love! But vengeance pursues—they are heating the cauldron!

KO. Katisha—behold a suppliant at your feet! Katisha—mercy!

KAT. Mercy? Had you mercy on him? See here, you! You have slain my love. He did not love *me*, but he would have loved me in time. I am an acquired taste—only the educated palate can appreciate *me*. I was educating *his* palate when he left me. Well, he is dead, and where shall I find another? It takes years to train a man to love me. Am I to go through the weary round again, and, at the same time, implore mercy for you who robbed me of my prey—I mean my pupil—just as his education was on the point of completion? Oh, where shall I find another?

KO. (*suddenly, and with great vehemence*). Here!—Here!

KAT. What!!!

KO. (*with intense passion*). Katisha, for years I have loved you with a white-hot passion that is slowly but surely consuming my very vitals! Ah, shrink not from me! If there is aught of woman's mercy in your heart, turn not away from a love-sick suppliant whose every fibre thrills at your tiniest touch! True it is that, under a poor mask of disgust, I have endeavoured to conceal a passion whose inner fires are broiling the soul within me! But the fire will not be smothered—it defies all attempts at extinction, and, breaking forth, all the more eagerly for its long restraint, it declares itself in words that will not be weighed—that cannot be schooled—that should not be too severely criticised. Katisha, I dare not hope for your love—but I will not live without it! Darling!

KAT. You, whose hands still reek with the blood of my betrothed, dare to address words of passion to the woman you have so foully wronged!

KO. I do—accept my love, or I perish on the spot!

KAT.   Go to! Who knows so well as I that no one ever yet died of a broken heart!

KO.   You know not what you say.   Listen!

SONG—KO-KO.

On a tree by a river a little tom-tit
      Sang " Willow, titwillow, titwillow! "
And I said to him, " Dicky-bird, why do you sit
      Singing ' Willow, titwillow, titwillow ' ? "
" Is it weakness of intellect, birdie ? " I cried,
" Or a rather tough worm in your little inside ? "
With a shake of his poor little head, he replied,
      " Oh, willow, titwillow, titwillow! "

He slapped at his chest, as he sat on that bough,
      Singing " Willow, titwillow, titwillow! "
And a cold perspiration bespangled his brow,
      Oh, willow, titwillow, titwillow!
He sobbed and he sighed, and a gurgle he gave,
Then he plunged himself into the billowy wave,
And an echo arose from the suicide's grave—
      " Oh, willow, titwillow, titwillow! "

Now I feel just as sure as I'm sure that my name
      Isn't Willow, titwillow, titwillow,
That 'twas blighted affection that made him exclaim
      " Oh, willow, titwillow, titwillow! "
And if you remain callous and obdurate, I
Shall perish as he did, and you will know why,
Though I probably shall not exclaim as I die,
      " Oh, willow, titwillow, titwillow! "

(*During this song* KATISHA *has been greatly affected, and at the end is almost in tears.*)

KAT. (*whimpering*).   Did he really die of love ?

KO.   He really did.

KAT.   All on account of a cruel little hen ?

KO.   Yes.

Kat. Poor little chap !

Ko. It's an affecting tale, and quite true. I knew the bird intimately.

Kat. Did you ? He must have been very fond of her.

Ko. His devotion was something extraordinary.

Kat. (*still whimpering*). Poor little chap ! And—and if I refuse you, will you go and do the same ?

Ko. At once.

Kat. No, no—you mustn't ! Anything but that ! (*Falls on his breast.*) Oh, I'm a silly little goose !

Ko. (*making a wry face*). You are !

Kat. And you won't hate me because I'm just a little teeny weeny wee bit bloodthirsty, will you ?

Ko. Hate you ? Oh, Katisha ! is there not beauty even in bloodthirstiness ?

Kat. My idea exactly.

DUET—Katisha *and* Ko-Ko.

Kat. There is beauty in the bellow of the blast,
There is grandeur in the growling of the gale,
There is eloquent outpouring
When the lion is a-roaring,
And the tiger is a-lashing of his tail !

Ko. Yes, I like to see a tiger
From the Congo or the Niger,
And especially when lashing of his tail !

Kat. Volcanoes have a splendour that is grim,
And earthquakes only terrify the dolts,
But to him who's scientific
There's nothing that's terrific
In the falling of a flight of thunderbolts !

Ko. Yes, in spite of all my meekness,
If I have a little weakness,
It's a passion for a flight of thunderbolts !

Both. If that is so,
Sing derry down derry !
It's evident, very,
Our tastes are one.

> Away we'll go,
>> And merrily marry,
>> Nor tardily tarry
>>> Till day is done !

Ko.   There is beauty in extreme old age—
>> Do you fancy you are elderly enough ?
>>> Information I'm requesting
>>> On a subject interesting :
>> Is a maiden all the better when she's tough ?

Kat.   Throughout this wide dominion
>>> It's the general opinion
>> That she'll last a good deal longer when she's tough.

Ko.   Are you old enough to marry, do you think ?
>> Won't you wait till you are eighty in the shade ?
>>> There's a fascination frantic
>>> In a ruin that's romantic ;
>> Do you think you are sufficiently decayed ?

Kat.   To the matter that you mention
>>> I have given some attention,
>> And I think I am sufficiently decayed.

Both.   If that is so,
>>> Sing derry down derry !
>>> It's evident, very,
>>>> Our tastes are one !
>> Away we'll go,
>>> And merrily marry,
>>> Nor tardily tarry
>>>> Till day is done !

[Exeunt together.

Flourish. Enter the Mikado, *attended by* Pish-Tush *and Court.*

Mik. Now then, we've had a capital lunch, and we're quite ready. Have all the painful preparations been made?

Pish. Your Majesty, all is prepared.

Mik. Then produce the unfortunate gentleman and his two well-meaning but misguided accomplices.

Enter Ko-Ko, Katisha, Pooh-Bah, *and* Pitti-Sing.
They throw themselves at the Mikado's *feet.*

Kat.   Mercy!   Mercy for Ko-Ko!   Mercy for Pitti-Sing!   Mercy even for Pooh-Bah!

Mik.   I beg your pardon, I don't think I quite caught that remark.

Pooh.   Mercy even for Pooh-Bah.

Kat.   Mercy!   My husband that was to have been is dead, and I have just married this miserable object.

Mik.   Oh!   You've not been long about it!

Ko.   We were married before the Registrar.

Pooh.   *I* am the Registrar.

Mik.   I see.   But my difficulty is that, as you have slain the Heir Apparent——

Enter Nanki-Poo *and* Yum-Yum.   *They kneel.*

Nanki.   The Heir Apparent is *not* slain.

Mik.   Bless my heart, my son!

Yum.   And your daughter-in-law elected!

Kat. (*seizing* Ko-Ko).   Traitor, you have deceived me!

Mik.   Yes, you are entitled to a little explanation, but I think he will give it better whole than in pieces.

Ko.   Your Majesty, it's like this: It is true that I stated that I had killed Nanki-Poo——

Mik.   Yes, with most affecting particulars.

Pooh.   Merely corroborative detail intended to give artistic verisimilitude to a bald and——

Ko.   *Will* you refrain from putting in your oar? (*To* Mikado.)   It's like this: When your Majesty says, "Let a thing be done," it's as good as done—practically, it *is* done—because your Majesty's will is law.   Your Majesty says, "Kill a gentleman," and a gentleman is told off to be killed.   Consequently, that gentleman is as good as dead—practically, he *is* dead—and if he is dead, why not say so?

Mik.   I see.   Nothing could possibly be more satisfactory!

FINALE.

PITTI.　For he's gone and married Yum-Yum—

ALL.　　　　　　　　　Yum-Yum !

PITTI.　　　　Your anger pray bury,
　　　　　　　For all will be merry,
　　I think you had better succumb—

ALL.　　　　　　　　　Cumb—cumb !

PITTI.　　　And join our expressions of glee !

KO.　On this subject I pray you be dumb—

ALL.　　　　　　　　　Dumb—dumb !

KO.　　　Your notions, though many,
　　　　　Are not worth a penny,
　The word for your guidance is " Mum "—

ALL.　　　　　　　　　Mum—Mum !

KO.　You've a very good bargain in me.

ALL.　On this subject we pray you be dumb—
　　　　　　　　　Dumb—dumb !
　We think you had better succumb—
　　　　　　　　　Cumb—cumb !
　　　　You'll find there are many
　　　　Who'll wed for a penny,
　　There are lots of good fish in the sea.

YUM. *and* NANK.　The threatened cloud has passed away,
　　　　　　And brightly shines the dawning day ;
　　　　　　What though the night may come too soon,
　　　　　　We've years and years of afternoon !

ALL.　　　　　　　Then let the throng
　　　　　　　　Our joy advance,
　　　　　　With laughing song
　　　　　　　　And merry dance,
　　　　With joyous shout and ringing cheer,
　　　　Inaugurate our new career !
　　　　　Then let the throng, etc.

CURTAIN.

RUDDIGORE

OR

THE WITCH'S CURSE

DRAMATIS PERSONÆ.

MORTALS.

SIR RUTHVEN MURGATROYD (*disguised as Robin Oakapple, a Young Farmer*).

RICHARD DAUNTLESS (*his Foster-Brother—a Man-o'-war's-man*).

SIR DESPARD MURGATROYD, OF RUDDIGORE (*a Wicked Baronet*).

OLD ADAM GOODHEART (*Robin's Faithful Servant*).

ROSE MAYBUD (*a Village Maiden*).

MAD MARGARET.

DAME HANNAH (*Rose's Aunt*).

ZORAH ⎫ (*Professional Bridesmaids*).
RUTH ⎭

GHOSTS.

SIR RUPERT MURGATROYD (*the First Baronet*).

SIR JASPER MURGATROYD (*the Third Baronet*).

SIR LIONEL MURGATROYD (*the Sixth Baronet*).

SIR CONRAD MURGATROYD (*the Twelfth Baronet*).

SIR DESMOND MURGATROYD (*the Sixteenth Baronet*).

SIR GILBERT MURGATROYD (*the Eighteenth Baronet*).

SIR MERVYN MURGATROYD (*the Twentieth Baronet*),

AND

SIR RODERIC MURGATROYD (*the Twenty-first Baronet*).

Chorus of Officers, Ancestors, Professional Bridesmaids, and Villagers.

ACT I.—The Fishing Village of Rederring, in Cornwall.

ACT II.—The Picture Gallery in Ruddigore Castle.

Time—Early in the 19th century.

First produced at the Savoy Theatre on January 22, 1887.

374

370   THE SAVOY OPERAS

        Hour by hour and day by day,
        Several months have passed away,
        Though she, the fairest flower that blows,
        No one has married Rose.

                CHORUS.

            Rose, all glowing
                With virgin blushes, say—
            To marry to-day?

RUDDIGORE

OR

THE WITCH'S CURSE

ACT I.

SCENE.—*The fishing village of Rederring (in Cornwall).*
ROSE MAYBUD'S *cottage is seen* L.

*Enter Chorus of Bridesmaids. They range themselves in
front of* ROSE'S *cottage.*

CHORUS OF BRIDESMAIDS.

Fair is Rose as the bright May-day;
    Soft is Rose as the warm west-wind;
Sweet is Rose as the new-mown hay—
    Rose is the queen of maiden-kind!
            Rose, all glowing
                With virgin blushes, say—
            Is anybody going
                To marry you to-day?

SOLO—ZORAH.

Every day, as the days roll on,
Bridesmaids' garb we gaily don,
Sure that a maid so fairly famed
Can't long remain unclaimed.

375

Hour by hour and day by day,
Several months have passed away,
Though she's the fairest flower that blows,
No one has married Rose !

CHORUS.

Rose, all glowing
    With virgin blushes, say—
Is anybody going
    To marry you to-day ?

Enter DAME HANNAH, *from cottage.*

HANNAH.   Nay, gentle maidens, you sing well but
vainly, for Rose is still heart-free, and looks but coldly
upon her many suitors.

ZORAH.   It's very disappointing.   Every young man
in the village is in love with her, but they are appalled by
her beauty and modesty, and won't declare themselves ;
so, until she makes her own choice, there's no chance for
anybody else.

RUTH.   This is, perhaps, the only village in the world
that possesses an endowed corps of professional bridesmaids who are bound to be on duty every day from ten
to four—and it is at least six months since our services
were required.   The pious charity by which we exist is
practically wasted !

ZOR.   We shall be disendowed—that will be the end
of it !   Dame Hannah—you're a nice old person—*you*
could marry if you liked.   There's old Adam—Robin's
faithful servant—he loves you with all the frenzy of a boy
of fourteen.

HAN.   Nay—that may never be, for I am pledged !

ALL.   To whom ?

HAN.   To an eternal maidenhood !   Many years ago
I was betrothed to a god-like youth who woo'd me under
an assumed name.   But on the very day upon which our
wedding was to have been celebrated, I discovered that

he was no other than Sir Roderic Murgatroyd, one of the bad Baronets of Ruddigore, and the uncle of the man who now bears that title. As a son of that accursed race he was no husband for an honest girl, so, madly as I loved him, I left him then and there. He died but ten years since, but I never saw him again.

ZOR. But why should you not marry a bad Baronet of Ruddigore?

RUTH. All baronets are bad; but was he worse than other baronets?

HAN. My child, he was accursed.

ZOR. But who cursed him? Not you, I trust!

HAN. The curse is on all his line and has been, ever since the time of Sir Rupert, the first Baronet. Listen, and you shall hear the legend:

LEGEND—HANNAH.

Sir Rupert Murgatroyd
  His leisure and his riches
He ruthlessly employed
  In persecuting witches.
With fear he'd make them quake—
He'd duck them in his lake—
    He'd break their bones
    With sticks and stones,
And burn them at the stake!

CHORUS.
        This sport he much enjoyed,
        Did Rupert Murgatroyd—
          No sense of shame
          Or pity came
        To Rupert Murgatroyd!

Once, on the village green,
  A palsied hag he roasted,
And what took place, I ween,
  Shook his composure boasted;

For, as the torture grim
Seized on each withered limb,
    The writhing dame
    'Mid fire and flame
Yelled forth this curse on him :

" Each lord of Ruddigore,
    Despite his best endeavour,
Shall do one crime, or more,
    Once, every day, for ever !
This doom he can't defy,
However he may try,
        For should he stay
        His hand, that day
In torture he shall die ! "

The prophecy came true :
    Each heir who held the title
Had, every day, to do
    Some crime of import vital ;
Until, with guilt o'erplied,
" I'll sin no more ! " he cried,
        And on the day
        He said that say,
In agony he died !

CHORUS.   And thus, with sinning cloyed,
Has died each Murgatroyd,
        And so shall fall,
        Both one and all,
Each coming Murgatroyd !

[*Exeunt Chorus of Bridesmaids.*

Enter ROSE MAYBUD *from cottage, with small basket
on her arm.*

HAN. Whither away, dear Rose ? On some errand
of charity, as is thy wont ?

ROSE. A few gifts, dear aunt, for deserving villagers. Lo, here is some peppermint rock for old gaffer Gadderby, a set of false teeth for pretty little Ruth Rowbottom, and a pound of snuff for the poor orphan girl on the hill.

HAN. Ah, Rose, pity that so much goodness should not help to make some gallant youth happy for life ! Rose, why dost thou harden that little heart of thine ? Is there none hereaway whom thou couldst love ?

ROSE. And if there were such an one, verily it would ill become me to tell him so.

HAN. Nay, dear one, where true love is, there is little need of prim formality.

ROSE. Hush, dear aunt, for thy words pain me sorely. Hung in a plated dish-cover to the knocker of the work-house door, with naught that I could call mine own, save a change of baby-linen and a book of etiquette, little wonder if I have always regarded that work as a voice from a parent's tomb. This hallowed volume (*producing a book of etiquette*), composed, if I may believe the title-page, by no less an authority than the wife of a Lord Mayor, has been, through life, my guide and monitor. By its solemn precepts I have learnt to test the moral worth of all who approach me. The man who bites his bread, or eats peas with a knife, I look upon as a lost creature, and he who has not acquired the proper way of entering and leaving a room is the object of my pitying horror. There are those in this village who bite their nails, dear aunt, and nearly all are wont to use their pocket combs in public places. In truth I could pursue this painful theme much further, but behold, I have said enough.

HAN. But is there not one among them who is faultless, in thine eyes ? For example—young Robin. He combines the manners of a Marquis with the morals of a Methodist. Couldst thou not love *him* ?

ROSE. And even if I could, how should I confess it unto him ? For lo, he is shy, and sayeth naught !

BALLAD—Rose.

If somebody there chanced to be
Who loved me in a manner true,
My heart would point him out to me,
And I would point him out to you.

(Referring   But here it says of those who point,
to book.)   Their manners must be out of joint—
You *may* not point—
You *must* not point—
It's manners out of joint, to point !
Had I the love of such as he,
Some quiet spot he'd take me to,
Then he could whisper it to me,
And I could whisper it to you.

(Referring   But whispering, I've somewhere met,
to book.)   Is contrary to etiquette :
Where can it be ?   *(Searching book.)*
Now let me see—*(Finding reference.)*
Yes, yes !
It's contrary to etiquette !

(Showing it to HANNAH.)

If any well-bred youth I knew,
Polite and gentle, neat and trim,
Then I would hint as much to you,
And you could hint as much to him.

(Referring   But here it says, in plainest print,
to book.)   " It's most unladylike to hint "—
You *may* not hint,
. You *must* not hint—
It says you mustn't hint, in print !
And if I loved him through and through—
(True love and not a passing whim),
Then I could speak of it to you,
And you could speak of it to him.

(Referring   But here I find it doesn't do
to book.)   To speak until you're spoken to.

Where can it be ?   (*Searching book.*)
Now let me see— (*Finding reference.*)
Yes, yes !
" Don't speak until you're spoken to ! "

              [*Exit* HANNAH.

ROSE.   Poor aunt ! Little did the good soul think, when she breathed the hallowed name of Robin, that he would do even as well as another. But he resembleth all the youths in this village, in that he is unduly bashful in my presence, and lo, it is hard to bring him to the point. But soft, he is here !

(ROSE *is about to go when* ROBIN *enters and calls her.*)

ROBIN.   Mistress Rose !
ROSE.   (*Surprised.*)   Master Robin !
ROB.   I wished to say that—it is fine.
ROSE.   It is passing fine.
ROB.   But we do want rain.
ROSE.   Aye, sorely ! Is that all ?
ROB.   (*Sighing.*) That is all.
ROSE.   Good day, Master Robin !
ROB.   Good day, Mistress Rose ! (*Both going—both stop.*)
ROSE. ⎫   I crave pardon, I——
ROB. ⎬   I beg pardon, I——
ROSE.   You were about to say ?——
ROB.   I would fain consult you——
ROSE.   Truly ?
ROB.   It is about a friend.
ROSE.   In truth I have a friend myself.
ROB.   Indeed ?   I mean, of course——
ROSE.   And I would fain consult you——
ROB.   (*Anxiously.*) About him ?
ROSE.   (*Prudishly.*) About *her.*
ROB.   (*Relieved.*) Let us consult one another.

DUET—ROBIN *and* ROSE.

ROB.   I know a youth who loves a little maid—
          (Hey, but his face is a sight for to see !)
      Silent is he, for he's modest and afraid—
          (Hey, but he's timid as a youth can be !)

ROSE.   I know a maid who loves a gallant youth,
          (Hey, but she sickens as the days go by !)
      She cannot tell him all the sad, sad truth—
          (Hey, but I think that little maid will die !)

ROB.   Poor little man !

ROSE.   Poor little maid !

ROB.   Poor little man !

ROSE.   Poor little maid !

BOTH.   Now tell me pray, and tell me true,
      What in the world should the $\left\{ {young\ man \atop maiden} \right\}$ do ?

ROB.   He cannot eat and he cannot sleep—
          (Hey, but his face is a sight for to see !)
      Daily he goes for to wail—for to weep
          (Hey, but he's wretched as a youth can be !)

ROSE.   She's very thin and she's very pale—
          (Hey, but she sickens as the days go by !)
      Daily she goes for to weep—for to wail—
          (Hey, but I think that little maid will die !)

ROB.   Poor little maid !

ROSE.   Poor little man !

ROB.   Poor little maid !

ROSE.   Poor little man !

BOTH.   Now tell me pray, and tell me true,
      What in the world should the $\left\{ {young\ man \atop maiden} \right\}$ do ?

Rose.   If I were the youth I should offer her my
                name—
                (Hey, but her face is a sight for to see !)
Rob.   If I were the maid I should fan his honest
                flame—
                (Hey, but he's bashful as a youth can be !)
Rose.   If I were the youth I should speak to her
                to-day—
                (Hey, but she sickens as the days go by !)
Rob.   If I were the maid I should meet the lad half
                way—
                (For I really do believe that timid youth will
                die !)

Rose.   Poor little man !

Rob.   Poor little maid !

Rose.   Poor little man !

Rob.   Poor little maid !

Both.   I thank you, $\left\{ {\text{miss,} \atop \text{sir,}} \right\}$ for your counsel true ;

          I'll tell that $\left\{ {\text{youth} \atop \text{maid}} \right\}$ what $\left\{ {\text{he} \atop \text{she}} \right\}$ ought to do !

                                              [*Exit* Rose.

Rob.   Poor child ! I sometimes think that if she
wasn't quite so particular I might venture—but no, no—
even then I should be unworthy of her !

He sits desponding.   Enter Old Adam.

Adam.   My kind master is sad ! Dear Sir Ruthven
Murgatroyd——
Rob.   Hush ! As you love me, breathe not that hated
name. Twenty years ago, in horror at the prospect of
inheriting that hideous title, and with it the ban that
compels all who succeed to the baronetcy to commit at
least one deadly crime per day, for life, I fled my home,
and concealed myself in this innocent village under the

name of Robin Oakapple. My younger brother, Despard, believing me to be dead, succeeded to the title and its attendant curse. For twenty years I have been dead and buried. Don't dig me up now.

ADAM. Dear master, it shall be as you wish, for have I not sworn to obey you for ever in all things ? Yet, as we are here alone, and as I belong to that particular description of good old man to whom the truth is a refreshing novelty, let me call you by your own right title once more ! (ROBIN *assents*.) Sir Ruthven Murgatroyd ! Baronet ! Of Ruddigore ! Whew ! It's like eight hours at the seaside !

ROB. My poor old friend ! Would there were more like you !

ADAM. Would there were indeed ! But I bring you good tidings. Your foster - brother, Richard, has returned from sea—his ship the *Tom-Tit* rides yonder at anchor, and he himself is even now in this very village !

ROB. My beloved foster-brother ? No, no—it cannot be !

ADAM. It is even so—and see, he comes this way !

[*Exeunt together.*

Enter Chorus of Bridesmaids.

CHORUS.

From the briny sea
          Comes young Richard, all victorious !
Valorous is he—
          His achievements all are glorious !
Let the welkin ring
With the news we bring
          Sing it—shout it—
          Tell about it—
Safe and sound returneth he,
All victorious from the sea !

Enter RICHARD. *The girls welcome him as he greets old acquaintances.*

BALLAD—RICHARD.

I shipped, d'ye see, in a Revenue sloop,
   And, off Cape Finistere,
      A merchantman we see,
      A Frenchman, going free,
So we made for the bold Mounseer,
         D'ye see ?
We made for the bold Mounseer.
But she proved to be a Frigate—and she up with her ports,
   And fires with a thirty-two !
      It come uncommon near,
      But we answered with a cheer,
Which paralysed the Parley-voo,
         D'ye see ?
Which paralysed the Parley-voo !

Then our Captain he up and he says, says he,
   " That chap we need not fear,—
      We can take her, if we like,
      She is sartin for to strike,
For she's only a darned Mounseer,
         D'ye see ?
She's only a darned Mounseer !
But to fight a French fal-lal—it's like hittin' of a gal—
   It's a lubberly thing for to do ;
      For we, with all our faults,
      Why we're sturdy British salts,
While she's only a Parley-voo,
         D'ye see ?
While she's only a Parley-voo ! "

So we up with our helm, and we scuds before the breeze
   As we gives a compassionating cheer ;

Froggee answers with a shout
As he sees us go about,
Which was grateful of the poor Mounseer,
                    D'ye see ?
Which was grateful of the poor Mounseer !
And I'll wager in their joy they kissed each other's
                    cheek
(Which is what them furriners do),
            And they blessed their lucky stars
            We were hardy British tars
Who had pity on a poor Parley-voo,
                    D'ye see ?
Who had pity on a poor Parley-voo !
                    (HORNPIPE.)

                                        [*Exeunt* CHORUS.

Enter ROBIN.

ROB.   Richard !
RICH.   Robin !
ROB.   My beloved foster-brother, and very dearest
friend, welcome home again after ten long years at sea !
It is such deeds as yours that cause our flag to be loved
and dreaded throughout the civilized world !

RICH.   Why, lord love ye, Rob, that's but a trifle to
what we *have* done in the way of sparing life ! I believe
I may say, without exaggeration, that the marciful little
Tom-Tit has spared more French frigates than any craft
afloat ! But 'taint for a British seaman to brag, so I'll
just stow my jawin' tackle and belay. (ROBIN *sighs*.)
But 'vast heavin', messmate, what's brought *you* all
a-cockbill ?

ROB.   Alas, Dick, I love Rose Maybud, and love in
vain !

RICH.   *You* love in vain ? Come, that's too good !
Why, you're a fine strapping muscular young fellow—
tall and strong as a to'-gall'n'-m'st — taut as a fore-

stay—aye, and a barrowknight to boot, if all had their rights!

ROB. Hush, Richard—not a word about my true rank, which none here suspect. Yes, I know well enough that few men are better calculated to win a woman's heart than I. I'm a fine fellow, Dick, and worthy any woman's love—happy the girl who gets me, say I. But I'm timid, Dick; shy—nervous—modest—retiring—diffident—and I cannot tell her, Dick, I cannot tell her! Ah, you've no idea what a poor opinion I have of myself, and how little I deserve it.

RICH. Robin, do you call to mind how, years ago, we swore that, come what might, we would always act upon our hearts' dictates?

ROB. Aye, Dick, and I've always kept that oath. In doubt, difficulty, and danger I've always asked my heart what I should do, and it has never failed me.

RICH. Right! Let your heart be your compass, with a clear conscience for your binnacle light, and you'll sail ten knots on a bowline, clear of shoals, rocks, and quicksands! Well, now, what does my heart say in this here difficult situation? Why, it says, "Dick," it says—(it calls me Dick acos it's known me from a babby)—"Dick," it says, "you ain't shy—you ain't modest—speak you up for him as is!" Robin, my lad, just you lay me alongside, and when she's becalmed under my lee, I'll spin her a yarn that shall sarve to fish you two together for life!

ROB. Will you do this thing for me? Can you, do you think? Yes (feeling his pulse). There's no false modesty about you. Your—what I would call bumptious self-assertiveness (I mean the expression in its complimentary sense) has already made you a bos'n's mate, and it will make an admiral of you in time, if you work it properly, you dear, incompetent old impostor! My dear fellow, I'd give my right arm for one tenth of your modest assurance!

SONG—Robin

My boy, you may take it from me,
    That of all the afflictions accurst
        With which a man's saddled
        And hampered and addled,
    A diffident nature's the worst.
Though clever as clever can be—
    A Crichton of early romance—
        You must stir it and stump it,
        And blow your own trumpet,
    Or, trust me, you haven't a chance !

    If you wish in the world to advance,
    Your merits you're bound to enhance,
        You must stir it and stump it,
        And blow your own trumpet,
    Or, trust me, you haven't a chance !

    Now take, for example, *my* case :
        I've a bright intellectual brain—
            In all London city
            There's no one so witty—
        I've thought so again and again.
    I've a highly intelligent face—
        My features cannot be denied—
            But, whatever I try, sir,
            I fail in—and why, sir ?
        I'm modesty personified !

        If you wish in the world to advance, etc.

    As a poet, I'm tender and quaint—
        I've passion and fervour and grace—
            From Ovid and Horace
            To Swinburne and Morris,
        They all of them take a back place.

Then I sing and I play and I paint :
Though none are accomplished as I,
To say so were treason :
You ask me the reason ?
I'm diffident, modest, and shy !
If you wish in the world to advance, etc.

[*Exit* ROBIN.

RICH. (*looking after him*). Ah, it's a thousand pities
he's such a poor opinion of himself, for a finer fellow don't
walk ! Well, I'll do my best for him. " Plead for him
as though it was for your own father "—that's what my
heart's a-remarkin' to me just now. But here she comes !
Steady ! Steady it is ! (*Enter* ROSE—*he is much struck
by her.*) By the Port Admiral, but she's a tight little
craft ! Come, come, she's not for you, Dick, and yet—
she's fit to marry Lord Nelson ! By the Flag of Old
England, I can't look at her unmoved.

ROSE. Sir, you are agitated——

RICH. Aye, aye, my lass, well said ! I am agitated,
true enough !—took flat aback, my girl ; but 'tis naught—
'twill pass. (*Aside.*) This here heart of mine's a-dictatin'
to me like anythink. Question is, Have I a right to
disregard its promptings ?

ROSE. Can I do aught to relieve thine anguish, for
it seemeth to me that thou art in sore trouble ? This
apple—(*offering a damaged apple*).

RICH. (*looking at it and returning it*). No, my lass,
'taint that : I'm—I'm took flat aback—I never see
anything like you in all my born days. Parbuckle me,
if you ain't the loveliest gal I've ever set eyes on. There—
I can't say fairer than that, can I ?

ROSE. No. (*Aside.*) The question is, Is it meet that
an utter stranger should thus express himself ? (*Refers
to book.*) Yes—" Always speak the truth."

RICH. I'd no thoughts of sayin' this here to you on
my own account, for, truth to tell, I was chartered by
another ; but when I see you my heart it up and it says,

says it, " This is the very lass for *you*, Dick "—" speak up to her, Dick," it says—(it calls me Dick acos we was at school together)—" tell her all, Dick," it says, " never sail under false colours—it's mean ! " *That's* what my heart tells me to say, and in my rough, common-sailor fashion, I've said it, and I'm a-waiting for your reply. I'm a-tremblin', miss. Lookye here—(*holding out his hand*). That's narvousness !

ROSE (*aside*). Now, how should a maiden deal with such an one ? (*Consults book.*) " Keep no one in unnecessary suspense." (*Aloud.*) Behold, I will not keep you in unnecessary suspense. (*Refers to book.*) " In accepting an offer of marriage, do so with apparent hesitation." (*Aloud.*) I take you, but with a certain show of reluctance. (*Refers to book.*) " Avoid any appearance of eagerness." (*Aloud.*) Though you will bear in mind that I am far from anxious to do so. (*Refers to book.*) " A little show of emotion will not be misplaced ! " (*Aloud.*) Pardon this tear ! (*Wipes her eye.*)

RICH. Rose, you've made me the happiest blue-jacket in England ! I wouldn't change places with the Admiral of the Fleet, no matter who he's a-huggin' of at this present moment ! But, axin' your pardon, miss (*wiping his lips with his hand*), might I be permitted to salute the flag I'm a-goin' to sail under ?

ROSE (*referring to book*). " An engaged young lady should not permit too many familiarities." (*Aloud.*) Once ! (RICHARD *kisses her.*)

DUET—RICHARD *and* ROSE.

RICH.   The battle's roar is over,
O my love !
Embrace thy tender lover,
O my love !
From tempests' welter,
From war's alarms,
O give me shelter
Within those arms !

Thy smile alluring,
All heart-ache curing,
Gives peace enduring,
O my love !

ROSE.   If heart both true and tender,
O my love !
A life-love can engender,
O my love !
A truce to sighing
And tears of brine,
For joy undying
Shall aye be mine,
And thou and I, love,
Shall live and die, love,
Without a sigh, love—
My own, my love !

Enter ROBIN, *with* CHORUS OF BRIDESMAIDS.

CHORUS.

If well his suit has sped,
Oh, may they soon be wed !
Oh, tell us, tell us, pray,
What doth the maiden say ?
In singing are we justified,
Hail the Bridegroom—hail the Bride !
Let the nuptial knot be tied :
In fair phrases
Hymn their praises,
Hail the Bridegroom—hail the Bride ?

ROB.   Well—what news ?   Have you spoken to her ?
RICH.   Aye, my lad, I have—so to speak—spoke her.
ROB.   And she refuses ?
RICH.   Why, no, I can't truly say she do.
ROB.   Then she accepts! My darling! (*Embraces her.*)

BRIDESMAIDS.
Hail the Bridegroom—hail the Bride ! etc.

Rose (*aside, referring to her book*). Now, what should a maiden do when she is embraced by the wrong gentleman?

Rich.   Belay, my lad, belay. You don't understand.

Rose.   Oh, sir, belay, I beseech you!

Rich.   You see, it's like this : she accepts—but it's *me*!

Rob.   You! (Richard *embraces* Rose.)

Bridesmaids.

Hail the Bridegroom—hail the Bride!
When the nuptial knot is tied——

Rob. (*interrupting angrily*). Hold your tongues, will you! Now then, what does this mean?

Rich.   My poor lad, my heart grieves for thee, but it's like this : the moment I see her, and just as I was a-goin' to mention your name, my heart it up and it says, says it—" Dick, you've fell in love with her yourself," it says ; " Be honest and sailor-like—don't skulk under false colours—speak up," it says, " take her, you dog, and with her my blessin' ! "

Bridesmaids.

Hail the Bridegroom—hail the Bride!——

Rob.   Will you be quiet! Go away! (Chorus *make faces at him and exeunt*.) Vulgar girls!

Rich.   What could I do? I'm bound to obey my heart's dictates.

Rob.   Of course—no doubt. It's quite right—I don't mind—that is, not particularly—only it's—it *is* disappointing, you know.

Rose (*to* Robin). Oh, but, sir, I knew not that thou didst seek me in wedlock, or in very truth I should not have hearkened unto this man, for behold, he is but a lowly mariner, and very poor withal, whereas thou art a tiller of the land, and thou hast fat oxen, and many sheep and swine, a considerable dairy farm and much corn and oil!

Rich.   That's true, my lass, but it's done now, ain't it, Rob?

Rose. Still it may be that I should not be happy in thy love. I am passing young and little able to judge. Moreover, as to thy character I know naught!

Rob. Nay, Rose, I'll answer for that. Dick has won thy love fairly. Broken-hearted as I am, I'll stand up for Dick through thick and thin!

Rich. (*with emotion*). Thankye, messmate! that's well said. That's spoken honest. Thankye, Rob! (*Grasps his hand.*)

Rose. Yet methinks I have heard that sailors are but worldly men, and little prone to lead serious and thoughtful lives!

Rob. And what then? Admit that Dick is *not* a steady character, and that when he's excited he uses language that would make your hair curl. Grant that— he does. It's the truth, and I'm not going to deny it. But look at his *good* qualities. He's as nimble as a pony, and his hornpipe is the talk of the Fleet!

Rich. Thankye, Rob! That's well spoken. Thankye, Rob!

Rose. But it may be that he drinketh strong waters which do bemuse a man, and make him even as the wild beasts of the desert!

Rob. Well, suppose he does, and I don't say he don't, for rum's his bane, and ever has been. He *does* drink— I won't deny it. But what of that? Look at his arms— tattooed to the shoulder! (Rich. *rolls up his sleeves.*) No, no—I won't hear a word against Dick!

Rose. But they say that mariners are but rarely true to those whom they profess to love!

Rob. Granted—granted—and I don't say that Dick isn't as bad as any of 'em. (Rich. *chuckles.*) You are, you know you are, you dog! a devil of a fellow—a regular out-and-out Lothario! But what then? You can't have everything, and a better hand at turning-in a dead-eye don't walk a deck! And what an accomplishment *that* is in a family man! No, no—not a word against Dick. I'll stick up for him through thick and thin!

RICH. Thankye, Rob, thankye. You're a true friend. I've acted accordin' to my heart's dictates, and such orders as them no man should disobey.

ENSEMBLE—RICHARD, ROBIN, ROSE.

In sailing o'er life's ocean wide
Your heart should be your only guide ;
With summer sea and favouring wind,
Yourself in port you'll surely find.

SOLO—RICHARD.

My heart says, " To this maiden strike—
　　She's captured you.
She's just the sort of girl you like—
　　You know you do.
If other man her heart should gain,
　　I shall resign."
That's what it says to me quite plain,
　　This heart of mine.

SOLO—ROBIN.

My heart says, " You've a prosperous lot,
　　With acres wide ;
You mean to settle all you've got
　　Upon your bride."
It don't pretend to shape my acts
　　By word or sign ;
It merely states these simple facts,
　　This heart of mine !

SOLO—ROSE.

Ten minutes since my heart said " white "—
　　It now says " black ".
It then said " left "—it now says " right "—
　　Hearts often tack.

I must obey its latest strain——
    You tell me so. (*To* RICHARD.)
But should it change its mind again,
    I'll let you know.
(*Turning from* RICHARD *to* ROBIN, *who embraces her.*)

ENSEMBLE.

In sailing o'er life's ocean wide
No doubt the heart should be your guide ;
But it is awkward when you find
A heart that does not know its mind !

    [*Exeunt* ROBIN *with* ROSE L., *and* RICHARD,
      weeping, R.

Enter MAD MARGARET. *She is wildly dressed in
picturesque tatters, and is an obvious caricature of
theatrical madness.*

SCENA—MARGARET.

Cheerily carols the lark
    Over the cot.
Merrily whistles the clerk
    Scratching a blot.
      But the lark
      And the clerk,
      I remark,
    Comfort me not !

Over the ripening peach
    Buzzes the bee.
Splash on the billowy beach
    Tumbles the sea.
      But the peach
      And the beach
      They are each
    Nothing to me !

And why ?
Who am I ?
Daft Madge !   Crazy Meg !
Mad Margaret !   Poor Peg !
He ! he ! he ! he ! he ! (*chuckling*).

Mad, I ?
Yes, very !
But why ?
Mystery !
Don't call !
Whisht ! whisht !

No crime—
'Tis only
That I'm
Love—lonely !
That's all !

BALLAD.

To a garden full of posies
    Cometh one to gather flowers,
    And he wanders through its bowers
Toying with the wanton roses,
    Who, uprising from their beds,
    Hold on high their shameless heads
With their pretty lips a-pouting,
Never doubting—never doubting
    That for Cytherean posies
    He would gather aught but roses !

In a nest of weeds and nettles
    Lay a violet, half-hidden,
    Hoping that his glance unbidden
Yet might fall upon her petals.
    Though she lived alone, apart,
    Hope lay nestling at her heart,

But, alas, the cruel awaking
Set her little heart a-breaking,
For he gathered for his posies
Only roses—only roses !

(*Bursts into tears.*)

Enter ROSE.

ROSE. A maiden, and in tears ? Can I do aught to
soften thy sorrow ? This apple—(*offering apple*).

MAR. (*Examines it and rejects it.*) No ! (*Mysteri-ously.*) Tell me, are you mad ?

ROSE. I ? No ! That is, I think not.

MAR. That's well ! Then you don't love Sir Despard
Murgatroyd ? All mad girls love him. *I* love him. I'm
poor Mad Margaret—Crazy Meg—Poor Peg ! He ! he !
he ! he ! (*chuckling*).

ROSE. Thou lovest the bad Baronet of Ruddigore ?
Oh, horrible—too horrible !

MAR. You pity me ? Then be my mother ! The
squirrel had a mother, but she drank and the squirrel
fled ! Hush ! They sing a brave song in our parts—it
runs somewhat thus : (*Sings.*)

" The cat and the dog and the little puppee
    Sat down in a—down in a—in a—— "

I forget what they sat down in, but so the song goes !
Listen—I've come to pinch her !

ROSE. Mercy, whom ?

MAR. You mean " who ".

ROSE. Nay ! it is the accusative after the verb.

MAR. True. (*Whispers melodramatically.*) I have
come to pinch Rose Maybud !

ROSE. (*Aside, alarmed.*) Rose Maybud !

MAR. Aye ! I love him—he loved me once. But
that's all gone, Fisht ! He gave me an Italian glance—
thus—(*business*)—and made me his. He will give *her*
an Italian glance, and make *her* his. But it shall not be,

for I'll stamp on her—stamp on her—stamp on her! Did you ever kill anybody? No? Why not? Listen—I killed a fly this morning! It buzzed, and I wouldn't have it. So it died—pop! So shall she!

Rose. But, behold, *I* am Rose Maybud, and I would fain not die " pop ".

Mar. You are Rose Maybud?

Rose. Yes, sweet Rose Maybud!

Mar. Strange! They told me she was beautiful! And *he* loves *you*! No, no! If I thought that, I would treat you as the auctioneer and land-agent treated the lady-bird—I would rend you asunder!

Rose. Nay, be pacified, for behold I am pledged to another, and lo, we are to be wedded this very day!

Mar. Swear me that! Come to a Commissioner and let me have it on affidavit! *I* once made an affidavit—but it died—it died—it died! But see, they come—Sir Despard and his evil crew! Hide, hide—they are all mad—quite mad!

Rose. What makes you think that?

Mar. Hush! They sing choruses in public. That's mad enough, I think! Go—hide away, or they will seize you! Hush! Quite softly—quite, quite softly!

[*Exeunt together, on tiptoe.*

*Enter Chorus of Bucks and Blades, heralded
by Chorus of Bridesmaids.*

Chorus of Bridesmaids.

Welcome, gentry,
For your entry
Sets our tender hearts a-beating.
Men of station,
Admiration
Prompts this unaffected greeting.
Hearty greeting offer we!

Chorus of Bucks and Blades.

When thoroughly tired
Of being admired
By ladies of gentle degree—degree,
With flattery sated,
High-flown and inflated,
Away from the city we flee—we flee !

From charms intramural
To prettiness rural
The sudden transition
Is simply Elysian,
So come, Amaryllis,
Come, Chloe and Phyllis,
Your slaves, for the moment, are we !

ALL.   From charms intramural, etc.

Chorus of Bridesmaids.

The sons of the tillage
Who dwell in this village
Are people of lowly degree—degree.
Though honest and active,
They're most unattractive,
And awkward as awkward can be—can be.
They're clumsy clodhoppers
With axes and choppers,
And shepherds and ploughmen
And drovers and cowmen
And hedgers and reapers
And carters and keepers,
And never a lover for me !

Bridesmaids.

So, welcome, gentry, etc.

BUCKS AND BLADES.

When thoroughly tired, etc.

Enter SIR DESPARD MURGATROYD.

SONG AND CHORUS—SIR DESPARD.

SIR D.   Oh, why am I moody and sad?
CH.   Can't guess!
SIR D.   And why am I guiltily mad?
CH.   Confess!
SIR D.   Because I am thoroughly bad!
CH.   Oh yes—
SIR D.   You'll see it at once in my face.
         Oh, why am I husky and hoarse?
CH.   Ah, why?
SIR D.   It's the workings of conscience, of course.
CH.   Fie, fie!
SIR D.   And huskiness stands for remorse,
CH.   Oh my!
SIR D.   At least it does so in my case!

SIR D.   When in crime one is fully employed—
CH.   Like you—
SIR D.   Your expression gets warped and destroyed :
CH.   It do.
SIR D.   It's a penalty none can avoid ;
CH.   How true!
SIR D.   I once was a nice-looking youth ;
         But like stone from a strong catapult—
CH. (*explaining to each other*).   A trice—
SIR D.   I rushed at my terrible cult—
CH. (*explaining to each other*).   That's vice—
SIR D.   Observe the unpleasant result !
CH.   Not nice.
SIR D.   Indeed I am telling the truth !

Sir D. Oh, innocent, happy though poor !
Ch.   That's we—
Sir D. If I had been virtuous, I'm sure—
Ch.   Like me—
Sir D. I should be as nice-looking as you're !
Ch.   May be.
Sir D.   You are very nice-looking indeed !
          Oh, innocents, listen in time—
Ch.   We *doe*,
Sir D. Avoid an existence of crime—
Ch.   Just so—
Sir D. Or you'll be as ugly as I'm—
Ch. (*loudly*).   No ! No !
Sir D.   And now, if you please, we'll proceed.

(*All the Girls express their horror of* Sir Despard. *As he approaches them they fly from him, terror-stricken, leaving him alone on the stage.*)

Sir D. Poor children, how they loathe me—me whose hands are certainly steeped in infamy, but whose heart is as the heart of a little child ! But what *is* a poor baronet to do, when a whole picture gallery of ancestors step down from their frames and threaten him with an excruciating death if he hesitate to commit his daily crime ? But ha ! ha ! I am even with them ! (*Mysteriously*.) I get my crime over the first thing in the morning, and then, ha ! ha ! for the rest of the day I do good—I do good—I do good ! (*Melodramatically*.) Two days since, I stole a child and built an orphan asylum. Yesterday I robbed a bank and endowed a bishopric. To-day I carry off Rose Maybud and atone with a cathedral ! This is what it is to be the sport and toy of a Picture Gallery ! But I will be bitterly revenged upon them ! I will give them all to the Nation, and nobody shall ever look upon their faces again !

Enter Richard.

Rich. Ax your honour's pardon, but——

Sir D. Ha! observed! And by a mariner! What would you with me, fellow?

Rich. Your honour, I'm a poor man-o'-war's man, becalmed in the doldrums——

Sir D. I don't know them.

Rich. And I make bold to ax your honour's advice. Does your honour know what it is to have a heart?

Sir D. My honour knows what it is to have a complete apparatus for conducting the circulation of the blood through the veins and arteries of the human body.

Rich. Aye, but has your honour a heart that ups and looks you in the face, and gives you quarter-deck orders that it's life and death to disobey?

Sir D. I have not a heart of that description, but I have a Picture Gallery that presumes to take that liberty.

Rich. Well, your honour, it's like this—Your honour had an elder brother——

Sir D. It had.

Rich. Who should have inherited your title and, with it, its cuss.

Sir D. Aye, but he died. Oh, Ruthven!——

Rich. He didn't.

Sir D. He did *not*?

Rich. He didn't. On the contrary, he lives in this here very village, under the name of Robin Oakapple, and he's a-going to marry Rose Maybud this very day.

Sir D. Ruthven alive, and going to marry Rose Maybud! Can this be possible?

Rich. Now the question I was going to ask your honour is—Ought I to tell your honour this?

Sir D. I don't know. It's a delicate point. I think you ought. Mind, I'm not sure, but I think so.

Rich. That's what my heart says. It says, "Dick," it says (it calls me Dick acos it's entitled to take that liberty), "that there young gal would recoil from him if she knowed what he really were. Ought you to stand off and on, and let this young gal take this false step and never fire a shot across her bows to bring her to? No,"

it says, " you did *not* ought." And I won't ought, accordin'.

Sir D.   Then you really feel yourself at liberty to tell me that my elder brother lives—that I may charge him with his cruel deceit, and transfer to his shoulders the hideous thraldom under which I have laboured for so many years ! Free—free at last ! Free to live a blameless life, and to die beloved and regretted by all who knew me !

DUET—Sir Despard *and* Richard.

Rich.   You understand ?
Sir D.   I think I do ;
             With vigour unshaken
             This step shall be taken.
         It's neatly planned.
Rich.   I think so too ;
             I'll readily bet it
             You'll never regret it !

Both.   For duty, duty must be done ;
        The rule applies to every one,
        And painful though that duty be,
        To shirk the task were fiddle-de-dee !

Sir D.   The bridegroom comes—
Rich.   Likewise the bride—
             The maidens are very
             Elated and merry ;
         They are her chums.
Sir D.   To lash their pride
             Were almost a pity,
             The pretty committee !

Both.   But duty, duty must be done ;
        The rule applies to every one,
        And painful though that duty be,
        To shirk the task were fiddle-de-dee !

             [*Exeunt* Richard *and* Sir Despard.

Enter Chorus of Bridesmaids and Bucks.

CHORUS OF BRIDESMAIDS.

Hail the bride of seventeen summers :
In fair phrases
Hymn her praises ;
Lift your song on high, all comers.
She rejoices
In your voices.
Smiling summer beams upon her,
Shedding every blessing on her :
Maidens greet her—
Kindly treat her—
You may all be brides some day !

CHORUS OF BUCKS.

Hail the bridegroom who advances,
Agitated,
Yet elated.
He's in easy circumstances,
Young and lusty,
True and trusty.

Enter ROBIN, *attended by* RICHARD *and* OLD ADAM, *meeting* ROSE, *attended by* ZORAH *and* DAME HANNAH. ROSE *and* ROBIN *embrace*.

MADRIGAL.

ROSE.	When the buds are blossoming,
	Smiling welcome to the spring,
	Lovers choose a wedding day—
	Life is love in merry May !
GIRLS.	Spring is green—Fal lal la !
	Summer's rose—Fal lal la !
ALL.	It is sad when summer goes,
	Fal la !
MEN.	Autumn's gold—Fal lal la !
	Winter's grey—Fal lal la !
ALL.	Winter still is far away—
	Fal la !

Leaves in autumn fade and fall,
Winter is the end of all.
Spring and summer teem with glee :
Spring and summer, then, for me !
                Fal la !

HANNAH. In the spring-time seed is sown :
            In the summer grass is mown :
            In the autumn you may reap :
            Winter is the time for sleep.

GIRLS.   Spring is hope—Fal lal la !
                  Summer's joy—Fal lal la !
ALL.   Spring and summer never cloy.
                  Fal la !

MEN.   Autumn, toil—Fal lal la !
                  Winter, rest—Fal lal la !
ALL.   Winter, after all, is best—
                  Fal la !

ALL.   Spring and summer pleasure you,
            Autumn, aye, and winter too—
            Every season has its cheer,
            Life is lovely all the year !
                  Fal la !

GAVOTTE.

After Gavotte, enter SIR DESPARD.

SIR D. Hold, bride and bridegroom, ere you wed each
        other,
      I claim young Robin as my elder brother !
      His rightful title I have long enjoyed :
      I claim him as Sir Ruthven Murgatroyd !

ALL. O wonder !
ROSE (*wildly*). Deny the falsehood, Robin, as you should,
                It is a plot !
ROB.   I would, if conscientiously I could,
               But I cannot !
ALL.   Ah, base one !

SOLO—ROBIN.

As pure and blameless peasant,
　　I cannot, I regret,
Deny a truth unpleasant,
　　I am that Baronet !

ALL.　　　　　He is that Baronet !

But when completely rated
　　Bad Baronet am I,
That I am what he's stated
　　I'll recklessly deny !

ALL.　　　　　He'll recklessly deny !

ROB.　When I'm a bad Bart. I will tell taradiddles !
ALL.　　He'll tell taradiddles when he's a bad Bart.
ROB.　I'll play a bad part on the falsest of fiddles.
ALL.　　On very false fiddles he'll play a bad part !
ROB.　But until that takes place I must be conscientious—
ALL.　　He'll be conscientious until that takes place.
ROB.　Then adieu with good grace to my morals
　　　　sententious !
ALL.　To morals sententious adieu with good grace !

ZOR.　Who is the wretch who hath betrayed thee ?
　　　　　　Let him stand forth !
RICH. (*coming forward*).　'Twas I !
ALL.　　Die, traitor !
RICH.　　　　　　　　Hold ! my conscience made me !
　　　　　　Withhold your wrath !

SOLO—RICHARD.

Within this breast there beats a heart
　　Whose voice can't be gainsaid.
It bade me thy true rank impart,
　　And I at once obeyed.

I knew 'twould blight thy budding fate—
I knew 'twould cause thee anguish great—
But did I therefore hesitate ?
   No ! I at once obeyed !

ALL.   Acclaim him who, when his true heart
Bade him young Robin's rank impart,
   Immediately obeyed !

SOLO—ROSE (*addressing* ROBIN).

   Farewell !
Thou hadst my heart—
   'Twas quickly won !
But now we part—
   Thy face I shun !
   Farewell !

Go bend the knee
   At Vice's shrine,
Of life with me
   All hope resign.
   Farewell !

(*To* SIR DESPARD.)   Take me—I am thy bride !

BRIDESMAIDS.

Hail the Bridegroom—hail the Bride !
When the nuptial knot is tied ;
Every day will bring some joy
That can never, never cloy !

Enter MARGARET, *who listens.*

SIR D.   Excuse me, I'm a virtuous person now—
ROSE.   That's why I wed you !
SIR D.   And I to Margaret must keep my vow !
MAR.   Have I misread you ?
Oh, joy ! with newly kindled rapture warmed,
   I kneel before you ! (*Kneels.*)
SIR D.   I once disliked you ; now that I've reformed,
   How I adore you ! (*They embrace.*)

BRIDESMAIDS.

Hail the Bridegroom—hail the Bride !
When the nuptial knot is tied ;
Every day will bring some joy
That can never, never cloy !

ROSE.　　Richard, of him I love bereft,
　　　　　　　Through thy design,
　　　　Thou art the only one that's left,
　　　　　　　So I am thine !　(*They embrace.*)

BRIDESMAIDS.

Hail the Bridegroom—hail the Bride !
Let the nuptial knot be tied !

DUET—ROSE *and* RICHARD.

Oh, happy the lily
　　　When kissed by the bee ;
And, sipping tranquilly,
　　　Quite happy is he ;
And happy the filly
　　　That neighs in her pride ;
But happier than any,
A pound to a penny,
A lover is, when he
　　　Embraces his bride !

DUET—SIR DESPARD *and* MARGARET.

Oh, happy the flowers
　　　That blossom in June,
And happy the bowers
　　　That gain by the boon,
But happier by hours
　　　The man of descent,
Who, folly regretting,
Is bent on forgetting
His bad baronetting,
　　　And means to repent !

TRIO—HANNAH, ADAM, *and* ZORAH.

Oh, happy the blossom
    That blooms on the lea,
Likewise the opossum
    That sits on a tree,
But when you come across 'em,
    They cannot compare
With those who are treading
The dance at a wedding,
While people are spreading
    The best of good fare !

SOLO—ROBIN.

Oh, wretched the debtor
    Who's signing a deed !
And wretched the letter
    That no one can read !
But very much better
    Their lot it must be
Than that of the person
I'm making this verse on,
Whose head there's a curse on—
    Alluding to me !

Repeat ensemble with Chorus.

DANCE.

At the end of the dance ROBIN *falls senseless
on the stage.   Picture.*

END OF ACT I.

ACT II.

SCENE.—*Picture Gallery in Ruddigore Castle. The walls are covered with full-length portraits of the Baronets of Ruddigore from the time of* JAMES I.—*the first being that of* SIR RUPERT, *alluded to in the legend; the last, that of the last deceased Baronet,* SIR RODERIC.

Enter ROBIN *and* ADAM *melodramatically. They are greatly altered in appearance,* ROBIN *wearing the haggard aspect of a guilty roué;* ADAM, *that of the wicked steward to such a man.*

DUET—ROBIN *and* ADAM.

ROB.   I once was as meek as a new-born lamb,
        I'm now Sir Murgatroyd—ha! ha!
          With greater precision
          (Without the elision),
        Sir Ruthven Murgatroyd—ha! ha!

ADAM.   And I, who was once his *valley-de-sham*,
        As steward I'm now employed—ha! ha!
          The dickens may take him—
          I'll never forsake him!
        As steward I'm now employed—ha! ha!

BOTH.   How dreadful when an innocent heart
        Becomes, perforce, a bad young Bart.,
        And still more hard on old Adam,
        His former faithful *valley-de-sham*!

ROB.   This is a painful state of things, old Adam!

410

ADAM. Painful, indeed! Ah, my poor master, when I swore that, come what would, I would serve you in all things for ever, I little thought to what a pass it would bring me! The confidential adviser to the greatest villain unhung! Now, sir, to business. What crime do you propose to commit to-day?

ROB. How should I know? As my confidential adviser, it's your duty to suggest something.

ADAM. Sir, I loathe the life you are leading, but a good old man's oath is paramount, and I obey. Richard Dauntless is here with pretty Rose Maybud, to ask your consent to their marriage. Poison their beer.

ROB. No—not that—I know I'm a bad Bart., but I'm not as bad a Bart. as all that.

ADAM. Well, there you are, you see! It's no use my making suggestions if you don't adopt them.

ROB. (*melodramatically*). How would it be, do you think, were I to lure him here with cunning wile—bind him with good stout rope to yonder post—and then, by making hideous faces at him, curdle the heart-blood in his arteries, and freeze the very marrow in his bones? How say you, Adam, is not the scheme well planned?

ADAM. It would be simply rude—nothing more. But soft—they come!

ADAM *and* ROBIN *retire up as* RICHARD *and* ROSE *enter, preceded by Chorus of Bridesmaids.*

DUET—RICHARD *and* ROSE.

RICH.
> Happily coupled are we,
> > You see—
> I am a jolly Jack Tar,
> > My star,
> And you are the fairest,
> The richest and rarest
> Of innocent lasses you are,
> > By far—
> Of innocent lasses you are!

Fanned by a favouring gale,
You'll sail
Over life's treacherous sea
With me,
And as for bad weather,
We'll brave it together,
And you shall creep under my lee,
My wee !
And you shall creep under my lee !

For you are such a smart little craft—
Such a neat little, sweet little craft,
Such a bright little, tight little,
Slight little, light little,
Trim little, prim little craft !

CHORUS.   For she is such, etc.

ROSE.   My hopes will be blighted, I fear,
My dear ;
In a month you'll be going to sea,
Quite free,
And all of my wishes
You'll throw to the fishes
As though they were never to be ;
Poor me !
As though they were never to be.
And I shall be left all alone
To moan,
And weep at your cruel deceit,
Complete ;
While you'll be asserting
Your freedom by flirting
With every woman you meet,
You cheat—
With every woman you meet !

Though I am such a smart little craft—
Such a neat little, sweet little craft,
  Such a bright little, tight little,
  Slight little, light little,
Trim little, prim little craft!

CHORUS.   Though she is such, etc.

Enter ROBIN.

ROB. Soho! pretty one—in my power at last, eh?
Know ye not that I have those within my call who, at my
lightest bidding, would immure ye in an uncomfortable
dungeon? (*Calling.*) What ho! within there!

RICH. Hold—we are prepared for this (*producing a
Union Jack*). Here is a flag that none dare defy (*all
kneel*), and while this glorious rag floats over Rose Maybud's head, the man does not live who would dare to lay
unlicensed hand upon her!

ROB. Foiled—and by a Union Jack! But a time
will come, and then——

ROSE. Nay, let me plead with him. (*To* ROBIN.) Sir
Ruthven, have pity. In my book of etiquette the case of
a maiden about to be wedded to one who unexpectedly
turns out to be a baronet with a curse on him is not
considered. Time was when you loved me madly. Prove
that this was no selfish love by according your consent to
my marriage with one who, if he be not you yourself, is
the next best thing—your dearest friend!

BALLAD—ROSE.

In bygone days I had thy love—
  Thou hadst my heart.
But Fate, all human vows above,
  Our lives did part!
By the old love thou hadst for me—
By the fond heart that beat for thee—
By joys that never now can be,
  Grant thou my prayer!

ALL (*kneeling*).   Grant thou her prayer !

ROB. (*recit*.).   Take her—I yield !

ALL (*recit*.).   Oh, rapture !

CHORUS.   Away to the parson we go—
                      Say we're solicitous very
              That he will turn two into one—
                      Singing hey, derry down derry !

RICH.   For she *is* such a smart little craft—
ROSE.   Such a neat little, sweet little craft—
RICH.   Such a bright little—
ROSE.   Tight little—
RICH.   Slight little—
ROSE.   Light little—
BOTH.   Trim little, slim little craft !

CHORUS.   For she *is* such a smart little craft, etc.

                                        [*Exeunt all but* ROBIN.

ROB.   For a week I have fulfilled my accursed doom !
I have duly committed a crime a day ! Not a great crime,
I trust, but still, in the eyes of one as strictly regulated
as I used to be, a crime. But will my ghostly ancestors
be satisfied with what I have done, or will they regard it
as an unworthy subterfuge ? (*Addressing Pictures*.) Oh,
my forefathers, wallowers in blood, there came at last a
day when, sick of crime, you, each and every, vowed to
sin no more, and so, in agony, called welcome Death to
free you from your cloying guiltiness. Let the sweet
psalm of that repentant hour soften your long-dead hearts,
and tune your souls to mercy on your poor posterity !
(*kneeling*).

(*The stage darkens for a moment. It becomes light again,
    and the Pictures are seen to have become animated.*)

CHORUS OF FAMILY PORTRAITS.

Painted emblems of a race,
 All accurst in days of yore,
Each from his accustomed place
 Steps into the world once more.

(*The Pictures step from their frames and march
round the stage.*)

Baronet of Ruddigore,
 Last of our accursèd line,
Down upon the oaken floor—
 Down upon those knees of thine.

Coward, poltroon, shaker, squeamer,
Blockhead, sluggard, dullard, dreamer,
Shirker, shuffler, crawler, creeper,
Sniffler, snuffler, wailer, weeper,
Earthworm, maggot, tadpole, weevil!
Set upon thy course of evil,
Lest the King of Spectre-Land
Set on thee his grisly hand!

(*The Spectre of* SIR RODERIC *descends from his frame.*)

SIR ROD. Beware! beware! beware!

ROB.   Gaunt vision, who art thou
  That thus, with icy glare
   And stern relentless brow,
   Appearest, who knows how?

SIR ROD. I am the spectre of the late
   Sir Roderic Murgatroyd,
  Who comes to warn thee that thy fate
   Thou canst not now avoid.

ROB.   Alas, poor ghost!

SIR ROD.   The pity you
                    Express for nothing goes :
                 We spectres are a jollier crew
                    Than you, perhaps, suppose !

CHORUS.   We spectres are a jollier crew
                    Than you, perhaps, suppose !

SONG—SIR RODERIC.

When the night wind howls in the chimney cowls, and the
    bat in the moonlight flies,
And inky clouds, like funeral shrouds, sail over the mid-
    night skies—
When the footpads quail at the night-bird's wail, and
    black dogs bay at the moon,
Then is the spectres' holiday—then is the ghosts' high-
    noon !

    CHORUS.   Ha ! ha !
                Then is the ghosts' high-noon !

As the sob of the breeze sweeps over the trees, and the
    mists lie low on the fen,
From grey tomb-stones are gathered the bones that once
    were women and men,
And away they go, with a mop and a mow, to the revel
    that ends too soon,
For cockcrow limits our holiday—the dead of the night's
    high-noon !

    CHORUS.   Ha ! ha !
                The dead of the night's high-noon !

And then each ghost with his ladye-toast to their church-
    yard beds takes flight,
With a kiss, perhaps, on her lantern chaps, and a grisly
    grim " good-night " ;
Till the welcome knell of the midnight bell rings forth
    its jolliest tune,
And ushers in our next high holiday—the dead of the
    night's high-noon !

CHORUS.   Ha ! ha !
             The dead of the night's high-noon !

ROB.   I recognize you now—you are the picture that hangs at the end of the gallery.

SIR ROD.   In a bad light. I am.

ROB.   Are you considered a good likeness ?

SIR ROD.   Pretty well. Flattering.

ROB.   Because as a work of art you are poor.

SIR ROD.   I am crude in colour, but I have only been painted ten years. In a couple of centuries I shall be an Old Master, and then you will be sorry you spoke lightly of me.

ROB.   And may I ask why you have left your frames ?

SIR ROD.   It is our duty to see that our successors commit their daily crimes in a conscientious and workman-like fashion. It is our duty to remind you that you are evading the conditions under which you are permitted to exist.

ROB.   Really, I don't know what you'd have. I've only been a bad baronet a week, and I've committed a crime punctually every day.

SIR ROD.   Let us inquire into this. Monday ?

ROB.   Monday was a Bank Holiday.

SIR ROD.   True. Tuesday ?

ROB.   On Tuesday I made a false income-tax return.

ALL.   Ha ! ha !

1ST GHOST.   That's nothing.

2ND GHOST.   Nothing at all.

3RD GHOST.   Everybody does that.

4TH GHOST.   It's expected of you.

SIR ROD.   Wednesday ?

ROB.   (*melodramatically*). On Wednesday I forged a will.

SIR ROD.   Whose will ?

ROB.   My own.

SIR ROD.   My good sir, you can't forge your own will !

ROB.   Can't I, though ! I like that ! I *did* ! Besides, if a man can't forge his own will, whose will can he forge ?

P

1st Ghost.   There's something in that.

2nd Ghost.   Yes, it seems reasonable.

3rd Ghost.   At first sight it does.

4th Ghost.   Fallacy somewhere, I fancy!

Rob.   A man can do what he likes with his own?

Sir Rod.   I suppose he can.

Rob.   Well, then, he can forge his own will, stoopid!
On Thursday I shot a fox.

1st Ghost.   Hear, hear!

Sir Rod.   That's better (*addressing Ghosts*).   Pass the
fox, I think?   (*They assent.*)   Yes, pass the fox.   Friday?

Rob.   On Friday I forged a cheque.

Sir Rod.   Whose cheque?

Rob.   Old Adam's.

Sir Rod.   But Old Adam hasn't a banker.

Rob.   I didn't say I forged his banker—I said I
forged his cheque.   On Saturday I disinherited my only
son.

Sir Rod.   But you haven't got a son.

Rob.   No—not yet.   I disinherited him in advance, to
save time.   You see—by this arrangement—he'll be born
ready disinherited.

Sir Rod.   I see.   But I don't think you can do that.

Rob.   My good sir, if I can't disinherit my own unborn
son, whose unborn son can I disinherit?

Sir Rod.   Humph!   These arguments sound very
well, but I can't help thinking that, if they were reduced
to syllogistic form, they wouldn't hold water.   Now quite
understand us.   We are foggy, but we don't permit our
fogginess to be presumed upon.   Unless you undertake
to—well, suppose we say, carry off a lady?   (*Addressing
Ghosts.*)   Those who are in favour of his carrying off a
lady?   (*All hold up their hands except a Bishop.*)   Those
of the contrary opinion?   (*Bishop holds up his hands.*)
Oh, you're never satisfied!   Yes, unless you undertake
to carry off a lady at once—I don't care what lady—any
lady—choose your lady—you perish in inconceivable
agonies.

Rob. Carry off a lady? Certainly not, on any account. I've the greatest respect for ladies, and I wouldn't do anything of the kind for worlds! No, no. I'm not that kind of baronet, I assure you! If that's all you've got to say, you'd better go back to your frames.

Sir Rod. Very good—then let the agonies commence.

(*Ghosts make passes.* Robin *begins to writhe in agony*.)

Rob. Oh! Oh! Don't do that! I can't stand it!
Sir Rod. Painful, isn't it? It gets worse by degrees.
Rob. Oh—Oh! Stop a bit! Stop it, will you? I want to speak.

(Sir Roderic *makes signs to Ghosts, who resume their attitudes*.)

Sir Rod. Better?
Rob. Yes—better now! Whew!
Sir Rod. Well, do you consent?
Rob. But it's such an ungentlemanly thing to do!
Sir Rod. As you please. (*To Ghosts.*) Carry on!
Rob. Stop—I can't stand it! I agree! I promise! It shall be done!
Sir Rod. To-day?
Rob. To-day!
Sir Rod. At once?
Rob. At once! I retract! I apologize! I had no idea it was anything like that!

Chorus.

He yields! He answers to our call!
    We do not ask for more.
A sturdy fellow, after all,
    This latest Ruddigore!
All perish in unheard-of woe
    Who dare our wills defy;

We want your pardon, ere we go,
For having agonized you so—
            So pardon us—
            So pardon us—
            So pardon us—
                        Or die !

ROB.   I pardon you !
                I pardon you !

ALL.   He pardons us—
                        Hurrah !

(*The Ghosts return to their frames.*)

CHORUS.   Painted emblems of a race,
                All accurst in days of yore,
            Each to his accustomed place
                Steps unwillingly once more !

(*By this time the Ghosts have changed to pictures
again.   ROBIN is overcome by emotion.*)

Enter ADAM.

ADAM.   My poor master, you are not well——
ROB.   Gideon Crawle, it won't do—I've seen 'em—all
my ancestors—they're just gone.   They say that I must
do something desperate at once, or perish in horrible
agonies.   Go—go to yonder village—carry off a maiden—
bring her here at once—any one—I don't care which——
ADAM.   But——
ROB.   Not a word, but obey !   Fly !

                                    [*Exit* ADAM.

RECIT. AND SONG—ROBIN.

Away, Remorse !
            Compunction, hence !
Go, Moral Force !
            Go, Penitence !

To Virtue's plea
      A long farewell—
Propriety,
        I ring your knell !
Come, guiltiness of deadliest hue !
Come, desperate deeds of derring-do !

Henceforth all the crimes that I find in the *Times*,
    I've promised to perpetrate daily ;
To-morrow I start, with a petrified heart,
    On a regular course of Old Bailey.
There's confidence tricking, bad coin, pocket-picking,
    And several other disgraces—
There's postage-stamp prigging, and then, thimble-rigging,
    The three-card delusion at races !
Oh ! a baronet's rank is exceedingly nice,
But the title's uncommonly dear at the price !

Ye well-to-do squires, who live in the shires,
    Where petty distinctions are vital,
Who found Athenæums and local museums,
    With views to a baronet's title—
Ye butchers and bakers and candlestick makers
    Who sneer at all things that are tradey,
Whose middle-class lives are embarrassed by wives
    Who long to parade as " My Lady ",
Oh ! allow me to offer a word of advice,
The title's uncommonly dear at the price !

Ye supple M.P.'s, who go down on your knees,
    Your precious identity sinking,
And vote black or white as your leaders indite
    (Which saves you the trouble of thinking),
For your country's good fame, her repute, or her shame,
    You don't care the snuff of a candle—
But you're paid for your game when you're told that your name
    Will be graced by a baronet's handle—
Oh ! allow me to give *you* a word of advice—
The title's uncommonly dear at the price !

                           [*Exit* ROBIN.

Enter DESPARD *and* MARGARET. *They are both dressed in sober black of formal cut, and present a strong contrast to their appearance in Act I.*

DUET.

DES.	I once was a very abandoned person—
MAR.	Making the most of evil chances.
DES.	Nobody could conceive a worse 'un—
MAR.	Even in all the old romances.
DES.	I blush for my wild extravagances,
	But be so kind
	To bear in mind,
MAR.	We were the victims of circumstances !

(Dance.)

That is one of our blameless dances.

MAR.	I was once an exceedingly odd young lady—
DES.	Suffering much from spleen and vapours.
MAR.	Clergymen thought my conduct shady—
DES.	She didn't spend much upon linen-drapers.
MAR.	It certainly entertained the gapers.
	My ways were strange
	Beyond all range—
DES.	Paragraphs got into all the papers.

(Dance.)

DES.	We only cut respectable capers.

DES.	I've given up all my wild proceedings.
MAR.	My taste for a wandering life is waning.
DES.	Now I'm a dab at penny readings.
MAR.	They are not remarkably entertaining.
DES.	A moderate livelihood we're gaining.
MAR.	In fact we rule
	A National School.
DES.	The duties are dull, but I'm not complaining.

(Dance.)

This sort of thing takes a deal of training !

DES. We have been married a week.

MAR. One happy, happy week !

DES. Our new life——

MAR. Is delightful indeed !

DES. So calm !

MAR. So unimpassioned ! (*wildly*). Master, all this I owe to you ! See, I am no longer wild and untidy. My hair is combed. My face is washed. My boots fit !

DES. Margaret, don't. Pray restrain yourself. Remember, you are now a district visitor.

MAR. A gentle district visitor !

DES. You are orderly, methodical, neat ; you have your emotions well under control.

MAR. I have ! (*wildly*). Master, when I think of all you have done for me, I fall at your feet. I embrace your ankles. I hug your knees ! (*Doing so.*)

DES. Hush. This is not well. This is calculated to provoke remark. Be composed, I beg !

MAR. Ah ! you are angry with poor little Mad Margaret !

DES. No, not angry ; but a district visitor should learn to eschew melodrama. Visit the poor, by all means, and give them tea and barley-water, but don't do it as if you were administering a bowl of deadly nightshade. It upsets them. Then when you nurse sick people, and find them not as well as could be expected, why go into hysterics ?

MAR. Why not ?

DES. Because it's too jumpy for a sick-room.

MAR. How strange ! Oh, Master ! Master !—how shall I express the all-absorbing gratitude that—(*about to throw herself at his feet*).

DES. Now ! (*warningly*).

MAR. Yes, I know, dear—it shan't occur again. (*He is seated—she sits on the ground by him.*) Shall I tell you one of poor Mad Margaret's odd thoughts ? Well, then, when I am lying awake at night, and the pale

moonlight streams through the latticed casement, strange
fancies crowd upon my poor mad brain, and I sometimes think that if we could hit upon some word for
you to use whenever I am about to relapse—some word
that teems with hidden meaning—like "Basingstoke"
—it might recall me to my saner self. For, after all,
I am only Mad Margaret! Daft Meg! Poor Meg!
He! he! he!

DES.   Poor child, she wanders! But soft—some one
comes—Margaret—pray recollect yourself—Basingstoke,
I beg! Margaret, if you don't Basingstoke at once, I
shall be seriously angry.

MAR. (*recovering herself*).   Basingstoke it is!

DES.   Then make it so.

Enter ROBIN.   *He starts on seeing them.*

ROB.   Despard! And his young wife! This visit is
unexpected.

MAR.   Shall I fly at him? Shall I tear him limb
from limb? Shall I rend him asunder? Say but the
word and——

DES.   Basingstoke!

MAR. (*suddenly demure*).   Basingstoke it is!

DES. (*aside*).   Then make it so. (*Aloud.*) My
brother—I call you brother still, despite your horrible
profligacy—we have come to urge you to abandon
the evil courses to which you have committed yourself, and at any cost to become a pure and blameless
ratepayer.

ROB.   But I've done no wrong yet.

MAR. (*wildly*).   No wrong! He has done no wrong!
Did you hear that!

DES.   Basingstoke!

MAR. (*recovering herself*).   Basingstoke it is!

DES.   My brother—I still call you brother, you
observe—you forget that you have been, in the eye of
the law, a Bad Baronet of Ruddigore for ten years—and
you are therefore responsible—in the eye of the law—for

all the misdeeds committed by the unhappy gentleman who occupied your place.

ROB. I see! Bless my heart, I never thought of that! Was I very bad?

DES. Awful. Wasn't he? (*to* MARGARET).

ROB. And I've been going on like this for how long?

DES. Ten years! Think of all the atrocities you have committed—by attorney as it were—during that period. Remember how you trifled with this poor child's affections —how you raised her hopes on high (don't cry, my love— Basingstoke, you know), only to trample them in the dust when they were at the very zenith of their fullness. Oh fie, sir, fie—she trusted you!

ROB. Did she? What a scoundrel I must have been! There, there—don't cry, my dear (*to* MARGARET, *who is sobbing on* ROBIN'S *breast*), it's all right now. Birmingham, you know—Birmingham——

MAR. (*sobbing*). It's Ba—Ba—Basingstoke!

ROB. Basingstoke! of course it is—Basingstoke.

MAR. Then make it so!

ROB. There, there—it's all right—he's married you now—that is, *I've* married you (*turning to* DESPARD)— I say, which of us has married her?

DES. Oh, *I've* married her.

ROB. (*aside*). Oh, I'm glad of that. (*To* MARGARET.) Yes, *he's* married you now (*passing her over to* DESPARD), and anything more disreputable than my conduct seems to have been I've never even heard of. But my mind is made up—I *will* defy my ancestors. I *will* refuse to obey their behests, thus, by courting death, atone in some degree for the infamy of my career!

MAR. I knew it — I knew it — God bless you — (*hysterically*).

DES. Basingstoke!

MAR. Basingstoke it is! (*Recovers herself.*)

PATTER-TRIO.

ROBIN, DESPARD, *and* MARGARET.

ROB. My eyes are fully open to my awful situation—
  I shall go at once to Roderic and make him an
    oration.
  I shall tell him I've recovered my forgotten moral
    senses,
  And I don't care twopence - halfpenny for any
    consequences.
  Now I do not want to perish by the sword or by
    the dagger,
  But a martyr may indulge a little pardonable
    swagger,
  And a word or two of compliment my vanity would
    flatter,
  But I've got to die to-morrow, so it really doesn't
    matter !

DES.   So it really doesn't matter—

MAR.   So it really doesn't matter—

ALL. So it really doesn't matter, matter, matter, matter,
    matter !

MAR. If I were not a little mad and generally silly
  I should give you my advice upon the subject,
    willy-nilly ;
  I should show you in a moment how to grapple
    with the question,
  And you'd really be astonished at the force of my
    suggestion.
  On the subject I shall write you a most valuable
    letter,
  Full of excellent suggestions when I feel a little
    better,
  But at present I'm afraid I am as mad as any
    hatter,
  So I'll keep 'em to myself, for my opinion doesn't
    matter !

DES.	Her opinion doesn't matter—
ROB.	Her opinion doesn't matter—
ALL.	Her opinion doesn't matter, matter, matter, matter, matter!

DES.   If I had been so lucky as to have a steady brother
Who could talk to me as we are talking now to one another—
Who could give me good advice when he discovered I was erring
(Which is just the very favour which on you I am conferring),
My story would have made a rather interesting idyll,
And I might have lived and died a very decent indiwiddle.
This particularly rapid, unintelligible patter
Isn't generally heard, and if it is it doesn't matter!

ROB.	If it is it doesn't matter—
MAR.	If it ain't it doesn't matter—

ALL.   If it is it doesn't matter, matter, matter, matter, matter!

                     [*Exeunt* DESPARD *and* MARGARET.

                  Enter ADAM.

ADAM (*guiltily*).   Master—the deed is done!

ROB.   What deed?

ADAM.   She is here—alone, unprotected——

ROB.   Who?

ADAM.   The maiden. I've carried her off—I had a hard task, for she fought like a tiger-cat!

ROB.   Great heaven, I had forgotten her! I had hoped to have died unspotted by crime, but I am foiled again—and by a tiger-cat! Produce her—and leave us!

        [ADAM *introduces* DAME HANNAH, *very much excited, and exit.*

ROB. Dame Hannah ! This is—this is not what I expected.

HAN. Well, sir, and what would you with me ? Oh, you have begun bravely—bravely indeed ! Unappalled by the calm dignity of blameless womanhood, your minion has torn me from my spotless home, and dragged me, blindfold and shrieking, through hedges, over stiles, and across a very difficult country, and left me, helpless and trembling, at your mercy ! Yet not helpless, coward sir, for approach one step—nay, but the twentieth part of one poor inch—and this poniard (*produces a very small dagger*) shall teach ye what it is to lay unholy hands on old Stephen Trusty's daughter !

ROB. Madam, I am extremely sorry for this. It is not at all what I intended—anything more correct— more deeply respectful than my intentions towards you, it would be impossible for any one—however particular— to desire.

HAN. Bah, I am not to be tricked by smooth words, hypocrite ! But be warned in time, for there are, without, a hundred gallant hearts whose trusty blades would hack him limb from limb who dared to lay unholy hands on old Stephen Trusty's daughter !

ROB. And this is what it is to embark upon a career of unlicensed pleasure !

(HANNAH, *who has taken a formidable dagger from one of the armed figures, throws her small dagger to* ROBIN.)

HAN. Harkye, miscreant, you have secured me, and I am your poor prisoner ; but if you think I cannot take care of myself you are very much mistaken. Now then, it's one to one, and let the best man win !

(*Making for him.*)

ROB. (*in an agony of terror*). Don't ! don't look at me like that ! I can't bear it ! Roderic ! Uncle ! Save me !

RODERIC *enters, from his picture. He comes down
the stage.*

ROD. What is the matter? Have you carried her
off?

ROB. I have—she is there—look at her—she terrifies
me!

ROD. (*looking at* HANNAH). Little Nannikin!

HAN. (*amazed*). Roddy-doddy!

ROD. My own old love! Why, how came *you*
here?

HAN. This brute—he carried me off! Bodily! But
I'll show him! (*about to rush at* ROBIN).

ROD. Stop! (*To* ROB.) What do you mean by
carrying off this lady? Are you aware that once upon
a time she was engaged to be married to me? I'm very
angry—very angry indeed.

ROB. Now I hope this will be a lesson to you in
future not to——

ROD. Hold your tongue, sir.

ROB. Yes, uncle.

ROD. Have you given him any encouragement?

HAN. (*to* ROB.). Have I given you any encouragement?
Frankly now, have I?

ROB. No. Frankly, you have not. Anything more
scrupulously correct than your conduct, it would be
impossible to desire.

ROD. You go away.

ROB. Yes, uncle. [*Exit* ROBIN.

ROD. This is a strange meeting after so many
years!

HAN. Very. I thought you were dead.

ROD. I am. I died ten years ago.

HAN. And are you pretty comfortable?

ROD. Pretty well—that is—yes, pretty well.

HAN. You don't deserve to be, for I loved you all the
while, dear; and it made me dreadfully unhappy to hear
of all your goings-on, you bad, bad boy!

BALLAD—Hannah.

There grew a little flower
　　　'Neath a great oak tree :
When the tempest 'gan to lower
　　　Little heeded she :
No need had she to cower,
For she dreaded not its power—
She was happy in the bower
　　　Of her great oak tree !
　　　　　Sing hey,
　　　　　Lackaday !
　　Let the tears fall free
For the pretty little flower and the great oak tree!

Вотн.　　　　　　　Sing hey,
　　　　　　　　Lackaday, etc.

When she found that he was fickle,
　　　Was that great oak tree,
She was in a pretty pickle,
　　　As she well might be—
But his gallantries were mickle,
For Death followed with his sickle,
And her tears began to trickle
　　　For her great oak tree !
Вотн.　　　　　　　Sing hey,
　　　　　　　　Lackaday ! etc.

Said she, " He loved me never,
　　　Did that great oak tree,
But I'm neither rich nor clever,
　　　And so why should he ?
But though fate our fortunes sever,
To be constant I'll endeavour,
Aye, for ever and for ever,
　　　To my great oak tree ! "
Вотн.　　　　　　　Sing hey,
　　　　　　　　Lackaday ! etc.

(*Falls weeping on* Roderic's *bosom.*)

Enter ROBIN, *excitedly, followed by all the characters and Chorus of Bridesmaids.*

ROB.   Stop a bit—both of you.

ROD.   This intrusion is unmannerly.

HAN.   I'm surprised at you.

ROB.   I can't stop to apologize—an idea has just occurred to me. A Baronet of Ruddigore can only die through refusing to commit his daily crime.

ROD.   No doubt.

ROB.   Therefore, to refuse to commit a daily crime is tantamount to suicide !

ROD.   It would seem so.

ROB.   But suicide is, itself, a crime—and so, by your own showing, you ought never to have died at all !

ROD.   I see—I understand ! Then I'm practically alive !

ROB.   Undoubtedly ! (SIR RODERIC *embraces* HANNAH.) Rose, when you believed that I was a simple farmer, I believe you loved me ?

ROSE.   Madly, passionately !

ROB.   But when I became a bad baronet, you very properly loved Richard instead ?

ROSE.   Passionately, madly !

ROB.   But if I should turn out *not* to be a bad baronet after all, how would you love me then ?

ROSE.   Madly, passionately !

ROB.   As before ?

ROSE.   Why, of course !

ROB.   My darling ! (*They embrace.*)

RICH.   Here, I say, belay !

ROSE.   Oh sir, belay, if it's absolutely necessary !

ROB.   Belay ? Certainly not !

FINALE.

ROB   Having been a wicked baronet a week.
   Once again a modest livelihood I seek,
    Agricultural employment
    Is to me a keen enjoyment,
   For I'm naturally diffident and meek !

ROSE. When a man has been a naughty baronet,
And expresses his repentance and regret,
 You should help him, if you're able,
 Like the mousie in the fable,
That's the teaching of my Book of Etiquette.

RICH. If you ask me why I do not pipe my eye,
Like an honest British sailor, I reply,
 That with Zorah for my missis,
 There'll be bread and cheese and kisses,
Which is just the sort of ration I enjye !

DES. *and* MAR. Prompted by a keen desire to evoke,
All the blessed calm of matrimony's yoke,
 We shall toddle off to-morrow,
 From this scene of sin and sorrow,
For to settle in the town of Basingstoke !

ALL.   For happy the lily
   That's kissed by the bee ;
  And, sipping tranquilly,
   Quite happy is he ;
  And happy the filly
   That neighs in her pride ;
  But happier than any,
  A pound to a penny,
  A lover is, when he
   Embraces his bride !

CURTAIN.

THE YEOMEN OF THE GUARD

OR

THE MERRYMAN AND HIS MAID

DRAMATIS PERSONÆ.

SIR RICHARD CHOLMONDELEY (*Lieutenant of the Tower*).
COLONEL FAIRFAX (*under sentence of death*).
SERGEANT MERYLL (*of the Yeomen of the Guard*).
LEONARD MERYLL (*his Son*).
JACK POINT (*a Strolling Jester*).
WILFRED SHADBOLT (*Head Jailer and Assistant Tormentor*).
THE HEADSMAN.
FIRST YEOMAN.
SECOND YEOMAN.
FIRST CITIZEN.
SECOND CITIZEN.
ELSIE MAYNARD (*a Strolling Singer*).
PHŒBE MERYLL (*Sergeant Meryll's Daughter*).
DAME CARRUTHERS (*Housekeeper to the Tower*).
KATE (*her Niece*).
Chorus of Yeomen of the Guard, Gentlemen, Citizens, etc.

SCENE.—Tower Green.

Date, 16th Century.

First produced at the Savoy Theatre on October 3, 1888.

THE YEOMEN OF THE GUARD

OR

THE MERRYMAN AND HIS MAID

ACT I.

SCENE.—Tower Green.

PHŒBE discovered spinning.

SONG—PHŒBE.

When maiden loves, she sits and sighs,
    She wanders to and fro ;
Unbidden tear-drops fill her eyes,
And to all questions she replies
      With a sad " heigho ! "
    'Tis but a little word—" heigho ! "
    So soft, 'tis scarcely heard—" heigho ! "
      An idle breath—
      Yet life and death
    May hang upon a maid's " heigho ! "

When maiden loves, she mopes apart,
    As owl mopes on a tree ;
Although she keenly feels the smart,
She cannot tell what ails her heart,
      With its sad " Ah me ! "

435

> 'Tis but a foolish sigh—" Ah me ! "
> Born but to droop and die—" Ah me ! "
>   Yet all the sense
>   Of eloquence
> Lies hidden in a maid's " Ah me ! " (*weeps*).

Enter WILFRED.

WIL.   Mistress Meryll !

PHŒ. (*looking up*).   Eh !   Oh ! it's you, is it ?   You may go away, if you like.   Because I don't want you, you know.

WIL.   Haven't you anything to say to me ?

PHŒ.   Oh yes !   Are the birds all caged ?   The wild beasts all littered down ?   All the locks, chains, bolts, and bars in good order ?   Is the Little Ease sufficiently uncomfortable ?   The racks, pincers, and thumbscrews all ready for work ?   Ugh ! you brute !

WIL.   These allusions to my professional duties are in doubtful taste.   I didn't become a head-jailer because I like head-jailing.   I didn't become an assistant-tormentor because I like assistant-tormenting.   We can't *all* be sorcerers, you know.   (PHŒBE *annoyed*.)   Ah ! you brought that upon yourself.

PHŒ.   Colonel Fairfax is *not* a sorcerer.   He's a man of science and an alchemist.

WIL.   Well, whatever he is, he won't be one long, for he's to be beheaded to-day for dealings with the devil. His master nearly had him last night, when the fire broke out in the Beauchamp Tower.

PHŒ.   Oh ! how I wish he had escaped in the confusion !   But take care ; there's still time for a reply to his petition for mercy.

WIL.   Ah ! I'm content to chance that.   This evening at half-past seven—ah !

PHŒ.   You're a cruel monster to speak so unfeelingly of the death of a young and handsome soldier.

WIL.   Young and handsome !   How do *you* know he's young and handsome ?

PHŒ. Because I've seen him every day for weeks past taking his exercise on the Beauchamp Tower.

WIL. Curse him!

PHŒ. There, I believe you're jealous of *him*, now. Jealous of a man I've never spoken to! Jealous of a poor soul who's to die in an hour!

WIL. I am! I'm jealous of everybody and everything. I'm jealous of the very words I speak to you—because they reach your ears—and I mustn't go near 'em!

PHŒ. How unjust you are! Jealous of the words you speak to me! Why, you know as well as I do that I don't even like them.

WIL. You used to like 'em.

PHŒ. I used to *pretend* I liked them. It was mere politeness to comparative strangers.

[*Exit* PHŒBE, *with spinning wheel.*

WIL. I don't believe you know what jealousy is! I don't believe you know how it eats into a man's heart— and disorders his digestion—and turns his interior into boiling lead. Oh, you are a heartless jade to trifle with the delicate organization of the human interior!

[*Exit* WILFRED.

Enter Crowd of Men and Women, followed by Yeomen of the Guard.

CHORUS (*as Yeomen march on*).
Tower Warders,
Under orders,
Gallant pikemen, valiant sworders!
Brave in bearing,
Foemen scaring,
In their bygone days of daring!
Ne'er a stranger
There to danger—
Each was o'er the world a ranger;
To the story
Of our glory
Each a bold contributory!

CHORUS OF YEOMEN.

In the autumn of our life,
   Here at rest in ample clover,
   We rejoice in telling over
      Our impetuous May and June.
In the evening of our day,
   With the sun of life declining,
   We recall without repining
      All the heat of bygone noon.

SOLO—2ND YEOMAN.

This the autumn of our life,
   This the evening of our day ;
Weary we of battle strife,
   Weary we of mortal fray.
But our year is not so spent,
   And our days are not so faded,
But that we with one consent,
   Were our lovèd land invaded,
      Still would face a foreign foe,
      As in days of long ago.

CHORUS.   Still would face a foreign foe,
          As in days of long ago.

PEOPLE.	YEOMEN.
Tower Warders,	This the autumn of our life, etc.
Under orders, etc.	

[*Exeunt Crowd. Manent Yeomen.*

Enter DAME CARRUTHERS.

DAME.   A good day to you !

2ND YEOMAN.   Good day, Dame Carruthers.   Busy to-day ?

DAME.   Busy, aye ! the fire in the Beauchamp last night has given me work enough.   A dozen poor prisoners —Richard Colfax, Sir Martin Byfleet, Colonel Fairfax,

Warren the preacher-poet, and half-a-score others—all packed into one small cell, not six feet square. Poor Colonel Fairfax, who's to die to-day, is to be removed to No. 14 in the Cold Harbour that he may have his last hour alone with his confessor; and I've to see to that.

2ND YEO. Poor gentleman! He'll die bravely. I fought under him two years since, and he valued his life as it were a feather!

PHŒ. He's the bravest, the handsomest, and the best young gentleman in England! He twice saved my father's life; and it's a cruel thing, a wicked thing, and a barbarous thing that so gallant a hero should lose his head—for it's the handsomest head in England!

DAME. For dealings with the devil. Aye! if all were beheaded who dealt with *him*, there'd be busy doings on Tower Green.

PHŒ. You know very well that Colonel Fairfax is a student of alchemy—nothing more, and nothing less; but this wicked Tower, like a cruel giant in a fairy-tale, must be fed with blood, and that blood must be the best and bravest in England, or it's not good enough for the old Blunderbore. Ugh!

DAME. Silence, you silly girl; you know not what you say. I was born in the old keep, and I've grown grey in it, and, please God, I shall die and be buried in it; and there's not a stone in its walls that is not as dear to me as my own right hand.

SONG WITH CHORUS—DAME CARRUTHERS
and YEOMEN.

When our gallant Norman foes
    Made our merry land their own,
        And the Saxons from the Conqueror were flying,
At his bidding it arose,
    In its panoply of stone,
        A sentinel unliving and undying.

Insensible, I trow,
  As a sentinel should be,
    Though a queen to save her head should come a-suing,
There's a legend on its brow
  That is eloquent to me,
    And it tells of duty done and duty doing.

      " The screw may twist and the rack may turn,
        And men may bleed and men may burn,
          O'er London town and its golden hoard
          I keep my silent watch and ward ! "

CHORUS.   The screw may twist, etc.

Within its wall of rock
  The flower of the brave
    Have perished with a constancy unshaken.
From the dungeon to the block,
  From the scaffold to the grave,
    Is a journey many gallant hearts have taken.
And the wicked flames may hiss
  Round the heroes who have fought
    For conscience and for home in all its beauty,
But the grim old fortalice
  Takes little heed of aught
    That comes not in the measure of its duty.

      " The screw may twist and the rack may turn,
        And men may bleed and men may burn,
          O'er London town and its golden hoard
          I keep my silent watch and ward ! "

CHORUS.   The screw may twist, etc.

                    [*Exeunt all but* PHŒBE. *Enter* SERGEANT
                        MERYLL.

  PHŒ. Father ! Has no reprieve arrived for the poor
gentleman ?
  MER. No, my lass ; but there's one hope yet. Thy
brother Leonard, who, as a reward for his valour in saving

his standard and cutting his way through fifty foes who would have hanged him, has been appointed a Yeoman of the Guard, will arrive to-day ; and as he comes straight from Windsor, where the Court is, it may be —it *may* be—that he will bring the expected reprieve with him.

PHŒ. Oh, that he may !

MER. Amen to that ! For the Colonel twice saved my life, and I'd give the rest of my life to save his ! And wilt thou not be glad to welcome thy brave brother, with the fame of whose exploits all England is a-ringing ?

PHŒ. Aye, truly, if he brings the reprieve.

MER. And not otherwise ?

PHŒ. Well, he's a brave fellow indeed, and I love brave men.

MER. *All* brave men ?

PHŒ. Most of them, I verily believe ! But I hope Leonard will not be too strict with me—they say he is a very dragon of virtue and circumspection ! Now, my dear old father is kindness itself, and——

MER. And leaves thee pretty well to thine own ways, eh ? Well, I've no fears for thee ; thou hast a feather-brain, but thou'rt a good lass.

PHŒ. Yes, that's all very well, but if Leonard is going to tell me that I may not do this and I may not do that, and I must not talk to this one, or walk with that one, but go through the world with my lips pursed up and my eyes cast down, like a poor nun who has renounced mankind—why, as I have *not* renounced mankind, and don't mean to renounce mankind, I won't have it—there !

MER. Nay, he'll not check thee more than is good for thee, Phœbe ! He's a brave fellow, and bravest among brave fellows, and yet it seems but yesterday that he robbed the Lieutenant's orchard.

Enter LEONARD MERYLL.

LEON. Father !

MER. Leonard! my brave boy! I'm right glad to see thee, and so is Phœbe!

PHŒ. Aye—hast thou brought Colonel Fairfax's reprieve?

LEON. Nay, I have here a despatch for the Lieutenant, but no reprieve for the Colonel!

PHŒ. Poor gentleman! poor gentleman!

LEON. Aye, I would I had brought better news. I'd give my right hand—nay, my body—my life, to save his!

MER. Dost thou speak in earnest, my lad?

LEON. Aye, father—I'm no braggart. Did he not save thy life? and am I not his foster-brother?

MER. Then hearken to me. Thou hast come to join the Yeomen of the Guard!

LEON. Well?

MER. None has seen thee but ourselves?

LEON. And a sentry, who took but scant notice of me.

MER. Now to prove thy words. Give me the despatch, and get thee hence at once! Here is money, and I'll send thee more. Lie hidden for a space, and let no one know. I'll convey a suit of Yeoman's uniform to the Colonel's cell—he shall shave off his beard, so that none shall know him, and I'll own him as my son, the brave Leonard Meryll, who saved his flag and cut his way through fifty foes who thirsted for his life. He will be welcomed without question by my brother-Yeomen, I'll warrant that. Now, how to get access to the Colonel's cell? (*To* PHŒBE.) The key is with thy sour-faced admirer, Wilfred Shadbolt.

PHŒ. (*demurely*). I think—I say, I *think*—I can get anything I want from Wilfred. I think—mind I say, I *think*—you may leave that to me.

MER. Then get thee hence at once, lad—and bless thee for this sacrifice.

PHŒ. And take my blessing, too, dear, dear Leonard!

LEON. And thine, eh? Humph! Thy love is new-born; wrap it up carefully, lest it take cold and die.

TRIO—Phœbe, Leonard, Meryll.

Phœ.   Alas! I waver to and fro!
          Dark danger hangs upon the deed!

All.   Dark danger hangs upon the deed!

Leon.   The scheme is rash and well may fail,
          But ours are not the hearts that quail,
          The hands that shrink, the cheeks that pale
                    In hours of need!

All.   No, ours are not the hearts that quail,
          The hands that shrink, the cheeks that pale
                    In hours of need!

Mer.   The air I breathe to him I owe:
          My life is his—I count it naught!

Phœ. and Leon.   That life is his—so count it naught!

Mer.   And shall I reckon risks I run
          When services are to be done
          To save the life of such an one?
                    Unworthy thought!

Phœ. and Leon.   And shall we reckon risks we run
          To save the life of such an one?

All.   Unworthy thought!
          We may succeed—who can foretell?
          May heaven help our hope—farewell!

          [Leonard *embraces* Meryll *and* Phœbe, *and
          then exit.* Phœbe *weeping.*

Mer.   Nay, lass, be of good cheer, we may save him
yet.

Phœ.   Oh! see, father—they bring the poor gentleman
from the Beauchamp! Oh, father! his hour is not yet
come?

Mer.   No, no,—they lead him to the Cold Harbour
Tower to await his end in solitude. But softly—the
Lieutenant approaches! He should not see thee weep.

Enter FAIRFAX, *guarded. The* LIEUTENANT *enters,
meeting him.*

LIEUT. Halt ! Colonel Fairfax, my old friend, we meet but sadly.

FAIR. Sir, I greet you with all good-will ; and I thank you for the zealous care with which you have guarded me from the pestilent dangers which threaten human life outside. In this happy little community, Death, when he comes, doth so in punctual and business-like fashion ; and, like a courtly gentleman, giveth due notice of his advent, that one may not be taken unawares.

LIEUT. Sir, you bear this bravely, as a brave man should.

FAIR. Why, sir, it is no light boon to die swiftly and surely at a given hour and in a given fashion ! Truth to tell, I would gladly have my life ; but if that may not be, I have the next best thing to it, which is death. Believe me, sir, my lot is not so much amiss !

PHŒ. (*aside to* MERYLL). Oh, father, father, I cannot bear it !

MER. My poor lass !

FAIR. Nay, pretty one, why weepest thou ? Come, be comforted. Such a life as mine is not worth weeping for. (*Sees* MERYLL.) Sergeant Meryll, is it not ? (*To* LIEUT.) May I greet my old friend ? (*Shakes* MERYLL'S *hand.*) Why, man, what's all this ? Thou and I have faced the grim old king a dozen times, and never has his majesty come to me in such goodly fashion. Keep a stout heart, good fellow—we are soldiers, and we know how to die, thou and I. Take my word for it, it is easier to die well than to live well—for, in sooth, I have tried both.

BALLAD—FAIRFAX.

Is life a boon ?
    If so, it must befall
    That Death, whene'er he call,
Must call too soon.

> Though fourscore years he give,
> > Yet one would pray to live
> Another moon !
> > What kind of plaint have I,
> > Who perish in July ?
> > I might have had to die,
> Perchance, in June !
>
> Is life a thorn ?
> > Then count it not a whit !
> > Man is well done with it ;
> Soon as he's born
> > He should all means essay
> > To put the plague away ;
> And I, war-worn,
> > Poor captured fugitive,
> > My life most gladly give—
> > I might have had to live
> Another morn !

[*At the end*, PHŒBE *is led off, weeping, by* MERYLL.

FAIR.   And now, Sir Richard, I have a boon to beg. I am in this strait for no better reason than because my kinsman, Sir Clarence Poltwhistle, one of the Secretaries of State, has charged me with sorcery, in order that he may succeed to my estate, which devolves to him provided I die unmarried.

LIEUT.   As thou wilt most surely do.

FAIR.   Nay, as I will most surely *not* do, by your worship's grace ! I have a mind to thwart this good cousin of mine.

LIEUT.   How ?

FAIR.   By marrying forthwith, to be sure !

LIEUT.   But heaven ha' mercy, whom wouldst thou marry ?

FAIR.   Nay, I am indifferent on that score. Coming Death hath made of me a true and chivalrous knight,

who holds all womankind in such esteem that the oldest, and the meanest, and the worst-favoured of them is good enough for him. So, my good Lieutenant, if thou wouldst serve a poor soldier who has but an hour to live, find me the first that comes—my confessor shall marry us, and her dower shall be my dishonoured name and a hundred crowns to boot. No such poor dower for an hour of matrimony !

LIEUT. A strange request. I doubt that I should be warranted in granting it.

FAIR. There never was a marriage fraught with so little of evil to the contracting parties. In an hour she'll be a widow, and I—a bachelor again for aught I know !

LIEUT. Well, I will see what can be done, for I hold thy kinsman in abhorrence for the scurvy trick he has played thee.

FAIR. A thousand thanks, good sir ; we meet again on this spot in an hour or so. I shall be a bridegroom then, and your worship will wish me joy. Till then, farewell. (*To Guard.*) I am ready, good fellows.

[*Exit with Guard into Cold Harbour Tower.*

LIEUT. He is a brave fellow, and it is a pity that he should die. Now, how to find him a bride at such short notice ? Well, the task should be easy !

[*Exit.*

Enter JACK POINT *and* ELSIE MAYNARD, *pursued by a crowd of men and women.* POINT *and* ELSIE *are much terrified ;* POINT, *however, assuming an appearance of self-possession.*

CHORUS.

Here's a man of jollity,
Jibe, joke, jollify !
Give us of your quality,
Come, fool, follify !

If you vapour vapidly,
River runneth rapidly,
    Into it we fling
    Bird who doesn't sing !

Give us an experiment
In the art of merriment ;
    Into it we throw
    Cock who doesn't crow !

Banish your timidity,
And with all rapidity
Give us quip and quiddity—
    Willy-nilly, O !

River none can mollify ;—
    Into it we throw
Fool who doesn't follify,
    Cock who doesn't crow !

POINT (*alarmed*). My masters, I pray you bear with us, and we will satisfy you, for we are merry folk who would make all merry as ourselves. For, look you, there is humour in all things, and the truest philosophy is that which teaches us to find it and to make the most of it.

ELSIE (*struggling with one of the crowd*). Hands off, I say, unmannerly fellow !

POINT (*to 1st Citizen*). Ha ! Didst thou hear her say, " Hands off " ?

1ST CIT. Aye, I heard her say it, and I felt her do it ! What then ?

POINT. Thou dost not see the humour of that ?

1ST CIT. Nay, if I do, hang me !

POINT. Thou dost not ? Now observe. She said, " Hands off ! " Whose hands ? Thine. Off whom ? Off *her*. Why ? Because she is a woman. Now, had she *not* been a woman, thine hands had not been set upon her at all. So the reason for the laying on of hands is the reason for the taking off of hands, and herein is

contradiction contradicted ! It is the very marriage of *pro*
with *con* ; and no such lopsided union either, as times go,
for *pro* is not more unlike *con* than man is unlike woman—
yet men and women marry every day with none to say,
" Oh, the pity of it ! " but I and fools like me ! Now
wherewithal shall we please you ? We can rhyme you
couplet, triolet, quatrain, sonnet, rondolet, ballade, what
you will. Or we can dance you saraband, gondolet, carole,
pimpernel, or Jumping Joan.

ELSIE. Let us give them the singing farce of the
Merryman and his Maid—therein is song and dance too.

ALL. Aye, the Merryman and his Maid !

DUET—ELSIE *and* POINT.

POINT. 　　　　　　I have a song to sing, O !

ELSIE. 　　　　　　Sing me your song, O !

POINT. 　　　　　　　　It is sung to the moon
　　　　　　　　　　　By a love-lorn loon,
　　　　　　Who fled from the mocking throng, O !
　　　It's a song of a merryman, moping mum,
　　Whose soul was sad, and whose glance was glum,
　　Who sipped no sup, and who craved no crumb,
　　　　　　As he sighed for the love of a ladye.
　　　　　　　　　Heighdy ! heighdy !
　　　　　　　　Misery me, lackadaydee !
　　He sipped no sup, and he craved no crumb,
　　　　As he sighed for the love of a ladye.

ELSIE. 　　　　I have a song to sing, O !

POINT. 　　　　　What is your song, O ?

ELSIE. 　　　　　　　It is sung with the ring
　　　　　　　　　　Of the songs maids sing
　　　　　　Who love with a love life-long, O !
　　It's the song of a merrymaid, peerly proud,
　　Who loved a lord, and who laughed aloud

At the moan of the merryman, moping mum,
Whose soul was sad, and whose glance was glum,
Who sipped no sup, and who craved no crumb,
    As he sighed for the love of a ladye !
        Heighdy ! heighdy !
        Misery me, lackadaydee !
          He sipped no sup, etc.

POINT.   I have a song to sing, O !

ELSIE.   Sing me your song, O !

POINT.   It is sung to the knell
             Of a churchyard bell,
      And a doleful dirge, ding dong, O !
It's a song of a popinjay, bravely born,
Who turned up his noble nose with scorn
At the humble merrymaid, peerly proud,
Who loved a lord, and who laughed aloud
At the moan of the merryman, moping mum,
Whose soul was sad, and whose glance was glum,
Who sipped no sup, and who craved no crumb,
    As he sighed for the love of a ladye !

BOTH.   Heighdy ! heighdy !
            Misery me, lackadaydee !
              He sipped no sup, etc.

ELSIE.   I have a song to sing, O !

POINT.   Sing me your song, O !

ELSIE.   It is sung with a sigh
            And a tear in the eye,
      For it tells of a righted wrong, O !
It's a song of the merrymaid, once so gay,
Who turned on her heel and tripped away
From the peacock popinjay, bravely born,
Who turned up his noble nose with scorn
At the humble heart that he did not prize :
So she begged on her knees, with downcast eyes,

                                    Q

> For the love of the merryman, moping mum,
> Whose soul was sad, and whose glance was glum,
> Who sipped no sup, and who craved no crumb,
>   As he sighed for the love of a ladye !

BOTH.   Heighdy ! heighdy !
                         Misery me, lackadaydee !
> His pains were o'er, and he sighed no more,
>   For he lived in the love of a ladye !

1ST CIT. Well sung and well danced !

2ND CIT. A kiss for that, pretty maid !

ALL. Aye, a kiss all round.

ELSIE (*drawing dagger*). Best beware !   I am armed !

POINT. Back, sirs—back ! This is going too far.

2ND CIT. Thou dost not see the humour of it, eh ?
Yet there is humour in all things—even in this. (*Trying
to kiss her.*)

ELSIE. Help ! help !

Enter LIEUTENANT *with Guard. Crowd falls back.*

LIEUT. What is this pother ?

ELSIE. Sir, we sang to these folk, and they would
have repaid us with gross courtesy, but for your honour's
coming.

LIEUT. (*to Mob*). Away with ye ! Clear the rabble.
(*Guards push Crowd off, and go off with them.*) Now,
my girl, who are you, and what do you here ?

ELSIE. May it please you, sir, we are two strolling
players, Jack Point and I, Elsie Maynard, at your worship's
service. We go from fair to fair, singing, and dancing,
and playing brief interludes ; and so we make a poor living.

LIEUT. You two, eh ? Are ye man and wife ?

POINT. No, sir ; for though I'm a fool, there is a
limit to my folly. Her mother, old Bridget Maynard,
travels with us (for Elsie is a good girl), but the old woman
is a-bed with fever, and we have come here to pick up
some silver to buy an electuary for her.

LIEUT. Hark ye, my girl ! Your mother is ill ?

ELSIE.   Sorely ill, sir.

LIEUT.   And needs good food, and many things that thou canst not buy?

ELSIE.   Alas! sir, it is too true.

LIEUT.   Wouldst thou earn an hundred crowns?

ELSIE.   An hundred crowns! They might save her life!

LIEUT.   Then listen! A worthy but unhappy gentleman is to be beheaded in an hour on this very spot. For sufficient reasons, he desires to marry before he dies, and he hath asked me to find him a wife. Wilt thou be that wife?

ELSIE.   The wife of a man I have never seen!

POINT.   Why, sir, look you, I am concerned in this; for though I am not yet wedded to Elsie Maynard, time works wonders, and there's no knowing what may be in store for us. Have we your worship's word for it that this gentleman will die to-day?

LIEUT.   Nothing is more certain, I grieve to say.

POINT.   And that the maiden will be allowed to depart the very instant the ceremony is at an end?

LIEUT.   The very instant. I pledge my honour that it shall be so.

POINT.   An hundred crowns?

LIEUT.   An hundred crowns!

POINT.   For my part, I consent. It is for Elsie to speak.

TRIO—ELSIE, POINT, *and* LIEUTENANT.

LIEUT.   How say you, maiden, will you wed
        A man about to lose his head?
           For half an hour
             You'll be a wife,
           And then the dower
             Is yours for life.
        A headless bridegroom why refuse?
          If truth the poets tell,
       Most bridegrooms, ere they marry, lose
         Both head and heart as well!

ELSIE.   A strange proposal you reveal,
          It almost makes my senses reel.
          Alas! I'm very poor indeed,
          And such a sum I sorely need.
            My mother, sir, is like to die,
            This money life may bring.
            Bear this in mind, I pray, if I
            Consent to do this thing!

POINT.   Though as a general rule of life
          I don't allow my promised wife,
          My lovely bride that is to be,
          To marry any one but me,
            Yet if the fee is promptly paid,
            And he, in well-earned grave,
          Within the hour is duly laid,
            Objection I will waive!
            Yes, objection I will waive!

ALL.   Temptation, oh, temptation,
                Were we, I pray, intended
              To shun, whate'er our station,
                Your fascinations splendid;
              Or fall, whene'er we view you,
              Head over heels into you?
                  Temptation, oh, temptation, etc.

(*During this, the* LIEUTENANT *has whispered to* WILFRED
   (*who has entered*). WILFRED *binds* ELSIE'S *eyes with
   a kerchief, and leads her into the Cold Harbour Tower.*)

   LIEUT.   And so, good fellow, you are a jester?
   POINT.   Aye, sir, and, like some of my jests, out of place.
   LIEUT.   I have a vacancy for such an one. Tell me,
what are your qualifications for such a post?
   POINT.   Marry, sir, I have a pretty wit. I can rhyme
you extempore; I can convulse you with quip and conundrum; I have the lighter philosophies at my tongue's
tip; I can be merry, wise, quaint, grim, and sardonic,

one by one, or all at once ; I have a pretty turn for anecdote;
I know all the jests—ancient and modern—past, present,
and to come ; I can riddle you from dawn of day to set
of sun, and, if that content you not, well on to midnight
and the small hours. Oh, sir, a pretty wit, I warrant you—
a pretty, pretty wit !

RECITATIVE AND SONG—POINT.

I've jibe and joke
And quip and crank
For lowly folk
And men of rank.
I ply my craft
And know no fear,
But aim my shaft
At prince or peer.
At peer or prince—at prince or peer,
I aim my shaft and know no fear !

I've wisdom from the East and from the West,
That's subject to no academic rule ;
You may find it in the jeering of a jest,
Or distil it from the folly of a fool.
I can teach you with a quip, if I've a mind ;
I can trick you into learning with a laugh ;
Oh, winnow all my folly, and you'll find
A grain or two of truth among the chaff !

I can set a braggart quailing with a quip,
The upstart I can wither with a whim ;
He may wear a merry laugh upon his lip,
But his laughter has an echo that is grim !
When they're offered to the world in merry guise,
Unpleasant truths are swallowed with a will—
For he who'd make his fellow-creatures wise
Should always gild the philosophic pill !

LIEUT. And how came you to leave your last employ ?

POINT. Why, sir, it was in this wise. My Lord was the Archbishop of Canterbury, and it was considered that one of my jokes was unsuited to His Grace's family circle. In truth, I ventured to ask a poor riddle, sir—Wherein lay the difference between His Grace and poor Jack Point? His Grace was pleased to give it up, sir. And thereupon I told him that whereas His Grace was paid £10,000 a year for being good, poor Jack Point was good—for nothing. 'Twas but a harmless jest, but it offended His Grace, who whipped me and set me in the stocks for a scurril rogue, and so we parted. I had as lief not take post again with the dignified clergy.

LIEUT. But I trust you are very careful not to give offence. I have daughters.

POINT. Sir, my jests are most carefully selected, and anything objectionable is expunged. If your honour pleases, I will try them first on your honour's chaplain.

LIEUT. Can you give me an example? Say that I had sat me down hurriedly on something sharp?

POINT. Sir, I should say that you had sat down on the spur of the moment.

LIEUT. Humph! I don't think much of that. Is that the best you can do?

POINT. It has always been much admired, sir, but we will try again.

LIEUT. Well, then, I am at dinner, and the joint of meat is but half cooked.

POINT. Why then, sir, I should say that what is *under*done cannot be helped.

LIEUT. I see. I think that manner of thing would be somewhat irritating.

POINT. At first, sir, perhaps; but use is everything, and you would come in time to like it.

LIEUT. We will suppose that I caught you kissing the kitchen wench under my very nose.

POINT. Under *her* very nose, good sir—not under yours! *That* is where *I* would kiss her. Do you take me? Oh, sir, a pretty wit—a pretty, pretty wit!

LIEUT. The maiden comes. Follow me, friend, and we will discuss this matter at length in my library.

POINT. I am your worship's servant. That is to say, I trust I soon shall be. But, before proceeding to a more serious topic, can you tell me, sir, why a cook's brain-pan is like an overwound clock ?

LIEUT. A truce to this fooling—follow me.

POINT. Just my luck ; my best conundrum wasted !

[*Exeunt.*

Enter ELSIE *from Tower, led by* WILFRED, *who removes the bandage from her eyes, and exit.*

RECITATIVE AND SONG—ELSIE.

'Tis done ! I am a bride ! Oh, little ring,
   That bearest in thy circlet all the gladness
That lovers hope for, and that poets sing,
   What bringest thou to me but gold and sadness ?
A bridegroom all unknown, save in this wise,
To-day he dies ! To-day, alas, he dies !

    Though tear and long-drawn sigh
      Ill fit a bride,
    No sadder wife than I
      The whole world wide !
        Ah me ! Ah me !
        Yet maids there be
    Who would consent to lose
      The very rose of youth,
        The flower of life,
      To be, in honest truth,
        A wedded wife,
          No matter whose !

    Ah me ! what profit we,
      O maids that sigh,
    Though gold, though gold should live
      If wedded love must die ?

Ere half an hour has rung,
    A widow I !
Ah, heaven, he is too young,
    Too brave to die !
        Ah me ! Ah me !
        Yet wives there be
    So weary worn, I trow,
    That they would scarce complain,
        So that they could
        In half an hour attain
            To widowhood,
                No matter how !

    O weary wives
        Who widowhood would win,
    Rejoice that ye have time
        To weary in.

[*Exit* ELSIE *as* WILFRED *re-enters.*

WIL. (*looking after* ELSIE). 'Tis an odd freak, for a dying man and his confessor to be closeted alone with a strange singing girl. I would fain have espied them, but they stopped up the keyhole. *My* keyhole !

Enter PHŒBE *with* MERYLL. MERYLL *remains in the background, unobserved by* WILFRED.

PHŒ. (*aside*). Wilfred—and alone !

WIL. Now what could he have wanted with her ? That's what puzzles me !

PHŒ. (*aside*). Now to get the keys from him. (*Aloud.*) Wilfred—has no reprieve arrived ?

WIL. None. Thine adored Fairfax is to die.

PHŒ. Nay, thou knowest that I have naught but pity for the poor condemned gentleman.

WIL. I know that he who is about to die is more to thee than I, who am alive and well.

PHŒ. Why, that were out of reason, dear Wilfred. Do they not say that a live ass is better than a dead lion ? No, I don't mean that !

Wil. Oh, they say that, do they?

Phœ. It's unpardonably rude of them, but I believe they put it in that way. Not that it applies to thee, who art clever beyond all telling!

Wil. Oh yes, as an assistant-tormentor.

Phœ. Nay, as a wit, as a humorist, as a most philosophic commentator on the vanity of human resolution.

(Phœbe *slyly takes bunch of keys from* Wilfred's *waistband and hands them to* Meryll, *who enters the Tower, unnoticed by* Wilfred.)

Wil. Truly, I have seen great resolution give way under my persuasive methods (*working a small thumbscrew*). In the nice regulation of a thumbscrew—in the hundredth part of a single revolution lieth all the difference between stony reticence and a torrent of impulsive unbosoming that the pen can scarcely follow. Ha! ha! I am a mad wag.

Phœ. (*with a grimace*). Thou art a most light-hearted and delightful companion, Master Wilfred. Thine anecdotes of the torture-chamber are the prettiest hearing.

Wil. I'm a pleasant fellow an I choose. I believe I am the merriest dog that barks. Ah, we might be passing happy together——

Phœ. Perhaps. I do not know.

Wil. For thou wouldst make a most tender and loving wife.

Phœ. Aye, to one whom I really loved. For there is a wealth of love within this little heart—saving up for— I wonder whom? Now, of all the world of men, I wonder whom? To think that he whom I am to wed is now alive and somewhere! Perhaps far away, perhaps close at hand! And I know him not! It seemeth that I am wasting time in not knowing him.

Wil. Now say that it is I—nay! suppose it for the nonce. Say that we are wed—suppose it only—say that thou art my very bride, and I thy cheery, joyous, bright, frolicsome husband—and that, the day's work being done,

and the prisoners stored away for the night, thou and I are alone together—with a long, long evening before us !

PHŒ. (*with a grimace*). It is a pretty picture—but I scarcely know. It cometh so unexpectedly—and yet—and yet—*were* I thy bride——

WIL. Aye !—wert thou my bride——?

PHŒ. Oh, how I would love thee !

SONG—PHŒBE.

Were I thy bride,
Then all the world beside
Were not too wide
    To hold my wealth of love—
Were I thy bride !

Upon thy breast
My loving head would rest,
As on her nest
    The tender turtle dove—
Were I thy bride !

This heart of mine
Would be one heart with thine,
And in that shrine
    Our happiness would dwell—
Were I thy bride !

And all day long
Our lives should be a song :
No grief, no wrong
    Should make my heart rebel—
Were I thy bride !

The silvery flute,
The melancholy lute,
Were night-owl's hoot
    To my low-whispered coo—
Were I thy bride !

> The skylark's trill
> Were but discordance shrill
> To the soft thrill
> Of wooing as I'd woo—
> Were I thy bride !

MERYLL *re-enters ; gives keys to* PHŒBE, *who replaces them at* WILFRED'S *girdle, unnoticed by him. Exit* MERYLL.

> The rose's sigh
> Were as a carrion's cry
> To lullaby
> Such as I'd sing to thee,
> Were I thy bride !

> A feather's press
> Were leaden heaviness
> To my caress.
> But then, of course, you see,
> I'm not thy bride !

[*Exit* PHŒBE.

WIL. No, thou'rt not—not yet ! But, Lord, how she woo'd ! I should be no mean judge of wooing, seeing that I have been more hotly woo'd than most men. I have been woo'd by maid, widow, and wife. I have been woo'd boldly, timidly, tearfully, shyly—by direct assault, by suggestion, by implication, by inference, and by innuendo. But this wooing is not of the common order : it is the wooing of one who must needs woo me, if she die for it !

[*Exit* WILFRED.

Enter MERYLL, *cautiously, from Tower.*

MER. (*looking after them*). The deed is, so far, safely accomplished. The slyboots, how she wheedled him ! What a helpless ninny is a love-sick man ! He is but as a lute in a woman's hands—she plays upon him whatever tune she will. But the Colonel comes. I' faith, he's just in time, for the Yeomen parade here for his execution in two minutes !

Enter FAIRFAX, *without beard and moustache,
and dressed in Yeoman's uniform.*

FAIR. My good and kind friend, thou runnest a grave risk for me !

MER. Tut, sir, no risk. I'll warrant none here will recognise you. You make a brave Yeoman, sir ! So—this ruff is too high ; so—and the sword should hang thus. Here is your halbert, sir; carry it thus.   The Yeomen come. Now remember, you are my brave son, Leonard Meryll.

FAIR. If I may not bear mine own name, there is none other I would bear so readily.

MER. Now, sir, put a bold face on it, for they come.

FINALE—ACT I.

Enter Yeomen of the Guard.

CHORUS.

Oh, Sergeant Meryll, is it true—
　　The welcome news we read in orders ?
Thy son, whose deeds of derring-do
Are echoed all the country through,
　　Has come to join the Tower Warders ?
If so, we come to meet him,
That we may fitly greet him,
And welcome his arrival here
With shout on shout and cheer on cheer.
　　　　Hurrah !   Hurrah !   Hurrah !

RECITATIVE—SERGEANT MERYLL.

Ye Tower Warders, nursed in war's alarms,
　　Suckled on gunpowder, and weaned on glory,
Behold my son, whose all-subduing arms
　　Have formed the theme of many a song and story !
Forgive his aged father's pride ; nor jeer
　　His aged father's sympathetic tear !
　　　　　　　(*Pretending to weep.*)

CHORUS.

Leonard Meryll !
Leonard Meryll !
Dauntless he in time of peril !
Man of power,
Knighthood's flower,
Welcome to the grim old Tower,
To the Tower, welcome thou !

RECITATIVE—FAIRFAX.

Forbear, my friends, and spare me this ovation,
I have small claim to such consideration ;
The tales that of my prowess are narrated
Have been prodigiously exaggerated !

CHORUS.

'Tis ever thus !
Wherever valour true is found,
True modesty will there abound.

COUPLETS.

1ST YEOMAN.   Didst thou not, oh, Leonard Meryll !
    Standard lost in last campaign,
Rescue it at deadly peril—
    Bear it safely back again ?

CHORUS.   Leonard Meryll, at his peril,
    Bore it safely back again !

2ND YEOMAN.   Didst thou not, when prisoner taken,
    And debarred from all escape,
Face, with gallant heart unshaken,
    Death in most appalling shape ?

CHORUS.   Leonard Meryll faced his peril,
    Death in most appalling shape !

FAIR. (*aside*).   Truly I was to be pitied,
      Having but an hour to live,
     I reluctantly submitted,
      I had no alternative !

(*Aloud.*)   Oh ! the tales that are narrated
      Of my deeds of derring-do
     Have been much exaggerated,
     Very much exaggerated,
      Scarce a word of them is true !

CHORUS.   They are not exaggerated, etc.

     Enter PHŒBE.   *She rushes to* FAIRFAX.
         Enter WILFRED.

RECITATIVE.

PHŒ. Leonard !
FAIR. (*puzzled*). I beg your pardon ?
PHŒ.   Don't you know me ?
   I'm little Phœbe !
FAIR. (*still puzzled*).   Phœbe ?   Is this Phœbe ?
   What ! little Phœbe ?   (*Aside.*)   Who the deuce
     may *she* be ?
   It can't be Phœbe, surely ?
WIL.   Yes, 'tis Phœbe——
   Your sister Phœbe !   Your own little sister !
ALL.   Aye, he speaks the truth ;
   'Tis Phœbe !
FAIR. (*pretending to recognise her*). Sister Phœbe !
PHŒ.   Oh, my brother !
FAIR. Why, how you've grown !   I did not recognise you !
PHŒ. So many years !   Oh, brother !
FAIR.   Oh, my sister !
WIL. Aye, hug him, girl !   There are three thou mayst
   hug——
   Thy father and thy brother and—myself !
FAIR. Thyself, forsooth ?   And who art thou thyself ?

WIL.	Good sir, we are betrothed. (FAIRFAX *turns inquiringly to* PHŒBE.)
PHŒ.	Or more or less—— But rather less than more !
WIL.	To thy fond care I do commend thy sister. Be to her An ever-watchful guardian—eagle-eyed ! And when she feels (as sometimes she does feel) Disposed to indiscriminate caress, Be thou at hand to take those favours from her !
ALL.	Be thou at hand to take those favours from her !
PHŒ.	Yes, yes. Be thou at hand to take those favours from me !

TRIO—WILFRED, FAIRFAX, *and* PHŒBE.

WIL.	To thy fraternal care Thy sister I commend ; From every lurking snare Thy lovely charge defend : And to achieve this end, Oh ! grant, I pray, this boon— She shall not quit thy sight : From morn to afternoon— From afternoon to night— From seven o'clock to two— From two to eventide— From dim twilight to 'leven at night She shall not quit thy side !
ALL.	From morn to afternoon, etc.
PHŒ.	So amiable I've grown, So innocent as well, That if I'm left alone The consequences fell No mortal can foretell. So grant, I pray, this boon— I shall not quit thy sight :

> From morn to afternoon—
> From afternoon to night—
> From seven o'clock to two—
> From two to eventide—
> From dim twilight to 'leven at night
> I shall not quit thy side.

ALL.   From morn to afternoon, etc.

FAIR.   With brotherly readiness,
> For my fair sister's sake,
> At once I answer " Yes "—
> That task I undertake—
> My word I never break.
> I freely grant that boon,
> And I'll repeat my plight.
> From morn to afternoon—   (*kiss*)
> From afternoon to night—   (*kiss*)
> From seven o'clock to two—   (*kiss*)
> From two to evening meal—   (*kiss*)
> From dim twilight to 'leven at night
> That compact I will seal.   (*kiss*)

ALL.   From morn to afternoon, etc.

*The bell of St. Peter's begins to toll. The Crowd enters ;
the block is brought on to the stage, and the Headsman
takes his place. The Yeomen of the Guard form up.
The* LIEUTENANT *enters and takes his place, and tells
off* FAIRFAX *and two others to bring the prisoner to
execution.* WILFRED, FAIRFAX, *and two Yeomen
exeunt to Tower.*

CHORUS (*to tolling accompaniment*).

The prisoner comes to meet his doom ;
The block, the headsman, and the tomb.
The funeral bell begins to toll—
May Heaven have mercy on his soul !

SOLO—ELSIE, *with* CHORUS.

Oh, Mercy, thou whose smile has shone
So many a captive heart upon ;
Of all immured within these walls,
To-day the very worthiest falls !

Enter FAIRFAX *and two other Yeomen from Tower
in great excitement.*

FAIR.   My lord ! I know not how to tell
The news I bear !
I and my comrades sought the prisoner's cell—
He is not there !

ALL.   He is not there !
They sought the prisoner's cell—he is not there !

TRIO—FAIRFAX *and two Yeomen.*

As escort for the prisoner
We sought his cell, in duty bound ;
The double gratings open were,
No prisoner at all we found !

We hunted high, we hunted low,
We hunted here, we hunted there—
The man we sought with anxious care
Had vanished into empty air !

[*Exit* LIEUTENANT.

GIRLS.   Now, by my troth, the news is fair,
The man has vanished into air !

ALL.   As escort for the prisoner
They sought his cell in duty bound, etc.

Enter WILFRED, *followed by* LIEUTENANT.

LIEUT.   Astounding news !   The prisoner fled !
(*To* WILFRED.) Thy life shall forfeit be instead !

(WILFRED *is arrested.*)

WIL.   My lord, I did not set him free,
        I hate the man—my rival he !

                        (WILFRED *is taken away*.)

MER.   The prisoner gone—I'm all agape !
        Who could have helped him to escape ?

PHŒ.   Indeed I can't imagine who !
        I've no idea at all—have you ?

                Enter JACK POINT.

DAME.   Of his escape no traces lurk,
        Enchantment must have been at work !

ELSIE (*aside to* POINT).
        What have I done !   Oh, woe is me !
        I am his wife, and he is free !

POINT. Oh, woe is *you* ?   Your anguish sink !
        Oh, woe is *me*, I rather think !
        Oh, woe is *me*, I rather think !
        Yes, woe is *me*, I rather think !
                Whate'er betide
                You are his bride,
                And I am left
                Alone—bereft !
        Yes, woe is *me*, I rather think !
        Yes, woe is *me*, I rather think !

ENSEMBLE—LIEUTENANT *and* CHORUS.

        All frenzied with despair I rave,
            The grave is cheated of its due.
        Who is the misbegotten knave
            Who hath contrived this deed to do ?
        Let search be made throughout the land,
            Or $\begin{Bmatrix} his \\ my \end{Bmatrix}$ vindictive anger dread—

        A thousand marks to him $\begin{Bmatrix} he'll \\ I'll \end{Bmatrix}$ hand
        Who brings him here, alive or dead.

At the end, ELSIE *faints in* FAIRFAX'S *arms ; all the Yeomen and populace rush off the stage in different directions, to hunt for the fugitive, leaving only the Headsman on the stage, and* ELSIE *insensible in* FAIRFAX'S *arms.*

END OF ACT I.

ACT II.

SCENE.—*The same.—Moonlight.*

Two days have elapsed.

Women and Yeomen of the Guard discovered.

CHORUS.
Night has spread her pall once more,
    And the prisoner still is free :
Open is his dungeon door,
    Useless now his dungeon key !
He has shaken off his yoke—
    How, no mortal man can tell !
Shame on loutish jailer-folk—
    Shame on sleepy sentinel !

Enter DAME CARRUTHERS *and* KATE.

SOLO—DAME CARRUTHERS.
    Warders are ye ?
        Whom do ye ward ?
    Bolt, bar, and key,
        Shackle and cord,
    Fetter and chain,
        Dungeon of stone,
    All are in vain—
        Prisoner's flown !
Spite of ye all, he is free—he is free !
Whom do ye ward ?   Pretty warders are ye !

CHORUS OF WOMEN.   Pretty warders are ye, etc.

CHORUS.

YEOMEN.   Up and down, and in and out,
           Here and there, and round about ;
           Every chamber, every house,
           Every chink that holds a mouse,
           Every crevice in the keep,
           Where a beetle black could creep,
           Every outlet, every drain,
           Have we searched, but all in vain.

WOMEN.   Warders are ye ?
              Whom do ye ward ? etc.

[Exeunt all.

Enter JACK POINT, *in low spirits, reading
from a huge volume.*

POINT (*reads*). " The Merrie Jestes of Hugh Ambrose.
No. 7863. The Poor Wit and the Rich Councillor. A
certayne poor wit, being an-hungered, did meet a well-fed
councillor. ' Marry, fool,' quoth the councillor, ' whither
away ? ' ' In truth,' said the poor wag, ' in that I have
eaten naught these two dayes, I do wither away, and that
right rapidly ! ' The councillor laughed hugely, and gave
him a sausage." Humph ! The councillor was easier to
please than my new master the Lieutenant. I would like
to take post under that councillor. Ah ! 'tis but melancholy
mumming when poor heart-broken, jilted Jack Point must
needs turn to Hugh Ambrose for original light humour !

Enter WILFRED, *also in low spirits.*

WIL. (*sighing*). Ah, Master Point !
POINT (*changing his manner*). Ha ! friend jailer !
Jailer that wast—jailer that never shalt be more ! Jailer
that jailed not, or that jailed, if jail he did, so unjailerly
that 'twas but jerry-jailing, or jailing in joke—though no
joke to him who, by unjailerlike jailing, did so jeopardise

his jailership. Come, take heart, smile, laugh, wink, twinkle, thou tormentor that tormentest none—thou racker that rackest not—thou pincher out of place—come, take heart, and be merry, as I am!—(*aside, dolefully*)—as I am!

WIL. Aye, it's well for thee to laugh. Thou hast a good post, and hast cause to be merry.

POINT (*bitterly*). Cause? Have we not all cause? Is not the world a big butt of humour, into which all who will may drive a gimlet? See, I am a salaried wit; and is there aught in nature more ridiculous? A poor, dull, heart-broken man, who must needs be merry, or he will be whipped; who must rejoice, lest he starve; who must jest you, jibe you, quip you, crank you, wrack you, riddle you, from hour to hour, from day to day, from year to year, lest he dwindle, perish, starve, pine, and die! Why, when there's naught else to laugh at, I laugh at myself till I ache for it!

WIL. Yet I have often thought that a jester's calling would suit me to a hair.

POINT. Thee? Would suit *thee*, thou death's head and cross-bones?

WIL. Aye, I have a pretty wit—a light, airy, joysome wit, spiced with anecdotes of prison cells and the torture chamber. Oh, a very delicate wit! I have tried it on many a prisoner, and there have been some who smiled. Now it is not easy to make a prisoner smile. And it should not be difficult to be a good jester, seeing that thou art one.

POINT. Difficult? Nothing easier. Nothing easier. Attend, and I will prove it to thee!

SONG—POINT.

Oh! a private buffoon is a light-hearted loon,
    If you listen to popular rumour;
From the morn to the night he's so joyous and bright,
    And he bubbles with wit and good humour!

He's so quaint and so terse, both in prose and in verse ;
   Yet though people forgive his transgression,
There are one or two rules that all family fools
   Must observe, if they love their profession.
           There are one or two rules,
             Half a dozen, may be,
           That all family fools,
             Of whatever degree,
    Must observe, if they love their profession.

If you wish to succeed as a jester, you'll need
   To consider each person's auricular :
What is all right for B would quite scandalise C
   (For C is so very particular) ;
And D may be dull, and E's very thick skull
   Is as empty of brains as a ladle ;
While F is F sharp, and will cry with a carp
   That he's known your best joke from his cradle !
           When your humour they flout,
             You can't let yourself go ;
           And it *does* put you out
             When a person says, " Oh,
    I have known that old joke from my cradle ! "

If your master is surly, from getting up early
   (And tempers are short in the morning),
An inopportune joke is enough to provoke
   Him to give you, at once, a month's warning.
Then if you refrain, he is at you again,
   For he likes to get value for money ;
He'll ask then and there, with an insolent stare,
   " If you know that you're paid to be funny ? "
           It adds to the tasks
             Of a merryman's place,
           When your principal asks,
             With a scowl on his face,
    If you know that you're paid to be funny ?

Comes a Bishop, maybe, or a solemn D.D.—
    Oh, beware of his anger provoking !
Better not pull his hair—don't stick pins in his chair ;
    He don't understand practical joking.
If the jests that you crack have an orthodox smack,
    You may get a bland smile from these sages ;
But should they, by chance, be imported from France,
    Half-a-crown is stopped out of your wages !
            It's a general rule,
               Though your zeal it may quench,
            If the family fool
               Tells a joke that's too French,
       Half-a-crown is stopped out of his wages !

Though your head it may rack with a bilious attack,
    And your senses with toothache you're losing,
Don't be mopy and flat—they don't fine you for that,
    If you're properly quaint and amusing !
Though your wife ran away with a soldier that day,
    And took with her your trifle of money ;
Bless your heart, they don't mind—they're exceedingly
    kind—
    They don't blame you—as long as you're funny !
            It's a comfort to feel,
               If your partner should flit,
            Though *you* suffer a deal,
               They don't mind it a bit—
    They don't blame you—so long as you're funny !

    POINT.   And so thou wouldst be a jester, eh ?
    WIL.   Aye !
    POINT.   Now, listen ! My sweetheart, Elsie Maynard,
was secretly wed to this Fairfax half an hour ere he
escaped.
    WIL.   She did well.
    POINT.   She did nothing of the kind, so hold thy
peace and perpend. Now, while he liveth she is dead to

me and I to her, and so, my jibes and jokes notwithstanding, I am the saddest and the sorriest dog in England !

WIL.   Thou art a very dull dog indeed.

POINT.   Now, if thou wilt swear that thou didst shoot this Fairfax while he was trying to swim across the river— it needs but the discharge of an arquebus on a dark night— and that he sank and was seen no more, I'll make thee the very Archbishop of jesters, and that in two days' time ! Now, what sayest thou ?

WIL.   I am to lie ?

POINT.   Heartily.   But thy lie must be a lie of circumstance, which I will support with the testimony of eyes, ears, and tongue.

WIL.   And thou wilt qualify me as a jester ?

POINT.   As a jester among jesters.   I will teach thee all my original songs, my self-constructed riddles, my own ingenious paradoxes ; nay, more, I will reveal to thee the source whence I get them.   Now, what sayest thou ?

WIL.   Why, if it be but a lie thou wantest of me, I hold it cheap enough, and I say yes, it is a bargain !

DUET—POINT *and* WILFRED.

BOTH.   Hereupon we're both agreed,
                        All that we two
                        Do agree to
                We'll secure by solemn deed,
                        To prevent all
                        Error mental.

POINT.   I on Elsie am to call
                        With a story
                        Grim and gory ;

WIL.   How this Fairfax died, and all
                        I declare to
                        You're to swear to.

BOTH.   Tell a tale of cock and bull,
                            Of convincing detail full
                                Tale tremendous,
                                    Heaven defend us !
                    What a tale of cock and bull !

BOTH.   In return for $\left\{\begin{matrix} your \\ my \end{matrix}\right\}$ own part

                    You are $\left.\begin{matrix} \\ \end{matrix}\right\}$ making
                    I am $\left.\begin{matrix} \\ \end{matrix}\right\}$
                    Undertaking

                To instruct $\left\{\begin{matrix} me \\ you \end{matrix}\right\}$ in the art

                    (Art amazing,
                    Wonder raising)

POINT.   Of a jester, jesting free.
                    Proud position—
                    High ambition !

WIL.   And a lively one I'll be,
                    Wag-a-wagging,
                    Never flagging !

BOTH.   Tell a tale of cock and bull, etc.

                                            [*Exeunt together.*

                            Enter FAIRFAX.

FAIR.   Two days gone, and no news of poor Fairfax.
The dolts ! They seek him everywhere save within a
dozen yards of his dungeon. So I am free ! Free, but
for the cursed haste with which I hurried headlong into
the bonds of matrimony with—Heaven knows whom ! As
far as I remember, she should have been young ; but
even had not her face been concealed by her kerchief,
I doubt whether, in my then plight, I should have taken
much note of her. Free ? Bah ! The Tower bonds
were but a thread of silk compared with these conjugal
fetters which I, fool that I was, placed upon mine own

hands. From the one I broke readily enough—how to break the other !

BALLAD—Fairfax.

Free from his fetters grim—
  Free to depart ;
Free both in life and limb—
  In all but heart !
Bound to an unknown bride
  For good and ill ;
Ah, is not one so tied
  A prisoner still ?

Free, yet in fetters held
  Till his last hour,
Gyves that no smith can weld,
  No rust devour !
Although a monarch's hand
  Had set him free,
Of all the captive band
  The saddest he !

Enter MERYLL.

FAIR. Well, Sergeant Meryll, and how fares thy pretty charge, Elsie Maynard ?

MER. Well enough, sir. She is quite strong again, and leaves us to-night.

FAIR. Thanks to Dame Carruthers' kind nursing, eh ?

MER. Aye, deuce take the old witch ! Ah, 'twas but a sorry trick you played me, sir, to bring the fainting girl to me. It gave the old lady an excuse for taking up her quarters in my house, and for the last two years I've shunned her like the plague. Another day of it and she would have married me ! (*Enter* DAME CARRUTHERS *and* KATE.) Good Lord, here she is again ! I'll e'en go. (*Going*.)

DAME. Nay, Sergeant Meryll, don't go. I have something of grave import to say to thee.

MER. (*aside*). It's coming.

FAIR. (*laughing*). I'faith, I think I'm not wanted here. (*Going.*)

DAME. Nay, Master Leonard, I've naught to say to thy father that his son may not hear.

FAIR. (*aside*). True. I'm one of the family; I had forgotten!

DAME. 'Tis about this Elsie Maynard. A pretty girl, Master Leonard.

FAIR. Aye, fair as a peach blossom—what then?

DAME. She hath a liking for thee, or I mistake not.

FAIR. With all my heart. She's as dainty a little maid as you'll find in a midsummer day's march.

DAME. Then be warned in time, and give not thy heart to her. Oh, *I* know what it is to give my heart to one who will have none of it!

MER. (*aside*). Aye, *she* knows all about that. (*Aloud.*) And why is my boy to take heed of her? She's a good girl, Dame Carruthers.

DAME. Good enough, for aught I know. But she's no girl. She's a married woman.

MER. A married woman! Tush, old lady—she's promised to Jack Point, the Lieutenant's new jester.

DAME. Tush in thy teeth, old man! As my niece Kate sat by her bedside to-day, this Elsie slept, and as she slept she moaned and groaned, and turned this way and that way—and, "How shall I marry one I have never seen?" quoth she—then, "An hundred crowns!" quoth she—then, "Is it certain he will die in an hour?" quoth she—then, "I love him not, and yet I am his wife," quoth she! Is it not so, Kate?

KATE. Aye, aunt, 'tis even so.

FAIR. Art thou sure of all this?

KATE. Aye, sir, for I wrote it all down on my tablets.

DAME. Now, mark my words: it was of this Fairfax she spake, and he is her husband, or I'll swallow my kirtle!

MER. (*aside*). Is it true, sir?

FAIR. (*aside to* MERYLL). True? Why, the girl was raving! (*Aloud.*) Why should she marry a man who had but an hour to live?

DAME. Marry? There be those who would marry but for a minute, rather than die old maids.

MER. (*aside*). Aye, I know one of them!

QUARTET—FAIRFAX, SERGEANT MERYLL, DAME CARRUTHERS, *and* KATE.

Strange adventure! Maiden wedded
　　To a groom she's never seen—
　　　　Never, never, never seen!
Groom about to be beheaded,
　　In an hour on Tower Green!
　　　　Tower, Tower, Tower Green!
Groom in dreary dungeon lying,
Groom as good as dead, or dying,
For a pretty maiden sighing—
　　Pretty maid of seventeen!
　　　　Seven—seven—seventeen!

Strange adventure that we're trolling:
　　Modest maid and gallant groom—
　　　　Gallant, gallant, gallant groom!—
While the funeral bell is tolling,
　　Tolling, tolling, Bim-a-boom!
　　　　Bim-a, Bim-a, Bim-a-boom!
Modest maiden will not tarry;
Though but sixteen years she carry,
She must marry, she must marry,
　　Though the altar be a tomb—
　　　　Tower—Tower—Tower tomb!

[*Exeunt* DAME CARRUTHERS, MERYLL, *and* KATE.

FAIR. So my mysterious bride is no other than this winsome Elsie! By my hand, 'tis no such ill plunge in

Fortune's lucky bag! I might have fared worse with my eyes open! But she comes. Now to test her principles. 'Tis not every husband who has a chance of wooing his own wife!

Enter ELSIE.

FAIR. Mistress Elsie!

ELSIE. Master Leonard!

FAIR. So thou leavest us to-night?

ELSIE. Yes, Master Leonard. I have been kindly tended, and I almost fear I am loth to go.

FAIR. And this Fairfax. Wast thou glad when he escaped?

ELSIE. Why, truly, Master Leonard, it is a sad thing that a young and gallant gentleman should die in the very fullness of his life.

FAIR. Then when thou didst faint in my arms, it was for joy at his safety?

ELSIE. It may be so. I was highly wrought, Master Leonard, and I am but a girl, and so, when I am highly wrought, I faint.

FAIR. Now, dost thou know, I am consumed with a parlous jealousy?

ELSIE. Thou? And of whom?

FAIR. Why, of this Fairfax, surely!

ELSIE. Of Colonel Fairfax?

FAIR. Aye. Shall I be frank with thee? Elsie—I love thee, ardently, passionately! (ELSIE *alarmed and surprised*.) Elsie, I have loved thee these two days— which is a long time—and I would fain join my life to thine!

ELSIE. Master Leonard! Thou art jesting!

FAIR. Jesting? May I shrivel into raisins if I jest! I love thee with a love that is a fever—with a love that is a frenzy—with a love that eateth up my heart! What sayest thou? Thou wilt not let my heart be eaten up?

ELSIE (*aside*). Oh, mercy! What am I to say?

FAIR. Dost thou love me, or hast thou been insensible these two days?

ELSIE. I love all brave men.

FAIR. Nay, there is love in excess. I thank heaven there are many brave men in England; but if thou lovest them all, I withdraw my thanks.

ELSIE. I love the bravest best. But, sir, I may not listen—I am not free—I—I am a wife!

FAIR. Thou a wife? Whose? His name? His hours are numbered—nay, his grave is dug and his epitaph set up! Come, his name?

ELSIE. Oh, sir! keep my secret—it is the only barrier that Fate could set up between us. My husband is none other than Colonel Fairfax!

FAIR. The greatest villain unhung! The most ill-favoured, ill-mannered, ill-natured, ill-omened, ill-tempered dog in Christendom!

ELSIE. It is very like. He is naught to me—for I never saw him. I was blindfolded, and he was to have died within the hour; and he did not die—and I am wedded to him, and my heart is broken!

FAIR. He was to have died, and he did *not* die? The scoundrel! The perjured, traitorous villain! Thou shouldst have insisted on his dying first, to make sure. 'Tis the only way with these Fairfaxes.

ELSIE. I now wish I had!

FAIR. (*aside*). Bloodthirsty little maiden! (*Aloud*.) A fig for this Fairfax! Be mine—he will never know— he dares not show himself; and if he dare, what art thou to him? Fly with me, Elsie—we will be married to-morrow, and thou shalt be the happiest wife in England!

ELSIE. Master Leonard! I am amazed! Is it thus that brave soldiers speak to poor girls? Oh! for shame, for shame! I am wed—not the less because I love not my husband. I am a wife, sir, and I have a duty, and— oh, sir! thy words terrify me—they are not honest—they are wicked words, and unworthy thy great and brave heart! Oh, shame upon thee! shame upon thee!

FAIR. Nay, Elsie, I did but jest. I spake but to try
thee—— (*Shot heard.*)

Enter MERYLL *hastily.*

MER. (*recit.*). Hark! What was that, sir?
FAIR. Why, an arquebus—
Fired from the wharf, unless I much mistake.
MER. Strange—and at such an hour! What can it
mean?

Enter CHORUS.

CHORUS.

Now what can that have been—
A shot so late at night,
Enough to cause a fright!
What can the portent mean?

Are foemen in the land?
Is London to be wrecked?
What are we to expect?
What danger is at hand?
Let us understand
What danger is at hand!

LIEUTENANT *enters, also* POINT *and* WILFRED.

RECITATIVE.

LIEUT. Who fired that shot? At once the truth declare!
WIL. My lord, 'twas I—to rashly judge forbear!
POINT. My lord, 'twas he—to rashly judge forbear!

DUET AND CHORUS—WILFRED *and* POINT.

WIL. Like a ghost his vigil keeping—
POINT. Or a spectre all-appalling—
WIL. I beheld a figure creeping—
POINT. I should rather call it crawling—
WIL. He was creeping—
POINT. He was crawling—

WIL.   He was creeping, creeping—

POINT.   Crawling !

WIL.   He was creeping—

POINT.   He was crawling—

WIL.   He was creeping, creeping—

POINT.   Crawling !

WIL.   Not a moment's hesitation—
           I myself upon him flung,
       With a hurried exclamation
           To his draperies I hung ;
       Then we closed with one another
       In a rough-and-tumble smother ;
       Colonel Fairfax and no other
           Was the man to whom I clung !

ALL.   Colonel Fairfax and no other
           Was the man to whom he clung !

WIL.   After mighty tug and tussle—

POINT.   It resembled more a struggle—

WIL.   He, by dint of stronger muscle—

POINT.   Or by some infernal juggle—

WIL.   From my clutches quickly sliding—

POINT.   I should rather call it slipping—

WIL.   With a view, no doubt, of hiding—

POINT.   Or escaping to the shipping—

WIL.   With a gasp, and with a quiver—

POINT.   I'd describe it as a shiver—

WIL.   Down he dived into the river,
           And, alas, I cannot swim.

ALL.   It's enough to make one shiver—
       With a gasp and with a quiver,
       Down he dived into the river ;
           It was very brave of him !

R

WIL.   Ingenuity is catching ;
              With the view my king of pleasing,
              Arquebus from sentry snatching—

POINT.   I should rather call it seizing—

WIL.   With an ounce or two of lead
                I despatched him through the head !

ALL.   With an ounce or two of lead
                He despatched him through the head !

WIL.   I discharged it without winking,
            Little time I lost in thinking,
            Like a stone I saw him sinking—

POINT.   I should say a lump of lead.

ALL.   He discharged it without winking,
            Little time he lost in thinking.

WIL.   Like a stone I saw him sinking—

POINT.   I should say a lump of lead.

WIL.   Like a stone, my boy, I said—

POINT.   Like a heavy lump of lead.

WIL.   Anyhow, the man is dead,
            Whether stone or lump of lead !

ALL.   Anyhow, the man is dead,
                Whether stone or lump of lead !
            Arquebus from sentry seizing,
            With the view his king of pleasing,
                Wilfred shot him through the head,
                And he's very, very dead.
And it matters very little whether stone or lump of lead ;
It is very, very certain that he's very, very dead !

RECITATIVE—LIEUTENANT.

The river must be dragged—no time be lost ;
The body must be found, at any cost.
To this attend without undue delay ;
So set to work with what despatch ye may !

                           [*Exit*.

ALL.   Yes, yes,
    We'll set to work with what despatch we may !

(*Four men raise* WILFRED, *and carry him off
            on their shoulders.*)

CHORUS.

Hail the valiant fellow who
Did this deed of derring-do !
Honours wait on such an one ;
By my head, 'twas bravely done !
Now, by my head, 'twas bravely done !

[*Exeunt all but* ELSIE, POINT, FAIRFAX, *and*
                POINT.

POINT (*to* ELSIE, *who is weeping*). Nay, sweetheart,
be comforted. This Fairfax was but a pestilent fellow,
and, as he had to die, he might as well die thus as any
other way. 'Twas a good death.

ELSIE. Still, he was my husband, and had he not
been, he was nevertheless a living man, and now he is
dead ; and so, by your leave, my tears may flow un-
chidden, Master Point.

FAIR. And thou didst see all this ?

POINT. Aye, with both eyes at once—this and that.
The testimony of one eye is naught—he may lie. But
when it is corroborated by the other, it is good evidence
that none may gainsay. Here are both present in court,
ready to swear to him !

PHŒ. But art thou sure it was Colonel Fairfax ?
Saw you his face ?

POINT. Aye, and a plaguey ill-favoured face too.
A very hang-dog face—a felon face—a face to fright the
headsman himself, and make him strike awry. Oh, a
plaguey, bad face, take my word for 't. (PHŒBE *and*
FAIRFAX *laugh.*) How they laugh ! 'Tis ever thus with
simple folk—an accepted wit has but to say " Pass the
mustard," and they roar their ribs out !

FAIR. (*aside*).   If ever I come to life again, thou shalt pay for this, Master Point !

POINT.   Now, Elsie, thou art free to choose again, so behold me :   I am young and well-favoured.   I have a pretty wit.   I can jest you, jibe you, quip you, crank you, wrack you, riddle you——

FAIR.   Tush, man, thou knowest not how to woo. 'Tis not to be done with time-worn jests and thread-bare sophistries ;   with quips, conundrums, rhymes, and para-doxes.   'Tis an art in itself, and must be studied gravely and conscientiously.

TRIO—ELSIE, PHŒBE, *and* FAIRFAX.

FAIR.   A man who would woo a fair maid
          Should 'prentice himself to the trade,
               And study all day,
               In methodical way,
          How to flatter, cajole, and persuade ;
          He should 'prentice himself at fourteen,
          And practise from morning to e'en ;
               And when he's of age,
               If he will, I'll engage,
          He may capture the heart of a queen !

ALL.   It is purely a matter of skill,
               Which all may attain if they will :
                    But every Jack,
                    He must study the knack
               If he wants to make sure of his Jill !

ELSIE.   If he's made the best use of his time,
          His twig he'll so carefully lime
               That every bird
               Will come down at his word,
          Whatever its plumage or clime.

He must learn that the thrill of a touch
May mean little, or nothing, or much :
  It's an instrument rare,
  To be handled with care,
And ought to be treated as such.

ALL.   It is purely a matter of skill, etc.

PHŒ. Then a glance may be timid or free,
It will vary in mighty degree,
  From an impudent stare
  To a look of despair
That no maid without pity can see !
And a glance of despair is no guide—
It may have its ridiculous side ;
  It may draw you a tear
  Or a box on the ear ;
You can never be sure till you've tried !

ALL.   It is purely a matter of skill, etc.

FAIR. (*aside to* POINT).   Now, listen to me—'tis done
thus—(*aloud*)—Mistress Elsie, there is one here who, as
thou knowest, loves thee right well !

POINT (*aside*).   That he does—right well !

FAIR.   He is but a man of poor estate, but he hath a
loving, honest heart.   He will be a true and trusty husband
to thee, and if thou wilt be his wife, thou shalt lie curled
up in his heart, like a little squirrel in its nest !

POINT (*aside*).   'Tis a pretty figure.   A maggot in a
nut lies closer, but a squirrel will do.

FAIR.   He knoweth that thou wast a wife—an unloved
and unloving wife, and his poor heart was near to breaking.
But now that thine unloving husband is dead, and thou
art free, he would fain pray that thou wouldst hearken
unto him, and give him hope that thou wouldst one day
be his !

PHŒ. (*alarmed*).   He presses her hands — and he

whispers in her ear! Ods bodikins, what does it mean?

FAIR. Now, sweetheart, tell me—wilt thou be this poor good fellow's wife?

ELSIE. If the good, brave man—*is* he a brave man?

FAIR. So men say.

POINT (*aside*). That's not true, but let it pass.

ELSIE. If the brave man will be content with a poor, penniless, untaught maid——

POINT (*aside*). Widow—but let *that* pass.

ELSIE. I will be his true and loving wife, and that with my heart of hearts!

FAIR. My own dear love! (*Embracing her.*)

PHŒ. (*in great agitation*). Why, what's all this? Brother—brother—it is not seemly!

POINT (*also alarmed, aside*). Oh, I can't let *that* pass! (*Aloud.*) Hold, enough, Master Leonard! An advocate should have his fee, but methinks thou art over-paying thyself!

FAIR. Nay, that is for Elsie to say. I promised thee I would show thee how to woo, and herein lies the proof of the virtue of my teaching. Go thou, and apply it elsewhere! (PHŒBE *bursts into tears*.)

QUARTET—ELSIE, PHŒBE, FAIRFAX, *and* POINT.

ELSIE *and* FAIR.   When a wooer
      Goes a-wooing,
    Naught is truer
      Than his joy.
    Maiden hushing
      All his suing—
    Boldly blushing—
      Bravely coy!

ALL.   Oh, the happy days of doing!
          Oh, the sighing and the suing!
          When a wooer goes a-wooing,
          Oh, the sweets that never cloy!

PHŒ. (*weeping*).   When a brother
           Leaves his sister
        For another,
           Sister weeps.
        Tears that trickle,
           Tears that blister—
        'Tis but mickle
           Sister reaps !

ALL.   Oh, the doing and undoing,
        Oh, the sighing and the suing,
        When a brother goes a-wooing,
           And a sobbing sister weeps !

POINT.   When a jester
           Is outwitted,
        Feelings fester,
           Heart is lead !
        Food for fishes
           Only fitted,
        Jester wishes
           He was dead !

ALL.   Oh, the doing and undoing,
        Oh, the sighing and the suing,
        When a jester goes a-wooing,
           And he wishes he was dead !

[*Exeunt all but* PHŒBE, *who remains weeping*.

PHŒ. And I helped that man to escape, and I've kept his secret, and pretended that I was his dearly loving sister, and done everything I could think of to make folk believe I *was* his loving sister, and this is his gratitude ! Before I pretend to be sister to anybody again, I'll turn nun, and be sister to everybody—one as much as another !

Enter WILFRED.

WIL. In tears, eh ? What a plague art thou grizzling for now ?

PHŒ. Why am I grizzling? Thou hast often wept for jealousy—well, 'tis for jealousy I weep now. Aye, yellow, bilious, jaundiced jealousy. So make the most of that, Master Wilfred.

WIL. But I have never given thee cause for jealousy. The Lieutenant's cook-maid and I are but the merest gossips!

PHŒ. Jealous of thee! Bah! I'm jealous of no craven cock-on-a-hill, who crows about what he'd do an he dared! I am jealous of another and a better man than thou—set that down, Master Wilfred. And he is to marry Elsie Maynard, the little pale fool—set that down, Master Wilfred — and my heart is wellnigh broken! There, thou hast it all! Make the most of it!

WIL. The man thou lovest is to marry Elsie Maynard? Why, that is no other than thy brother, Leonard Meryll!

PHŒ. (aside). Oh, mercy! what have I said?

WIL. Why, what manner of brother is this, thou lying little jade? Speak! Who is this man whom thou hast called brother, and fondled, and coddled, and kissed!— with my connivance, too! Oh Lord! with my connivance! Ha! should it be this Fairfax! (PHŒBE starts.) It is! It is this accursed Fairfax! It's Fairfax! Fairfax, who——

PHŒ. Whom thou hast just shot through the head, and who lies at the bottom of the river!

WIL. A—I—I may have been mistaken. We are but fallible mortals, the best of us. But I'll make sure—I'll make sure. (Going.)

PHŒ. Stay—one word. I think it cannot be Fairfax— mind, I say I *think*—because thou hast just slain Fairfax. But whether he be Fairfax or no Fairfax, he is to marry Elsie—and—and—as thou hast shot him through the head, and he is dead, be content with that, and I will be thy wife!

WIL. Is that sure?

PHŒ. Aye, sure enough, for there's no help for it! Thou art a very brute—but even brutes must marry, I suppose.

WIL.   My beloved ! (*Embraces her.*)

PHŒ. (*aside*).   Ugh !

Enter LEONARD, *hastily*.

LEON.   Phœbe, rejoice, for I bring glad tidings. Colonel Fairfax's reprieve was signed two days since, but it was foully and maliciously kept back by Secretary Poltwhistle, who designed that it should arrive after the Colonel's death.   It hath just come to hand, and it is now in the Lieutenant's possession !

PHŒ.   Then the Colonel is free ?   Oh, kiss me, kiss me, my dear !   Kiss me, again, and again !

WIL. (*dancing with fury*).   Ods bobs, death o' my life !   Art thou mad ?   Am *I* mad ?   Are we *all* mad ?

PHŒ.   Oh, my dear—my dear, I'm wellnigh crazed with joy !   (*Kissing* LEONARD.)

WIL.   Come away from him, thou hussy—thou jade—thou kissing, clinging cockatrice !   And as for thee, sir, devil take thee, I'll rip thee like a herring for this !   I'll skin thee for it !   I'll cleave thee to the chine !   I'll—oh ! Phœbe !   Phœbe !   Who is this man ?

PHŒ.   Peace, fool.   He is my brother !

WIL.   Another brother !   Are there any more of them ?   Produce them all at once, and let me know the worst !

PHŒ.   This is the real Leonard, dolt ; the other was but his substitute.   The *real* Leonard, I say—my father's own son.

WIL.   How do I know this ?   Has he " brother " writ large on his brow ?   I mistrust thy brothers !   Thou art but a false jade !   [*Exit* LEONARD.

PHŒ.   Now, Wilfred, be just.   Truly I did deceive thee before—but it was to save a precious life—and to save it, not for me, but for another.   They are to be wed this very day.   Is not this enough for thee ?   Come—I am thy Phœbe—thy very own—and we will be wed in a year—or two—or three, at the most.   Is not that enough for thee ?

Enter MERYLL, *excitedly, followed by* DAME CARRUTHERS
(*who listens, unobserved*).

MER.   Phœbe, hast thou heard the brave news?

PHŒ. (*still in* WILFRED'S *arms*).   Aye, father.

MER.   I'm nigh mad with joy! (*Seeing* WILFRED.)
Why, what's all this?

PHŒ.   Oh, father, he discovered our secret through
my folly, and the price of his silence is——

WIL.   Phœbe's heart.

PHŒ.   Oh dear, no——Phœbe's hand.

WIL.   It's the same thing!

PHŒ.   *Is* it?   [*Exeunt* WILFRED *and* PHŒBE.

MER. (*looking after them*).   'Tis pity, but the Colonel
had to be saved at any cost, and as thy folly revealed our
secret, thy folly must e'en suffer for it! (DAME CAR-
RUTHERS *comes down*.)   Dame Carruthers!

DAME.   So this is a plot to shield this arch-fiend, and
I have detected it.   A word from me, and three heads
besides his would roll from their shoulders!

MER.   Nay, Colonel Fairfax is reprieved. (*Aside*.)   Yet,
if my complicity in his escape were known!   Plague on
the old meddler!   There's nothing for it——(*aloud*)——Hush,
pretty one!   Such bloodthirsty words ill become those
cherry lips!   (*Aside*.)   Ugh!

DAME (*bashfully*).   Sergeant Meryll!

MER.   Why, look ye, chuck—for many a month I've—
I've thought to myself—" There's snug love saving up in
that middle-aged bosom for some one, and why not for
thee—that's me—so take heart and tell her—that's thee—
that thou—that's me—lovest her—thee—and—and—well,
I'm a miserable old man, and I've done it—and that's me!"
But not a word about Fairfax!   The price of thy silence
is——

DAME.   Meryll's heart?

MER.   No, Meryll's *hand*.

DAME.   It's the same thing!

MER.   *Is* it!

DUET—Dame Carruthers *and* Sergeant Meryll.

DAME. Rapture, rapture !
   When love's votary,
  Flushed with capture,
   Seeks the notary,
    Joy and jollity
    Then is polity ;
    Reigns frivolity !
  Rapture, rapture !

MER. Doleful, doleful !
   When humanity,
  With its soul full
   Of satanity,
    Courting privity,
    Down declivity
    Seeks captivity !
  Doleful, doleful !

DAME. Joyful, joyful !
   When virginity
  Seeks, all coyful,
   Man's affinity ;
    Fate all flowery,
    Bright and bowery,
    Is her dowery !
  Joyful, joyful !

MER. Ghastly, ghastly !
   When man, sorrowful,
  Firstly, lastly,
   Of to-morrow full,
    After tarrying,
    Yields to harrying—
    Goes a-marrying.
  Ghastly, ghastly !

BOTH. Rapture, etc.

       [*Exeunt* DAME *and* MERYLL.

FINALE.

Enter Yeomen and Women.

CHORUS OF WOMEN.

(ELEGIACS.)

Comes the pretty young bride, a-blushing, timidly
        shrinking—
Set all thy fears aside—cheerily, pretty young bride !
Brave is the youth to whom thy lot thou art willingly
        linking !
Flower of valour is he—loving as loving can be !
    Brightly thy summer is shining,
    Fair as the dawn of the day ;
      Take him, be true to him—
      Tender his due to him—
    Honour him, love and obey !

Enter DAME, PHŒBE, *and* ELSIE *as Bride.*

TRIO—PHŒBE, ELSIE, *and* DAME CARRUTHERS.

    'Tis said that joy in full perfection
      Comes only once to womankind—
    That, other times, on close inspection,
      Some lurking bitter we shall find.
    If this be so, and men say truly,
    My day of joy has broken duly.

    With happiness $\begin{cases} my \\ her \end{cases}$ soul is cloyed—

    This is $\begin{cases} my \\ her \end{cases}$ joy-day unalloyed !

ALL.   Yes, yes, with happiness her soul is cloyed !
        This is her joy-day unalloyed !

Flourish. Enter LIEUTENANT.

LIEUT. Hold, pretty one ! I bring to thee
        News—good or ill, it is for thee to say.

> Thy husband lives—and he is free,
>   And comes to claim his bride this very day !

ELSIE.   No ! no ! recall those words—it cannot be !

ENSEMBLE.

KATE *and* CHORUS.	DAME CARRUTHERS *and* PHŒBE.
Oh, day of terror ! Day of tears !	Oh, day of terror ! Day of tears !
Who is the man who, in his pride,	The man to whom thou art allied
Claims thee as his bride ?	Appears to claim thee as his bride.

LIEUT., MERYLL, *and* WILFRED.	ELSIE.
Come, dry these unbecoming tears,	Oh, Leonard, come thou to my side,
Most joyful tidings greet thine ears,	And claim me as thy loving bride !
The man to whom thou art allied	Oh, day of terror ! Day of tears !
Appears to claim thee as his bride	

Flourish.   Enter COLONEL FAIRFAX, *handsomely dressed, and attended by other Gentlemen.*

FAIR. (*sternly*).   All thought of Leonard Meryll set aside.
          Thou art mine own !   I claim thee as my bride.

ALL.   Thou art his own !   Alas ! he claims thee as his bride.

ELSIE.   A suppliant at thy feet I fall ;
          Thine heart will yield to pity's call !

FAIR.   Mine is a heart of massive rock,
          Unmoved by sentimental shock !

ALL.   Thy husband he !

ELSIE (*aside*).   Leonard, my loved one—come to me.
          They bear me hence away !
          But though they take me far from thee,
            My heart is thine for aye !
              My bruised heart,
               My broken heart,
        Is thine, my own, for aye !

(*To* FAIRFAX.) Sir, I obey!
> I am thy bride;
> But ere the fatal hour
> I said the say
> That placed me in thy power
> Would I had died!
> Sir, I obey!
> I am thy bride!

(*Looks up and recognises* FAIRFAX.)　　Leonard!

FAIR.　　　　　　　　　　　　　　　　　　My own!

ELSIE.　　　　　　　　　　　　　　　Ah!　(*Embrace.*)

ELSIE *and*　⎰ With happiness my soul is cloyed,
　FAIR.　　⎱ This is our joy-day unalloyed!

ALL.　　　　　　　　　　　　Yes, yes!
> With happiness their souls are cloyed,
> This is their joy-day unalloyed!

Enter JACK POINT.

POINT　　　　　Oh, thoughtless crew!
> Ye know not what ye do!
> Attend to me, and shed a tear or two—
> For I have a song to sing, O!

ALL.　　　　　　Sing me your song, O!

POINT.　　　　　　　It is sung to the moon
> By a love-lorn loon,
> Who fled from the mocking throng, O!
> It's the song of a merryman, moping mum,
> Whose soul was sad, and whose glance was glum,
> Who sipped no sup, and who craved no crumb,
> As he sighed for the love of a ladye!

ALL.　　　　　　Heighdy! heighdy!
> Misery me, lackadaydee!
> He sipped no sup, and he craved no crumb,
> As he sighed for the love of a ladye!

ELSIE.   I have a song to sing, O !

ALL.   What is your song, O ?

ELSIE.   It is sung with the ring
                                Of the songs maids sing
                     Who love with a love life-long, O !
                     It's the song of a merrymaid, nestling near,
                     Who loved her lord—but who dropped a tear
                     At the moan of the merryman, moping mum,
                     Whose soul was sad, and whose glance was glum,
                     Who sipped no sup, and who craved no crumb,
                           As he sighed for the love of a ladye !

ALL.   Heighdy ! heighdy !
                                Misery me, lackadaydee !
                     He sipped no sup, and he craved no crumb,
                           As he sighed for the love of a ladye !

FAIRFAX *embraces* ELSIE *as* POINT *falls insensible
                     at their feet.*

CURTAIN.

THE GONDOLIERS

OR

THE KING OF BARATARIA

DRAMATIS PERSONÆ.

THE DUKE OF PLAZA-TORO (*a Grandee of Spain*).

LUIZ (*his Attendant*).

DON ALHAMBRA DEL BOLERO (*the Grand Inquisitor*).

MARCO PALMIERI
GIUSEPPE PALMIERI
ANTONIO
FRANCESCO   } (*Venetian Gondoliers*).
GIORGIO
ANNIBALE

THE DUCHESS OF PLAZA-TORO.

CASILDA (*her Daughter*).

GIANETTA
TESSA
FIAMETTA   } (*Contadine*).
VITTORIA
GIULIA

INEZ (*the King's Foster-mother*).

Chorus of Gondoliers and Contadine, Men-at-Arms, Heralds, and Pages.

ACT I.—The Piazzetta, Venice.

ACT II.—Pavilion in the Palace of Barataria.

(*An interval of three months is supposed to elapse between Acts I. and II.*)

Date 1750.

First produced at the Savoy Theatre on December 7, 1889.

THE GONDOLIERS

OR

THE KING OF BARATARIA

ACT I.

Scene.—The Piazzetta, Venice. *The Ducal Palace on the right.*

Fiametta, Giulia, Vittoria, *and other Contadine discovered, each tying a bouquet of roses.*

Chorus of Contadine.

List and learn, ye dainty roses,
　　Roses white and roses red,
Why we bind you into posies
　　Ere your morning bloom has fled.
By a law of maiden's making,
Accents of a heart that's aching,
Even though that heart be breaking,
　　Should by maiden be unsaid :
Though they love with love exceeding,
They must seem to be unheeding—
Go ye then and do their pleading,
　　Roses white and roses red !

FIAMETTA.

Two there are for whom, in duty,
           Every maid in Venice sighs—
Two so peerless in their beauty
           That they shame the summer skies.
We have hearts for them, in plenty,
           They have hearts, but all too few,
We, alas, are four-and-twenty !
           They, alas, are only two !
We, alas !

CHORUS.   Alas !

FIA.   Are four-and-twenty,
           They, alas !

CHORUS.   Alas !

FIA.   Are only two.

CHORUS.   They, alas, are only two, alas !
           Now ye know, ye dainty roses,
           Why we bind you into posies,
                    Ere your morning bloom has fled,
                    Roses white and roses red !

During this chorus ANTONIO, FRANCESCO, GIORGIO, *and
other Gondoliers have entered unobserved by the
Girls—at first two, then two more, then four, then
half a dozen, then the remainder of the Chorus.*

SOLI.

FRANC. Good morrow, pretty maids ; for whom prepare ye
        These floral tributes extraordinary ?

FIA.   For Marco and Giuseppe Palmieri,
          The pink and flower of all the Gondolieri.

GIU.   They're coming here, as we have heard but lately,
          To choose two brides from us who sit sedately.

ANT.   Do all you maidens love them ?

ALL.   Passionately !

ANT.   These gondoliers are to be envied greatly !

GIOR. But what of us, who one and all adore you ?
Have pity on our passion, we implore you !

FIA. These gentlemen must make their choice before
you ;

VIT. In the meantime we tacitly ignore you.

GIU. When they have chosen two that leaves you
plenty—
Two dozen we, and ye are four-and-twenty.

FIA. *and* VIT. Till then, enjoy your *dolce far niente.*

ANT. With pleasure, nobody *contradicente* !

SONG—ANTONIO *and* CHORUS.

For the merriest fellows are we, tra la,
That ply on the emerald sea, tra la ;
With loving and laughing,
And quipping and quaffing,
We're happy as happy can be, tra la—
As happy as happy can be !

With sorrow we've nothing to do, tra la,
And care is a thing to pooh-pooh, tra la ;
And Jealousy yellow,
Unfortunate fellow,
We drown in the shimmering blue, tra la—
We drown in the shimmering blue !

FIA. (*looking off*). See, see, at last they come to make
their choice—
Let us acclaim them with united voice.

(MARCO *and* GIUSEPPE *appear in gondola at back.*)

CHORUS (*Girls*). Hail, hail ! gallant gondolieri, ben
venuti !
Accept our love, our homage, and our duty.

(MARCO *and* GIUSEPPE *jump ashore—the Girls
salute them.*)

DUET—Marco *and* Giuseppe,
with Chorus of Girls.

Mar. *and* Giu.	Buon' giorno, signorine !
Girls.	Gondolieri carissimi ! Siamo contadine !
Mar. *and* Giu. (*bowing*).	Servitori umilissimi ! Per chi questi fiori— Questi fiori bellissimi ?
Girls.	Per voi, bei signori O eccellentissimi !

(*The Girls present their bouquets to* Marco *and* Giuseppe,
*who are overwhelmed with them, and carry them
with difficulty.*)

Mar. *and* Giu. (*their arms full of flowers*).	O ciel' !
Girls.	Buon' giorno, cavalieri !
Mar. *and* Giu. (*deprecatingly*). (*To* Fia. *and* Vit.)	Siamo gondolieri. Signorina, io t' amo !
Girls (*deprecatingly*).	Contadine siamo.
Mar. *and* Giu.	Signorine !
Girls (*deprecatingly*).	Contadine !
(*Curtseying to* Mar. *and* Giu.)	Cavalieri.
Mar. *and* Giu. (*deprecatingly*).	Gondolieri ! Poveri gondolieri !
Chorus.	Buon' giorno, signorine, etc.

DUET—Marco *and* Giuseppe.

We're called *gondolieri*,
But that's a vagary,
It's quite honorary
        The trade that we ply.
For gallantry noted
Since we were short-coated,
To beauty devoted,
        Guiseppe }and I ;
        Are Marco}

When morning is breaking,
Our couches forsaking,
To greet their awaking
  With carols we come.
At summer day's nooning,
When weary lagooning,
Our mandolins tuning,
  We lazily thrum.
When vespers are ringing,
To hope ever clinging,
With songs of our singing
  A vigil we keep,
When daylight is fading,
Enwrapt in night's shading,
With soft serenading
  We sing them to sleep.

We're called *gondolieri*, etc.

RECIT.—MARCO *and* GIUSEPPE.

MAR. And now to choose our brides !

GIU.   As all are young and fair,
And amiable besides,

BOTH.   We really do not care
  A preference to declare.

MAR. A bias to disclose
  Would be indelicate—

GIU. And therefore we propose
  To let impartial Fate
  Select for us a mate !

ALL.   Viva !

GIRLS. A bias to disclose
  Would be indelicate—

MEN. But how do they propose
  To let impartial Fate
  Select for them a mate ?

GIU.   These handkerchiefs upon our eyes be good enough
            to bind,

MAR.   And take good care that both of us are absolutely
            blind ;

BOTH.   Then turn us round—and we, with all convenient
            despatch,
            Will undertake to marry any two of you we catch !

ALL.   Viva !

    They undertake to marry any two of ⎰ us they catch !
                                        ⎱ them they catch !

(*The Girls prepare to bind their eyes as directed.*)

FIA. (*to* MARCO). Are you peeping ?
                        Can you see me ?

MAR.   Dark I'm keeping,
                        Dark and dreamy !

                            (MARCO *slyly lifts bandage.*)

VIT. (*to* GIUSEPPE). If you're blinded
                        Truly, say so.

GIU.   All right-minded
                        Players play so ! (*slyly lifts bandage*).

FIA. (*detecting* MARCO).   Conduct shady !
                        They are cheating !
                    Surely they de-
                        Serve a beating !   (*replaces bandage*).

VIT. (*detecting* GIUSEPPE).   This too much is ;
                        Maidens mocking—
                    Conduct such is
                        Truly shocking !   (*replaces bandage*).

ALL.   You can spy, sir !
                        Shut your eye, sir !
                    You may use it by and by, sir !
                        You can see, sir !
                        Don't tell me, sir !
                    That will do—now let it be, sir !

CHORUS OF   My papa he keeps three horses,
 GIRLS.   Black, and white, and dapple grey, sir ;
    Turn three times, then take your courses,
     Catch whichever girl you may, sir !

CHORUS OF MEN. My papa, etc.

(MARCO *and* GIUSEPPE *turn round, as directed, and try
 to catch the girls. Business of blind-man's buff.
 Eventually* MARCO *catches* GIANETTA, *and* GIUSEPPE
 catches* TESSA. *The two girls try to escape, but in
 vain. The two men pass their hands over the girls'
 faces to discover their identity.*)

GIU.   I've at length achieved a capture !
 (*Guessing.*) This is Tessa ! (*removes bandage*). Rapture,
    rapture !

MAR. (*guessing*). To me Gianetta fate has granted !
     (*removes bandage*)
    Just the very girl I wanted !

GIU. (*politely to* MAR.). If you'd rather change——

TESS.   My goodness !
    This indeed is simple rudeness.

MAR. (*politely to* GIU.). I've no preference whatever—

GIA.   Listen to him ! Well, I never !
    (*Each man kisses each girl.*)

GIA.   Thank you, gallant *gondolieri* !
    In a set and formal measure
   It is scarcely necessary
     To express our pleasure.
     Each of us to prove a treasure,
   Conjugal and monetary,
     Gladly will devote our leisure,
   Gay and gallant *gondolieri.*
    Tra, la, la, la, la, la, etc.

TESS. Gay and gallant *gondolieri*,
    Take us both and hold us tightly,
 You have luck extraordinary ;
    We might both have been unsightly !
    If we judge your conduct rightly,
 'Twas a choice involuntary ;
    Still we thank you most politely,
 Gay and gallant *gondolieri* !
    Tra, la, la, la, la, la, etc.

CHORUS OF Thank you, gallant *gondolieri* ;
 GIRLS.   In a set and formal measure,
 It is scarcely necessary
    To express our pleasure.
    Each of us to prove a treasure
    Gladly will devote our leisure,
 Gay and gallant *gondolieri* !
    Tra, la, la, la, la, la, etc.

ALL. Fate in this has put his finger—
    Let us bow to Fate's decree,
 Then no longer let us linger,
    To the altar hurry we !

*[They all dance off two and two—*GIANETTA
with MARCO, TESSA *with* GIUSEPPE.

*Flourish. A gondola arrives at the Piazzetta steps, from
which enter the* DUKE OF PLAZA-TORO, *the* DUCHESS,
their daughter CASILDA, *and their attendant* LUIZ,
*who carries a drum. All are dressed in pompous
but old and faded clothes.*

Entrance of DUKE, DUCHESS, CASILDA, *and* LUIZ.

DUKE. From the sunny Spanish shore,
   The Duke of Plaza-Tor'—

DUCH. And His Grace's Duchess true—

CAS. And His Grace's daughter, too—

LUIZ.   And His Grace's private drum
          To Venetia's shores have come :

ALL.   If ever, ever, ever
                         They get back to Spain,
                     They will never, never, never
                         Cross the sea again—

DUKE.   Neither that Grandee from the Spanish shore,
          The noble Duke of Plaza Tor'—

DUCH.   Nor His Grace's Duchess, staunch and true—

CAS.   You may add, His Grace's daughter, too—

LUIZ.   Nor His Grace's own particular drum
          To Venetia's shores will come :

ALL.   If ever, ever, ever
                         They get back to Spain,
                     They will never, never, never
                         Cross the sea again !

DUKE.   At last we have arrived at our destination.
This is the Ducal Palace, and it is here that the Grand
Inquisitor resides.   As a Castilian hidalgo of ninety-five
quarterings, I regret that I am unable to pay my state
visit on a horse.   As a Castilian hidalgo of that description,
I should have preferred to ride through the streets of
Venice ; but owing, I presume, to an unusually wet
season, the streets are in such a condition that equestrian
exercise is impracticable.   No matter.   Where is our
suite ?

LUIZ (coming forward).   Your Grace, I am here.

DUCH.   Why do you not do yourself the honour to
kneel when you address His Grace ?

DUKE.   My love, it is so small a matter !   (To LUIZ.)
Still, you may as well do it.   (LUIZ kneels.)

CAS.   The young man seems to entertain but an
imperfect appreciation of the respect due from a menial
to a Castilian hidalgo.

DUKE.   My child, you are hard upon our suite.

CAS.   Papa, I've no patience with the presumption of persons in his plebeian position.   If he does not appreciate that position, let him be whipped until he does.

DUKE.   Let us hope the omission was not intended as a slight.   I should be much hurt if I thought it was.   So would he.   (*To* LUIZ.)   Where are the halberdiers who were to have had the honour of meeting us here, that our visit to the Grand Inquisitor might be made in becoming state ?

LUIZ.   Your Grace, the halberdiers are mercenary people who stipulated for a trifle on account.

DUKE.   How tiresome !   Well, let us hope the Grand Inquisitor is a blind gentleman.   And the band who were to have had the honour of escorting us ?   I see no band !

LUIZ.   Your Grace, the band are sordid persons who required to be paid in advance.

DUCH.   That's so like a band !

DUKE (*annoyed*).   Insuperable difficulties meet me at every turn !

DUCH.   But surely they know His Grace ?

LUIZ.   Exactly—they know His Grace.

DUKE.   Well, let us hope that the Grand Inquisitor is a deaf gentleman.   A cornet-à-piston would be something.   You do not happen to possess the accomplishment of tootling like a cornet-à-piston ?

LUIZ.   Alas, no, Your Grace !   But I can imitate a farmyard.

DUKE (*doubtfully*).   I don't see how that would help us.   I don't see how we could bring it in.

CAS.   It would not help us in the least.   We are not a parcel of graziers come to market, dolt !

DUKE.   My love, our suite's feelings !   (*To* LUIZ.) Be so good as to ring the bell and inform the Grand Inquisitor that his Grace the Duke of Plaza-Toro, Count Matadoro, Baron Picadoro——

DUCH.   And suite—

DUKE. And suite—have arrived at Venice, and seek——

CAS. Desire—

DUCH. Demand !

DUKE. And demand an audience.

LUIZ. Your Grace has but to command. (*Rising.*)

DUKE (*much moved*). I felt sure of it—I felt sure of it ! (*Exit* LUIZ *into Ducal Palace.*) And now, my love— (*aside to* DUCHESS) Shall we tell her ? I think so— (*aloud to* CASILDA) And now, my love, prepare for a magnificent surprise. It is my agreeable duty to reveal to you a secret which should make you the happiest young lady in Venice !

CAS. A secret ?

DUCH. A secret which, for State reasons, it has been necessary to preserve for twenty years.

DUKE. When you were a prattling babe of six months old you were married by proxy to no less a personage than the infant son and heir of His Majesty the immeasurably wealthy King of Barataria !

CAS. Married to the infant son of the King of Barataria ? Was I consulted ? (DUKE *shakes his head*.) Then it was a most unpardonable liberty !

DUKE. Consider his extreme youth and forgive him. Shortly after the ceremony that misguided monarch abandoned the creed of his forefathers, and became a Wesleyan Methodist of the most bigoted and persecuting type. The Grand Inquisitor, determined that the innovation should not be perpetuated in Barataria, caused your smiling and unconscious husband to be stolen and conveyed to Venice. A fortnight since the Methodist Monarch and all his Wesleyan Court were killed in an insurrection, and we are here to ascertain the whereabouts of your husband, and to hail you, our daughter, as Her Majesty, the reigning Queen of Barataria ! (*Kneels.*)

During this speech LUIZ *re-enters.*

DUCH. Your Majesty ! (*Kneels.*)

DUKE. It is at such moments as these that one feels how necessary it is to travel with a full band.

CAS. I, the Queen of Barataria! But I've nothing to wear! We are practically penniless!

DUKE. That point has not escaped me. Although I am unhappily in straitened circumstances at present, my social influence is something enormous; and a Company, to be called the Duke of Plaza-Toro, Limited, is in course of formation to work me. An influential directorate has been secured, and I shall myself join the Board after allotment.

CAS. Am I to understand that the Queen of Barataria may be called upon at any time to witness her honoured sire in process of liquidation?

DUCH. The speculation is not exempt from that drawback. If your father should stop, it will, of course, be necessary to wind him up.

CAS. But it's so undignified—it's so degrading! A Grandee of Spain turned into a public company! Such a thing was never heard of!

DUKE. My child, the Duke of Plaza-Toro does not follow fashions—he leads them. He always leads everybody. When he was in the army he led his regiment. He occasionally led them into action. He invariably led them out of it.

SONG—DUKE OF PLAZA-TORO.

In enterprise of martial kind,
    When there was any fighting,
He led his regiment from behind—
    He found it less exciting.
But when away his regiment ran,
    His place was at the fore, O—
        That celebrated,
        Cultivated,
        Underrated
            Nobleman,
    The Duke of Plaza-Toro!

ALL. In the first and foremost flight, ha, ha !
You always found that knight, ha, ha !
  That celebrated,
   Cultivated,
   Underrated
    Nobleman,
  The Duke of Plaza-Toro !

When, to evade Destruction's hand,
 To hide they all proceeded,
No soldier in that gallant band
 Hid half as well as he did.
He lay concealed throughout the war,
 And so preserved his gore, O !
  That unaffected,
   Undetected,
   Well-connected
    Warrior,
  The Duke of Plaza-Toro !

ALL. In every doughty deed, ha, ha !
He always took the lead, ha, ha !
  That unaffected,
   Undetected,
   Well-connected
    Warrior,
  The Duke of Plaza-Toro !

When told that they would all be shot
 Unless they left the service,
That hero hesitated not,
 So marvellous his nerve is.
He sent his resignation in,
 The first of all his corps, O !
  That very knowing,
   Overflowing,
   Easy-going
    Paladin,
  The Duke of Plaza-Toro !

ALL.   To men of grosser clay, ha, ha !
              He always showed the way, ha, ha !
                      That very knowing,
                      Overflowing,
                      Easy-going
                          Paladin,
              The Duke of Plaza-Toro !

> [*Exeunt* DUKE *and* DUCHESS *into Grand
> Ducal Palace. As soon as they have
> disappeared,* LUIZ *and* CASILDA *rush to
> each other's arms.*

RECIT. AND DUET—CASILDA *and* LUIZ.

O rapture, when alone together
    Two loving hearts and those that bear them
May join in temporary tether,
    Though Fate apart should rudely tear them.

CAS.   Necessity, Invention's mother,
             Compelled me to a course of feigning—
         But, left alone with one another,
             I will atone for my disdaining !

                  Ah, well-beloved,
                  Mine angry frown
                  Is but a gown
                  That serves to dress
                  My gentleness !

LUIZ.   Ah, well-beloved,
                  Thy cold disdain,
                  It gives no pain—
                  'Tis mercy, played
                  In masquerade !

BOTH.   Ah, well-beloved, etc.

    CAS.   O Luiz, Luiz—what have you said ?   What have
I done ?   What have I allowed you to do ?

Luiz.   Nothing, I trust, that you will ever have reason to repent. (*Offering to embrace her.*)

Cas. (*withdrawing from him*).   Nay, Luiz, it may not be. I have embraced you for the last time.

Luiz (*amazed*).   Casilda!

Cas.   I have just learnt, to my surprise and indignation, that I was wed in babyhood to the infant son of the King of Barataria!

Luiz.   The son of the King of Barataria?   The child who was stolen in infancy by the Inquisition?

Cas.   The same.   But, of course, you know his story.

Luiz.   Know his story?   Why, I have often told you that my mother was the nurse to whose charge he was entrusted!

Cas.   True.   I had forgotten.   Well, he has been discovered, and my father has brought me here to claim his hand.

Luiz.   But you will not recognize this marriage?   It took place when you were too young to understand its import.

Cas.   Nay, Luiz, respect my principles and cease to torture me with vain entreaties.   Henceforth my life is another's.

Luiz.   But stay—the present and the future—*they* are another's; but the past—that at least is ours, and none can take it from us.   As we may revel in naught else, let us revel in that!

Cas.   I don't think I grasp your meaning.

Luiz.   Yet it is logical enough.   You say you cease to love me?

Cas. (*demurely*).   I say I *may* not love you.

Luiz.   Ah, but you do not say you *did* not love me?

Cas.   I loved you with a frenzy that words are powerless to express—and that but ten brief minutes since!

Luiz.   Exactly.   My own—that is, until ten minutes since, my own—my lately loved, my recently adored—tell me that untii, say a quarter of an hour ago, I was all in all to thee!   (*Embracing her.*)

s

Cas. I see your idea. It's ingenious, but don't do that. (*Releasing herself.*)

Luiz. There can be no harm in revelling in the past.

Cas. None whatever, but an embrace cannot be taken to act retrospectively.

Luiz. Perhaps not !

Cas. We may recollect an embrace—I recollect many —but we must not repeat them.

Luiz. Then let us recollect a few ! (*A moment's pause, as they recollect, then both heave a deep sigh.*)

Luiz. Ah, Casilda, you were to me as the sun is to the earth !

Cas. A quarter of an hour ago ?

Luiz. About that.

Cas. And to think that, but for this miserable discovery, you would have been my own for life !

Luiz. Through life to death—a quarter of an hour ago !

Cas. How greedily my thirsty ears would have drunk the golden melody of those sweet words a quarter—well, it's now about twenty minutes since. (*Looking at her watch.*)

Luiz. About that. In such a matter one cannot be too precise.

Cas. And now our love, so full of life, is but a silent, solemn memory !

Luiz. Must it be so, Casilda ?

Cas. Luiz, it must be so !

DUET—Casilda *and* Luiz.

Luiz.
     There was a time—
         A time for ever gone—ah, woe is me !
     It was no crime
         To love but thee alone—ah, woe is me !
     One heart, one life, one soul,
         One aim, one goal—
     Each in the other's thrall,
         Each all in all, ah, woe is me !

Both.   Oh, bury, bury—let the grave close o'er
        The days that were—that never will be more !
        Oh, bury, bury love that all condemn,
        And let the whirlwind mourn its requiem !

Cas.   Dead as the last year's leaves—
            As gathered flowers—ah, woe is me !
        Dead as the garnered sheaves,
            That love of ours—ah, woe is me !
        Born but to fade and die
            When hope was high,
        Dead and as far away
            As yesterday !—ah, woe is me !

Both.   Oh, bury, bury—let the grave close o'er, etc.

Re-enter from the Ducal Palace the Duke *and* Duchess,
    followed by Don Alhambra del Bolero, *the Grand
    Inquisitor.*

Duke.   My child, allow me to present to you His
Distinction Don Alhambra del Bolero, the Grand Inquisitor
of Spain. It was His Distinction who so thoughtfully
abstracted your infant husband and brought him to Venice.

Don Al.   So this is the little lady who is so unexpectedly called upon to assume the functions of Royalty !
And a very nice little lady, too !

Duke.   Jimp, isn't she ?

Don Al.   Distinctly jimp. Allow me ! (*Offers his
hand. She turns away scornfully.*) Naughty temper !

Duke.   You must make some allowance. Her
Majesty's head is a little turned by her access of dignity.

Don Al.   I could have wished that Her Majesty's
access of dignity had turned it in this direction.

Duch.   Unfortunately, if I am not mistaken, there
appears to be some little doubt as to His Majesty's
whereabouts.

Cas. (*aside*).   A doubt as to his whereabouts ? Then
we may yet be saved !

Don Al.   A doubt ? Oh dear, no—no doubt at all !

He is here, in Venice, plying the modest but picturesque
calling of a gondolier. I can give you his address—I see
him every day ! In the entire annals of our history there
is absolutely no circumstance so entirely free from all
manner of doubt of any kind whatever ! Listen, and I'll
tell you all about it.

SONG—Don Alhambra (*with* Duke, Duchess,
Casilda, *and* Luiz).

I stole the Prince, and brought him here,
　　And left him gaily prattling
With a highly respectable gondolier,
Who promised the Royal babe to rear,
And teach him the trade of a timoneer
　　With his own beloved bratling.

　　　Both of the babes were strong and stout,
　　　　And, considering all things, clever.
　　　Of that there is no manner of doubt—
　　　No probable, possible shadow of doubt—
　　　　No possible doubt whatever.

But owing, I'm much disposed to fear,
　　To his terrible taste for tippling,
That highly respectable gondolier
Could never declare with a mind sincere
Which of the two was his offspring dear,
　　And which the Royal stripling !

　　　Which was which he could never make out
　　　　Despite his best endeavour.
　　　Of *that* there is no manner of doubt—
　　　No probable, possible shadow of doubt—
　　　　No possible doubt whatever.

Time sped, and when at the end of a year
　　I sought that infant cherished,
That highly respectable gondolier
Was lying a corpse on his humble bier—
I dropped a Grand Inquisitor's tear—
　　That gondolier had perished.

A taste for drink, combined with gout,
    Had doubled him up for ever.
Of *that* there is no manner of doubt—
No probable, possible shadow of doubt—
    No possible doubt whatever.

The children followed his old career—
    (This statement can't be parried)
Of a highly respectable gondolier :
Well, one of the two (who will soon be here)—
But *which* of the two is not quite clear—
    Is the Royal Prince you married !

      Search in and out and round about,
        And you'll discover never
      A tale so free from every doubt—
      All probable, possible shadow of doubt—
        All possible doubt whatever !

CAS. Then do you mean to say that I am married to one of two gondoliers, but it is impossible to say which ?

DON AL. Without any doubt of any kind whatever. But be reassured : the nurse to whom your husband was entrusted is the mother of the musical young man who is such a past-master of that delicately modulated instrument (*indicating the drum*). She can, no doubt, establish the King's identity beyond all question.

LUIZ. Heavens, how did he know that ?

DON AL. My young friend, a Grand Inquisitor is always up to date. (*To* CAS.) His mother is at present the wife of a highly respectable and old-established brigand, who carries on an extensive practice in the mountains around Cordova. Accompanied by two of my emissaries, he will set off at once for his mother's address. She will return with them, and if she finds any difficulty in making up her mind, the persuasive influence of the torture chamber will jog her memory.

RECIT.—CASILDA *and* DON ALHAMBRA.

CAS.   But, bless my heart, consider my position !
              I am the wife of one, that's very clear ;
              But who can tell, except by intuition,
                Which is the Prince, and which the Gondolier ?

DON AL. Submit to Fate without unseemly wrangle :
              Such complications frequently occur—
              Life is one closely complicated tangle :
                Death is the only true unraveller !

QUINTET—DUKE, DUCHESS, CASILDA, LUIZ,
        and GRAND INQUISITOR.

ALL.   Try we life-long, we can never
                Straighten out life's tangled skein,
              Why should we, in vain endeavour,
                Guess and guess and guess again ?

LUIZ.   Life's a pudding full of plums,

DUCH.   Care's a canker that benumbs.

ALL.   Life's a pudding full of plums,
                Care's a canker that benumbs.
              Wherefore waste our elocution
              On impossible solution ?
              Life's a pleasant institution,
                Let us take it as it comes !

              Set aside the dull enigma,
                We shall guess it all too soon ;
              Failure brings no kind of stigma—
                Dance we to another tune !

LUIZ.   String the lyre and fill the cup,

DUCH.   Lest on sorrow we should sup.

ALL.   String the lyre and fill the cup,
                Lest on sorrow we should sup.

Hop and skip to Fancy's fiddle,
Hands across and down the middle—
Life's perhaps the only riddle
    That we shrink from giving up !

[*Exeunt all into Ducal Palace except* LUIZ,
   who goes off in gondola.

Enter Gondoliers and Contadine, followed by MARCO,
   GIANETTA, GIUSEPPE, *and* TESSA.

CHORUS.

Bridegroom and bride !
   Knot that's insoluble,
   Voices all voluble
Hail it with pride.
Bridegroom and bride !
   We in sincerity
   Wish you prosperity,
Bridegroom and bride !

SONG—TESSA.

TESS.   When a merry maiden marries,
Sorrow goes and pleasure tarries ;
   Every sound becomes a song,
   All is right, and nothing's wrong !
From to-day and ever after
Let our tears be tears of laughter.
   Every sigh that finds a vent
   Be a sigh of sweet content !
When you marry, merry maiden,
Then the air with love is laden ;
   Every flower is a rose,
      Every goose becomes a swan,
   Every kind of trouble goes
      Where the last year's snows have gone !

CHORUS.   Sunlight takes the place of shade
When you marry, merry maid !

TESS.   When a merry maiden marries,
          Sorrow goes and pleasure tarries ;
             Every sound becomes a song,
             All is right, and nothing's wrong.
          Gnawing Care and aching Sorrow,
          Get ye gone until to-morrow ;
             Jealousies in grim array,
             Ye are things of yesterday !
          When you marry, merry maiden,
          Then the air with joy is laden ;
             All the corners of the earth
               Ring with music sweetly played,
             Worry is melodious mirth,
               Grief is joy in masquerade ;

CHORUS.   Sullen night is laughing day—
          All the year is merry May !

At the end of the song, DON ALHAMBRA *enters at back. The Gondoliers and Contadine shrink from him, and gradually go off, much alarmed.*

GIU. And now our lives are going to begin in real earnest ! What's a bachelor ? A mere nothing—he's a chrysalis. He can't be said to live—he exists.

MAR. What a delightful institution marriage is ! Why have we wasted all this time ? Why didn't we marry ten years ago ?

TESS. Because you couldn't find anybody nice enough.

GIA. Because you were waiting for *us.*

MAR. I suppose that *was* the reason. We were waiting for you without knowing it. (DON ALHAMBRA *comes forward.*) Hallo !

DON AL. Good morning.

GIU. If this gentleman is an undertaker, it's a bad omen.

DON AL. Ceremony of some sort going on ?

GIU. (*aside*). He *is* an undertaker ! (*Aloud.*) No— a little unimportant family gathering. Nothing in *your* line.

Don Al. Somebody's birthday, I suppose?

Gia. Yes, mine!

Tess. And mine!

Mar. And mine!

Giu. And mine!

Don Al. Curious coincidence! And how old may you all be?

Tess. It's a rude question—but about ten minutes.

Don Al. Remarkably fine children! But surely you are jesting?

Tess. In other words, we were married about ten minutes since.

Don Al. Married! You don't mean to say you are married?

Mar. Oh yes, we are married.

Don Al. What, both of you?

All. All four of us.

Don Al. (*aside*). Bless my heart, how extremely awkward!

Gia. You don't mind, I suppose?

Tess. You were not thinking of either of us for yourself, I presume? Oh, Giuseppe, look at him—he was. He's heart-broken!

Don Al. No, no, I wasn't! I wasn't!

Giu. Now, my man (*slapping him on the back*), we don't want anything in your line to-day, and if your curiosity's satisfied—you can go!

Don Al. You mustn't call me your man. It's a liberty. I don't think you know who I am.

Giu. Not we, indeed! We are jolly gondoliers, the sons of Baptisto Palmieri, who led the last revolution. Republicans, heart and soul, we hold all men to be equal. As we abhor oppression, we abhor kings: as we detest vain-glory, we detest rank: as we despise effeminacy, we despise wealth. We are Venetian gondoliers—your equals in everything except our calling, and in that at once your masters and your servants.

Don Al. Bless my heart, how unfortunate! One of

you may be Baptisto's son, for anything I know to the contrary ; but the other is no less a personage than the only son of the late King of Barataria.

ALL. What !

DON AL. And I trust—I *trust* it was that one who slapped me on the shoulder and called me his man !

GIU. One of us a king !

MAR. Not brothers !

TESS. The King of Barataria ! } *Together.*

GIA. Well, who'd have thought it ! }

MAR. But which is it ?

DON AL. What does it matter ? As you are both Republicans, and hold kings in detestation, of course you'll abdicate at once. Good morning ! (*Going.*)

GIA. *and* TESS. Oh, don't do that ! (MARCO *and* GIUSEPPE *stop him.*)

GIU. Well, as to that, of course there are kings and kings. When I say that I detest kings, I mean I detest *bad* kings.

DON AL. I see. It's a delicate distinction.

GIU. Quite so. Now I can conceive a kind of king— an ideal king—the creature of my fancy, you know—who would be absolutely unobjectionable. A king, for instance, who would abolish taxes and make everything cheap, except gondolas——

MAR. And give a great many free entertainments to the gondoliers——

GIU. And let off fireworks on the Grand Canal, and engage all the gondolas for the occasion——

MAR. And scramble money on the Rialto among the gondoliers.

GIU. Such a king would be a blessing to his people, and if I were a king, that is the sort of king I would be.

MAR. And so would I !

DON AL. Come, I'm glad to find your objections are not insuperable.

MAR. *and* GIU. Oh, they're not insuperable.

GIA. *and* TESS.   No, they're not insuperable.

GIU.   Besides, we are open to conviction.

GIA.   Yes ; they are open to conviction.

TESS.   Oh ! they've often been convicted.

GIU.   Our views may have been hastily formed on insufficient grounds.   They may be crude, ill-digested, erroneous.   I've a very poor opinion of the politician who is not open to conviction.

TESS. (*to* GIA.).   Oh, he's a fine fellow !

GIA.   Yes, that's the sort of politician for *my* money !

DON AL.   Then we'll consider it settled.   Now, as the country is in a state of insurrection, it is absolutely necessary that you should assume the reins of Government at once ; and, until it is ascertained which of you is to be king, I have arranged that you will reign jointly, so that no question can arise hereafter as to the validity of any of your acts.

MAR.   As one individual ?

DON AL.   As one individual.

GIU. (*linking himself with* MARCO).   Like this ?

DON AL.   Something like that.

MAR.   And we may take our friends with us, and give them places about the Court ?

DON AL.   Undoubtedly.   That's always done !

MAR.   I'm convinced !

GIU.   So am I !

TESS.   Then the sooner we're off the better.

GIA.   We'll just run home and pack up a few things (*going*)——

DON AL.   Stop, stop—that won't do at all—ladies are not admitted.

ALL.   What !

DON AL.   Not admitted.   Not at present.   Afterwards, perhaps.   We'll see.

GIU.   Why, you don't mean to say you are going to separate us from our wives !

DON AL. (*aside*).   This is very awkward !   (*Aloud*.)

Only for a time—a few months.   After all, what is a few months ?

TESS.   But we've only been married half an hour ! (*Weeps*.)

FINALE, ACT I.

SONG—GIANETTA.

Kind sir, you cannot have the heart
Our lives to part
From those to whom an hour ago
We were united !
Before our flowing hopes you stem,
Ah, look at them,
And pause before you deal this blow,
All uninvited !
You men can never understand
That heart and hand
Cannot be separated when
We go a-yearning ;
You see, you've only women's eyes
To idolize
And only women's hearts, poor men,
To set *you* burning !
Ah me, you men will never understand
That woman's heart is one with woman's hand !

Some kind of charm you seem to find
In womankind—
Some source of unexplained delight
(Unless you're jesting),
But what attracts you, I confess,
I cannot guess,
To me a woman's face is quite
Uninteresting !
If from my sister I were torn,
It could be borne—
I should, no doubt, be horrified,
But I could bear it ;—

But Marco's quite another thing—
He is my King,
He has my heart and none beside
Shall ever share it !
Ah me, you men will never understand
That woman's heart is one with woman's hand !

RECIT.—Don Alhambra.

Do not give way to this uncalled-for grief,
Your separation will be very brief.
To ascertain which is the King
And which the other,
To Barataria's Court I'll bring
His foster-mother ;
Her former nurseling to declare
She'll be delighted.
That settled, let each happy pair
Be reunited.

Mar., Giu., Gia.,   Viva !   His argument is strong !
Tess.   Viva !   We'll not be parted long !
            Viva !   It will be settled soon !
            Viva !   Then comes our honeymoon !

[*Exit* Don Alhambra.

QUARTET—Marco, Giuseppe, Gianetta, Tessa.

Gia.   Then one of us will be a Queen,
And sit on a golden throne,
With a crown instead
Of a hat on her head,
And diamonds all her own !
With a beautiful robe of gold and green,
I've always understood ;
I wonder whether
She'd wear a feather ?
I rather think she should !

ALL.   Oh, 'tis a glorious thing, I ween,
        To be a regular Royal Queen !
        No half-and-half affair, I mean,
        But a right-down regular Royal Queen !

MAR.   She'll drive about in a carriage and pair,
            With the King on her left-hand side,
                And a milk-white horse,
                As a matter of course,
            Whenever she wants to ride !
        With beautiful silver shoes to wear
            Upon her dainty feet ;
                With endless stocks
                Of beautiful frocks
            And as much as she wants to eat !

ALL.   Oh, 'tis a glorious thing, I ween, etc.

TESS.   Whenever she condescends to walk,
            Be sure she'll shine at that,
                With her haughty stare
                And her nose in the air,
            Like a well-born aristocrat !
        At elegant high society talk
            She'll bear away the bell,
                With her " How de do ? "
                And her " How are you ? "
            And " I trust I see you well ! "

ALL.   Oh, 'tis a glorious thing, I ween, etc.

GIU.   And noble lords will scrape and bow,
            And double themselves in two,
                And open their eyes
                In blank surprise
            At whatever she likes to do.
        And everybody will roundly vow
            She's fair as flowers in May,
                And say, " How clever ! "
                At whatsoever
            She condescends to say !

ALL.   Oh, 'tis a glorious thing, I ween,
            To be a regular Royal Queen !
            No half-and-half affair, I mean,
            But a right-down regular Royal Queen !

Enter Chorus of Gondoliers and Contadine.

CHORUS.

Now, pray, what is the cause of this remarkable hilarity ?
    This sudden ebullition of unmitigated jollity ?
Has anybody blessed you with a sample of his charity ?
    Or have you been adopted by a gentleman of quality ?

MAR. *and* GIU.   Replying, we sing
                As one individual,
            As I find I'm a king,
                To my kingdom I bid you all.
            I'm aware you object
                To pavilions and palaces,
            But you'll find I respect
                Your Republican fallacies.

CHORUS.   As they know we object
                To pavilions and palaces,
            How can they respect
                Our Republican fallacies ?

MARCO *and* GIUSEPPE.

MAR.   For every one who feels inclined,
        Some post we undertake to find
        Congenial with his frame of mind—
            And all shall equal be.

GIU.   The Chancellor in his peruke—
        The Earl, the Marquis, and the Dook,
        The Groom, the Butler, and the Cook—
            They all shall equal be.

MAR.   The Aristocrat who banks with Coutts—
        The Aristocrat who hunts and shoots—
        The Aristocrat who cleans our boots—
            They all shall equal be !

GIU.   The Noble Lord who rules the State—
        The Noble Lord who cleans the plate—

MAR.   The Noble Lord who scrubs the grate—
            They all shall equal be !

GIU.   The Lord High Bishop orthodox—
        The Lord High Coachman on the box—

MAR.   The Lord High Vagabond in the stocks—
            They all shall equal be !

BOTH.   For every one, etc.

            Sing high, sing low,
            Wherever they go,
                They all shall equal be !

CHORUS.   Sing high, sing low,
            Wherever they go,
                They all shall equal be !

        The Earl, the Marquis, and the Dook,
        The Groom, the Butler, and the Cook,
        The Aristocrat who banks with Coutts,
        The Aristocrat who cleans the boots,
        The Noble Lord who rules the State,
        The Noble Lord who scrubs the grate,
        The Lord High Bishop orthodox,
        The Lord High Vagabond in the stocks—

        For every one, etc.

            Sing high, sing low,
            Wherever they go,
                They all shall equal be !

            Then hail ! O King,
            Whichever you may be,
            To you we sing,
                But do not bend the knee.
            Then hail ! O King.

MARCO *and* GIUSEPPE (*together*).

Come, let's away—our island crown awaits me—
    Conflicting feelings rend my soul apart !
The thought of Royal dignity elates me,
    But leaving thee behind me breaks my heart !
           (*Addressing* GIANETTA *and* TESSA.)

GIANETTA *and* TESSA (*together*).

Farewell, my love ; on board you must be getting ;
    But while upon the sea you gaily roam,
Remember that a heart for thee is fretting—
    The tender little heart you've left at home !

GIA.   Now, Marco dear,
                My wishes hear :
                    While you're away
                It's understood
                You will be good,
                    And not too gay.
                To every trace
                Of maiden grace
                    You will be blind,
                And will not glance
                By any chance
                    On womankind !

                If you are wise,
                You'll shut your eyes
                    Till we arrive,
                And not address
                A lady less
                    Than forty-five.
                You'll please to frown
                On every gown
                    That you may see ;
                And, O my pet,
                You won't forget
                    You've married me !

And O my darling, O my pet,
Whatever else you may forget,
In yonder isle beyond the sea,
Do not forget you've married me !

TESS.   You'll lay your head
                Upon your bed
                    At set of sun.
                You will not sing
                Of anything
                    To any one.
                You'll sit and mope
                All day, I hope,
                    And shed a tear
                Upon the life
                Your little wife
                    Is passing here.

                And if so be
                You think of me,
                    Please tell the moon !
                I'll read it all
                In rays that fall
                    On the lagoon :
                You'll be so kind
                As tell the wind
                    How you may be,
                And send me words
                By little birds
                    To comfort me !

And O my darling, O my pet,
Whatever else you may forget,
In yonder isle beyond the sea,
Do not forget you've married me .

QUARTET.   O my darling, O my pet, etc.

CHORUS (*during which a " Xebeque " is hauled
          alongside the quay*).

Then away we go to an island fair
  That lies in a Southern sea :
We know not where, and we don't much care,
  Wherever that isle may be.

THE MEN (*hauling on boat*).   One, two, three,
                              Haul !
                            One, two, three,
                              Haul !
                            One, two, three,
                              Haul !
                          With a will !

ALL.   When the breezes are a-blowing
  The ship will be going,
        When they don't we shall all stand still !
Then away we go to an island fair,
We know not where, and we don't much care,
        Wherever that isle may be.

SOLO—MARCO.

Away we go
  To a balmy isle,
Where the roses blow
  All the winter while.

ALL (*hoisting sail*).   Then away we go to an island fair
                      That lies in a Southern sea :
                    Then away we go to an island fair,
                      Then away, then away, then away !

(*The men embark on the " Xebeque ".* MARCO *and*
    GIUSEPPE *embracing* GIANETTA *and* TESSA. *The
    girls wave a farewell to the men as the curtain falls.*)

END OF ACT I.

ACT II.

SCENE.—*Pavilion in the Court of Barataria.* MARCO *and* GIUSEPPE, *magnificently dressed, are seated on two thrones, occupied in cleaning the crown and the sceptre. The Gondoliers are discovered, dressed, some as courtiers, officers of rank, etc., and others as private soldiers and servants of various degrees. All are enjoying themselves without reference to social distinctions—some playing cards, others throwing dice, some reading, others playing cup and ball, "morra", etc.*

CHORUS OF MEN *with* MARCO *and* GIUSEPPE.

Of happiness the very pith
> In Barataria you may see:
A monarchy that's tempered with
> Republican Equality.
This form of government we find
The beau-ideal of its kind—
A despotism strict, combined
> With absolute equality!

MARCO *and* GIUSEPPE.

Two kings, of undue pride bereft,
> Who act in perfect unity,
Whom you can order right and left
> With absolute impunity.

532

      Who put their subjects at their ease
      By doing all they can to please !
      And thus, to earn their bread-and-cheese,
          Seize every opportunity.

CHORUS.   Of happiness the very pith, etc.

MAR. Gentlemen, we are much obliged to you for your expressions of satisfaction and good feeling—I say, we are much obliged to you for your expressions of satisfaction and good feeling.

ALL. We heard you.

MAR. We are delighted, at any time, to fall in with sentiments so charmingly expressed.

ALL. That's all right.

GIU. At the same time there is just one little grievance that we should like to ventilate.

ALL (*angrily*). What ?

GIU. Don't be alarmed—it's not serious. It is arranged that, until it is decided which of us two is the actual King, we are to act as one person.

GIORGIO. Exactly.

GIU. Now, although we act as *one* person, we are, in point of fact, *two* persons.

ANNIBALE. Ah, I don't think we can go into that. It is a legal fiction, and legal fictions are solemn things. Situated as we are, we can't recognize two independent responsibilities.

GIU. No ; but you can recognize two independent appetites. It's all very well to say we act as one person, but when you supply us with only one ration between us, I should describe it as a legal fiction carried a little too far.

ANNI. It's rather a nice point. I don't like to express an opinion off-hand. Suppose we reserve it for argument before the full Court ?

MAR. Yes, but what are we to do in the meantime ?

MAR. *and* GIU. We want our tea.

ANNI. I think we may make an interim order for double rations on their Majesties entering into the usual

undertaking to indemnify in the event of an adverse decision ?

GIOR.   That, I think, will meet the case.   But you must work hard—stick to it—nothing like work.

GIU.   Oh, certainly.   We quite understand that a man who holds the magnificent position of King should do something to justify it.   We are called " Your Majesty ", we are allowed to buy ourselves magnificent clothes, our subjects frequently nod to us in the streets, the sentries always return our salutes, and we enjoy the inestimable privilege of heading the subscription lists to all the principal charities.   In return for these advantages the least we can do is to make ourselves useful about the Palace.

SONG—GIUSEPPE with CHORUS.

Rising early in the morning,
    We proceed to light the fire,
Then our Majesty adorning
    In its workaday attire,
        We embark without delay
        On the duties of the day.

First, we polish off some batches
Of political despatches,
    And foreign politicians circumvent ;
Then, if business isn't heavy,
We may hold a Royal *levée,*
    Or ratify some Acts of Parliament.
Then we probably review the household troops—
With the usual " Shalloo humps ! " and " Shalloo hoops ! "
Or receive with ceremonial and state
An interesting Eastern potentate.
        After that we generally
        Go and dress our private *valet*—
(It's a rather nervous duty—he's a touchy little man)—
        Write some letters literary
        For our private secretary—
He is shaky in his spelling, so we help him if we can.

Then, in view of cravings inner,
　　We go down and order dinner ;
Then we polish the Regalia and the Coronation Plate—
　　Spend an hour in titivating
　　All our Gentlemen-in-Waiting ;
Or we run on little errands for the Ministers of State.

　　Oh, philosophers may sing
　　Of the troubles of a King ;
Yet the duties are delightful, and the privileges great ;
　　But the privilege and pleasure
　　That we treasure beyond measure
Is to run on little errands for the Ministers of State.

CHORUS.　　Oh, philosophers may sing, etc.

After luncheon (making merry
On a bun and glass of sherry),
　　If we've nothing in particular to do,
We may make a Proclamation,
Or receive a deputation—
　　Then we possibly create a Peer or two.
Then we help a fellow-creature on his path
With the Garter or the Thistle or the Bath,
Or we dress and toddle off in semi-state
To a festival, a function, or a *fête*.
　　Then we go and stand as sentry
　　At the Palace (private entry),
Marching hither, marching thither, up and down and to
　　　　and fro,
　　While the warrior on duty
　　Goes in search of beer and beauty
(And it generally happens that he hasn't far to go).
　　He relieves us, if he's able,
　　Just in time to lay the table,
Then we dine and serve the coffee, and at half-past twelve
　　　　or one,
　　With a pleasure that's emphatic,
　　We retire to our attic
With the gratifying feeling that our duty has been done !

Oh, philosophers may sing
Of the troubles of a King,
But of pleasures there are many and of worries there are
none ;
And the culminating pleasure
That we treasure beyond measure
Is the gratifying feeling that our duty has been done !

CHORUS.   Oh, philosophers may sing, etc.

[*Exeunt all but* MARCO *and* GIUSEPPE.

GIU.   Yes, it really is a very pleasant existence.
They're all so singularly kind and considerate.   You don't
find them wanting to do this, or wanting to do that, or
saying " It's my turn now."   No, they let us have all the
fun to ourselves, and never seem to grudge it.

MAR.   It makes one feel quite selfish.   It almost seems
like taking advantage of their good nature.

GIU.   How nice they were about the double rations.

MAR.   Most considerate.   Ah ! there's only one thing
wanting to make us thoroughly comfortable.

GIU.   And that is ?

MAR.   The dear little wives we left behind us three
months ago.

GIU.   Yes, it *is* dull without female society.   We
can do without everything else, but we can't do without
that.

MAR.   And if we have that in perfection, we have
everything.   There is only one recipe for perfect happiness.

SONG—MARCO.

Take a pair of sparkling eyes,
Hidden, ever and anon,
In a merciful eclipse—
Do not heed their mild surprise—
Having passed the Rubicon,
Take a pair of rosy lips ;

Take a figure trimly planned—
    Such as admiration whets
        (Be particular in this) ;
Take a tender little hand,
    Fringed with dainty fingerettes,
        Press it—in parenthesis ;—
Ah !   Take all these, you lucky man—
Take and keep them, if you can !

Take a pretty little cot—
    Quite a miniature affair—
        Hung about with trellised vine,
Furnish it upon the spot
    With the treasures rich and rare
        I've endeavoured to define.
Live to love and love to live—
    You will ripen at your ease,
        Growing on the sunny side—
Fate has nothing more to give.
        You're a dainty man to please
        If you are not satisfied.
Ah !   Take my counsel, happy man ;
Act upon it, if you can !

Enter Chorus of Contadine, running in, led by FIAMETTA
and VITTORIA. *They are met by all the Ex-Gondoliers,
who welcome them heartily.*

SCENA—CHORUS OF GIRLS, QUARTET, DUET
    and CHORUS.

Here we are, at the risk of our lives,
From ever so far, and we've brought your wives—
And to that end we've crossed the main,
And don't intend to return again !

FIA.   Though obedience is strong,
                    Curiosity's stronger—
                We waited for long,
                    Till we couldn't wait longer.

VIT.   It's imprudent, we know,
                   But without your society
              Existence was slow,
                   And we wanted variety—

ALL. So here we are, at the risk of our lives,
       From ever so far, and we've brought your wives—
       And to that end we've crossed the main,
       And don't intend to return again !

Enter GIANETTA *and* TESSA. *They rush to the arms
             of* MARCO *and* GIUSEPPE.

GIU.   Tessa !
TESS.   Giuseppe !
GIA.   Marco !   } *Embrace.*
MAR.   Gianetta !

                   TESSA *and* GIANETTA.

TESS.   After sailing to this island—
GIA.   Tossing in a manner frightful,
TESS.   We are all once more on dry land—
GIA.   And we find the change delightful,
TESS.   As at home we've been remaining—
             We've not seen you both for ages,
GIA.   Tell me, are you fond of reigning ?—
             How's the food, and what's the wages ?
TESS.   Does your new employment please ye ?—
GIA.   How does Royalizing strike you ?
TESS.   Is it difficult or easy ?—
GIA.   Do you think your subjects like you ?
TESS.   I am anxious to elicit,
             Is it plain and easy steering ?
GIA.   Take it altogether, is it—
             Better fun than gondoliering ?
BOTH.   We shall both go on requesting
             Till you tell us, never doubt it ;
         Everything is interesting,
             Tell us, tell us all about it !

CHORUS. They will both go on requesting, etc.

Tess.	Is the populace exacting ?
Gia.	Do they keep you at a distance ?
Tess.	All unaided are you acting,
Gia.	Or do they provide assistance ?
Tess.	When you're busy, have you got to
	Get up early in the morning ?
Gia.	If you do what you ought not to,
	Do they give the usual warning ?
Tess.	With a horse do they equip you ?
Gia.	Lots of trumpeting and drumming ?
Tess.	Do the Royal tradesmen tip you ?
Gia.	Ain't the livery becoming !
Tess.	Does your human being inner
	Feed on everything that nice is ?
Gia.	Do they give you wine for dinner ;
	Peaches, sugar-plums, and ices ?
Both.	We shall both go on requesting
	Till you tell us, never doubt it ;
	Everything is interesting,
	Tell us, tell us all about it !

Chorus. They will both go on requesting, etc.

Mar. This is indeed a most delightful surprise !

Tess. Yes, we thought you'd like it. You see, it was like this. After you left we felt very dull and mopey, and the days crawled by, and you never wrote ; so at last I said to Gianetta, " I can't stand this any longer ; those two poor Monarchs haven't got any one to mend their stockings or sew on their buttons or patch their clothes— at least, I hope they haven't—let us all pack up a change and go and see how they're getting on." And she said, " Done," and they all said, " Done " ; and we asked old Giacopo to lend us his boat, and *he* said, " Done " ; and we've crossed the sea, and, thank goodness, *that's* done ; and here we are, and—and—*I've* done !

Gia. And now—which of you is King ?

Tess. And which of us is Queen ?

Giu. That we shan't know until Nurse turns up.

But never mind that—the question is, how shall we celebrate the commencement of our honeymoon ? Gentlemen, will you allow us to offer you a magnificent banquet ?

ALL. We will !

GIU. Thanks very much ; and, ladies, what do you say to a dance ?

TESS. A banquet *and* a dance ! Oh, it's too much happiness !

CHORUS *and* DANCE.

Dance a cachucha, fandango, bolero,
Xeres we'll drink—Manzanilla, Montero—
Wine, when it runs in abundance, enhances
The reckless delight of that wildest of dances !
To the pretty pitter-pitter-patter,
And the clitter-clitter-clitter-clatter—
Clitter—clitter—clatter,
Pitter—pitter—patter,
Patter, patter, patter, patter, we'll dance.
Old Xeres we'll drink—Manzanilla, Montero ;
For wine, when it runs in abundance, enhances
The reckless delight of that wildest of dances !

CACHUCHA.

The dance is interrupted by the unexpected appearance of DON ALHAMBRA, *who looks on with astonishment.* MARCO *and* GIUSEPPE *appear embarrassed. The others run off, except Drummer Boy, who is driven off by* DON ALHAMBRA.

DON AL. Good evening. Fancy ball ?

GIU. No, not exactly. A little friendly dance. That's all. Sorry you're late.

DON AL. But I saw a groom dancing, and a footman !

MAR. Yes. That's the Lord High Footman.

DON AL. And, dear me, a common little drummer boy !

GIU. Oh no ! That's the Lord High Drummer Boy.

Don Al. But surely, surely the servants'-hall is the place for these gentry?

Giu. Oh dear no! *We* have appropriated the servants'-hall. It's the Royal Apartment, and accessible only by tickets obtainable at the Lord Chamberlain's office.

Mar. We really must have some place that we can call our own.

Don Al. (*puzzled*). I'm afraid I'm not quite equal to the intellectual pressure of the conversation.

Giu. You see, the Monarchy has been re-modelled on Republican principles.

Don Al. What!

Giu. All departments rank equally, and everybody is at the head of his department.

Don Al. I see.

Mar. I'm afraid you're annoyed.

Don Al. No. I won't say that. It's not quite what I expected.

Giu. I'm awfully sorry.

Mar. So am I.

Giu. By the by, can I offer you anything after your voyage? A plate of macaroni and a rusk?

Don Al. (*preoccupied*). No, no—nothing—nothing.

Giu. Obliged to be careful?

Don Al. Yes—gout. You see, in every Court there are distinctions that must be observed.

Giu. (*puzzled*). There are, are there?

Don Al. Why, of course. For instance, you wouldn't have a Lord High Chancellor play leapfrog with his own cook.

Mar. Why not?

Don Al. Why not! Because a Lord High Chancellor is a personage of great dignity, who should never, under any circumstances, place himself in the position of being told to tuck in his tuppenny, except by noblemen of his own rank. A Lord High Archbishop, for instance, might tell a Lord High Chancellor to tuck in his tuppenny, but certainly not a cook, gentlemen, certainly not a cook.

Giu.   Not even a Lord High Cook ?

Don Al.   My good friend, that is a rank that is not recognized at the Lord Chamberlain's office.   No, no, it won't do.   I'll give you an instance in which the experiment was tried.

SONG—Don Alhambra, *with* Marco *and* Giuseppe.

Don Al.   There lived a King, as I've been told,
                       In the wonder-working days of old,
                       When hearts were twice as good as gold,
                            And twenty times as mellow.
                       Good-temper triumphed in his face,
                       And in his heart he found a place
                       For all the erring human race
                            And every wretched fellow.
                       When he had Rhenish wine to drink
                       It made him very sad to think
                       That some, at junket or at jink,
                            Must be content with toddy.

Mar. *and* Giu.   With toddy, must be content with toddy.

Don Al.   He wished all men as rich as he
                       (And he was rich as rich could be),
                       So to the top of every tree
                            Promoted everybody.

Mar. *and* Giu.   Now, that's the kind of King for me—
                       He wished all men as rich as he,
                       So to the top of every tree
                            Promoted everybody !

Don Al.   Lord Chancellors were cheap as sprats,
                       And Bishops in their shovel hats
                       Were plentiful as tabby cats—
                            In point of fact, too many.
                       Ambassadors cropped up like hay,
                       Prime Ministers and such as they
                       Grew like asparagus in May,
                            And Dukes were three a penny.

On every side Field-Marshals gleamed,
Small beer were Lords-Lieutenant deemed,
With Admirals the ocean teemed
    All round his wide dominions.

MAR. *and* GIU. With Admirals all round his wide do-
    minions.

DON AL. And Party Leaders you might meet
In twos and threes in every street
Maintaining, with no little heat,
    Their various opinions.

MAR. *and* GIU. Now that's a sight you couldn't beat—
Two Party Leaders in each street
Maintaining, with no little heat,
    Their various opinions.

DON AL. That King, although no one denies
His heart was of abnormal size,
Yet he'd have acted otherwise
    If he had been acuter.
The end is easily foretold,
When every blessed thing you hold
Is made of silver, or of gold,
    You long for simple pewter.
When you have nothing else to wear
But cloth of gold and satins rare,
For cloth of gold you cease to care—
    Up goes the price of shoddy.

MAR. *and* GIU. Of shoddy, up goes the price of shoddy.

DON AL. In short, whoever you may be,
To this conclusion you'll agree,
When every one is somebodee,
    Then no one's anybody !

MAR. *and* GIU. Now that's as plain as plain can be,
To this conclusion we agree—

ALL. When every one is somebodee,
    Then no one's anybody !

GIANETTA *and* TESSA *enter unobserved. The two girls, impelled by curiosity, remain listening at the back of the stage.*

DON AL. And now I have some important news to communicate. His Grace the Duke of Plaza-Toro, Her Grace the Duchess, and their beautiful daughter Casilda— I say their beautiful daughter Casilda——

GIU. We heard you.

DON AL. Have arrived at Barataria, and may be here at any moment.

MAR. The Duke and Duchess are nothing to us.

DON AL. But the daughter—the beautiful daughter ! Aha ! Oh, you're a lucky dog, one of you !

GIU. I think you're a very incomprehensible old gentleman.

DON AL. Not a bit—I'll explain. Many years ago when you (whichever you are) were a baby, you (whichever you are) were married to a little girl who has grown up to be the most beautiful young lady in Spain. That beautiful young lady will be here to claim you (whichever you are) in half an hour, and I congratulate that one (whichever it is) with all my heart.

MAR. Married when a baby !

GIU. But we were married three months ago !

DON AL. One of you—only one. The other (whichever it is) is an unintentional bigamist.

GIA. *and* TESS. (*coming forward*). Well, upon my word !

DON AL. Eh ? Who are these young people ?

TESS. Who are we ? Why, their wives, of course. We've just arrived.

DON AL. Their wives ! Oh dear, this is very unfortunate ! Oh dear, this complicates matters ! Dear, dear, what will Her Majesty say ?

GIA. And do you mean to say that one of these Monarchs was already married ?

TESS. And that neither of us will be a Queen ?

Don Al. That is the idea I intended to convey. (Tessa *and* Gianetta *begin to cry*.)

Giu. (*to* Tessa). Tessa, my dear, dear child——

Tess. Get away ! perhaps it's you !

Mar. (*to* Gia.). My poor, poor little woman !

Gia. Don't ! Who knows whose husband you are ?

Tess. And pray, why didn't you tell us all about it before they left Venice ?

Don Al. Because, if I had, no earthly temptation would have induced these gentlemen to leave two such extremely fascinating and utterly irresistible little ladies !

Tess. There's something in that.

Don Al. I may mention that you will not be kept long in suspense, as the old lady who nursed the Royal child is at present in the torture chamber, waiting for me to interview her.

Giu. Poor old girl. Hadn't you better go and put her out of her suspense ?

Don Al. Oh no—there's no hurry—she's all right. She has all the illustrated papers. However, I'll go and interrogate her, and, in the meantime, may I suggest the absolute propriety of your regarding yourselves as single young ladies. Good evening !

[*Exit* Don Alhambra.

Gia. Well, here's a pleasant state of things !

Mar. Delightful. One of us is married to two young ladies, and nobody knows which ; and the other is married to one young lady whom nobody can identify !

Gia. And one of us is married to one of you, and the other is married to nobody.

Tess. But which of you is married to which of us, and what's to become of the other ? (*About to cry*.)

Giu. It's quite simple. Observe. Two husbands have managed to acquire three wives. Three wives— two husbands. (*Reckoning up*.) That's two-thirds of a husband to each wife.

Tess. O Mount Vesuvius, here we are in arithmetic ! My good sir, one can't marry a vulgar fraction !

T

GIU.   You've no right to call me a vulgar fraction.

MAR.   We are getting rather mixed. The situation entangled. Let's try and comb it out.

QUARTET—MARCO, GIUSEPPE, GIANETTA, TESSA.

In a contemplative fashion,
    And a tranquil frame of mind,
Free from every kind of passion,
    Some solution let us find.
Let us grasp the situation,
    Solve the complicated plot—
Quiet, calm deliberation
    Disentangles every knot.

TESS. I, no doubt, Giuseppe wedded—
    That's, of course, a slice of luck.
He is rather dunder-headed,
    Still distinctly, he's a duck.

THE OTHERS.   In a contemplative fashion, etc.

GIA. I, a victim, too, of Cupid,
    Marco married—that is clear.
He's particularly stupid,
    Still distinctly, he's a dear.

THE OTHERS.   Let us grasp the situation, etc.

MAR. To Gianetta I was mated ;
    I can prove it in a trice :
Though her charms are overrated,
    Still I own she's rather nice.

THE OTHERS.   In a contemplative fashion, etc.

GIU. I to Tessa, willy-nilly,
    All at once a victim fell.
She is what is called a silly,
    Still she answers pretty well.

THE OTHERS.   Let us grasp the situation, etc.

MAR.   Now when we were pretty babies
    Some one married us, that's clear—

GIA.   And if I can catch her
    I'll pinch her and scratch her,
And send her away with a flea in her ear.

GIU.   He whom that young lady married,
    To receive her can't refuse.

TESS.   If I overtake her
                     I'll warrant I'll make her
               To shake in her aristocratical shoes !

GIA. (*to* TESS.). If she married your Giuseppe
                    You and he will have to part—

TESS. (*to* GIA.).   If I have to do it
                      I'll warrant she'll rue it—
               I'll teach her to marry the man of my heart !

TESS. (*to* GIA.). If she married Messer Marco
                    You're a spinster, that is plain—

GIA. (*to* TESS.).   No matter—no matter
                      If I can get at her
               I doubt if her mother will know her again !

ALL.   Quiet, calm deliberation
               Disentangles every knot !

                                        [*Exeunt, pondering*

MARCH. *Enter procession of Retainers, heralding
         approach of* DUKE, DUCHESS, *and* CASILDA. *All
         three are now dressed with the utmost magnificence.*

     CHORUS OF MEN, *with* DUKE *and* DUCHESS.

            With ducal pomp and ducal pride
                   (Announce these comers,
                     O ye kettle-drummers !)
            Comes Barataria's high-born bride.
                   (Ye sounding cymbals clang !)
            She comes to claim the Royal hand—
                   (Proclaim their Graces,
                     O ye double basses !)
            Of the King who rules this goodly land.
                   (Ye brazen brasses bang !)

DUKE *and*   This polite attention touches
  DUCH.   Heart of Duke and heart of Duchess,
           Who resign their pet
           With profound regret.
       She of beauty was a model
       When a tiny tiddle-toddle,
           And at twenty-one
           She's excelled by none !

CHORUS.   With ducal pomp and ducal pride, etc.

DUKE (*to his attendants*).   Be good enough to inform His Majesty that His Grace the Duke of Plaza-Toro, Limited, has arrived, and begs——

CAS.   Desires——

DUCH.   Demands——

DUKE.   And demands an audience. (*Exeunt attendants.*)   And now, my child, prepare to receive the husband to whom you were united under such interesting and romantic circumstances.

CAS.   But which is it ?   There are two of them !

DUKE.   It is true that at present His Majesty is a double gentleman ; but as soon as the circumstances of his marriage are ascertained, he will, *ipso facto*, boil down to a single gentleman—thus presenting a unique example of an individual who becomes a single man and a married man by the same operation.

DUCH. (*severely*).   I have known instances in which the characteristics of both conditions existed concurrently in the same individual.

DUKE.   Ah, he couldn't have been a Plaza-Toro.

DUCH.   Oh ! couldn't he, though !

CAS.   Well, whatever happens, I shall, of course, be a dutiful wife, but I can never love my husband.

DUKE.   I don't know. It's extraordinary what unprepossessing people one can love if one gives one's mind to it.

DUCH.   I loved your father.

DUKE.   My love—that remark is a little hard, I think ?

Rather cruel, perhaps ? Somewhat uncalled-for, I venture
to believe ?

DUCH.   It was very difficult, my dear ; but I said to
myself, " That man is a Duke, and I *will* love him."
Several of my relations bet me I couldn't, but I did—
desperately !

SONG—DUCHESS.

On the day when I was wedded
　　To your admirable sire,
I acknowledge that I dreaded
　　An explosion of his ire.
I was overcome with panic—
For his temper was volcanic,
　　And I didn't dare revolt,
　　For I feared a thunderbolt !
I was always very wary,
　　For his fury was ecstatic—
His refined vocabulary
　　Most unpleasantly emphatic.
　　　　To the thunder
　　　　　　Of this Tartar
　　　　I knocked under
　　　　　　Like a martyr ;
　　　　When intently
　　　　　　He was fuming,
　　　　I was gently
　　　　　　Unassuming—
　　　　When reviling
　　　　　　Me completely,
　　　　I was smiling
　　　　　　Very sweetly :
Giving him the very best, and getting back the very worst—
That is how I tried to tame your great progenitor—at first !

But I found that a reliance
　　On my threatening appearance,
And a resolute defiance
　　Of marital interference,

And a gentle intimation
    Of my firm determination
        To see what I could do
        To be wife and husband too
    Was the only thing required
        For to make his temper supple,
    And you couldn't have desired
        A more reciprocating couple.
            Ever willing
                To be wooing,
            We were billing—
                We were cooing;
            When I merely
                From him parted,
            We were nearly
                Broken-hearted—
            When in sequel
                Reunited,
            We were equal-
                Ly delighted.

So with double-shotted guns and colours nailed unto the
    mast,
I tamed your insignificant progenitor—at last !

CAS. My only hope is that when my husband sees
what a shady family he has married into he will repudiate
the contract altogether.

DUKE. Shady ? A nobleman shady, who is blazing
in the lustre of unaccustomed pocket-money ? A nobleman shady, who can look back upon ninety-five quarterings?
It is not every nobleman who is ninety-five quarters in
arrear—I mean, who can look back upon ninety-five of
them ! And this, just as I have been floated at a premium !
Oh fie !

DUCH. Your Majesty is surely unaware that directly
Your Majesty's father came before the public he was
applied for over and over again.

DUKE. My dear, Her Majesty's father was in the habit

of being applied for over and over again—and very urgently applied for, too—long before he was registered under the Limited Liability Act.

RECIT.—DUKE.

To help unhappy commoners, and add to their enjoyment,
Affords a man of noble rank congenial employment ;
Of our attempts we offer you examples illustrative :
The work is light, and, I may add, it's most remunerative.

DUET—DUKE *and* DUCHESS.

DUKE.   Small titles and orders
          For Mayors and Recorders
              I get—and they're highly delighted—

DUCH.   They're highly delighted !

DUKE.   M.P.'s baronetted,
          Sham Colonels gazetted,
              And second-rate Aldermen knighted—

DUCH.   Yes, Aldermen knighted.

DUKE.   Foundation-stone laying
          I find very paying :
              It adds a large sum to my makings—

DUCH.   Large sums to his makings.

DUKE.   At charity dinners
          The best of speech-spinners,
              I get ten per cent on the takings—

DUCH.   One-tenth of the takings.

DUCH.   I present any lady
          Whose conduct is shady
              Or smacking of doubtful propriety—

DUKE.   Doubtful propriety.

DUCH. When Virtue would quash her,
   I take and whitewash her,
    And launch her in first-rate society—

DUKE.   First-rate society !

DUCH. I recommend acres
   Of clumsy dressmakers—
    Their fit and their finishing touches—

DUKE.   Their finishing touches.

DUCH. A sum in addition
   They pay for permission
    To say that they make for the Duchess—

DUKE.   They make for the Duchess !

DUKE. Those pressing prevailers,
   The ready-made tailors,
    Quote me as their great double-barrel—

DUCH.   Their great double-barrel.

DUKE. I allow them to do so,
   Though Robinson Crusoe
    Would jib at their wearing apparel—

DUCH.   Such wearing apparel !

DUKE. I sit, by selection,
   Upon the direction
    Of several Companies bubble—

DUCH.   All Companies bubble !

DUKE. As soon as they're floated
   I'm freely bank-noted—
    I'm pretty well paid for my trouble—

DUCH.   He's paid for his trouble !

DUCH. At middle-class party
   I play at *écarté*—
    And I'm by no means a beginner—

DUKE (*significantly*).   She's not a beginner.

Duch.   To one of my station
            The remuneration—
                Five guineas a night and my dinner—

Duke.   And wine with her dinner.

Duch.   I write letters blatant
            On medicines patent—
                And use any other you mustn't—

Duke.   Believe me, you mustn't—

Duch.   And vow my complexion
            Derives its perfection
                From somebody's soap—which it doesn't—

Duke (*significantly*).   It certainly doesn't !

Duke.   We're ready as witness
            To any one's fitness
                To fill any place or preferment—

Duch.   A place or preferment.

Duch.   We're often in waiting
            At junket or *fêting*,
                And sometimes attend an interment—

Duke.   We enjoy an interment.

Both.   In short, if you'd kindle
            The spark of a swindle,
                Lure simpletons into your clutches—
                    Yes ; into your clutches.
            Or hoodwink a debtor,
            You cannot do better

Duch.   Than trot out a Duke or a Duchess—

Duke.   A Duke or a Duchess !

Enter MARCO *and* GIUSEPPE.

Duke.   Ah ! Their Majesties. Your Majesty ! (*Bows with great ceremony.*)

Mar.   The Duke of Plaza-Toro, I believe ?

Duke. The same. (Marco *and* Giuseppe *offer to shake hands with him. The* Duke *bows ceremoniously. They endeavour to imitate him.*) Allow me to present——

Giu. The young lady one of us married?

(Marco *and* Giuseppe *offer to shake hands with her.* Casilda *curtsies formally. They endeavour to imitate her.*)

Cas. Gentlemen, I am the most obedient servant of one of you. (*Aside.*) Oh, Luiz!

Duke. I am now about to address myself to the gentleman whom my daughter married; the other may allow his attention to wander if he likes, for what I am about to say does not concern him. Sir, you will find in this young lady a combination of excellences which you would search for in vain in any young lady who had not the good fortune to be my daughter. There is some little doubt as to which of you is the gentleman I am addressing, and which is the gentleman who is allowing his attention to wander; but when that doubt is solved, I shall say (still addressing the attentive gentleman), " Take her, and may she make you happier than her mother has made me."

Duch. Sir!

Duke. If possible. And now there is a little matter to which I think I am entitled to take exception. I come here in state with Her Grace the Duchess and Her Majesty my daughter, and what do I find? Do I find, for instance, a guard of honour to receive me? No!

Mar. *and* Giu. No.

Duke. The town illuminated? No!

Mar. *and* Giu. No.

Duke. Refreshment provided? No!

Mar. *and* Giu. No.

Duke. A Royal salute fired? No!

Mar. *and* Giu. No.

Duke. Triumphal arches erected? No!

Mar. *and* Giu. No.

DUKE.   The bells set ringing ?

MAR. *and* GIU.   No.

DUKE.   Yes—one—the Visitors', and I rang it myself. It is not enough !   It is not enough !

GIU.   Upon my honour, I'm very sorry ; but you see, I was brought up in a gondola, and my ideas of politeness are confined to taking off my cap to my passengers when they tip me.

DUCH.   That's all very well in its way, but it is not enough.

GIU.   I'll take off anything else in reason.

DUKE.   But a Royal Salute to my daughter—it costs so little.

CAS.   Papa, I don't want a salute.

GIU.   My dear sir, as soon as we know which of us is entitled to take that liberty she shall have as many salutes as she likes.

MAR.   As for guards of honour and triumphal arches, you don't know our people—they wouldn't stand it.

GIU.   They are very off-hand with us—very off-hand indeed.

DUKE.   Oh, but you mustn't allow that—you must keep them in proper discipline, you must impress your Court with your importance.   You want deportment—carriage——

GIU.   We've got a carriage.

DUKE.   Manner—dignity.   There must be a good deal of this sort of thing—(*business*)—and a little of this sort of thing—(*business*)—and possibly just a *soupçon* of this sort of thing !—(*business*)—and so on.   Oh, it's very useful, and most effective.   Just attend to me.   You are a King—I am a subject.   Very good——

GAVOTTE.

DUKE, DUCHESS, CASILDA, MARCO, GIUSEPPE.

DUKE.   I am a courtier grave and serious
                    Who is about to kiss your hand :
                    Try to combine a pose imperious
                    With a demeanour nobly bland.

MAR. *and*   Let us combine a pose imperious
GIU.   With a demeanour nobly bland.

    (MARCO *and* GIUSEPPE *endeavour to carry out
his instructions.*)

DUKE.   That's, if anything, *too* unbending—
            Too aggressively stiff and grand ;

    (*They suddenly modify their attitudes.*)

           Now to the other extreme you're tending—
           Don't be so deucedly condescending !

DUCH. *and* Now to the other extreme you're tending—
CAS.   Don't be so dreadfully condescending !

MAR. *and*   Oh, hard to please some noblemen seem !
GIU.   At first, if anything, *too* unbending ;
           Off we go to the other extreme—
           Too confoundedly condescending !

DUKE.   Now a gavotte perform sedately—
           Offer your hand with conscious pride ;
      Take an attitude not too stately,
           Still sufficiently dignified.

MAR. *and*   Now for an attitude not too stately,
GIU.   Still sufficiently dignified.

    (*They endeavour to carry out his instructions.*)

DUKE (*beating time*).
           Oncely, twicely—oncely, twicely—
           Bow impressively ere you glide.

                       (*They do so.*)

           Capital both—you've caught it nicely !
           That is the style of thing precisely !

DUCH. *and* Capital both—they've caught it nicely !
CAS.   That is the style of thing precisely !

MAR. *and*   Oh, sweet to earn a nobleman's praise !
  GIU.   Capital both—we've caught it nicely !
                Supposing he's right in what he says,
                  This is the style of thing precisely !

     [GAVOTTE. *At the end exeunt* DUKE *and*
          DUCHESS, *leaving* CASILDA *with* MARCO
          and GIUSEPPE.

GIU. (*to* MARCO).   The old birds have gone away and left the young chickens together.   That's called tact.

MAR.   It's very awkward.   We really ought to tell her how we are situated.   It's not fair to the girl.

GIU.   Then why don't you do it ?

MAR.   I'd rather not—you.

GIU.   I don't know how to begin.   (*To* CASILDA.) A—Madam—I—we, that is, several of us——

CAS.   Gentlemen, I am bound to listen to you ; but it is right to tell you that, not knowing I was married in infancy, I am over head and ears in love with somebody else.

GIU.   Our case exactly !   *We* are over head and ears in love with somebody else !   (*Enter* GIANETTA *and* TESSA.)   In point of fact, with our wives !

CAS.   Your wives !   Then you are married ?

TESS.   It's not our fault.

GIA.   We knew nothing about it.

BOTH.   We are sisters in misfortune.

CAS.   My good girls, I don't blame you.   Only before we go any further we must really arrive at some satisfactory arrangement, or we shall get hopelessly complicated.

QUINTET AND FINALE.

MARCO, GIUSEPPE, CASILDA, GIANETTA, TESSA.

ALL.   Here is a case unprecedented !
           Here are a King and Queen ill-starred !
        Ever since marriage was first invented
           Never was known a case so hard !

MAR. *and*   I may be said to have been bisected,
GIU.   By a profound catastrophe !

CAS., GIA., Through a calamity unexpected
TESS.   I am divisible into three !

ALL.   O moralists all,
             How can you call
          Marriage a state of unitee,
     When excellent husbands are bisected,
          And wives divisible into three ?
          O moralists all,
             How can you call
          Marriage a state of union true ?

CAS., GIA., One-third of myself is married to half of ye
TESS.   or you,
MAR. *and*   When half of myself has married one-third
GIU.   of ye or you ?

Enter DON ALHAMBRA, *followed by* DUKE, DUCHESS,
and all the CHORUS.

FINALE.

RECIT.—DON ALHAMBRA.

Now let the loyal lieges gather round—
The Prince's foster-mother has been found !
She will declare, to silver clarion's sound,
The rightful King—let him forthwith be crowned !

CHORUS.   She will declare, etc.

(DON ALHAMBRA *brings forward* INEZ, *the Prince's
foster-mother.*)

TESS.   Speak, woman, speak—
DUKE.   We're all attention !
GIA.   The news we seek—
DUCH.   This moment mention.

CAS.	To us they bring—
DON AL.	His foster-mother.
MAR.	Is he the King ?
GIU.	Or this my brother ?
ALL.	Speak, woman, speak, etc.

RECIT.—INEZ.

The Royal Prince was by the King entrusted
To my fond care, ere I grew old and crusted ;
When traitors came to steal his son reputed,
My own small boy I deftly substituted !
The villains fell into the trap completely—
I hid the Prince away—still sleeping sweetly :
I called him " son " with pardonable slyness—
His name, Luiz !   Behold his Royal Highness !

(*Sensation.* LUIZ *ascends the throne, crowned
and robed as King.*)

CAS. (*rushing to his arms*).   Luiz !
LUIZ.   Casilda !   (*Embrace.*)

ALL.   Is this indeed the King ?
　　　　　Oh, wondrous revelation !
　　　Oh, unexpected thing !
　　　　　Unlooked-for situation !

MAR., GIA.,   This statement we receive
GIU., TESS.　　With sentiments conflicting ;
　　　Our hearts rejoice and grieve,
　　　　　Each other contradicting ;
　　　To those whom we adore
　　　　　We can be reunited—
　　　On one point rather sore,
　　　　　But, on the whole, delighted !

LUIZ.   When others claimed thy dainty hand,
　　　　　I waited—waited—waited,

DUKE.   As prudence (so I understand)
                    Dictated—tated—tated.

CAS.   By virtue of our early vow
                    Recorded—corded—corded,

DUCH.   Your pure and patient love is now
                    Rewarded—warded—warded.

ALL.   Then hail, O King of a Golden Land,
          And the high-born bride who claims his hand !
          The past is dead, and you gain your own,
          A royal crown and a golden throne !

                (*All kneel :* LUIZ *crowns* CASILDA.)

ALL.   Once more *gondolieri*,
                  Both skilful and wary,
                  Free from this quandary
                        Contented are we.
                  From Royalty flying,
                  Our gondolas plying,
                  And merrily crying
                        Our "*premé*," "*stalì !*"

          So good-bye, cachucha, fandango, bolero—
              We'll dance a farewell to that measure—
          Old Xeres, adieu—Manzanilla—Montero—
              We leave you with feelings of pleasure !

                        CURTAIN.

UTOPIA LIMITED

OR

THE FLOWERS OF PROGRESS

DRAMATIS PERSONÆ.

KING PARAMOUNT THE FIRST (*King of Utopia*).

SCAPHIO
PHANTIS } (*Judges of the Utopian Supreme Court*).

TARARA (*the Public Exploder*).

CALYNX (*the Utopian Vice-Chamberlain*).

IMPORTED FLOWERS OF PROGRESS.

LORD DRAMALEIGH (*a British Lord Chamberlain*).

CAPTAIN FITZBATTLEAXE (*First Life Guards*).

CAPTAIN SIR EDWARD CORCORAN, K.C.B. (*of the Royal Navy*).

MR. GOLDBURY (*a Company Promoter ; afterwards Comptroller of the Utopian Household*).

SIR BAILEY BARRE, Q.C., M.P.

MR. BLUSHINGTON (*of the County Council*).

————

THE PRINCESS ZARA (*Eldest Daughter of King Paramount*).

THE PRINCESS NEKAYA
THE PRINCESS KALYBA } (*her Younger Sisters*)

THE LADY SOPHY (*their English Gouvernante*).

SALATA
MELENE } (*Utopian Maidens*).
PHYLLA

————

ACT I.—A Utopian Palm Grove.

ACT II.—Throne Room in King Paramount's Palace.

First produced at the Savoy Theatre on October 7, 1893.

UTOPIA LIMITED

OR

THE FLOWERS OF PROGRESS

ACT I.

SCENE.—*A Utopian Palm Grove in the gardens of* KING PARAMOUNT'S *Palace, showing a picturesque and luxuriant tropical landscape, with the sea in the distance.* SALATA, MELENE, PHYLLA, *and other Maidens discovered, lying lazily about the stage and thoroughly enjoying themselves in lotus-eating fashion.*

OPENING CHORUS.

In lazy languor—motionless,
We lie and dream of nothingness ;
    For visions come
    From Poppydom
        Direct at our command :
Or, delicate alternative,
In open idleness we live,
    With lyre and lute
    And silver flute,
        The life of Lazyland !

SOLO—Phylla.

The song of birds
        In ivied towers ;
                The rippling play
                Of waterway ;
        The lowing herds ;
                The breath of flowers ;
                The languid loves
                Of turtle doves—
These simple joys are all at hand
Upon thy shores, O Lazyland !

Chorus.

In lazy languor, etc.

Enter Calynx.

Cal. Good news ! Great news ! His Majesty's
eldest daughter, Princess Zara, who left our shores five
years since to go to England—the greatest, the most
powerful, the wisest country in the world — has taken
a high degree at Girton, and is on her way home
again, having achieved a complete mastery over all
the elements that have tended to raise that glorious
country to her present pre - eminent position among
civilized nations !

Salata. Then in a few months Utopia may hope to
be completely Anglicized ?

Cal. Absolutely and without a doubt.

Melene (*lazily*). We are very well as we are. Life
without a care—every want supplied by a kind and fatherly
monarch, who, despot though he be, has no other thought
than to make his people happy—what have we to gain by
the great change that is in store for us ?

Sal. What have we to gain ? English institutions,
English tastes, and oh, English fashions !

CAL. England has made herself what she is because, in that favoured land, every one has to think for himself. Here we have no need to think, because our monarch anticipates all our wants, and our political opinions are formed for us by the journals to which we subscribe. Oh, think how much more brilliant this dialogue would have been, if we had been accustomed to exercise our reflective powers! They say that in England the conversation of the very meanest is a coruscation of impromptu epigram!

Enter TARARA *in a great rage.*

TAR. Lalabalele talala! Callabale lalabalica falahle!

CAL. (*horrified*). Stop—stop, I beg! (*All the ladies close their ears.*)

TAR. Callamalala galalate! Caritalla lalabalee kallalale poo!

LADIES. Oh, stop him! stop him!

CAL. My Lord, I'm surprised at you. Are you not aware that His Majesty, in his despotic acquiescence with the emphatic wish of his people, has ordered that the Utopian language shall be banished from his court, and that all communications shall henceforward be made in the English tongue?

TAR. Yes, I'm perfectly aware of it, although— (*suddenly presenting an explosive " cracker "*). Stop—allow me.

CAL. (*pulls it*). Now, what's that for?

TAR. Why, I've recently been appointed Public Exploder to His Majesty, and as I'm constitutionally nervous, I must accustom myself by degrees to the startling nature of my duties. Thank you. I was about to say that although, as Public Exploder, I am next in succession to the throne, I nevertheless do my best to fall in with the royal decree. But when I am overmastered by an indignant sense of overwhelming wrong, as I am now, I slip into my native tongue without knowing it. I am told that in the language of that great and pure nation,

strong expressions do not exist, consequently when I want to let off steam I have no alternative but to say, " Lalabalele molola lililah kallalale poo ! "

CAL.   But what is your grievance ?

TAR.   This—by our Constitution we are governed by a Despot who, although in theory absolute—is, in practice, nothing of the kind—being watched day and night by two Wise Men whose duty it is, on his very first lapse from political or social propriety, to denounce him to me, the Public Exploder, and it then becomes my duty to blow up His Majesty with dynamite—allow me. (*Presenting a cracker which* CALYNX *pulls.*)   Thank you—and, as some compensation to my wounded feelings, I reign in his stead.

CAL.   Yes.   After many unhappy experiments in the direction of an ideal Republic, it was found that what may be described as a Despotism tempered by Dynamite provides, on the whole, the most satisfactory description of ruler—an autocrat who dares not abuse his autocratic power.

TAR.   That's the theory—but in practice, how does it act ?   Now, do you ever happen to see the *Palace Peeper* ? (*producing a " Society " paper*).

CAL.   Never even heard of the journal.

TAR.   I'm not surprised, because His Majesty's agents always buy up the whole edition ; but I have an aunt in the publishing department, and she has supplied me with a copy.   Well, it actually teems with circumstantially convincing details of the King's abominable immoralities !   If this high-class journal may be believed, His Majesty is one of the most Heliogabalian profligates that ever disgraced an autocratic throne !   And *do* these Wise Men denounce him to me ?   Not a bit of it !   They wink at his immoralities !   Under the circumstances I really think I am justified in exclaiming " Lalabalele molola lililah kalabalele poo ! " (*All horrified.*)   I don't care—the occasion demands it.

[*Exit* TARARA.

March. Enter Guard, escorting SCAPHIO *and* PHANTIS.

CHORUS.

O make way for the Wise Men !
They are prizemen—
Double-first in the world's university !
For though lovely this island
(Which is *my* land),
She has no one to match them in *her* city.
They're the pride of Utopia—
Cornucopia
Is each in his mental fertility.
O they never make blunder,
And no wonder,
For they're triumphs of infallibility.

DUET—SCAPHIO *and* PHANTIS.

In every mental lore
(The statement smacks of vanity)
We claim to rank before
The wisest of humanity.
As gifts of head and heart
We wasted on " utility ",
We're " cast " to play a part
Of great responsibility.

Our duty is to spy
Upon our King's illicities,
And keep a watchful eye
On all his eccentricities.
If ever a trick he tries
That savours of rascality,
At our decree he dies
Without the least formality.

We fear no rude rebuff,
Or newspaper publicity ;
Our word is quite enough,
The rest is electricity.

A pound of dynamite
    Explodes in his auriculars ;
It's not a pleasant sight—
    We'll spare you the particulars.

Its force all men confess,
    The King needs no admonishing—
We may say its success
    Is something quite astonishing.
Our despot it imbues
    With virtues quite delectable,
He minds his P's and Q's,—
    And keeps himself respectable.

    Of a tyrant polite
    He's a paragon quite.
    He's as modest and mild
    In his ways as a child ;
    And no one ever met
    With an autocrat, yet,
    So delightfully bland
    To the least in the land !

            So make way for the wise men, etc.

[*Exeunt all but* SCAPHIO *and* PHANTIS.
        PHANTIS *is pensive.*

SCA.   Phantis, you are not in your customary exuberant
spirits.   What is wrong ?

PHAN.   Scaphio, I think you once told me that you
have never loved ?

SCA.   Never !   I have often marvelled at the fairy
influence which weaves its rosy web about the faculties
of the greatest and wisest of our race ; but I thank Heaven
I have never been subjected to its singular fascination.
For, oh, Phantis ! there is that within me that tells me that
when my time *does* come, the convulsion will be tremendous !
When *I* love, it will be with the accumulated fervour of

sixty - six years ! But I have an ideal — a semi-transparent Being, filled with an inorganic pink jelly—and I have never yet seen the woman who approaches within measurable distance of it. All are opaque — opaque — opaque !

PHAN. Keep that ideal firmly before you, and love not until you find her. Though but fifty-five, I am an old campaigner in the battle-fields of Love ; and, believe me, it is better to be as you are, heart-free and happy, than as I am—eternally racked with doubting agonies ! Scaphio, the Princess Zara returns from England to-day !

SCA. My poor boy, I see it all.

PHAN. Oh ! Scaphio, she is so beautiful. Ah ! you smile, for you have never seen her. She sailed for England three months before you took office.

SCA. Now tell me, is your affection requited ?

PHAN. I do not know—I am not sure. Sometimes I think it is, and then come these torturing doubts ! I feel sure that she does not regard me with absolute indifference, for she could never look at me without having to go to bed with a sick headache.

SCA. That is surely something. Come, take heart, boy ! you are young and beautiful. What more could maiden want ?

PHAN. Ah ! Scaphio, remember she returns from a land where every youth is as a young Greek god, and where such poor beauty as I can boast is seen at every turn.

SCA. Be of good cheer ! Marry her, boy, if so your fancy wills, and be sure that love will come.

PHAN. (overjoyed). Then you will assist me in this ?

SCA. Why, surely ! Silly one, what have you to fear ? We have but to say the word, and her father must consent. Is he not our very slave ? Come, take heart. I cannot bear to see you sad.

PHAN. Now I may hope, indeed ! Scaphio, you have placed me on the very pinnacle of human joy !

DUET—SCAPHIO *and* PHANTIS.

SCA. Let all your doubts take wing—
Our influence is great.
If Paramount our King
Presume to hesitate,
Put on the screw,
And caution him
That he will rue
Disaster grim
That must ensue
To life and limb,
Should he pooh-pooh
This harmless whim.

BOTH. This harmless whim—this harmless whim,

It is, as $\left\{\begin{array}{c} I \\ you \end{array}\right\}$ say, a harmless whim.

PHAN. (*dancing*). Observe this dance
Which I employ
When I, by chance,
Go mad with joy.
What sentiment
Does this express ?

(PHANTIS *continues his dance while* SCAPHIO *vainly
endeavours to discover its meaning.*)

Supreme content
And happiness !

BOTH. Of course it does ! Of course it does !
Supreme content and happiness !

PHAN. Your friendly aid conferred,
I need no longer pine.
I've but to speak the word,
And lo ! the maid is mine !

I do not choose
To be denied.
Or wish to lose
A lovely bride—
If to refuse
The King decide,
The Royal shoes
Then woe betide !

BOTH.　　Then woe betide—then woe betide !
The Royal shoes then woe betide !

SCA. (*dancing*).　　This step to use
I condescend
Whene'er I choose
To serve a friend.
What it implies
Now try to guess ;

(SCA. *continues his dance while* PHANTIS *is vainly endeavouring to discover its meaning*.)

It typifies
Unselfishness !

BOTH　　Of course it does !　Of course it does !
(*dancing*).　　It typifies unselfishness !

[*Exeunt* SCAPHIO *and* PHANTIS.

March.　Enter KING PARAMOUNT, *attended by guards and nobles, and preceded by girls dancing before him.*

CHORUS.

Quaff the nectar—cull the roses—
Gather fruit and flowers in plenty !
For our King no longer poses—
Sing the songs of *far niente* !
Wake the lute that sets us lilting,
Dance a welcome to each comer ;
Day by day our year is wilting—
Sing the sunny songs of summer !
La, la, la, la !

SONG—King.

A King of autocratic power we—
 A despot whose tyrannic will is law—
Whose rule is paramount o'er land and sea,
 A presence of unutterable awe !
But though the awe that I inspire
Must shrivel with imperial fire
 All foes whom it may chance to touch,
To judge by what I see and hear,
It does not seem to interfere
 With popular enjoyment, much.

CHORUS. No, no—it does not interfere
    With our enjoyment much.

Stupendous when we rouse ourselves to strike,
 Resistless when our tyrant thunder peals,
We often wonder what obstruction's like,
 And how a contradicted monarch feels.
But as it is our Royal whim
Our Royal sails to set and trim
 To suit whatever wind may blow—
What buffets contradiction deals
And how a thwarted monarch feels
 We probably shall never know.

CHORUS. No, no—what thwarted monarch feels
    You'll never, never know.

RECIT.—King.

My subjects all, it is your wish emphatic
That all Utopia shall henceforth be modelled
Upon that glorious country called Great Britain—
To which some add—but others do not—Ireland.

ALL. It is !

KING. That being so, as you insist upon it,
  We have arranged that our two younger daughters
  Who have been " finished " by an English Lady—
(*tenderly*) A grave, and good, and gracious English Lady—
  Shall daily be exhibited in public,
  That all may learn what, from the English stand-
   point,

Is looked upon as maidenly perfection !
Come hither, daughters !

Enter NEKAYA *and* KALYBA. *They are twins, about fifteen years old ; they are very modest and demure in their appearance, dress, and manner. They stand with their hands folded and their eyes cast down.*

CHORUS.

How fair ! how modest ! how discreet !
How bashfully demure !
See how they blush, as they've been taught,
At this publicity unsought !
How English and how pure !

DUET—NEKAYA *and* KALYBA.

BOTH. Although of native maids the cream,
We're brought up on the English scheme—
The best of all
For great and small
Who modesty adore.

NEK. For English girls are good as gold,
Extremely modest (so we're told),
Demurely coy—divinely cold—

KAL. And we are that—and more.

To please papa, who argues thus—
All girls should mould themselves on us
Because we are
By furlongs far
The best of all the bunch,
We show ourselves to loud applause
From ten to four without a pause—

NEK. Which is an awkward time because
It cuts into our lunch.

BOTH. Oh, maids of high and low degree,
Whose social code is rather free,
Please look at us and you will see
What good young ladies ought to be !

NEK.   And as we stand, like clockwork toys,
        A lecturer whom papa employs
                Proceeds to praise
                Our modest ways
                And guileless character—
KAL.   Our well-known blush—our downcast eyes—
        Our famous look of mild surprise
NEK.   (Which competition still defies)—
KAL.   Our celebrated " Sir ! ! ! "

        Then all the crowd take down our looks
        In pocket memorandum books.
                To diagnose
                Our modest pose
                The Kodaks do their best :
NEK.   If evidence you would possess
        Of what is maiden bashfulness,
        You only need a button press—
KAL.   And *we* do all the rest.

Enter LADY SOPHY—*an English lady of mature years and
    extreme gravity of demeanour and dress.   She carries
    a lecturer's wand in her hand.   She is led on by the*
    KING, *who expresses great regard and admiration for
    her.*

        RECIT.—LADY SOPHY.

    This morning we propose to illustrate
    A course of maiden courtship, from the start
    To the triumphant matrimonial finish.

(*Through the following song the two Princesses illustrate
    in gesture the description given by* LADY SOPHY.)

        SONG—LADY SOPHY.
            Bold-faced ranger
            (Perfect stranger)
    Meets two well-behaved young ladies.
            He's attractive,
            Young and active—
    Each a little bit afraid is.

Youth advances,
At his glances
To their danger they awaken ;
They repel him
As they tell him
He is very much mistaken.
Though they speak to him politely,
Please observe they're sneering slightly,
Just to show he's acting vainly.
This is Virtue saying plainly,
" Go away, young bachelor,
We are not what you take us for ! "
When addressed impertinently,
English ladies answer gently,
" Go away, young bachelor,
We are not what you take us for ! "

As he gazes,
Hat he raises,
Enters into conversation.
Makes excuses—
This produces
Interesting agitation.
He, with daring,
Undespairing,
Gives his card—his rank discloses.
Little heeding
This proceeding,
They turn up their little noses.
Pray observe this lesson vital—
When a man of rank and title
His position first discloses,
Always cock your little noses.
When at home, let all the class
Try this in the looking-glass.
English girls of well-bred notions
Shun all unrehearsed emotions.
English girls of highest class
Practise them before the glass.

His intentions
Then he mentions.
Something definite to go on—
Makes recitals
Of his titles,
Hints at settlements, and so on.
Smiling sweetly,
They, discreetly,
Ask for further evidences :
Thus invited,
He, delighted,
Gives the usual references.
This is business.   Each is fluttered
When the offer's fairly uttered.
" Which of them has his affection ? "
He declines to make selection.
Do they quarrel for his dross ?
Not a bit of it—they toss !
Please observe this cogent moral—
English ladies never quarrel.
When a doubt they come across,
English ladies always toss.

RECIT.—LADY SOPHY.

The lecture's ended.   In ten minutes' space
'Twill be repeated in the market-place !

[*Exit* LADY SOPHY, *followed by* NEKAYA *and*
KALYBA.

CHORUS.   Quaff the nectar—cull the roses—
Bashful girls will soon be plenty !
Maid who thus at fifteen poses
Ought to be divine at twenty !

[*Exit* CHORUS.   *Manet* KING.

KING.   I requested Scaphio and Phantis to be so good
as to favour me with an audience this morning. (*Enter*
SCAPHIO *and* PHANTIS.)   Oh, here they are !

SCA. Your Majesty wished to speak with us, I believe. You—you needn't keep your crown on, on our account, you know.

KING. I beg your pardon (*removes it*). I always forget that ! Odd, the notion of a King not being allowed to wear one of his own crowns in the presence of two of his own subjects.

PHAN. Yes—bizarre, is it not ?

KING. Most quaint. But then it's a quaint world.

PHAN. Teems with quiet fun. I often think what a lucky thing it is that you are blessed with such a keen sense of humour !

KING. Do you know, I find it invaluable. Do what I will, I *cannot* help looking at the humorous side of things — for, properly considered, everything has its humorous side—even the *Palace Peeper* (*producing it*). See here—" Another Royal Scandal ", by Junius Junior. " How long is this to last ? " by Senex Senior. " Ribald Royalty ", by Mercury Major. " Where is the Public Exploder ? " by Mephistopheles Minor. When I reflect that all these outrageous attacks on my morality are written by me, at your command—well, it's one of the funniest things that have come within the scope of my experience.

SCA. Besides, apart from that, they have a quiet humour of their own which is simply irresistible.

KING (*gratified*). Not bad, I think. Biting, trenchant sarcasm—the rapier, not the bludgeon—that's my line. But then it's so easy—I'm such a good subject—a bad King but a good Subject—ha ! ha !—a capital heading for next week's leading article ! (*makes a note*). And then the stinging little paragraphs about our Royal goings-on with our Royal Second Housemaid—delicately sub-acid, are they not ?

SCA. My dear King, in that kind of thing no one can hold a candle to you.

PHAN. But the crowning joke is the Comic Opera you've written for us—" King Tuppence, or A Good Deal

Less than Half a Sovereign "—in which the celebrated English tenor, Mr. Wilkinson, burlesques your personal appearance and gives grotesque imitations of your Royal peculiarities. It's immense !

KING. Ye—es—That's what I wanted to speak to you about. Now I've not the least doubt but that even *that* has its humorous side, too—if one could only see it. As a rule I'm pretty quick at detecting latent humour—but I confess I do *not* quite see where it comes in, in this particular instance. It's so horribly personal !

SCA. Personal ? Yes, of course it's personal—but consider the antithetical humour of the situation.

KING. Yes. I—I don't think I've quite grasped that.

SCA. No ? You surprise me. Why, consider. During the day thousands tremble at your frown, during the night (from 8 to 11) thousands roar at it. During the day your most arbitrary pronouncements are received by your subjects with abject submission—during the night, they shout with joy at your most terrible decrees. It's not every monarch who enjoys the privilege of undoing by night all the despotic absurdities he's committed during the day.

KING. Of course ! Now I see it ! Thank you very much. I was sure it had its humorous side, and it was very dull of me not to have seen it before. But, as I said just now, it's a quaint world.

PHAN. Teems with quiet fun.

KING. Yes. Properly considered, what a farce life is, to be sure !

SONG—KING.

First you're born—and I'll be bound you
Find a dozen strangers round you.
" Hallo," cries the new-born baby,
" Where's my parents ? which may they be ? "
Awkward silence—no reply—
Puzzled baby wonders why !

Father rises, bows politely—
Mother smiles (but not too brightly)—
Doctor mumbles like a dumb thing—
Nurse is busy mixing something.—
    Every symptom tends to show
    You're decidedly *de trop*—

ALL.
    Ho! ho! ho! ho! ho! ho! ho! ho!
      Time's teetotum,
        If you spin it,
      Gives its quotum
        Once a minute.
      I'll go bail
      You hit the nail,
      And if you fail
        The deuce is in it!

You grow up and you discover
What it is to be a lover.
Some young lady is selected—
Poor, perhaps, but well-connected,
    Whom you hail (for Love is blind)
    As the Queen of fairy kind.
Though she's plain—perhaps unsightly,
Makes her face up—laces tightly,
In her form your fancy traces
All the gifts of all the graces.
    Rivals none the maiden woo,
    So you take her and she takes you!

ALL.
    Ho! ho! ho! ho! ho! ho! ho! ho!
      Joke beginning,
        Never ceases,
      Till your inning
        Time releases,
      On your way
      You blindly stray,
      And day by day
        The joke increases!

Ten years later—Time progresses—
Sours your temper—thins your tresses ;
Fancy, then, her chain relaxes ;
Rates are facts and so are taxes.
        Fairy Queen's no longer young—
        Fairy Queen has got a tongue.
Twins have probably intruded—
Quite unbidden—just as you did—
They're a source of care and trouble—
Just as you were—only double.
        Comes at last the final stroke—
        Time has had his little joke !

ALL.   Ho ! ho ! ho ! ho ! ho ! ho ! ho ! ho !
                        Daily driven
                            (Wife as drover)
                        Ill you've thriven—
                            Ne'er in clover ;
                        Lastly, when
                        Three-score and ten
                        (And not till then),
                            The joke is over !
                        Ho ! ho ! ho ! ho ! ho ! ho ! ho ! ho !
                        Then—and then
                            The joke is over !

[*Exeunt* SCAPHIO *and* PHANTIS. *Manet* KING.

KING (*putting on his crown again*).   It's all very well.
I always like to look on the humorous side of things ;
but I do *not* think I ought to be required to write libels
on my own moral character.   Naturally, I see the joke
of it—anybody would—but Zara's coming home to-day ;
she's no longer a child, and I confess I should *not* like
her to see my Opera — though it's uncommonly well
written ; and I should be sorry if the *Palace Peeper* got
into her hands—though it's certainly smart—very smart
indeed.   It is almost a pity that I have to buy up the whole
edition, because it's really too good to be lost.   And Lady

Sophy—that blameless type of perfect womanhood! Great Heavens, what would *she* say if the Second Housemaid business happened to meet *her* pure blue eye!

Enter LADY SOPHY.

LADY S. My monarch is soliloquizing. I will withdraw (*going*).

KING. No—pray don't go. Now I'll give you fifty chances, and you won't guess whom I was thinking of.

LADY S. Alas, sir, I know too well. Ah! King, it's an old, old story, and I'm wellnigh weary of it! Be warned in time—from my heart I pity you, but I am not for you! (*going*).

KING. But hear what I have to say.

LADY S. It is useless. Listen. In the course of a long and adventurous career in the principal European Courts, it has been revealed to me that I unconsciously exercise a weird and supernatural fascination over all Crowned Heads. So irresistible is this singular property, that there is not a European Monarch who has not implored me, with tears in his eyes, to quit his kingdom, and take my fatal charms elsewhere. As time was getting on it occurred to me that by descending several pegs in the scale of Respectability I might qualify your Majesty for my hand. Actuated by this humane motive and happening to possess Respectability enough for Six, I consented to confer Respectability enough for Four upon your two younger daughters — but although I have, alas, only Respectability enough for Two left, there is still, as I gather from the public press of this country (*producing the " Palace Peeper "*), a considerable balance in my favour.

KING (*aside*). Da—! (*Aloud.*) May I ask how you came by this?

LADY S. It was handed to me by the officer who holds the position of Public Exploder to your Imperial Majesty.

KING. And surely, Lady Sophy, surely you are not

so unjust as to place any faith in the irresponsible gabble of the Society press !

LADY S. (*referring to paper*).   I read on the authority of Senex Senior that your Majesty was seen dancing with your Second Housemaid on the Oriental Platform of the Tivoli Gardens.   That is untrue ?

KING.   Absolutely.   Our Second Housemaid has only one leg.

LADY S. (*suspiciously*).   How do you know that ?

KING.   Common report, I give you my honour.

LADY S.   It may be so.   I further read—and the statement is vouched for by no less an authority than Mephistopheles Minor—that your Majesty indulges in a bath of hot rum-punch every morning.   I trust I do not lay myself open to the charge of displaying an indelicate curiosity as to the mysteries of the royal dressing-room when I ask if there is any foundation for this statement ?

KING.   None whatever.   When our medical adviser exhibits rum-punch it is as a draught, not as a fomentation. As to our bath, our valet plays the garden hose upon us every morning.

LADY S. (*shocked*).   Oh, pray—pray spare me these unseemly details.   Well, you are a Despot—have you taken steps to slay this scribbler ?

KING.   Well, no—I have *not* gone so far as that. After all, it's the poor devil's living, you know.

LADY S.   It is the poor devil's living that surprises me.   If this man lies, there is no recognized punishment that is sufficiently terrible for him.

KING.   That's precisely it.   I—I am waiting until a punishment is discovered that will exactly meet the enormity of the case.   I am in constant communication with the Mikado of Japan, who is a leading authority on such points ; and, moreover, I have the ground plans and sectional elevations of several capital punishments in my desk at this moment.   Oh, Lady Sophy, as you are powerful, be merciful !

DUET—KING *and* LADY SOPHY.

KING.   Subjected to your heavenly gaze
        (Poetical phrase),
      My brain is turned completely.
        Observe me now,
        No Monarch, I vow,
          Was ever so far afflicted !

LADY S.   I'm pleased with that poetical phrase,
        " A heavenly gaze ",
      But though you put it neatly,
        Say what you will,
        These paragraphs still
          Remain uncontradicted.

      Come, crush me this contemptible worm
        (A forcible term),
      If he's assailed you wrongly.
        The rage display,
        Which, as you say,
          Has moved your Majesty lately.

KING.   Though I admit that forcible term,
        " Contemptible worm ",
      Appeals to me most strongly,
        To treat this pest
        As you suggest
          Would pain my Majesty greatly.

LADY S.   This writer lies !
KING.   Yes, bother his eyes !
LADY S.   He lives, you say ?
KING.   In a sort of a way.
LADY S.   Then have him shot.
KING.   Decidedly not.
LADY S.   Or crush him flat.
KING.   I cannot do that.

BOTH.   O royal Rex,
          My ⎱
          Her ⎰ blameless sex
              Abhors such conduct shady.
          You ⎱
          I   ⎰ plead in vain,
          You ⎱
          I   ⎰ never will gain
              Respectable English lady !

          [*Dance of repudiation by* LADY SOPHY.   *Exit,
              followed by* KING.

*March.   Enter all the Court, heralding the arrival of
    the* PRINCESS ZARA, *who enters, escorted by* CAPTAIN
    FITZBATTLEAXE *and four Troopers, all in the full
    uniform of the First Life Guards.*

CHORUS.

Oh, maiden, rich
    In Girton lore,
That wisdom which
    We prized before,
We do confess
Is nothingness,
And rather less,
    Perhaps, than more.
On each of us
    Thy learning shed.
On calculus
    May we be fed.
And teach us, please,
To speak with ease
All languages,
    Alive and dead !

SOLO—Princess *and* Chorus.

ZARA.   Five years have flown since I took wing—
                Time flies, and his footstep ne'er retards—
           I'm the eldest daughter of your king.

TROOPERS.   And we are her escort—First Life Guards!
           On the royal yacht,
                When the waves were white,
                In a helmet hot
                And a tunic tight,
           And our great big boots,
                We defied the storm:
           For we're not recruits,
                And his uniform
           A well-drilled trooper ne'er discards—
           And we are her escort—First Life Guards!

ZARA.   These gentlemen I present to you,
                The pride and boast of their barrack-yards;
           They've taken, O! such care of me!

TROOPERS.   For we are her escort—First Life Guards!
           When the tempest rose,
                And the ship went *so*—
           Do you suppose
                We were ill? No, no!
           Though a qualmish lot
                In a tunic tight,
                And a helmet hot,
                And a breastplate bright
           (Which a well-drilled trooper ne'er discards),
           We stood as her escort—First Life Guards!

Full Chorus.

Knightsbridge nursemaids—serving fairies—
Stars of proud Belgravian airies;
At stern duty's call you leave them,
Though you know how that must grieve them!

U 2

ZARA.   Tantantarara-rara-rara !
CAPT. FITZ.   Trumpet-call of Princess Zara !
CHORUS.   That's trump-call, and they're all trump cards—
               They are her escort—First Life Guards !

ENSEMBLE.

CHORUS.	PRINCESS ZARA and FITZBATTLE-
LADIES.	AXE (*aside*).

Knightsbridge nursemaids, etc.	Oh ! the hours are gold,
	And the joys untold,
MEN.	When my eyes behold
When the tempest rose, etc.	My beloved Princess ;
	And the years will seem
	But a brief day-dream,
	In the joy extreme
	Of our happiness !

FULL CHORUS. Knightsbridge nursemaids, serving fairies,
              etc.

Enter KING, PRINCESSES NEKAYA *and* KALYBA, *and*
  LADY SOPHY. *As the* KING *enters the escort present
  arms.*

KING. Zara ! my beloved daughter ! Why, how well
you look and how lovely you have grown ! (*embraces her*).
  ZARA. My dear father ! (*embracing him*). And my
two beautiful little sisters ! (*embracing them*).
  NEK. Not beautiful.
  KAL. Nice-looking.
  ZARA. But first let me present to you the English
warrior who commands my escort, and who has taken,
O ! such care of me during the voyage—Captain Fitz-
battleaxe !
  TROOPERS.   The First Life Guards.
               When the tempest rose,
               And the ship went *so*—

(CAPT. FITZBATTLEAXE *motions them to be silent. The
  Troopers place themselves in the four corners of the*

stage, standing at ease, immovably, as if on sentry. Each is surrounded by an admiring group of young ladies, of whom they take no notice.)

KING (*to* CAPT. FITZ.). Sir, you come from a country where every virtue flourishes. We trust that you will not criticize too severely such shortcomings as you may detect in our semi-barbarous society.

FITZ. (*looking at* ZARA). Sir, I have eyes for nothing but the blameless and the beautiful.

KING. We thank you—he is really very polite ! (LADY SOPHY, *who has been greatly scandalized by the attentions paid to the Lifeguardsmen by the young ladies, marches the* PRINCESSES NEKAYA *and* KALYBA *towards an exit.*) Lady Sophy, do not leave us.

LADY S. Sir, your children are young, and, so far, innocent. If they are to remain so, it is necessary that they be at once removed from the contamination of their present disgraceful surroundings. (*She marches them off.*)

KING (*whose attention has thus been called to the proceedings of the young ladies—aside*). Dear, dear! They really shouldn't. (*Aloud.*) Captain Fitzbattleaxe——

FITZ. Sir.

KING. Your Troopers appear to be receiving a troublesome amount of attention from those young ladies. I know how strict you English soldiers are, and I should be extremely distressed if anything occurred to shock their puritanical British sensitiveness.

FITZ. Oh, I don't think there's any chance of that.

KING. You think not ? They won't be offended ?

FITZ. Oh no ! They are quite hardened to it. They get a good deal of that sort of thing, standing sentry at the Horse Guards.

KING. It's English, is it ?

FITZ. It's particularly English.

KING. Then, of course, it's all right. Pray proceed, ladies, it's particularly English. Come, my daughter, for we have much to say to each other.

ZARA. Farewell, Captain Fitzbattleaxe! I cannot thank you too emphatically for the devoted care with which you have watched over me during our long and eventful voyage.

DUET—ZARA and CAPTAIN FITZBATTLEAXE.

ZARA.   Ah! gallant soldier, brave and true
        In tented field and tourney,
    I grieve to have occasioned you
        So very long a journey.
    A British warrior gives up all—
        His home and island beauty—
    When summoned by the trumpet-call
        Of Regimental Duty!

ALL.   Tantantarara-rara-rara!
    Trumpet-call of Princess Zara!

ENSEMBLE.

MEN.	FITZBATTLEAXE and ZARA (aside).
A British warrior gives up all, etc.	Oh, my joy, my pride,
	My delight to hide,
LADIES.	Let us sing, aside,
Knightsbridge nursemaids, etc.	What in truth we feel.
	Let us whisper low
	Of our love's glad glow,
	Lest the truth we show
	We would fain conceal.

FITZ.   Such escort duty, as his due,
        To young Lifeguardsman falling
    Completely reconciles him to
        His uneventful calling.
    When soldier seeks Utopian glades
        In charge of Youth and Beauty,
    Then pleasure merely masquerades
        As Regimental Duty!

ALL.   Tantantarara-rara-rara!
    Trumpet-call of Princess Zara!

ENSEMBLE.

CHORUS.	FITZBATTLEAXE *and* ZARA (*aside*).
MEN.	Oh ! the hours are gold,
A British warrior, etc.	And the joys untold,
	When my eyes behold
WOMEN.	My beloved Princess ;
Knightsbridge nursemaids, etc.	And the years will seem
	But a brief day-dream,
	In the joy extreme
	Of our happiness !

[*Exeunt* KING *and* PRINCESS *in one direction,
Lifeguardsmen and crowd in opposite
direction. Enter, at back,* SCAPHIO *and*
PHANTIS, *who watch the* PRINCESS *as
she goes off.* SCAPHIO *is seated, shaking
violently, and obviously under the influence
of some strong emotion.*

PHAN.   There—tell me, Scaphio, is she not beautiful ?
Can you wonder that I love her so passionately ?

SCA.   No. She is extraordinarily—miraculously lovely !
Good heavens, what a singularly beautiful girl !

PHAN.   I knew you would say so !

SCA.   What exquisite charm of manner ! What
surprising delicacy of gesture ! Why, she's a goddess !
a very goddess !

PHAN.   (*rather taken aback*). Yes — she's — she's an
attractive girl.

SCA.   Attractive ? Why, you must be blind !—She's
entrancing—enthralling !—intoxicating ! (*Aside.*) God
bless my heart, what's the matter with me ?

PHAN.   (*alarmed*). Yes. You—you promised to help
me to get her father's consent, you know.

SCA.   Promised ! Yes, but the convulsion has come,
my good boy ! It is she—my ideal ! Why, what's this ?
(*staggering*). Phantis ! Stop me—I'm going mad—mad
with the love of her !

PHAN.   Scaphio, compose yourself, I beg. The girl

is perfectly opaque ! Besides, remember—each of us is helpless without the other. You can't succeed without my consent, you know.

Sca. And you dare to threaten ? Oh, ungrateful ! When you came to me, palsied with love for this girl, and implored my assistance, did I not unhesitatingly promise it ? And this is the return you make ? Out of my sight, ingrate ! (*Aside.*) Dear ! dear ! what is the matter with me ?

Enter Capt. Fitzbattleaxe *and* Zara.

Zara. Dear me. I'm afraid we are interrupting a *tête-à-tête.*

Sca. (*breathlessly*). No, no. You come very appropriately. To be brief, we—we love you—this man and I —madly—passionately !

Zara. Sir !

Sca. And we don't know how we are to settle which of us is to marry you.

Fitz. Zara, this is very awkward.

Sca. (*very much overcome*). I—I am paralysed by the singular radiance of your extraordinary loveliness. I know I am incoherent. I never was like this before— it shall not occur again. I—shall be fluent, presently.

Zara (*aside*). Oh, dear, Captain Fitzbattleaxe, what *is* to be done ?

Fitz. (*aside*). Leave it to me—I'll manage it. (*Aloud.*) It's a common situation. Why not settle it in the English fashion ?

Both. The English fashion ? What is that ?

Fitz. It's very simple. In England, when two gentlemen are in love with the same lady, and until it is settled which gentleman is to blow out the brains of the other, it is provided, by the Rival Admirers' Clauses Consolidation Act, that the lady shall be entrusted to an officer of Household Cavalry as stakeholder, who is bound to hand her over to the survivor (on the Tontine principle) in a good condition of substantial and decorative repair.

Sca. Reasonable wear and tear and damages by fire excepted ?

Fitz. Exactly.

Phan. Well, that seems very reasonable. (*To* Scaphio.) What do you say—Shall we entrust her to this officer of Household Cavalry ? It will give us time.

Sca. (*trembling violently*). I—I am not at present in a condition to think it out coolly—but if he *is* an officer of Household Cavalry, and if the Princess consents——

Zara. Alas, dear sirs, I have no alternative—under the Rival Admirers' Clauses Consolidation Act !

Fitz. Good—then that's settled.

QUARTET.

Fitzbattleaxe, Zara, Scaphio, *and* Phantis.

Fitz.   It's understood, I think, all round
           That, by the English custom bound
           I hold the lady safe and sound
               In trust for either rival,
           Until you clearly testify
           By sword or pistol, by and by,
           Which gentleman prefers to die,
               And which prefers survival.

ENSEMBLE.

Sca. *and* Phan.	Zara *and* Fitz. (*aside*).
It's clearly understood, all round,	We stand, I think, on safish ground,
That, by your English custom bound,	Our senses weak it will astound
He holds the lady safe and sound	If either gentleman is found
In trust for either rival,	Prepared to meet his rival.
Until we clearly testify	Their machinations we defy ;
By sword or pistol, by and by,	We won't be parted, you and I—
Which gentleman prefers to die,	Of bloodshed each is rather shy—
And which prefers survival.	They both prefer survival.

Phan.   If I should die and he should live,
(*aside to* Fitz.).   To you, without reserve, I give
              Her heart so young and sensitive,
                And all her predilections.

SCA.   If he should live and I should die,
(*aside to* FITZ.).   I see no kind of reason why
                            You should not, if you wish it, try
                                  To gain her young affections.

ENSEMBLE.

SCA. *and* PHAN. (*angrily to each other*).	FITZ. *and* ZARA (*aside*).
If I should die and you should live,	As both of us are positive
To this young officer I give	That both of them intend to live,
Her heart so soft and sensitive,	There's nothing in the case to give
And all her predilections.	Us cause for grave reflections.
If you should live and I should die,	As both will live and neither die
I see no kind of reason why	I see no kind of reason why
He should not, if he chooses, try	I should not, if I wish it, try
To win her young affections.	To gain your young affections!

[*Exeunt* SCAPHIO *and* PHANTIS *together.*

DUET—ZARA *and* FITZBATTLEAXE.

ENSEMBLE.

Oh, admirable art !
     Oh, neatly-planned intention !
          Oh, happy intervention—
               Oh, well-constructed plot !
When sages try to part
     Two loving hearts in fusion,
          Their wisdom's a delusion,
               And learning serves them not !

FITZ.   Until quite plain
                              Is their intent,
                        These sages twain
                              I represent.
                        Now please infer
                              That, nothing loth,
                        You're henceforth, as it were,
                              Engaged to marry both—
               Then take it that I represent the two—
                        On that hypothesis, what would you do ?

ZARA (*aside*). What would I do ? what would I do ?
(*To* FITZ.) In such a case,
   Upon your breast,
My blushing face
   I think I'd rest—(*doing so*).
Then perhaps I might
   Demurely say—
" I find this breastplate bright
   Is sorely in the way ! "

FITZ. Our mortal race
   Is never blest—
There's no such case
   As perfect rest ;
Some petty blight
   Asserts its sway—
Some crumpled roseleaf light
Is always in the way !

[*Exit* FITZBATTLEAXE. *Manet* ZARA.

Enter KING.

KING. My daughter ! At last we are alone to-gether.

ZARA. Yes, and I'm glad we are, for I want to speak to you very seriously. Do you know this paper ?

KING (*aside*). Da—! (*Aloud.*) Oh yes — I've — I've seen it. Where in the world did you get this from ?

ZARA. It was given to me by Lady Sophy—my sisters' governess.

KING (*aside*). Lady Sophy's an angel, but I do sometimes wish she'd mind her own business ! (*Aloud.*) It's—ha ! ha !—it's rather humorous.

ZARA. I see nothing humorous in it. I only see that you, the despotic King of this country, are made the

subject of the most scandalous insinuations. Why do you permit these things ?

KING. Well, they appeal to my sense of humour. It's the only really comic paper in Utopia, and I wouldn't be without it for the world.

ZARA. If it had any literary merit I could understand it.

KING. Oh, it *has* literary merit. Oh, distinctly, it has literary merit.

ZARA. My dear father, it's mere ungrammatical twaddle.

KING. Oh, it's not ungrammatical. I can't allow that. Unpleasantly personal, perhaps, but written with an epigrammatical point that is very rare nowadays—very rare indeed.

ZARA (*looking at cartoon*). Why do they represent you with such a big nose ?

KING (*looking at cartoon*). Eh ? Yes, it *is* a big one ! Why, the fact is that, in the cartoons of a comic paper, the size of your nose always varies inversely as the square of your popularity. It's the rule.

ZARA. Then you must be at a tremendous discount just now ! I see a notice of a new piece called " King Tuppence ", in which an English tenor has the audacity to personate you on a public stage. I can only say that I am surprised that any English tenor should lend himself to such degrading personalities.

KING. Oh, he's not really English. As it happens he's a Utopian, but he calls himself English.

ZARA. Calls himself English ?

KING. Yes. Bless you, they wouldn't listen to any tenor who didn't call himself English.

ZARA. And you permit this insolent buffoon to caricature you in a pointless burlesque ! My dear father—if you were a free agent, you would never permit these outrages.

KING (*almost in tears*). Zara—I—I admit I am not altogether a free agent. I—I am controlled. I try to make the best of it, but sometimes I find it very difficult— very difficult indeed. Nominally a Despot, I am, between

ourselves, the helpless tool of two unscrupulous Wise
Men, who insist on my falling in with all their wishes and
threaten to denounce me for immediate explosion if I
remonstrate ! (*Breaks down completely*.)

ZARA. My poor father ! Now listen to me. With a
view to remodelling the political and social institutions of
Utopia, I have brought with me six Representatives of
the principal causes that have tended to make England
the powerful, happy, and blameless country which the
consensus of European civilization has declared it to be.
Place yourself unreservedly in the hands of these gentlemen,
and they will reorganize your country on a footing that
will enable you to defy your persecutors. They are all
now washing their hands after their journey. Shall I
introduce them ?

KING. My dear Zara, how can I thank you ? I will
consent to anything that will release me from the abominable tyranny of these two men. (*Calling*.) What ho !
Without there ! (*Enter* CALYNX.) Summon my Court
without an instant's delay !
                                              [*Exit* CALYNX.

FINALE.

Enter every one, except the Flowers of Progress.

CHORUS.

Although your Royal summons to appear
From courtesy was singularly free,
Obedient to that summons we are here—
What would your Majesty ?

RECIT.—KING.

My worthy people, my beloved daughter
Most thoughtfully has brought with her from England
The types of all the causes that have made
That great and glorious country what it is.

CHORUS.   Oh, joy unbounded !

SCA., TAR., *and* PHAN. (*aside*). Why, what *does* this mean ?

RECIT.—Zara.

Attend to me, Utopian populace,
    Ye South Pacific Island viviparians;
All, in the abstract, types of courtly grace,
Yet, when compared with Britain's glorious race,
    But little better than half-clothed barbarians!

Chorus.

Yes! Contrasted when
    With Englishmen,
Are little better than half-clothed barbarians!

Enter all the Flowers of Progress, led by Fitzbattleaxe.

SOLO—Zara.

(*Presenting* Capt. Fitzbattleaxe.)

When Britain sounds the trump of war
    (And Europe trembles),
The army of that conqueror
    In serried ranks assembles;
'Tis then this warrior's eyes and sabre gleam
    For our protection—
He represents a military scheme
    In all its proud perfection!

Chorus.   Yes—yes—
He represents a military scheme
    In all its proud perfection!
    Ulahlica!   Ulahlica!   Ulahlica!

SOLO—Zara.

(*Presenting* Sir Bailey Barre, Q.C., M.P.)

A complicated gentleman allow me to present,
Of all the arts and faculties the terse embodiment,
He's a great Arithmetician who can demonstrate with ease
That two and two are three, or five, or anything you please;

An eminent Logician who can make it clear to you
That black is white—when looked at from the proper
    point of view ;
A marvellous Philologist who'll undertake to show
That " yes " is but another and a neater form of " no ".

SIR BAILEY.   Yes—yes—yes—
  " Yes " is but another and a neater form of " no ".
  All preconceived ideas on any subject I can scout,
  And demonstrate beyond all possibility of doubt,
  That whether you're an honest man or whether you're
    a thief
  Depends on whose solicitor has given me my brief.

CHORUS.   Yes—yes—yes—
        That whether you're an honest man, etc.
          Ulahlica !   Ulahlica !   Ulahlica !

SOLO—ZARA.

(*Presenting* LORD DRAMALEIGH *and County Councillor.*)

        What these may be, Utopians all,
           Perhaps you'll hardly guess—
        They're types of England's physical
           And moral cleanliness.
        This is a Lord High Chamberlain,
           Of purity the gauge—
        He'll cleanse our Court from moral stain
           And purify our Stage.

LORD D.   Yes—yes—yes—
           Court reputations I revise,
           And presentations scrutinize,
           New plays I read with jealous eyes,
             And purify the Stage.

CHORUS.   Court reputations, etc.

ZARA.   This County Councillor acclaim,
           Great Britain's latest toy—
        On anything you like to name
           His talents he'll employ—

> All streets and squares he'll purify
> Within your city walls,
> And keep meanwhile a modest eye
> On wicked music halls.

C. C.　　　　Yes—yes—yes—
> In towns I make improvements great,
> Which go to swell the County Rate—
> I dwelling-houses sanitate,
> And purify the Halls !

CHORUS.　In towns he makes improvements great, etc.
> Ulahlica !　Ulahlica !　Ulahlica !

SOLO—ZARA.

(*Presenting* MR. GOLDBURY.)

A Company Promoter this, with special education,
Which teaches what Contango means and also Back-
　　wardation—
To speculators he supplies a grand financial leaven,
Time was when *two* were company—but now it must
　　be seven.

MR. GOLD.　　Yes—yes—yes—
> Stupendous loans to foreign thrones
> I've largely advocated ;
> In ginger-pops and peppermint-drops
> I've freely speculated ;
> Then mines of gold, of wealth untold,
> Successfully I've floated,
> And sudden falls in apple-stalls
> Occasionally quoted :
> And soon or late I always call
> For Stock Exchange quotation—
> No schemes too great and none too small
> For Companification !

CHORUS.　Yes !　Yes !　Yes !　No schemes too great, etc.
> Ulahlica !　Ulahlica !　Ulahlica !

ZARA. (*Presenting* CAPT. SIR EDWARD CORCORAN, R.N.)

And lastly I present
    Great Britain's proudest boast,
Who from the blows
Of foreign foes
    Protects her sea-girt coast—
And if you ask him in respectful tone,
He'll show you how you may protect your own !

SOLO—CAPTAIN CORCORAN.

I'm Captain Corcoran, K.C.B.,
I'll teach you how we rule the sea,
    And terrify the simple Gauls ;
And how the Saxon and the Celt
Their Europe-shaking blows have dealt
With Maxim gun and Nordenfelt
    (Or will, when the occasion calls).
If sailor-like you'd play your cards,
Unbend your sails and lower your yards,
    Unstep your masts—you'll never want 'em more.
Though we're no longer hearts of oak,
Yet we can steer and we can stoke,
And, thanks to coal, and thanks to coke,
    We never run a ship ashore !

ALL. What never ?
CAPT.   No, never !
ALL. What *never* ?
CAPT.   Hardly ever !

ALL.   Hardly ever run a ship ashore !
        Then give three cheers, and three cheers more,
        For the tar who never runs his ship ashore ;
        Then give three cheers, and three cheers more,
        For he never runs his ship ashore !

CHORUS.

All hail, ye types of England's power—
    Ye heaven-enlightened band !

We bless the day, and bless the hour
That brought you to our land.

QUARTET.

Ye wanderers from a mighty State,
Oh, teach us how to legislate—
Your lightest word will carry weight
          In our attentive ears.
Oh, teach the natives of this land
(Who are not quick to understand)
How to work off their social and
          Political arrears !

CAPT. FITZ. Increase your army !
LORD D.   Purify your Court !
CAPT. COR. Get up your steam and cut your canvas short !
SIR B. BAR. To speak on both sides teach your sluggish
                          brains !
MR. B., C. C. Widen your thoroughfares, and flush your
                          drains !
MR. GOLD.   Utopia's much too big for one small head—
                    I'll float it as a Company Limited !

KING.   A Company Limited ? What may that be ?
                    The term, I rather think, is new to me.

CHORUS.   A Company Limited ? etc.

SCA., PHAN., *and* TAR. (*aside*).
              What does he mean ? What does he mean ?
                    Give us a kind of clue !
              What does he mean ?   What does he mean ?
                    What is he going to do ?

SONG—MR. GOLDBURY.

Some seven men form an Association
          (If possible, all Peers and Baronets),

They start off with a public declaration
    To what extent they mean to pay their debts.
That's called their Capital : if they are wary
    They will not quote it at a sum immense.
The figure's immaterial—it may vary
    From eighteen million down to eighteenpence.
        I should put it rather low ;
        The good sense of doing so
    Will be evident at once to any debtor.
        When it's left to you to say
        What amount you mean to pay,
    Why, the lower you can put it at, the better.

CHORUS.   When it's left to you to say, etc.

They then proceed to trade with all who'll trust 'em,
    Quite irrespective of their capital
(It's shady, but it's sanctified by custom) ;
    Bank, Railway, Loan, or Panama Canal.
You can't embark on trading too tremendous—
    It's strictly fair, and based on common sense—
If you succeed, your profits are stupendous—
    And if you fail, pop goes your eighteenpence.
        Make the money-spinner spin !
        For you only stand to win,
    And you'll never with dishonesty be twitted,
        For nobody can know,
        To a million or so,
    To what extent your capital's committed !

CHORUS.   No, nobody can know, etc.

If you come to grief, and creditors are craving
    (For nothing that is planned by mortal head
Is certain in this Vale of Sorrow—saving
    That one's Liability is Limited),—
Do you suppose that signifies perdition ?
    If so you're but a monetary dunce—
You merely file a Winding-Up Petition,
    And start another Company at once !

Though a Rothschild you may be
In your own capacity,
As a Company you've come to utter sorrow—
But the Liquidators say,
" Never mind—you needn't pay,"
So you start another Company to-morrow !

CHORUS.   But the Liquidators say, etc.

RECIT.

KING.   Well, at first sight it strikes us as dishonest,
But if it's good enough for virtuous England—
The first commercial country in the world—
It's good enough for us.

SCA., PHAN., *and* TAR. (*aside to* KING).
You'd best take care—
Please recollect *we* have not been consulted.

KING (*not heeding them*).
And do I understand you that Great Britain
Upon this Joint Stock principle is governed ?

MR. GOLD. We haven't come to that, exactly—but
We're tending rapidly in that direction.
The date's not distant.

KING (*enthusiastically*). We will be before you !
We'll go down to Posterity renowned
As the First Sovereign in Christendom
Who registered his Crown and Country under
The Joint Stock Company's Act of Sixty-Two.

ALL.   Ulahlica !

SOLO—KING.

Henceforward, of a verity,
With Fame ourselves we link—
We'll go down to Posterity
Of sovereigns all the pink !

SCA., PHAN., *and* TAR. (*aside to* KING).
If you've the mad temerity

> Our wishes thus to blink,
> You'll go down to Posterity
> Much earlier than you think !

TAR. (*correcting them*).
> He'll go *up* to Posterity,
> If *I* inflict the blow !

SCA. *and* PHAN. (*angrily*).
> He'll go *down* to Posterity—
> We think we ought to know !

TAR. (*explaining*).
> He'll go *up* to Posterity,
> Blown up with dynamite !

SCA. *and* PHAN. (*apologetically*),
> He'll go *up* to Posterity,
> Of course he will, you're right !

ENSEMBLE.

KING, LADY SOPHY, NEK., KAL, CALYNX, *and* CHORUS.	SCA., PHAN., *and* TAR. (*aside*).	FITZBATTLEAXE *and* ZARA (*aside*).
Henceforward, of a verity, With fame ourselves we link— And go down to Posterity, Of sovereigns all the pink !	If he has the temerity Our wishes thus to blink, He'll go up to Posterity Much earlier than they think !	Who love with all sincerity, Their lives may safely link ; And as for our Posterity— We don't care what they think !

CHORUS.

> Let's seal this mercantile pact—
> The step we ne'er shall rue—
> It gives whatever we lacked—
> The statement's strictly true.
> All hail, astonishing Fact !
> All hail, Invention new—
> The Joint Stock Company's Act—
> The Act of Sixty-Two !

END OF ACT I.

ACT II.

SCENE.—*Throne Room in the Palace. Night.*
FITZBATTLEAXE *discovered, singing to* ZARA.

RECIT.—FITZ.

Oh, Zara, my beloved one, bear with me !
Ah, do not laugh at my attempted C !
Repent not, mocking maid, thy girlhood's choice—
The fervour of my love affects my voice !

SONG—FITZ.

A tenor, all singers above
    (This doesn't admit of a question),
        Should keep himself quiet,
        Attend to his diet
    And carefully nurse his digestion ;
But when he is madly in love
    It's certain to tell on his singing—
        You can't do chromatics
        With proper emphatics
    When anguish your bosom is wringing !
When distracted with worries in plenty,
And his pulse is a hundred and twenty,
And his fluttering bosom the slave of mistrust is,
A tenor can't do himself justice.
    Now observe—(*sings a high note*),
You see, I can't do myself justice !

I could sing if my fervour were mock,
 It's easy enough if you're acting—
  But when one's emotion
  Is born of devotion
 You mustn't be over-exacting.
One ought to be firm as a rock
 To venture a shake in *vibrato*,
  When fervour's expected
  Keep cool and collected
 Or never attempt *agitato*.
But, of course, when his tongue is of leather,
And his lips appear pasted together,
And his sensitive palate as dry as a crust is,
A tenor can't do himself justice.
  Now observe—(*sings a cadence*),
 It's no use—I can't do myself justice !

ZARA. Why, Arthur, what *does* it matter ? When the higher qualities of the heart are all that can be desired, the higher notes of the voice are matters of comparative insignificance. Who thinks slightingly of the cocoanut because it is husky ? Besides (*demurely*), you are not singing for an engagement (*putting her hand in his*), you have that already !

FITZ. How good and wise you are ! How unerringly your practised brain winnows the wheat from the chaff— the material from the merely incidental !

ZARA. My Girton training, Arthur. At Girton all is wheat, and idle chaff is never heard within its walls ! But tell me, is not all working marvellously well ? Have not our Flowers of Progress more than justified their name ?

FITZ. We have indeed done our best. Captain Corcoran and I have, in concert, thoroughly remodelled the sister-services—and upon so sound a basis that the South Pacific trembles at the name of Utopia !

ZARA. How clever of you !

FITZ. Clever ? Not a bit. It's as easy as possible

when the Admiralty and Horse Guards are not there to interfere. And so with the others. Freed from the trammels imposed upon them by idle Acts of Parliament, all have given their natural talents full play and introduced reforms which, even in England, were never dreamt of!

ZARA.   But perhaps the most beneficent change of all has been effected by Mr. Goldbury, who, discarding the exploded theory that some strange magic lies hidden in the number Seven, has applied the Limited Liability principle to individuals, and every man, woman, and child is now a Company Limited with liability restricted to the amount of his declared Capital! There is not a christened baby in Utopia who has not already issued his little Prospectus!

FITZ.   Marvellous is the power of a Civilization which can transmute, by a word, a Limited Income into an Income Limited.

ZARA.   Reform has not stopped here—it has been applied even to the costume of our people. Discarding their own barbaric dress, the natives of our land have unanimously adopted the tasteful fashions of England in all their rich entirety. Scaphio and Phantis have undertaken a contract to supply the whole of Utopia with clothing designed upon the most approved English models —and the first Drawing-Room under the new state of things is to be held here this evening.

FITZ.   But Drawing-Rooms are always held in the afternoon.

ZARA.   Ah, we've improved upon that. We all look so much better by candle-light! And when I tell you, dearest, that my Court train has just arrived, you will understand that I am longing to go and try it on.

FITZ.   Then we must part?

ZARA.   Necessarily, for a time.

FITZ.   Just as I wanted to tell you, with all the passionate enthusiasm of my nature, how deeply, how devotedly I love you!

ZARA.   Hush! Are these the accents of a heart that

really feels ? True love does not indulge in declamation—
its voice is sweet, and soft, and low. The west wind
whispers when he woos the poplars !

DUET—Zara *and* Fitzbattleaxe.

ZARA.　Words of love too loudly spoken
　　　　　Ring their own untimely knell ;
　　　Noisy vows are rudely broken,
　　　　　Soft the song of Philomel.
　　　Whisper sweetly, whisper slowly,
　　　　　Hour by hour and day by day ;
　　　Sweet and low as accents holy
　　　　　Are the notes of lover's lay !

BOTH.　Sweet and low, etc.

FITZ.　Let the conqueror, flushed with glory,
　　　　　Bid his noisy clarions bray ;
　　　Lovers tell their artless story
　　　　　In a whispered virelay.
　　　False is he whose vows alluring
　　　　　Make the listening echoes ring ;
　　　Sweet and low when all-enduring
　　　　　Are the songs that lovers sing !

BOTH.　Sweet and low, etc.

[Exit ZARA.

Enter KING, *dressed as Field-Marshal.*

KING. To a Monarch who has been accustomed to
the uncontrolled use of his limbs, the costume of a British
Field - Marshal is, perhaps, at first, a little cramping.
Are you sure that this is all right ? It's not a practical
joke, is it ? No one has a keener sense of humour than
I have, but the First Statutory Cabinet Council of Utopia
Limited must be conducted with dignity and impress-
iveness. Now, where are the other five who signed the
Articles of Association ?

　　FITZ. Sir, they are here.

Enter LORD DRAMALEIGH, CAPTAIN CORCORAN, SIR
   BAILEY BARRE, MR. BLUSHINGTON, *and* MR. GOLD-
   BURY *from different entrances.*

KING. Oh! (*Addressing them.*) Gentlemen, our
daughter holds her first Drawing-Room in half an hour,
and we shall have time to make our half-yearly report
in the interval. I am necessarily unfamiliar with the
forms of an English Cabinet Council—perhaps the Lord
Chamberlain will kindly put us in the way of doing the
thing properly, and with due regard to the solemnity of
the occasion.

LORD D. Certainly—nothing simpler. Kindly bring
your chairs forward—His Majesty will, of course, preside.

(*They range their chairs across stage like Christy Minstrels.*
   KING *sits* C., LORD DRAMALEIGH *on his* L., MR.
   GOLDBURY *on his* R., CAPT. CORCORAN L. *of* LORD
   DRAMALEIGH, CAPT. FITZBATTLEAXE R. *of* MR.
   GOLDBURY, MR. BLUSHINGTON *extreme* R., SIR
   BAILEY BARRE *extreme* L.)

KING. Like this?
LORD D. Like this.
KING. We take your word for it that this is all right.
You are not making fun of us? This is in accordance
with the practice at the Court of St. James's?
LORD D. Well, it is in accordance with the practice
at the Court of St. James's Hall.
KING. Oh! it seems odd, but never mind.

SONG—KING.

Society has quite forsaken all her wicked courses,
   Which empties our police courts, and abolishes
      divorces.
CHORUS.   Divorce is nearly obsolete in England.
KING.   No tolerance we show to undeserving rank and
      splendour;
   For the higher his position is, the greater the
      offender.

CHORUS.   That's a maxim that is prevalent in England.

KING.   No peeress at our Drawing-room before the Presence passes
     Who wouldn't be accepted by the lower-middle classes.
     Each shady dame, whatever be her rank, is bowed out neatly.

CHORUS. In short, this happy country has been Anglicized completely !
     It really is surprising
     What a thorough Anglicizing
We have brought about—Utopia's quite another land ;
     In her enterprising movements,
     She is England—with improvements,
Which we dutifully offer to our mother-land !

KING.   Our city we have beautified—we've done it willy-nilly—
     And all that isn't Belgrave Square is Strand and Piccadilly.

CHORUS.   We haven't any slummeries in England !

KING.   We have solved the labour question with discrimination polished,
     So poverty is obsolete and hunger is abolished—

CHORUS.   We are going to abolish it in England.

KING.   The Chamberlain our native stage has purged, beyond a question,
     Of " risky " situation and indelicate suggestion ;
     No piece is tolerated if it's costumed indiscreetly—

CHORUS. In short, this happy country has been Anglicized completely !
     It really is surprising, etc.

KING.   Our Peerage we've remodelled on an intellectual basis,
     Which certainly is rough on our hereditary races—

CHORUS.   We are going to remodel it in England.

x

KING.   The Brewers and the Cotton Lords no longer
                  seek admission,
              And Literary Merit meets with proper recogni-
                  tion—
CHORUS.   As Literary Merit does in England !

KING.   Who knows but we may count among our
                  intellectual chickens,
              Like you, an Earl of Thackeray and p'r'aps a
                  Duke of Dickens—
              Lord Fildes and Viscount Millais (when they
                  come) we'll welcome sweetly—
CHORUS.   In short, this happy country has been Anglicized
                  completely !
              It really is surprising, etc.

(At the end all rise and replace their chairs.)

KING. Now, then, for our first Drawing-Room.
Where are the Princesses ? What an extraordinary thing
it is that since European looking-glasses have been supplied to the Royal bedrooms my daughters are invariably
late !

LORD D. Sir, their Royal Highnesses await your
pleasure in the Ante-room.

KING. Oh. Then request them to do us the favour
to enter at once.

MARCH. *Enter all the Royal Household, including
(besides the Lord Chamberlain) the Vice-Chamberlain,
the Master of the Horse, the Master of the Buckhounds,
the Lord High Treasurer, the Lord Steward, the
Comptroller of the Household, the Lord-in-Waiting,
the Groom-in-Waiting, the Field Officer in Brigade
Waiting, the Gold and Silver Stick, and the Gentlemen
Ushers.   Then enter the three Princesses (their trains
carried by Pages of Honour),* LADY SOPHY, *and the
Ladies-in-Waiting.*

KING. My daughters, we are about to attempt a very

solemn ceremonial, so no giggling, if you please.   Now, my Lord Chamberlain, we are ready.

LORD D.   Then, ladies and gentlemen, places, if you please.   His Majesty will take his place in front of the throne, and will be so obliging as to embrace all the *débutantes*.   (LADY SOPHY *much shocked*.)

KING.   What—must I really ?

LORD D.   Absolutely indispensable.

KING.   More jam for the *Palace Peeper* !

(*The* KING *takes his place in front of the throne, the* PRINCESS ZARA *on his left, the two younger Princesses on the left of* ZARA.)

KING.   Now, is every one in his place ?

LORD D.   Every one is in his place.

KING.   Then let the revels commence.

Enter the ladies attending the Drawing-Room. They give their cards to the Groom-in-Waiting, who passes them to the Lord-in-Waiting, who passes them to the Vice-Chamberlain, who passes them to the Lord Chamberlain, who reads the names to the KING *as each lady approaches.   The ladies curtsey in succession to the* KING *and the three Princesses, and pass out. When all the presentations have been accomplished, the* KING, *Princesses, and* LADY SOPHY *come forward, and all the ladies re-enter.*

RECIT.—KING.

This ceremonial our wish displays
To copy all Great Britain's courtly ways.
Though lofty aims catastrophe entail,
We'll gloriously succeed or nobly fail !

UNACCOMPANIED CHORUS.

Eagle high in cloudland soaring—
      Sparrow twittering on a reed—
Tiger in the jungle roaring—
      Frightened fawn in grassy mead—

> Let the eagle, not the sparrow,
> Be the object of your arrow—
>   Fix the tiger with your eye—
>   Pass the fawn in pity by.
>   Glory then will crown the day—
>   Glory, glory, anyway !

[Then exeunt all.

Enter SCAPHIO *and* PHANTIS, *now dressed as judges in red and ermine robes and undress wigs. They come down stage melodramatically—working together.*

DUET—SCAPHIO *and* PHANTIS.

SCA.   With fury deep we burn—
PHAN.   We do—
SCA.   We fume with smothered rage—
PHAN.   We do—
SCA.   These Englishmen who rule supreme,
          Their undertaking they redeem
          By stifling every harmless scheme
                In which we both engage—
PHAN.   They do—
SCA.   In which we both engage.
PHAN.   We think it is our turn—
SCA.   We do—
PHAN.   We think our turn has come—
SCA.   We do.
PHAN.   These Englishmen, they must prepare
          To seek at once their native air.
          The King as heretofore, we swear,
          Shall be beneath our thumb—
SCA.   He shall—
PHAN.   Shall be beneath our thumb—
SCA.   He shall.
BOTH (*with great energy*).
          For this mustn't be, and this won't do,
          If you'll back me, then I'll back you,
                No, this won't do,
                No, this mustn't be.

Enter the KING.

KING. Gentlemen, gentlemen—really! This unseemly display of energy within the Royal Precincts is altogether unpardonable. Pray, what do you complain of?

SCA. (*furiously*). What do we complain of? Why, through the innovations introduced by the Flowers of Progress all our harmless schemes for making a provision for our old age are ruined. Our Matrimonial Agency is at a standstill, our Cheap Sherry business is in bankruptcy, our Army Clothing contracts are paralysed, and even our Society paper, the *Palace Peeper*, is practically defunct!

KING. Defunct? Is that so? Dear, dear, I am truly sorry.

SCA. Are you aware that Sir Bailey Barre has introduced a law of libel by which all editors of scurrilous newspapers are publicly flogged—as in England? And six of our editors have resigned in succession! Now, the editor of a scurrilous paper can stand a good deal— he takes a private thrashing as a matter of course—it's considered in his salary—but no gentleman likes to be publicly flogged.

KING. Naturally. I shouldn't like it myself.

PHAN. Then our Burlesque Theatre is absolutely ruined!

KING. Dear me. Well, theatrical property is not what it was.

PHAN. Are you aware that the Lord Chamberlain, who has his own views as to the best means of elevating the national drama, has declined to license any play that is not in blank verse and three hundred years old—as in England?

SCA. And as if that wasn't enough, the County Councillor has ordered a four-foot wall to be built up right across the proscenium, in case of fire—as in England.

PHAN. It's so hard on the company—who are liable

to be roasted alive—and this has to be met by enormously increased salaries—as in England.

Sca. You probably know that we've contracted to supply the entire nation with a complete English outfit. But perhaps you do *not* know that, when we send in our bills, our customers plead liability limited to a declared capital of eighteenpence, and apply to be dealt with under the Winding-up Act—as in England?

King. Really, gentlemen, this is very irregular. If you will be so good as to formulate a detailed list of your grievances in writing, addressed to the Secretary of Utopia Limited, they will be laid before the Board, in due course, at their next monthly meeting.

Sca. Are we to understand that we are defied?

King. That is the idea I intended to convey.

Phan. Defied! We are defied!

Sca. (*furiously*). Take care—you know our powers. Trifle with us, and you die!

TRIO—Sca., Phan., *and* King.

Sca. If you think that, when banded in unity,
We may both be defied with impunity,
You are sadly misled of a verity!

Phan. If you value repose and tranquillity,
You'll revert to a state of docility,
Or prepare to regret your temerity!

King. If my speech is unduly refractory
You will find it a course satisfactory
At an early Board meeting to show it up.
Though if proper excuse you can trump any,
You may *wind* up a Limited Company,
You cannot conveniently *blow* it up!

(Scaphio *and* Phantis *thoroughly baffled.*)

King (*dancing quietly*).
Whene'er I chance to baffle you
I, also, dance a step or two—
Of this now guess the hidden sense:

(Scaphio *and* Phantis *consider the question as* King *continues dancing quietly—then give it up.*)

It means—complete indifference.

Sca. *and* Phan. Of course it does—indifference !
It means complete indifference !

(King *dancing quietly.* Sca. *and* Phan. *dancing furiously.*)

Sca. *and* Phan. As we've a dance for every mood
With *pas de trois* we will conclude.
What this may mean you all may guess—
It typifies remorselessness !

King. It means unruffled cheerfulness !

(King *dances off placidly as* Scaphio *and* Phantis *dance furiously.*)

Phan. (*breathless*). He's right—we are helpless ! He's no longer a human being—he's a Corporation, and so long as he confines himself to his Articles of Association we can't touch him ! What are we to do ?

Sca. Do ? Raise a Revolution, repeal the Act of Sixty-Two, reconvert him into an individual, and insist on his immediate explosion ! (Tarara *enters.*) Tarara, come here ; you're the very man we want.

Tar. Certainly, allow me. (*Offers a cracker to each ; they snatch them away impatiently.*) That's rude.

Sca. We have no time for idle forms. You wish to succeed to the throne ?

Tar. Naturally.

Sca. Then you won't unless you join us. The King has defied us, and, as matters stand, we are helpless. So are you. We must devise some plot at once to bring the people about his ears.

Tar. A plot ?

Phan. Yes, a plot of superhuman subtlety. Have you such a thing about you ?

Tar. (*feeling*). No, I think not. No. There's one on my dressing-table.

Sca. We can't wait—we must concoct one at once, and put it into execution without delay. There is not a moment to spare !

TRIO—Scaphio, Phantis, and Tarara.

ENSEMBLE.

> With wily brain upon the spot
>   A private plot we'll plan,
> The most ingenious private plot
>   Since private plots began.
> That's understood.   So far we've got
> And, striking while the iron's hot,
> We'll now determine like a shot
> The details of this private plot.

Sca.   I think we ought—(*whispers*).

Phan. *and* Tar.   Such bosh I never heard !

Phan.   Ah ! happy thought !—(*whispers*).

Sca. *and* Tar.   How utterly dashed absurd !

Tar.   *I'll* tell you how—(*whispers*).

Sca. *and* Phan.   Why, what put that in your head ?

Sca.   I've got it now—(*whispers*).

Phan. *and* Tar.   Oh, take him away to bed !

Phan.   Oh, put him to bed !

Tar.   Oh, put him to bed !

Sca.   What ! put *me* to bed ?

Phan. *and* Tar.   Yes, certainly put him to bed !

Sca.   But, bless me, don't you see—

Phan.   Do listen to me, I pray—

Tar.   It certainly seems to me—

Sca.   Bah—this is the only way !

Phan.   It's rubbish absurd you growl !

Tar.   You talk ridiculous stuff !

Sca.   You're a drivelling barndoor owl !

Phan.   You're a vapid and vain old muff !

(*All, coming down to audience.*)

So far we haven't quite solved the plot—
They're not a very ingenious lot—
    But don't be unhappy,
    It's still on the *tapis*,
We'll presently hit on a capital plot !

SCA.	Suppose we all—(*whispers*).
PHAN.	Now *there* I think you're right.
	Then we might all—(*whispers*).
TAR.	That's true—we certainly might.
	I'll tell you what—(*whispers*).
SCA.	We will if we possibly can.
	Then on the spot—(*whispers*).
PHAN. *and* TAR.	Bravo ! a capital plan !
SCA.	That's exceedingly neat and new !
PHAN.	Exceedingly new and neat.
TAR.	I fancy that that will do.
SCA.	It's certainly very complete.
PHAN.	Well done, you sly old sap !
TAR.	Bravo, you cunning old mole !
SCA.	You very ingenious chap !
PHAN.	You intellectual soul !

(*All, coming down and addressing audience.*)

At last a capital plan we've got ;
We won't say how and we won't say what :
    It's safe in my noddle—
    Now off we will toddle,
And slyly develop this capital plot !

[*Business. Exeunt* SCAPHIO *and* PHANTIS *in
one direction, and* TARARA *in the other.*

Enter LORD DRAMALEIGH *and* MR. GOLDBURY.

LORD D. Well, what do you think of our first South
Pacific Drawing-room ? Allowing for a slight difficulty
with the trains, and a little want of familiarity with the

x 2

use of the rouge-pot, it was, on the whole, a meritorious affair ?

GOLD. My dear Dramaleigh, it redounds infinitely to your credit.

LORD D. One or two judicious innovations, I think ?

GOLD. Admirable. The cup of tea and the plate of mixed biscuits were a cheap and effective inspiration.

LORD D. Yes—my idea entirely. Never been done before.

GOLD. Pretty little maids, the King's youngest daughters, but timid.

LORD D. That'll wear off. Young.

GOLD. *That'll* wear off. Ha ! here they come, by George ! And without the Dragon ! What can they have done with her ?

Enter NEKAYA *and* KALYBA, *timidly.*

NEK. Oh, if you please, Lady Sophy has sent us in here, because Zara and Captain Fitzbattleaxe are going on, in the garden, in a manner which no well-conducted young ladies ought to witness.

LORD D. Indeed, we are very much obliged to her Ladyship.

KAL. Are you ? I wonder why.

NEK. Don't tell us if it's rude.

LORD D. Rude ? Not at all. We are obliged to Lady Sophy because she has afforded us the pleasure of seeing you.

NEK. I don't think you ought to talk to us like that.

KAL. It's calculated to turn our heads.

NEK. Attractive girls cannot be too particular.

KAL. Oh pray, pray do not take advantage of our unprotected innocence.

GOLD. Pray be reassured—you are in no danger whatever.

LORD D. But may I ask—is this extreme delicacy— this shrinking sensitiveness—a general characteristic of Utopian young ladies ?

NEK. Oh no ; we are crack specimens.

KAL. We are the pick of the basket. *Would* you mind not coming quite so near ? Thank you.

NEK. And please don't look at us like that ; it unsettles us.

KAL. And we don't like it. At least, we *do* like it ; but it's wrong.

NEK. *We* have enjoyed the inestimable privilege of being educated by a most refined and easily shocked English lady, on the very strictest English principles.

GOLD. But, my dear young ladies——

KAL. Oh, don't ! You mustn't. It's too affectionate.

NEK. It really does unsettle us.

GOLD. Are you really under the impression that English girls are so ridiculously demure ? Why, an English girl of the highest type is the best, the most beautiful, the bravest, and the brightest creature that Heaven has conferred upon this world of ours. She is frank, open-hearted, and fearless, and never shows in so favourable a light as when she gives her own blameless impulses full play !

NEK. *and* KAL. Oh, you shocking story !

GOLD. Not at all. I'm speaking the strict truth. I'll tell you all about her.

SONG—MR. GOLDBURY.

A wonderful joy our eyes to bless,
In her magnificent comeliness,
Is an English girl of eleven stone two,
And five foot ten in her dancing shoe !
    She follows the hounds, and on she pounds—
        The " field " tails off and the muffs diminish—
    Over the hedges and brooks she bounds
        Straight as a crow, from find to finish.
    At cricket, her kin will lose or win—
        She and her maids, on grass and clover,
    Eleven maids out—eleven maids in—
        And perhaps an occasional " maiden over ! "

Go search the world and search the sea,
Then come you home and sing with me
There's no such gold and no such pearl
As a bright and beautiful English girl !

With a ten-mile spin she stretches her limbs,
She golfs, she punts, she rows, she swims—
She plays, she sings, she dances, too,
From ten or eleven till all is blue !
    At ball or drum, till small hours come
        (Chaperon's fan conceals her yawning)
    She'll waltz away like a teetotum,
        And never go home till daylight's dawning.
    Lawn-tennis may share her favours fair—
        Her eyes a-dance and her cheeks a-glowing—
    Down comes her hair, but what does she care ?
        It's all her own and it's worth the showing !
        Go search the world, etc.

Her soul is sweet as the ocean air,
For prudery knows no haven there ;
To find mock-modesty, please apply
To the conscious blush and the downcast eye.
    Rich in the things contentment brings,
        In every pure enjoyment wealthy,
    Blithe as a beautiful bird she sings,
        For body and mind are hale and healthy.
    Her eyes they thrill with right goodwill—
        Her heart is light as a floating feather—
    As pure and bright as the mountain rill
        That leaps and laughs in the Highland heather !
        Go search the world, etc.

QUARTET.

NEK.	Then I may sing and play ?	
LORD D.		You may !
KAL.	And I may laugh and shout ?	
GOLD.		No doubt !

NEK.   These maxims you endorse ?

LORD D.   Of course !

KAL.   You won't exclaim " Oh fie ! "

GOLD.   Not I !

GOLD.   Whatever you are—be that :
              Whatever you say—be true :
                  Straightforwardly act—
                  Be honest—in fact,
              Be nobody else but *you*.

LORD D.   Give every answer pat—
              Your character true unfurl ;
                  And when it is ripe,
                  You'll then be a type
              Of a capital English girl.

ALL.   Oh, sweet surprise—oh, dear delight,
             To find it undisputed quite,
             All musty, fusty rules despite,
             That Art is wrong and Nature right !

NEK.   When happy I,
              With laughter glad
                  I'll wake the echoes fairly,
       And only sigh
              When I am sad—
                  And that will be but rarely !

KAL.   I'll row and fish,
              And gallop, soon—
                  No longer be a prim one—
       And when I wish
              To hum a tune,
                  It needn't be a hymn one ?

GOLD. *and* LORD D.   No, no !
                  It needn't be a hymn one !

ALL   Oh, sweet surprise and dear delight
(*dancing*).   To find it undisputed quite—
               All musty, fusty rules despite—
               That Art is wrong and Nature right !

[*Dance, and off.*

Enter LADY SOPHY.

RECIT.—LADY SOPHY.

Oh, would some demon power the gift impart
To quell my over-conscientious heart—
Unspeak the oaths that never had been spoken,
And break the vows that never should be broken !

SONG—LADY SOPHY.

When but a maid of fifteen year,
       Unsought—unplighted—
Short-petticoated—and, I fear,
       Still shorter-sighted—
I made a vow, one early spring,
That only to some spotless King
Who proof of blameless life could bring
       I'd be united.
For I had read, not long before,
Of blameless kings in fairy lore,
And thought the race still flourished here—
       Well, well—
       I was a maid of fifteen year !

The KING *enters and overhears this verse.*

Each morning I pursued my game
       (An early riser) ;
For spotless monarchs I became
       An advertiser :
But all in vain I searched each land,
So, kingless, to my native strand
Returned, a little older, and
       A good deal wiser !

I learnt that spotless King and Prince
Have disappeared some ages since—
Even Paramount's angelic grace—
>   Ah, me !—
Is but a mask on Nature's face !

>   (KING *comes forward.*)

RECIT.

KING.   Ah, Lady Sophy—then you love me !
>   For so you sing—

LADY S.   (*indignant and surprised. Producing " Palace Peeper ".*).

>   No, by the stars that shine above me,
>   Degraded King !
For while these rumours, through the city bruited,
Remain uncontradicted, unrefuted,
The object thou of my aversion rooted,
>   Repulsive thing !

KING.   Be just——the time is now at hand
>   When truth may published be.
>   These paragraphs were written and
>   Contributed by me !

LADY S.   By you ? No, no !

KING.   >   Yes, yes, I swear, by me !
>   I, caught in Scaphio's ruthless toil,
>   Contributed the lot !

LADY S.   And *that* is why you did not boil
>   The author on the spot !

KING.   And *that* is why I did not boil
>   The author on the spot !

LADY S.   I *couldn't* think why you did not boil !

KING.   But *I* know why I did not boil
>   The author on the spot !

DUET—LADY SOPHY *and* KING.

LADY S.   Oh, the rapture unrestrained
>   Of a candid retractation !
>   For my sovereign has deigned
>   A convincing explanation—

And the clouds that gathered o'er,
    All have vanished in the distance,
And of Kings of fairy lore
    One, at least, is in existence!

KING.   Oh, the skies are blue above,
    And the earth is red and rosal,
Now the lady of my love
    Has accepted my proposal!
For that *asinorum pons*
    I have crossed without assistance,
And of prudish paragons
    One, at least, is in existence!

(KING *and* LADY SOPHY *dance gracefully. While this is going on* LORD DRAMALEIGH *enters unobserved with* NEKAYA *and* MR. GOLDBURY *with* KALYBA. *Then enter* ZARA *and* CAPT. FITZBATTLEAXE. *The two girls direct* ZARA'S *attention to the* KING *and* LADY SOPHY, *who are still dancing affectionately together. At this point the* KING *kisses* LADY SOPHY, *which causes the Princesses to make an exclamation. The* KING *and* LADY SOPHY *are at first much confused at being detected, but eventually throw off all reserve, and the four couples break into a wild Tarantella, and at the end exeunt severally.*)

Enter all the male Chorus, in great excitement, from various entrances, led by SCAPHIO, PHANTIS, *and* TARARA, *and followed by the female Chorus.*

CHORUS.
Upon our sea-girt land
At our enforced command
Reform has laid her hand
    Like some remorseless ogress—
And made us darkly rue
The deeds she dared to do—
And all is owing to
    Those hated Flowers of Progress!

> So down with them !
> So down with them !
> Reform's a hated ogress.
> So down with them !
> So down with them !
> Down with the Flowers of Progress !

Flourish.   Enter KING, *his three daughters*, LADY
SOPHY, *and the Flowers of Progress.*

KING. What means this most unmannerly irruption ?
       Is this your gratitude for boons conferred ?

SCA. Boons ?   Bah !   A fico for such boons, say we !
       These boons have brought Utopia to a standstill !
       Our pride and boast—the Army and the Navy—
       Have both been reconstructed and remodelled
       Upon so irresistible a basis
       That all the neighbouring nations have disarmed—
       And War's impossible !   Your County Councillor
       Has passed such drastic Sanitary laws
       That all the doctors dwindle, starve, and die !
       The laws, remodelled by Sir Bailey Barre,
       Have quite extinguished crime and litigation :
       The lawyers starve, and all the jails are let
       As model lodgings for the working-classes !
       In short—
       Utopia, swamped by dull Prosperity,
       Demands that these detested Flowers of Progress
       Be sent about their business, and affairs
       Restored to their original complexion !

KING (*to* ZARA). My daughter, this is a very unpleasant state of things.   What is to be done ?

ZARA. I don't know — I don't understand it.   We
must have omitted something.

KING. Omitted something ?   Yes, that's all very well,
but——

    (SIR BAILEY BARRE *whispers to* ZARA.)

ZARA (*suddenly*). Of course !   Now I remember !

Why, I had forgotten the most essential element of all !

KING.   And that is ?—

ZARA.   Government by Party ! Introduce that great and glorious element—at once the bulwark and foundation of England's greatness—and all will be well !   No political measures will endure, because one Party will assuredly undo all that the other Party has done ; and while grouse is to be shot, and foxes worried to death, the legislative action of the country will be at a standstill.   Then there will be sickness in plenty, endless lawsuits, crowded jails, interminable confusion in the Army and Navy, and, in short, general and unexampled prosperity !

ALL.   Ulahlica !   Ulahlica !

PHAN. (aside).   Baffled !

SCA.   But an hour will come !

KING.   Your hour has come already—away with them, and let them wait my will !   (SCAPHIO and PHANTIS are led off in custody.)   From this moment Government by Party is adopted, with all its attendant blessings ; and henceforward Utopia will no longer be a Monarchy Limited, but, what is a great deal better, a Limited Monarchy !

FINALE.

ZARA.   There's a little group of isles beyond the wave—
              So tiny, you might almost wonder where it is—
          That nation is the bravest of the brave,
              And cowards are the rarest of all rarities.
          The proudest nations kneel at her command ;
              She terrifies all foreign-born rapscallions ;
          And holds the peace of Europe in her hand
              With half a score invincible battalions !
                  Such, at least, is the tale
                  Which is borne on the gale,
                      From the island which dwells in the sea.
                  Let us hope, for her sake,
                  That she makes no mistake—
                      That she's all she professes to be !

KING.   Oh, may we copy all her maxims wise,
              And imitate her virtues and her charities ;
          And may we, by degrees, acclimatize
              Her Parliamentary peculiarities !
          By doing so, we shall, in course of time,
              Regenerate completely our entire land—
          Great Britain is that monarchy sublime,
              To which some add (but others do not) Ireland.
                  Such, at least, is the tale, etc.

                  CURTAIN.

THE GRAND DUKE

OR

THE STATUTORY DUEL

DRAMATIS PERSONÆ.

RUDOLPH (*Grand Duke of Pfennig Halbpfennig*).
ERNEST DUMMKOPF (*a Theatrical Manager*).
LUDWIG (*his Leading Comedian*).
DR. TANNHÄUSER (*a Notary*).
THE PRINCE OF MONTE CARLO.
VISCOUNT MENTONE.
BEN HASHBAZ (*a Costumier*).
HERALD.

———

THE PRINCESS OF MONTE CARLO (*betrothed to* RUDOLPH).
THE BARONESS VON KRAKENFELDT (*betrothed to* RUDOLPH).
JULIA JELLICOE (*an English Comédienne*).
LISA (*a Soubrette*).
OLGA
GRETCHEN
BERTHA } (*Members of Ernest Dummkopf's Company*).
ELSA
MARTHA

Chamberlains, Nobles, Actors, Actresses, etc.

———

ACT I.—Scene. Public Square of Speisesaal.
ACT II.—Scene. Hall in the Grand Ducal Palace.

Date 1750.

First produced at the Savoy Theatre on March 7, 1896.

THE GRAND DUKE

OR

THE STATUTORY DUEL

ACT I.

SCENE.—*Market-place of Speisesaal, in the Grand Duchy of Pfennig Halbpfennig. A well, with decorated iron-work, up* L.C. GRETCHEN, BERTHA, OLGA, MARTHA, *and other members of* ERNEST DUMMKOPF'S *theatrical company are discovered, seated at several small tables, enjoying a repast in honour of the nuptials of* LUDWIG, *his leading comedian, and* LISA, *his soubrette.*

CHORUS.

Won't it be a pretty wedding?
    Will not Lisa look delightful?
Smiles and tears in plenty shedding—
    Which in brides of course is rightful.
    One could say, if one were spiteful,
Contradiction little dreading,
    Her bouquet is simply frightful—
Still, 'twill be a pretty wedding!
Oh, it is a pretty wedding!
    Such a pretty, pretty wedding!

ELSA.   If her dress *is* badly fitting,
    Theirs the fault who made her *trousseau.*

BERTHA.　If her gloves *are* always splitting,
　　　　Cheap kid gloves, we know, will do so.

OLGA.　If upon her train she stumbled,
　　　　On one's train one's always treading.

GRET.　If her hair *is* rather tumbled,
　　　　Still, 'twill be a pretty wedding !

CHORUS.　　Such a pretty, pretty wedding !

CHORUS.

Here they come, the couple plighted—
　　On life's journey gaily start them.
Soon to be for aye united,
　　Till divorce or death shall part them.

(LUDWIG *and* LISA *come forward*.)

DUET—LUDWIG *and* LISA.

LUD.　　Pretty Lisa, fair and tasty,
　　　　Tell me now, and tell me truly,
　　Haven't you been rather hasty ?
　　　　Haven't you been rash unduly ?
　　Am I quite the dashing *sposo*
　　　　That your fancy could depict you ?
　　Perhaps you think I'm only so-so ?
　　　　　　(*She expresses admiration*.)
　　　　Well, I will not contradict you !

CHORUS.　　No, he will not contradict you !

LISA.　Who am I to raise objection ?
　　　　I'm a child, untaught and homely—
　　When you tell me you're perfection,
　　　　Tender, truthful, true, and comely—
　　That in quarrel no one's bolder,
　　　　Though dissensions always grieve you—
　　Why, my love, you're so much older
　　　　That, of course, I must believe you !

CHORUS.　　Yes, of course, she must believe you !

CHORUS.

If he ever acts unkindly,
Shut your eyes and love him blindly—
Should he call you names uncomely,
Shut your mouth and love him dumbly—
Should he rate you, rightly—leftly—
Shut your ears and love him deafly.
Ha! ha! ha! ha! ha! ha! ha!
Thus and thus and thus alone
Ludwig's wife may hold her own!

(LUDWIG *and* LISA *sit at table.*)

Enter NOTARY TANNHÄUSER.

NOT.   Hallo! Surely I'm not late? (*All chatter unintelligibly in reply.*)

NOT.   But, dear me, you're all at breakfast! Has the wedding taken place? (*All chatter unintelligibly in reply.*)

NOT.   My good girls, one at a time, I beg. Let me understand the situation. As solicitor to the conspiracy to dethrone the Grand Duke—a conspiracy in which the members of this company are deeply involved—I am invited to the marriage of two of its members. I present myself in due course, and I find, not only that the ceremony has taken place—which is not of the least consequence —but the wedding breakfast is half eaten—which is a consideration of the most serious importance.

(LUDWIG *and* LISA *come down.*)

LUD.   But the ceremony has *not* taken place. We can't get a parson!

NOT.   Can't get a parson! Why, how's that? They're three a penny!

LUD.   Oh, it's the old story—the Grand Duke!

ALL.   Ugh!

LUD.   It seems that the little imp has selected this,

our wedding day, for a convocation of all the clergy in the town to settle the details of his approaching marriage with the enormously wealthy Baroness von Krakenfeldt, and there won't be a parson to be had for love or money until six o'clock this evening !

LISA. And as we produce our magnificent classical revival of *Troilus and Cressida* to-night at seven, we have no alternative but to eat our wedding breakfast before we've earned it. So sit down, and make the best of it.

GRET. Oh, I should like to pull his Grand Ducal ears for him, that I should ! He's the meanest, the cruellest, the most spiteful little ape in Christendom !

OLGA. Well, we shall soon be freed from his tyranny. To-morrow the Despot is to be dethroned !

LUD. Hush, rash girl ! You know not what you say.

OLGA. Don't be absurd ! We're all in it—we're all tiled, here.

LUD. That has nothing to do with it. Know ye not that in alluding to our conspiracy without having first given and received the secret sign, you are violating a fundamental principle of our Association ?

SONG—LUDWIG.

By the mystic regulation
Of our dark Association,
Ere you open conversation
  With another kindred soul,
  You must eat a sausage-roll ! (*Producing one.*)

ALL.   You must eat a sausage-roll !

LUD.   If, in turn, he eats another,
That's a sign that he's a brother—
Each may fully trust the other.
  It is quaint and it is droll,
  But it's bilious on the whole.

ALL.   Very bilious on the whole.

SONG—ERNEST.

Were I a king in very truth,
And had a son—a guileless youth—
    In probable succession ;
To teach him patience, teach him tact,
How promptly in a fix to act,
He should adopt, in point of fact,
    A manager's profession.
To that condition he should stoop
    (Despite a too fond mother),
With eight or ten " stars " in his troupe,
    All jealous of each other !
Oh, the man who can rule a theatrical crew,
Each member a genius (and some of them two),
And manage to humour them, little and great,
    Can govern this tuppenny State !

ALL.   Oh, the man, etc.

Both A and B rehearsal slight—
They say they'll be " all right at night "
    (They've both to go to school yet) ;
C in each act *must* change her dress,
D *will* attempt to " square the press " ;
E won't play Romeo unless
    His grandmother plays Juliet ;
F claims all hoydens as her rights
    (She's played them thirty seasons) ;
And G must show herself in tights
    For two convincing reasons—
    Two very well-shaped reasons !
Oh, the man who can drive a theatrical team,
With wheelers and leaders in order supreme,
Can govern and rule, with a wave of his fin,
    All Europe—with Ireland thrown in !

ALL.   Oh, the man, etc.

                      [*Exeunt all but* ERNEST.

ERN.   Elected by my fellow-conspirators to be Grand

Duke of Pfennig Halbpfennig as soon as the contemptible little occupant of the historical throne is deposed—here is promotion indeed ! Why, instead of playing Troilus of Troy for a month, I shall play Grand Duke of Pfennig Halbpfennig for a lifetime ! Yet, am I happy ? No—far from happy ! The lovely English *comédienne*— the beautiful Julia, whose dramatic ability is so overwhelming that our audiences forgive even her strong English accent—that rare and radiant being treats my respectful advances with disdain unutterable ! And yet, who knows ? She is haughty and ambitious, and it may be that the splendid change in my fortunes may work a corresponding change in her feelings towards me !

Enter JULIA JELLICOE.

JULIA. Herr Dummkopf, a word with you, if you please.

ERN. Beautiful English maiden——

JULIA. No compliments, I beg. I desire to speak with you on a purely professional matter, so we will, if you please, dispense with allusions to my personal appearance, which can only tend to widen the breach which already exists between us.

ERN. (*aside*). My only hope shattered ! The haughty Londoner still despises me ! (*Aloud.*) It shall be as you will.

JULIA. I understand that the conspiracy in which we are all concerned is to develop to-morrow, and that the company is likely to elect you to the throne on the understanding that the posts about the Court are to be filled by members of your theatrical troupe, according to their professional importance.

ERN. That is so.

JULIA Then all I can say is that it places me in an extremely awkward position.

ERN. (*very depressed*). I don't see how it concerns you.

JULIA. Why, bless my heart, don't you see that, as

your leading lady, I am bound under a serious penalty to play the leading part in all your productions?

ERN. Well?

JULIA. Why, of course, the leading part in this production will be the Grand Duchess!

ERN. My wife?

JULIA. That is another way of expressing the same idea.

ERN. (*aside—delighted*). I scarcely dared even to hope for this!

JULIA. Of course, as your leading lady, you'll be mean enough to hold me to the terms of my agreement. Oh, that's so like a man! Well, I suppose there's no help for it—I shall have to do it!

ERN. (*aside*). She's mine! (*Aloud.*) But—do you really think you would care to play that part? (*Taking her hand.*)

JULIA (*withdrawing it*). Care to play it? Certainly not—but what am I to do? Business is business, and I am bound by the terms of my agreement.

ERN. It's for a long run, mind—a run that may last many, many years—no understudy—and once embarked upon there's no throwing it up.

JULIA. Oh, we're used to these long runs in England: they are the curse of the stage—but, you see, I've no option.

ERN. You think the part of Grand Duchess will be good enough for you?

JULIA. Oh, I think so. It's a very good part in Gerolstein, and oughtn't to be a bad one in Pfennig Halbpfennig. Why, what did you suppose I was going to play?

ERN. (*keeping up a show of reluctance*). But, considering your strong personal dislike to me and your persistent rejection of my repeated offers, won't you find it difficult to throw yourself into the part with all the impassioned enthusiasm that the character seems to demand? Remember, it's a strongly emotional part,

involving long and repeated scenes of rapture, tenderness, adoration, devotion—all in luxuriant excess, and all of the most demonstrative description.

JULIA. My good sir, throughout my career I have made it a rule never to allow private feeling to interfere with my professional duties. You may be quite sure that (however distasteful the part may be) if I undertake it, I shall consider myself professionally bound to throw myself into it with all the ardour at my command.

ERN. (aside—with effusion). I'm the happiest fellow alive! (Aloud.) Now—would you have any objection—to—to give me some idea—if it's only a mere sketch—as to how you would play it? It would be really interesting—to me—to know your conception of—of—the part of my wife.

JULIA. How would I play it? Now, let me see—let me see. (Considering.) Ah, I have it!

BALLAD—JULIA.

How would I play this part—
    The Grand Duke's Bride?
All rancour in my heart
        I'd duly hide—
I'd drive it from my recollection
And 'whelm you with a mock affection,
Well calculated to defy detection—
That's how I'd play this part—
        The Grand Duke's Bride.

With many a winsome smile
        I'd witch and woo;
With gay and girlish guile
        I'd frenzy you—
I'd madden you with my caressing,
Like turtle, her first love confessing—
That it was "mock", no mortal would be guessing,
With so much winsome wile
        I'd witch and woo!

Did any other maid
With you succeed,
I'd pinch the forward jade—
I would indeed !
With jealous frenzy agitated
(Which would, of course, be simulated),
I'd make her wish she'd never been created—
Did any other maid
With you succeed !

And should there come to me,
Some summers hence,
In all the childish glee
Of innocence,
Fair babes, aglow with beauty vernal,
My heart would bound with joy diurnal !
This sweet display of sympathy maternal,
Well, that would also be
A mere pretence !

My histrionic art
Though you deride,
That's how I'd play that part—
The Grand Duke's Bride !

ENSEMBLE.

ERNEST.	JULIA.
Oh joy ! when two glowing young hearts,	My boy, when two glowing young hearts,
From the rise of the curtain,	From the rise of the curtain,
Thus throw themselves into their parts,	Thus throw themselves into their parts,
Success is most certain !	Success is most certain !
If the *rôle* you're prepared to endow	The *rôle* I'm prepared to endow
With such delicate touches,	With most delicate touches,
By the heaven above us, I vow	By the heaven above us, I vow
You shall be my Grand Duchess !	I will be your Grand Duchess !

(*Dance.*)

Enter all the Chorus with LUDWIG, NOTARY,
and LISA—*all greatly agitated.*

Y

EXCITED CHORUS.

My goodness me ! what shall we do ?   Why, what
    a dreadful situation !
(*To* LUD.)   It's all your fault, you booby you—you lump
    of indiscrimination !
I'm sure I don't know where to go—it's put me into
    such a tetter—
But this at all events I know—the sooner we are
    off, the better !

ERN.   What means this *agitato* ?   What d'ye seek ?
    As your Grand Duke elect I bid you speak !

SONG—LUDWIG.

Ten minutes since I met a chap
    Who bowed an easy salutation—
Thinks I, " This gentleman, mayhap,
    Belongs to our Association."
        But, on the whole,
           Uncertain yet,
        A sausage-roll
           I took and eat—
That chap replied (I don't embellish)
By eating *three* with obvious relish.

CHORUS (*angrily*).   Why, gracious powers,
           No chum of ours
    Could eat three sausage-rolls with relish !

LUD. Quite reassured, I let him know
        Our plot—each incident explaining ;
That stranger chuckled much, as though
        He thought me highly entertaining.
        I told him all,
           Both bad and good ;
        I bade him call—
           He said he would :
I added much—the more I muckled,
The more that chuckling chummy chuckled !

ALL (*angrily*).   A bat could see
                      He couldn't be
           A chum of ours if he chuckled !

LUD.   Well, as I bowed to his applause,
               Down dropped he with hysteric bellow—
           And *that* seemed right enough, because
               I *am* a devilish funny fellow.
                   Then suddenly,
                       As still he squealed,
                   It flashed on me
                       That I'd revealed
           Our plot, with all details effective,
           To Grand Duke Rudolph's own detective !

ALL.   What folly fell,
                      To go and tell
           Our plot to any one's detective !

                      CHORUS.

(*Attacking* LUDWIG.) You booby dense—
                       You oaf immense,
                       With no pretence
                       To common sense !
                       A stupid muff
                       Who's made of stuff
                       Not worth a puff
                       Of candle-snuff !

Pack up at once and off we go, unless we're anxious to
     exhibit
Our fairy forms all in a row, strung up upon the Castle
     gibbet !

           [*Exeunt Chorus. Manent* LUDWIG, LISA,
               ERNEST, JULIA, *and* NOTARY.

   JULIA.   Well, a nice mess you've got us into !   There's
an end of our precious plot !   All up—pop—fizzle—
bang—done for !
   LUD.   Yes, but—ha ! ha !—fancy my choosing the

Grand Duke's private detective, of all men, to make a confidant of! When you come to think of it, it's really devilish funny!

ERN. (*angrily*). When you come to think of it, it's extremely injudicious to admit into a conspiracy every pudding-headed baboon who presents himself!

LUD. Yes—I should never do that. If I were chairman of this gang, I should hesitate to enrol *any* baboon who couldn't produce satisfactory credentials from his last Zoological Gardens.

LISA. Ludwig is far from being a baboon. Poor boy, he could not help giving us away—it's his trusting nature— he was deceived.

JULIA (*furiously*). His trusting nature! (*To* LUDWIG.) Oh, I should like to talk to you in my own language for five minutes—only five minutes! I know some good, strong, energetic English remarks that would shrivel your trusting nature into raisins—only you wouldn't understand them!

LUD. Here we perceive one of the disadvantages of a neglected education!

ERN. (*to* JULIA). And I suppose you'll never be my Grand Duchess now!

JULIA. Grand Duchess? My good friend, if you don't produce the piece how can I play the part?

ERN. True. (*To* LUDWIG.) You see what you've done.

LUD. But, my dear sir, you don't seem to understand that the man ate three sausage-rolls. Keep that fact steadily before you. Three large sausage-rolls.

JULIA. Bah!—Lots of people eat sausage-rolls who are not conspirators.

LUD. Then they shouldn't. It's bad form. It's not the game. When one of the Human Family proposes to eat a sausage-roll, it is his duty to ask himself, " Am I a conspirator ? " And if, on examination, he finds that he is *not* a conspirator, he is bound in honour to select some other form of refreshment.

LISA. Of course he is. One should always play the game. (*To* NOTARY, *who has been smiling placidly through this.*) What are you grinning at, you greedy old man ?

NOT. Nothing—don't mind me. It is always amusing to the legal mind to see a parcel of laymen bothering themselves about a matter which to a trained lawyer presents no difficulty whatever.

ALL. No difficulty !

NOT. None whatever ! The way out of it is quite simple.

ALL. Simple ?

NOT. Certainly ! Now attend. In the first place, you two men fight a Statutory Duel.

ERN. A Statutory Duel ?

JULIA. A Stat-tat-tatutory Duel ! Ach ! what a crack-jaw language this German is !

LUD. Never heard of such a thing.

NOT. It is true that the practice has fallen into abeyance through disuse. But all the laws of Pfennig Halbpfennig run for a hundred years, when they die a natural death, unless, in the meantime, they have been revived for another century. The Act that institutes the Statutory Duel was passed a hundred years ago, and as it has never been revived, it expires to-morrow. So you're just in time.

JULIA. But what is the use of talking to us about Statutory Duels when we none of us know what a Statutory Duel is ?

NOT. Don't you ? Then I'll explain.

SONG—NOTARY.

About a century since,
　The code of the duello
　　To sudden death
　　For want of breath
Sent many a strapping fellow.

> The then presiding Prince
>   (Who useless bloodshed hated).
>   He passed an Act,
>   Short and compact,
>   Which may be briefly stated.
> Unlike the complicated laws
> A Parliamentary draftsman draws,
>   It may be briefly stated.

ALL.   We know that complicated laws,
>   Such as a legal draftsman draws,
>   Cannot be briefly stated.

NOT.   By this ingenious law,
>   If any two shall quarrel,
>   They may not fight
>   With falchions bright
>   (Which seemed to him immoral) ;
> But each a card shall draw,
>   And he who draws the lowest
>   Shall (so 'twas said)
>   Be thenceforth dead—
>   In fact, a legal " ghoest "
> (When exigence of rhyme compels,
> Orthography forgoes her spells,
>   And " ghost " is written " ghoest ").

ALL (*aside*).   With what an emphasis he dwells
>   Upon " orthography " and " spells " !
>   That kind of fun's the lowest.

NOT.   When off the loser's popped
>   (By pleasing legal fiction),
>   And friend and foe
>   Have wept their woe
>   In counterfeit affliction,
> The winner must adopt
>   The loser's poor relations—
>   Discharge his debts,
>   Pay all his bets,
>   And take his obligations.

> In short, to briefly sum the case,
> The winner takes the loser's place,
> With all its obligations.

ALL.   How neatly lawyers state a case!
> The winner takes the loser's place,
> With all its obligations!

LUD.   I see.   The man who draws the lowest card——

NOT.   Dies, *ipso facto*, a social death.   He loses all his civil rights—his identity disappears—the Revising Barrister expunges his name from the list of voters, and the winner takes his place, whatever it may be, discharges all his functions, and adopts all his responsibilities.

ERN.   This is all very well, as far as it goes, but it only protects one of us.   What's to become of the survivor?

LUD.   Yes, that's an interesting point, because *I* might be the survivor.

NOT.   The survivor goes at once to the Grand Duke, and, in a burst of remorse, denounces the dead man as the moving spirit of the plot.   He is accepted as King's evidence, and, as a matter of course, receives a free pardon.   To-morrow, when the law expires, the dead man will, *ipso facto*, come to life again—the Revising Barrister will restore his name to the list of voters, and he will resume all his obligations as though nothing unusual had happened.

JULIA.   When he will be at once arrested, tried, and executed on the evidence of the informer!   Candidly, my friend, I don't think much of your plot!

NOT.   Dear, dear, dear, the ignorance of the laity! My good young lady, it is a beautiful maxim of our glorious Constitution that a man can only die once.   Death expunges crime, and when he comes to life again, it will be with a clean slate.

ERN.   It's really very ingenious.

LUD. (*to* NOTARY).   My dear sir, we owe you our lives!

LISA (*aside to* LUDWIG).   May I kiss him?

LUD. Certainly not : you're a big girl now. (*To* ERNEST.) Well, miscreant, are you prepared to meet me on the field of honour ?

ERN. At once. By Jove, what a couple of fire-eaters we are !

LISA. Ludwig doesn't know what fear is.

LUD. Oh, I don't mind this sort of duel !

ERN. It's not like a duel with swords. I hate a duel with swords. It's not the blade I mind—it's the blood.

LUD. And I hate a duel with pistols. It's not the ball I mind—it's the bang.

NOT. Altogether it is a great improvement on the old method of giving satisfaction.

QUINTET.

LUDWIG, LISA, NOTARY, ERNEST, JULIA.

Strange the views some people hold !
    Two young fellows quarrel—
Then they fight, for both are bold—
Rage of both is uncontrolled—
Both are stretched out, stark and cold !
    Prithee, where's the moral ?
        Ding dong ! Ding dong !
There's an end to further action,
And this barbarous transaction
Is described as " satisfaction " !
    Ha ! ha ! ha ! ha ! satisfaction !
        Ding dong ! Ding dong !
Each is laid in churchyard mould—
Strange the views some people hold !

Better than the method old,
    Which was coarse and cruel,
Is the plan that we've extolled.
Sing thy virtues manifold
(Better than refinèd gold),
    Statutory Duel !
        Sing song ! Sing song !

Sword or pistol neither uses—
Playing card he lightly chooses,
And the loser simply loses !
　　Ha ! ha ! ha ! ha ! simply loses.
　　　Sing song !　Sing song !
Some prefer the churchyard mould !
Strange the views some people hold !

NOT. (*offering a card to* ERNEST).
　　Now take a card and gaily sing
　　How little you care for Fortune's rubs—

ERN. (*drawing a card*).
　　Hurrah, hurrah !—I've drawn a King !

ALL.　　　He's drawn a King !
　　　　　He's drawn a King !
Sing Hearts and Diamonds, Spades and Clubs !

ALL (*dancing*).　He's drawn a King !
　　　　　　　　How strange a thing .
An excellent card—his chance it aids—
Sing Hearts and Diamonds, Spades and Clubs—
Sing Diamonds, Hearts and Clubs and Spades !

NOT. (*to* LUDWIG).
　　Now take a card with heart of grace—
　　(Whatever our fate, let's play our parts).

LUD. (*drawing card*).
　　Hurrah, hurrah !—I've drawn an Ace !

ALL.　　　He's drawn an Ace !
　　　　　He's drawn an Ace !
Sing Clubs and Diamonds, Spades and Hearts !

ALL (*dancing*).
　　　　　He's drawn an Ace !
　　　　　Observe his face—
Such very good fortune falls to few—
Sing Clubs and Diamonds, Spades and Hearts—
Sing Clubs, Spades, Hearts and Diamonds too !

NOT.   That both these maids may keep their troth,
          And never misfortune them befall,
       I'll hold 'em as trustee for both—

ALL.   He'll hold 'em both !
                  He'll hold 'em both !
       Sing Hearts, Clubs, Diamonds, Spades and all !

ALL (*dancing*).   By joint decree
                  As $\left\{\begin{array}{l}\text{our}\\\text{your}\end{array}\right\}$ trustee

       This Notary $\left\{\begin{array}{l}\text{we}\\\text{you}\end{array}\right\}$ will now instal—

       In custody let him keep $\left\{\begin{array}{l}\text{their}\\\text{our}\end{array}\right\}$ hearts,

       Sing Hearts, Clubs, Diamonds, Spades and all !

                    [*Dance and exeunt* LUDWIG, ERNEST, *and*
                      NOTARY *with the two Girls.*

          March.   Enter the seven Chamberlains of the
                  GRAND DUKE RUDOLPH.

               CHORUS OF CHAMBERLAINS.

The good Grand Duke of Pfennig Halbpfennig,
Though, in his own opinion, very very big,
In point of fact he's nothing but a miserable prig
Is the good Grand Duke of Pfennig Halbpfennig !

Though quite contemptible, as every one agrees,
We must dissemble if we want our bread and cheese,
So hail him in a chorus, with enthusiasm big,
The good Grand Duke of Pfennig Halbpfennig !

Enter the GRAND DUKE RUDOLPH. *He is meanly and
    miserably dressed in old and patched clothes, but
    blazes with a profusion of orders and decorations.
    He is very weak and ill, from low living.*

SONG—RUDOLPH.

A pattern to professors of monarchical autonomy,
I don't indulge in levity or compromising *bonhomie*,
But dignified formality, consistent with economy,
    Above all other virtues I particularly prize.
I never join in merriment—I don't see joke or jape any—
I never tolerate familiarity in shape any—
This, joined with an extravagant respect for tuppence-
    ha'penny,
    A keynote to my character sufficiently supplies.

(*Speaking.*) Observe. (*To Chamberlains.*) My snuff-box !

(*The snuff-box is passed with much ceremony from the
    Junior Chamberlain, through all the others, until it
    is presented by the Senior Chamberlain to* RUDOLPH,
    who uses it.)

    That incident a keynote to my character supplies.

RUD. I weigh out tea and sugar with precision mathe-
    matical—
    Instead of beer, a penny each—my orders are em-
    phatical—
    (Extravagance unpardonable, any more than that I
    call),
    But, on the other hand, my Ducal dignity to
    keep—
    All Courtly ceremonial—to put it comprehensively—
    I rigidly insist upon (but not, I hope, offensively)
    Whenever ceremonial can be practised inexpensively—
    And, when you come to think of it, it's really very
    cheap !

(*Speaking.*) Observe. (*To Chamberlains.*) My handker-
    chief !

(*Handkerchief is handed by Junior Chamberlain to the*

next in order, and so on until it reaches RUDOLPH,
who is much inconvenienced by the delay.)

It's sometimes inconvenient, but it's always very
cheap !

RUD. My Lord Chamberlain, as you are aware, my
marriage with the wealthy Baroness von Krakenfeldt will
take place to-morrow, and you will be good enough to see
that the rejoicings are on a scale of unusual liberality.
Pass that on. (*Chamberlain whispers to Vice-Chamberlain,
who whispers to the next, and so on.*) The sports will
begin with a Wedding Breakfast Bee. The leading
pastry-cooks of the town will be invited to compete, and
the winner will not only enjoy the satisfaction of seeing
his breakfast devoured by the Grand Ducal pair, but he
will also be entitled to have the Arms of Pfennig Halbpfennig tattoo'd between his shoulder-blades. The Vice-
Chamberlain will see to this. All the public fountains of
Speisesaal will run with Gingerbierheim and Currantwein-
milch at the public expense. The Assistant Vice-Chamberlain will see to this. At night, everybody will illuminate ;
and as I have no desire to tax the public funds unduly,
this will be done at the inhabitants' private expense. The
Deputy Assistant Vice-Chamberlain will see to this. All
my Grand Ducal subjects will wear new clothes, and the
Sub-Deputy Assistant Vice-Chamberlain will collect the
usual commission on all sales. Wedding presents (which,
on this occasion, should be on a scale of extraordinary
magnificence) will be received at the Palace at any hour
of the twenty-four, and the Temporary Sub-Deputy
Assistant Vice-Chamberlain will sit up all night for this
purpose. The entire population will be commanded to
enjoy themselves, and with this view the Acting Temporary
Sub-Deputy Assistant Vice-Chamberlain will sing comic
songs in the Market-place from noon to nightfall. Finally,
we have composed a Wedding Anthem, with which the
entire population are required to provide themselves. It

can be obtained from our Grand Ducal publishers at the usual discount price, and all the Chamberlains will be expected to push the sale. (*Chamberlains bow and exeunt.*) I don't feel at all comfortable. I hope I'm not doing a foolish thing in getting married. After all, it's a poor heart that never rejoices, and this wedding of mine is the first little treat I've allowed myself since my christening. Besides, Caroline's income is very considerable, and as her ideas of economy are quite on a par with mine, it ought to turn out well. Bless her tough old heart, she's a mean little darling! Oh, here she is, punctual to her appointment!

Enter BARONESS VON KRAKENFELDT.

BAR. Rudolph! Why, what's the matter?

RUD. Why, I'm not quite myself, my pet. I'm a little worried and upset. I want a tonic. It's the low diet, I think. I am afraid, after all, I shall have to take the bull by the horns and have an egg with my breakfast.

BAR. I shouldn't do anything rash, dear. Begin with a jujube. (*Gives him one.*)

RUD. (*about to eat it, but changes his mind*). I'll keep it for supper. (*He sits by her and tries to put his arm round her waist.*)

BAR. Rudolph, don't! What in the world are you thinking of?

RUD. I was thinking of embracing you, my sugarplum. Just as a little cheap treat.

BAR. What, here? In public? Really, you appear to have no sense of delicacy.

RUD. No sense of delicacy, Bon-bon!

BAR. No. I can't make you out. When you courted me, all your courting was done publicly in the Marketplace. When you proposed to me, you proposed in the Market-place. And now that we're engaged you seem to desire that our first *tête-à-tête* shall occur in the Marketplace! Surely you've a room in your Palace—with blinds—that would do?

Rud. But, my own, I can't help myself. I'm bound by my own decree.

Bar. Your own decree?

Rud. Yes. You see, all the houses that give on the Market-place belong to me, but the drains (which date back to the reign of Charlemagne) want attending to, and the houses wouldn't let—so, with a view to increasing the value of the property, I decreed that all love-episodes between affectionate couples should take place, in public, on this spot, every Monday, Wednesday, and Friday, when the band doesn't play.

Bar. Bless me, what a happy idea! So moral too! And have you found it answer?

Rud. Answer? The rents have gone up fifty per cent, and the sale of opera-glasses (which is a Grand Ducal monopoly) has received an extraordinary stimulus! So, under the circumstances, *would* you allow me to put my arm round your waist? As a source of income. Just once!

Bar. But it's so very embarrassing. Think of the opera-glasses!

Rud. My good girl, that's just what I *am* thinking of. Hang it all, we must give them *something* for their money! What's that?

Bar. (*unfolding paper, which contains a large letter, which she hands to him*). It's a letter which your detective asked me to hand to you. I wrapped it up in yesterday's paper to keep it clean.

Rud. Oh, it's only his report! That'll keep. But, I say, you've never been and bought a newspaper?

Bar. My dear Rudolph, do you think I'm mad? It came wrapped round my breakfast.

Rud. (*relieved*). I thought you were not the sort of girl to go and buy a newspaper! Well, as we've got it, we may as well read it. What does it say?

Bar. Why—dear me—here's your biography! " Our Detested Despot ! "

Rud. Yes—I fancy that refers to me.

BAR. And it says—Oh, it can't be !

RUD. What can't be ?

BAR. Why, it says that although you're going to marry me to-morrow, you were betrothed in infancy to the Princess of Monte Carlo !

RUD. Oh yes—that's quite right. Didn't I mention it ?

BAR. Mention it ! You never said a word about it !

RUD. Well, it doesn't matter, because, you see, it's practically off.

BAR. Practically off ?

RUD. Yes. By the terms of the contract the betrothal is void unless the Princess marries before she is of age. Now, her father, the Prince, is stony-broke, and hasn't left his house for years for fear of arrest. Over and over again he has implored me to come to him to be married—but in vain. Over and over again he has implored me to advance him the money to enable the Princess to come to me—but in vain. I am very young, but not as young as that ; and as the Princess comes of age at two to-morrow, why at two to-morrow I'm a free man, so I appointed that hour for our wedding, as I shall like to have as much marriage as I can get for my money.

BAR. I see. Of course, if the married state is a happy state, it's a pity to waste any of it.

RUD. Why, every hour we delayed I should lose a lot of you and you'd lose a lot of me !

BAR. My thoughtful darling ! Oh, Rudolph, we ought to be very happy !

RUD. If I'm not, it'll be my first bad investment. Still, there *is* such a thing as a slump even in Matrimonials.

BAR. I often picture us in the long, cold, dark December evenings, sitting close to each other and singing impassioned duets to keep us warm, and thinking of all the lovely things we could afford to buy if we chose, and, at the same time, planning out our lives in a spirit of the most rigid and exacting economy !

RUD. It's a most beautiful and touching picture of connubial bliss in its highest and most rarefied development!

DUET—Baroness *and* Rudolph.

BAR. As o'er our penny roll we sing,
                It is not reprehensive
         To think what joys our wealth would bring
         Were we disposed to do the thing
                Upon a scale extensive.
         There's rich mock-turtle—thick and clear—

RUD. (*confidentially*).   Perhaps we'll have it once a year !

BAR. (*delighted*).   You *are* an open-handed dear !

RUD.   Though, mind you, it's expensiv

BAR.   No doubt it *is* expensive.

BOTH. How fleeting are the glutton's joys !
         With fish and fowl he lightly toys,

RUD.   And pays for such expensive tricks
         Sometimes as much as two-and-six !

BAR.   As two-and-six ?

RUD.   As two-and-six—

BOTH. Sometimes as much as two-and-six !

BAR.   It gives him no advantage, mind—
         For you and he have only dined,
         And you remain when once it's down
         A better man by half-a-crown.

RUD.   By half-a-crown ?

BAR.   By half-a-crown.

BOTH. Yes, two-and-six is half-a-crown.
                Then let us be modestly merry,
                And rejoice with a derry down derry-
                        For to laugh and to sing
                        No extravagance bring—
                It's a joy economical, very !

BAR.   Although as you're of course aware
        (I never tried to hide it)
        I moisten my insipid fare
        With water—which I can't abear—

RUD.   Nor I—I can't abide it.

BAR.   This pleasing fact our souls will cheer,
        With fifty thousand pounds a year
        We *could* indulge in table beer !

RUD.   Get out !

BAR.   We could—I've tried it !

RUD.   Yes, yes, of course you've tried it !

BOTH.   Oh, he who has an income clear
        Of fifty thousand pounds a year—

BAR.   Can purchase all his fancy loves
        Conspicuous hats—

RUD.   Two-shilling gloves—

BAR. (*doubtfully*).   Two-shilling gloves ?

RUD. (*positively*).   Two-shilling gloves—

BOTH.   Yes, think of that, two-shilling gloves !

BAR.   Cheap shoes and ties of gaudy hue,
        And Waterbury watches, too—
        And think that he could buy the lot
        Were he a donkey—

RUD.   Which he's *not* !

BAR.   Oh no, he's *not* !

RUD.   Oh no, he's *not* !

BOTH (*dancing*).

        That kind of donkey he is *not* !
            Then let us be modestly merry,
            And rejoice with a derry down derry.
                For to laugh and to sing
                Is a rational thing—
            It's a joy economical, very !

                            [*Exit* BARONESS.

RUD. Oh, now for my detective's report. (*Opens letter.*) What's this! Another conspiracy! A conspiracy to depose *me*! And my private detective was so convulsed with laughter at the notion of a conspirator selecting him for a confidant that he was physically unable to arrest the malefactor! Why, it'll come off! This comes of engaging a detective with a keen sense of the ridiculous! For the future I'll employ none but Scotchmen. And the plot is to explode to-morrow! My wedding day! Oh, Caroline, Caroline! (*Weeps.*) This is perfectly frightful! What's to be done? I don't know! I ought to keep cool and think, but you *can't* think when your veins are full of hot soda-water, and your brain's fizzing like a firework, and all your faculties are jumbled in a perfect whirlpool of tumblication! And I'm going to be ill! I know I am! I've been living too low, and I'm going to be very ill indeed!

SONG—RUDOLPH.

When you find you're a broken-down critter,
Who is all of a trimmle and twitter,
With your palate unpleasantly bitter,
    As if you'd just eaten a pill—
When your legs are as thin as dividers,
And you're plagued with unruly insiders,
And your spine is all creepy with spiders,
    And you're highly gamboge in the gill—
When you've got a beehive in your head,
    And a sewing machine in each ear,
And you feel that you've eaten your bed,
    And you've got a bad headache *down here*—
    When such facts are about,
      And these symptoms you find
      In your body or crown—
    Well, you'd better look out,
      You may make up your mind
      You had better lie down!

When your lips are all smeary—like tallow,
And your tongue is decidedly yallow,
With a pint of warm oil in your swallow,
    And a pound of tin-tacks in your chest—
When you're down in the mouth with the vapours,
And all over your Morris wall-papers
Black-beetles are cutting their capers,
    And crawly things never at rest—
When you doubt if your head is your own,
    And you jump when an open door slams—
Then you've got to a state which is known
    To the medical world as " jim-jams ".
      If such symptoms you find
        In your body or head,
          They're not easy to quell—
      You may make up your mind
      You are better in bed,
        For you're not at all well !

(*Sinks exhausted and weeping at foot of well.*)

Enter LUDWIG.

LUD. Now for my confession and full pardon. They told me the Grand Duke was dancing duets in the Market-place, but I don't see him. (*Sees* RUDOLPH.) Hallo ! Who's this ? (*Aside.*) Why, it *is* the Grand Duke !

RUD. (*sobbing*). Who are you, sir, who presume to address me in person ? If you've anything to communicate, you must fling yourself at the feet of my Acting Temporary Sub-Deputy Assistant Vice-Chamberlain, who will fling himself at the feet of his immediate superior, and so on, with successive foot-flingings through the various grades—your communication will, in course of time, come to my august knowledge.

LUD. But when I inform your Highness that in me you see the most unhappy, the most unfortunate, the most completely miserable man in your whole dominion——

Rud. (*still sobbing*). *You* the most miserable man in my whole dominion? How can you have the face to stand there and say such a thing? Why, look at me! Look at me! (*Bursts into tears.*)

Lud. Well, I wouldn't be a cry-baby.

Rud. A cry-baby? If you had just been told that you were going to be deposed to-morrow, and perhaps blown up with dynamite for all I know, wouldn't *you* be a cry-baby? I do declare if I could only hit upon some cheap and painless method of putting an end to an existence which has become insupportable, I would unhesitatingly adopt it!

Lud. You would? (*Aside.*) I see a magnificent way out of this! By Jupiter, I'll try it! (*Aloud.*) Are you, by any chance, in earnest?

Rud. In earnest? Why, look at me!

Lud. If you are really in earnest—if you really desire to escape scot-free from this impending—this unspeakably horrible catastrophe—without trouble, danger, pain, or expense—why not resort to a Statutory Duel?

Rud. A Statutory Duel?

Lud. Yes. The Act is still in force, but it will expire to-morrow afternoon. You fight—you lose—you are dead for a day. To-morrow, when the Act expires, you will come to life again and resume your Grand Duchy as though nothing had happened. In the meantime, the explosion will have taken place and the survivor will have had to bear the brunt of it.

Rud. Yes, that's all very well, but who'll be fool enough to *be* the survivor?

Lud. (*kneeling*). Actuated by an overwhelming sense of attachment to your Grand Ducal person, I unhesitatingly offer myself as the victim of your subjects' fury.

Rud. You do? Well, really that's very handsome. I daresay being blown up is not nearly as unpleasant as one would think.

Lud. Oh, yes it is. It mixes one up, awfully!

THE GRAND DUKE

RUD. But suppose I were to lose?

LUD. Oh, that's easily arranged. (*Producing cards.*) I'll put an Ace up my sleeve—you'll put a King up yours. When the drawing takes place, I shall seem to draw the higher card and you the lower. And there you are!

RUD. Oh, but that's cheating.

LUD. So it is. I never thought of that. (*Going.*)

RUD. (*hastily*). Not that I mind. But I say—you won't take an unfair advantage of your day of office? You won't go tipping people, or squandering my little savings in fireworks, or any nonsense of that sort?

LUD. I am hurt—really hurt—by the suggestion.

RUD. You—you wouldn't like to put down a deposit, perhaps?

LUD. No. I don't think I should like to put down a deposit.

RUD. Or give a guarantee?

LUD. A guarantee would be equally open to objection.

RUD. It would be more regular. Very well, I suppose you must have your own way.

LUD. Good. I say—we must have a devil of a quarrel!

RUD. Oh, a devil of a quarrel!

LUD. Just to give colour to the thing. Shall I give you a sound thrashing before all the people? Say the word—it's no trouble.

RUD. No, I think not, though it would be very convincing and it's extremely good and thoughtful of you to suggest it. Still, a devil of a quarrel!

LUD. Oh, a devil of a quarrel!

RUD. No half measures. Big words—strong language —rude remarks. Oh, a devil of a quarrel!

LUD. Now the question is, how shall we summon the people?

RUD. Oh, there's no difficulty about that. Bless your heart, they've been staring at us through those windows for the last half-hour!

FINALE.

RUD.   Come hither, all you people—
            When you hear the fearful news,
        All the pretty women weep'll,
            Men will shiver in their shoes.

LUD.   And they'll all cry " Lord, defend us ! "
            When they learn the fact tremendous
                That to give this man his gruel
                In a Statutory Duel—

BOTH.   This plebeian man of shoddy—
                    This contemptible nobody—
                        Your Grand Duke does not refuse !

(*During this, Chorus of men and women have entered,
    all trembling with apprehension under the impression
    that they are to be arrested for their complicity in
    the conspiracy.*)

CHORUS.

    With faltering feet,
                            And our muscles in a quiver,
    Our fate we meet
                            With our feelings all unstrung !
    If our plot complete
                            He has managed to diskiver,
    There is no retreat—
                            We shall certainly be hung !

RUD. (*aside to* LUDWIG).
        Now *you* begin and pitch it strong—walk into me
            abusively—

LUD. (*aside to* RUDOLPH).
        I've several epithets that I've reserved for you
            exclusively.
        A choice selection I have here when you are ready
            to begin.

RUD.   Now *you* begin——

LUD.   No, *you* begin——

RUD.   No, *you* begin——

LUD.   No, *you* begin !

CHORUS (*trembling*).

> Has it happed as we expected ?
> Is our little plot detected ?

DUET—RUDOLPH *and* LUDWIG.

RUD. (*furiously*).

> Big bombs, small bombs, great guns and little ones !
>   Put him in a pillory !
>   Rack him with artillery !

LUD. (*furiously*).

> Long swords, short swords, tough swords and brittle ones !
>   Fright him into fits !
>   Blow him into bits !

RUD.   You muff, sir !

LUD.   You lout, sir !

RUD.   Enough, sir !

LUD.   Get out, sir !   (*Pushes him.*)

RUD.   A hit, sir ?

LUD.   Take that, sir !   (*Slaps him.*)

RUD.   It's tit, sir,

LUD.   For tat, sir !

CHORUS (*appalled*).

> When two doughty heroes thunder,
>   All the world is lost in wonder ;
>   When such men their temper lose,
>   Awful are the words they use !

LUD.   Tall snobs, small snobs, rich snobs and needy ones !

RUD. (*jostling him*).   Whom are you alluding to ?

LUD. (*jostling him*).   Where are you intruding to ?

RUD.   Fat snobs, thin snobs, swell snobs and seedy ones !

LUD. I rather think you err.
To whom do you refer ?

RUD. To you, sir !

LUD. To me, sir ?

RUD. I do, sir !

LUD. We'll see, sir !

RUD. I jeer, sir !

(*Makes a face at* LUDWIG.) Grimace, sir !

LUD. Look here, sir—

(*Makes a face at* RUDOLPH.) A face, sir !

CHORUS (*appalled*).
When two heroes, once pacific,
Quarrel, the effect's terrific !
What a horrible grimace !
What a paralysing face !

ALL. Big bombs, small bombs, etc.

LUD. *and* RUD. (*recit.*).
He has insulted me, and, in a breath,
This day we fight a duel to the death !

NOT. (*checking them*).
You mean, of course, by duel (*verbum sat.*),
A Statutory Duel.

ALL. Why, what's that ?

NOT. According to established legal uses,
A card apiece each bold disputant chooses—
Dead as a doornail is the dog who loses—
The winner steps into the dead man's shoeses !

ALL. The winner steps into the dead man's shoeses !

RUD. *and* LUD. Agreed ! Agreed !

RUD. Come, come—the pack !

LUD. (*producing one*). Behold it here !

RUD.   I'm on the rack!

LUD.   I quake with fear!

(NOTARY *offers card to* LUDWIG.)

LUD.   First draw to you!

RUD.   If that's the case,
            Behold the King! (*Drawing card from his sleeve.*)

LUD. (*same business*).   Behold the Ace!

CHORUS.   Hurrah, hurrah!   Our Ludwig's won.
                And wicked Rudolph's course is run—
                So Ludwig will as Grand Duke reign
                Till Rudolph comes to life again—

RUD.   Which will occur to-morrow!
                I come to life to-morrow!

GRET. (*with mocking curtsey*).
                My Lord Grand Duke, farewell!
                    A pleasant journey, very,
                To your convenient cell
                    In yonder cemetery!

LISA (*curtseying*).
                Though malcontents abuse you,
                We're much distressed to lose you!
                You were, when you were living,
                So liberal, so forgiving!

BERTHA.   So merciful, so gentle!
                So highly ornamental!

OLGA.   And now that you've departed,
                You leave us broken-hearted!

ALL (*pretending to weep*).   Yes, truly, truly, truly, truly—
                    Truly broken-hearted!
                Ha! ha! ha! ha! ha! ha! (*Mocking him.*)

RUD. (*furious*).   Rapscallions, in penitential fires,
                    You'll rue the ribaldry that from you falls!
                To-morrow afternoon the law expires.
                And then—look out for squalls!

                            [*Exit* RUDOLPH, *amid general ridicule.*

CHORUS.   Give thanks, give thanks to wayward fate—
                    By mystic fortune's sway,
                 Our Ludwig guides the helm of State
                 For one delightful day !

(*To* LUDWIG.)   We hail you, sir !
                         We greet you, sir !
                        Regale you, sir !
                         We treat you, sir !
                          Our ruler be
                          By fate's decree
                 For one delightful day !

NOT.   You've done it neatly ! Pity that your powers
            Are limited to four-and-twenty hours !

LUD.   No matter, though the time will quickly run,
            In hours twenty-four much may be done !

SONG—LUDWIG.

Oh, a Monarch who boasts intellectual graces
         Can do, if he likes, a good deal in a day—
He can put all his friends in conspicuous places,
         With plenty to eat and with nothing to pay !
You'll tell me, no doubt, with unpleasant grimaces,
To-morrow, deprived of your ribbons and laces,
You'll get your dismissal—with very long faces—
         But wait ! on that topic I've something to say !
(*Dancing.*) I've something to say—I've something to
         say—I've something to say !
Oh, our rule shall be merry—I'm not an ascetic—
         And while the sun shines we will get up our hay—
By a pushing young Monarch, of turn energetic,
         A very great deal may be done in a day !

CHORUS.   Oh, his rule will be merry, etc.

(*During this*, LUDWIG *whispers to* NOTARY, *who writes.*)

For instance, this measure (his ancestor drew it),

(*alluding to* NOTARY)

This law against duels—to-morrow will die—
The Duke will revive, and you'll certainly rue it—
He'll give you " what for " and he'll let you know why !
But in twenty-four hours there's time to renew it—
With a century's life I've the right to imbue it—
It's easy to do—and, by Jingo, I'll do it !

(*Signing paper, which* NOTARY *presents.*)

It's done !   Till I perish your Monarch am I !
Your Monarch am I—your Monarch am I—your Monarch
am I !
Though I do not pretend to be very prophetic,
I fancy I know what you're going to say—
By a pushing young Monarch, of turn energetic,
A very great deal may be done in a day !

ALL (*astonished*).
Oh, it's simply uncanny, his power prophetic—
It's perfectly right—we *were* going to say,
By a pushing, etc.

Enter JULIA, *at back.*

LUD. (*recit.*).   This very afternoon—at two (about)—
The Court appointments will be given out.
To each and all (for that was the condition)
According to professional position !

ALL.   Hurrah !

JULIA (*coming forward*).
According to professional position ?

LUD.   According to professional position !

JULIA.   Then, horror !

ALL.   Why, what's the matter ?   What's the matter ?
What's the matter ?

SONG—JULIA. (LISA *clinging to her*.)

Ah, pity me, my comrades true,
Who love, as well I know you do,
　　This gentle child,
　　　To me so fondly dear !

ALL.　　　　Why, what's the matter ?

JULIA.　Our sister love so true and deep
From many an eye unused to weep
　　Hath oft beguiled
　　　The coy reluctant tear !

ALL.　　　　Why, what's the matter ?

JULIA.　Each sympathetic heart 'twill bruise
When you have heard the frightful news
　　(O will it not ?)
　　　That I must now impart !

ALL.　　　　Why, what's the matter ?

JULIA.　Her love for him is all in all !
Ah, cursed fate ! that it should fall
　　Unto *my* lot
　　　To break my darling's heart !

ALL.　　　　Why, what's the matter ?

LUD.　　What means our Julia by those fateful looks ?
Please do not keep us all on tenter-hooks—
　　　Now, what's the matter ?

JULIA.　　　Our duty, if we're wise,
　　　　We never shun.
　　This Spartan rule applies
　　　　To every one.
　　In theatres, as in life,
　　　　Each has her line—
　　This part—the Grand Duke's wife
　　　　(Oh agony !) is mine !
　　A maxim new I do not start—
　　The canons of dramatic art
　　Decree that this repulsive part
　　　　(The Grand Duke's wife)
　　　　　Is mine !

ALL.   Oh, *that's* the matter !

LISA (*appalled, to* LUDWIG).   Can that be so ?

LUD.   I do not know—
                But time will show
                If that be so.

CHORUS.   Can that be so ? etc.

LISA (*recit.*).   Be merciful !

DUET—LISA *and* JULIA.

LISA.   Oh, listen to me, dear—
                I love him only, darling !
                    Remember, oh, my pet,
                    On him my heart is set !
            This kindness do me, dear—
                    Nor leave me lonely, darling !
                    Be merciful, my pet,
                    Our love do not forget !

JULIA.   Now don't be foolish, dear—
                You couldn't play it, darling !
                    It's " leading business ", pet.
                    And you're but a soubrette.
            So don't be mulish, dear—
                    Although I say it, darling,
                        It's not your line, my pet—
                        I play that part, you bet !
                        I play that part—
                        I play that part, you bet !

(LISA *overwhelmed with grief.*)

NOT. The lady's right.   Though Julia's engagement
                            Was for the stage meant—
        It certainly frees Ludwig from his
                            Connubial promise.
        Though marriage contracts—or whate'er you call
            'em—

Are very solemn,
Dramatic contracts (which you all adore so)
Are even more so !

ALL.   That's very true !
Though marriage contracts, etc.

SONG—LISA.

The die is cast,
My hope has perished !
Farewell, O Past,
Too bright to last,
Yet fondly cherished !
My light has fled.
My hope is dead,
Its doom is spoken—
My day is night,
My wrong is right
In all men's sight—
My heart is broken !

[*Exit weeping.*

LUD. (*recit.*).   Poor child, where will she go ? What
will she do ?

JULIA.   *That* isn't in your part, you know.

LUD. (*sighing*).   Quite true !
(*With an effort.*) Depressing topics we'll not touch upon—
Let us begin as we are going on !
For this will be a jolly Court, for little and for big !

ALL.   Sing hey, the jolly jinks of Pfennig Halbpfennig !

LUD.   From morn to night our lives shall be as merry as
a grig !

ALL.   Sing hey, the jolly jinks of Pfennig Halbpfennig !

LUD.   All state and ceremony we'll eternally abolish—
We don't mean to insist upon unnecessary polish—
And, on the whole, I rather think you'll find our
rule tollolish !

ALL.   Sing hey, the jolly jinks of Pfennig Halbpfennig !

JULIA.   But stay—your new-made Court
                Without a courtly coat is—
                    We shall require
                    Some Court attire,
                And at a moment's notice.
            In clothes of common sort
                Your courtiers must not grovel—
                    Your new *noblesse*
                    Must have a dress
                Original and novel !

LUD.   Old Athens we'll exhume !
                The necessary dresses,
                    Correct and true
                    And all brand-new,
                The company possesses :
            Henceforth our Court costume
                Shall live in song and story,
                    For we'll upraise
                    The dead old days
                Of Athens in her glory !

ALL.   Yes, let's upraise
                    The dead old days
                Of Athens in her glory !

ALL.   Agreed ! Agreed !
        For this will be a jolly Court for little and for big ! etc

(*They carry* LUDWIG *round stage and deposit him on the
    ironwork of well.* JULIA *stands by him, and the rest
    group round them.*)

                    END OF ACT I.